COMPREHENSIVE
CHESS
COURSE

VOLUME II

ROM BEGINNER TO TOURNAMENT PLAYER IN 12 LESSONS

W9-COV-298

BY ROMAN PELTS
AND GM LEV ALBURT,
three-time U.S. Chess Champion

HE COMPLETE, EASY-TO-USE PROGRAM FOR TEACHING AND SELF-STUDY

Volume II

Level Two
of
The Comprehensive Program of Chess Training

by Roman Pelts
and GM Lev Alburt, three-time U.S. Champion

Chess Information and Research Center
P.O. Box 534, Gracie Station, New York, NY 10028
For ordering information, see last page.

Library of Congress card number: 96-85860
ISBN 1-889323-01-2
Distribution to book trade in North America:
W.W. Norton, 500 Fifth Avenue, New York City.

Photographer: Nigel Eddis
Cover: Grandmaster Lev Alburt teaches chess to Timothy Eddis.

Printed in the United States of America.

TABLE OF CONTENTS

VOLUME II: AN INTRODUCTION

Welcome to Volume II, the second level, of our *Comprehensive Chess Course*. It is aimed at those students who have completed and mastered the lessons in Volume I. In addition to numerous corrections and alterations to this, the third edition, a new chapter has been added, "Moving On to Expert and Master." It addresses the concerns of many readers who want a guide for consolidating the progress made during the study of volumes I and II and concrete suggestions for advancing toward expert and master.

TEACHING INTERMEDIATE PLAYERS

Although Volume II is designed for players who are familiar with the main rules of play set forth in Volume I, teachers are advised to review these rules during the first lesson of the intermediate course. There are always a few players who do not know them thoroughly. Also during the first lesson, students will be introduced to the triple repetition and 50-move rules, which means that they will now know all the rules of chess play.

Experience has shown that the following lesson plan works well for intermediate level students:

1. Iron out difficulties, if any, in the homework assignments.
2. Review previously studied material.
3. Introduce and explain new subject matter.
4. Assign homework for the next lesson.
5. Supervise practice games, a portion of the lesson that should occupy half the time of the total lesson.

When discussing homework from the previous lesson, the teacher should consider not only questions asked by the students but also what he deems to be particularly interesting or instructive points in the assignment. Relevant positions should be set up on a demonstration board, and a student who has answered a given question correctly in the homework assignment ought to be asked to explain the solution to the entire class.

The next step in the lesson is to review previously studied materials, with special attention being given to mastery of the chessboard. Each chapter or lesson contains several review questions of varying difficulty. In most instances, the teacher should select three or four of these questions with which to drill the class. Direct the easier questions to weaker students (gradually leading up to more difficult exercises) and the tougher questions to the stronger students. The point behind this drill is not to stump students but to stimulate their thinking and, in the process, to activate their knowledge.

Following the review segment, new material should be presented. If during the introduction and explanation of this material, the students appear tired and begin to lose their concentration, then it is advisable to break off the theoretical portion of the lesson as soon as possible. Hand out homework assignments for the next lesson and begin the practical or game-playing portion of the lesson. (Course material that still remains to be explained can, if possible, be included in the homework assignment or be introduced at the next class session. Teachers must be certain that students assimilate the material even if it requires extra meetings for review purposes. It may happen, for example, that 12 class sessions are insufficient to cover the 12 lessons in Volume II. Frequently, coaches extend the number of classes to 15 or 16.)

Beginners are attracted to chess primarily as a game, and some of them have little patience for studying. Teachers need to convince students that the more they know about chess, the better they will play it and the greater they will enjoy it.

As already noted in the Introduction to Volume I, each student should be provided with a separate board and set so that he can follow the teacher's explanations during the theoretical portions of the lesson. The same goes for copies of *Comprehensive Chess Course*. If each student has his own copy, then the teacher's task will be both easier and less time-consuming. If that proves impossible, then teachers will have to make copies of homework assignments and distribute them *along with solutions to the questions*. We believe that students should not spend vast amounts of time trying to solve various problems. Five or ten minutes on an individual question is enough. Students should then consult the solution and endeavor to reason it out.

At the end of each lesson in Volume II, teachers will notice a section of supplementary material, which they may wish to incorporate into the lessons or use for class contests. For readers studying on their own, we suggest that they set up the positions on a board, devote no more than five to 10 minutes to any given position, consult the answers and discover the whys and wherefores. The benefits of this kind of independent work are considerable. About self-study, more a bit later.

If Volume II contains a huge amount of material (illustrated by nearly 800 diagrams!), the student can nonetheless master it successfully. Decades of experience in the former Soviet Union proved that anyone willing to work hard can reach advanced levels of play. The great Emanuel Lasker, for example, stated flatly that anyone this side of an imbecile could become a master. Moreover, by the word "master," Lasker did not mean someone who peaked at 2203; he meant someone who won at least one-third of his games, the famous *Meisterdrittel*, in a premier master event. For the moment, students need only do their homework assignments with gusto and activate their ever-increasing theoretical knowledge by playing several games each week between lessons.

Lesson 12, the final chapter of Volume II, consists of 20 separate tests with six questions each. The tests are of approximately equal difficulty. Students are allowed one hour to answer all six questions on a test. Those who fail to answer more than three questions correctly may be allowed to try another examination. The first five questions in each test count 15 percent each, and the final question (on pawn endings) is worth 25 percent.

Coaches must decide which students have adequately completed the second level of *Comprehensive Chess Course* and do not require further instruction with this manual.

SELF–STUDY FOR VOLUME II

As already noted in the Introduction to Volume I, *Comprehensive Chess Course* can be used profitably for serious self-study by both adults and children. The lessons are largely self-explanatory, and the tips given in the Volume I Introduction help players to create active knowledge which, as noted, is knowledge that can be readily applied in practice.

Still, students who learn in a classroom situation or with a personal coach possess certain advantages, including insider advice from veteran instructors about how to avoid accidents along the way. This advice includes such common-sense ideas as to count the material balance as it exists on the chessboard rather than count the captured pieces alongside the board. Another suggestion is that if a student tends to make elementary blunders, then when he is about to make a move, he should take a brief moment to look at the position with the *eyes of a complete beginner*. Forget about deeply laid plans and multi-move combinations and simply take a second or two to see if you are tossing away a piece, overlooking a back-rank checkmate and so on.

THE GREAT MEMORIZATION MISTAKE
Many instructional books begin with an explanation of the rules and follow this explanation with a section on opening theory, thereby beguiling beginners with the notion of being able to play correctly the first 10 to 15 moves of a game. So tempting and ultimately so wrong!

Unfortunately, opening theory is based on subtleties that can be grasped only by strong players. A weak player may be able to parrot opening variations, but he does not understand them. And since understanding — as evinced by thoughtful play — is the goal of every chess player, it follows that rote play is harmful. Players ought to know the purpose of every move that they make. What happens otherwise is the common case of amateurs who waste their time and energy memorizing opening variations, only to stumble pitifully the moment an opponent makes a move — good or bad — that is not in the books. Such well-booked amateurs are helpless even in simple positions.

Mindless memorization is inimical to good chess not only in the openings but also in the middlegame and endgame. What students need is to understand the principles of sound play

and the reasoning behind those principles. Once a student has developed this understanding, he will remember variations and specific endgames almost effortlessly.

Chess books usually tell students *what* to learn but say almost nothing about *how* to learn. These books are laid out in chapters. One chapter is devoted to the openings, another to the middlegame and still another to the endgame. But decades of chess teaching in the former Soviet Union demonstrated that beginners are far from keen about studying endgames. In *Comprehensive Chess Course*, we have tried an end run around this difficulty by devoting a section of each lesson to endings.

The lessons in both Volume I and Volume II place considerable emphasis on tactics, which is to say, combinations. The emphasis is not accidental. It is crucial for players to master the various tactical themes in order to make combinations, to find hidden possibilities in positions, to understand an opponent's plans, and to play creatively. Many outstanding chess masters began their careers as tacticians and only later mastered the nuances of positional play.

Keeping in mind our injunction against unthinkingly teaching opening variations to beginners, the initial lessons of the current course instead acquaint the student with general principles of piece development in the opening and give guidelines on how to avoid mistakes. For a beginner, the assimilation of these principles, along with assiduous study of middlegame and ending play, will prove quite enough to put up a good fight in most games.

SEEING THE WHOLE PICTURE
The ability to picture in the mind a position as it could be within a few moves is absolutely indispensable to chess players. Moreover, this feat of visualizing the chessboard with the position of the pieces changed from the way they are on the real board presents the greatest difficulty to beginners.

The specifically chess-related knack of being able to picture future positions can only be developed gradually. The first step for a beginner is to learn to visualize clearly all the squares of an *empty board*. A series of exercises have been devised to achieve this goal. Gradually — step by step — the board in our visualization exercises will be "peopled" by more and more chessmen, until the student develops the knack of forming mentally a clear picture of positions as they may become within a few moves.

PRACTICE AND ANALYSIS

A chess player can make progress only if he coordinates study with practice. Practice means playing games, and in a game, a player has to go through an opening, middlegame, and sometimes an endgame. That is why in each lesson of *Comprehensive Chess Course*, we provide information about the middlegame and endings. We also frequently present entire games so that students can get acquainted with openings placed in context.

About 100 games are presented in this course, with almost all of them specially annotated for students of Volume II. The games in each lesson have been chosen to illustrate the themes discussed in that lesson. For example, Lesson Eight contains games employing the theme of pinning. By studying these games and internalizing the pinning theme, students will be able to build their own combinations. Indeed, nice combinations such as the following pin, counter-pin, counter-counter pin passage of arms:

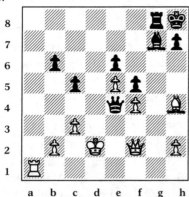

Michael Franklin–Harry Golombek
British Championship, 1962

Black had only a minute on his clock, but 60 seconds were more than enough time to force resignation by **1. ... Bxe5 2. fxe5 Rg2 3. Bf6+ Kg8 4. Rg1** (for a moment, White appears to win with this counter-pin, but...) **4. ... Qf4+!, White resigns.**

Another example of matching illustrative material with subject matter is Lesson 10, which concerns mates along the back rank. Students who master this useful theme will one day find themselves pulling off coups such as the following:

Mileika–Voitkevich
Riga, 1963

Frankly, a back rank mate seems impossible in this position. The more one looks at the position, the more one wonders what White can do, given that he is down a pawn. But the first player discovers a truly amazing line to divert the Black Queen from the d8 square. The winning line is **1. Ra7! Qb6 2. Rb7!!,** when Black must forfeit material because the Rook on b7 cannot be captured without permitting a back rank mate on d8.

Readers should not be surprised to find only one game by the great American world champion, Robert James Fischer. The reason is that some strong players have very complicated playing styles. Players studying Volume II would neither understand nor derive any benefit from such games. Later on, there will be plenty of time to discover the artwork of the genius Fischer.

In actual games, beginners frequently fail to perceive an opponent's threats. They often commit gross blunders. How often the authors of this volume have seen a player who is up several pieces suffer defeat because he falls into an elementary checkmate. To reduce such mistakes to a minimum, students must play often. And when they do play, they should always abide by the rules. During practice sessions, they should avoid playing numerous quick games and instead should play just one or two games in a serious manner. They ought to think out each move carefully.

CHESS APPRECIATION

Most good chess players take the time to learn something about the history of the game that they love. Beginners should also be introduced to chess history, but in a gradual fashion. For example, if a Fischer game is being studied, the teacher ought to explain who Fischer is and when he played chess. Or, to take another example, if a game opening with Philidor's Defense is under discussion, then the teacher can say a few words about Andre Philidor.

Another point behind developing chess appreciation among students is to cushion the impact of defeats. It happens not infrequently that several early defeats demoralize a child so much that he gives up chess. A modern aid to help us deal with this problem is the chess computer, to which a student can lose without his ego suffering too much! Still, the teacher ought to remind students constantly that they need not fear defeat because a player learns from his losses. The teacher can adduce the example of former world champion Jose Capablanca who said that he learned more from a single game that he lost than from many victories.

Students benefit greatly from an analysis of their games. Unfortunately, coaches cannot comment on every game played during practice sessions, though they should try to observe the play of every pupil. Common-sense advice to coaches is that they take note of particularly instructive ideas that occur and demonstrate them later to the class. For example, one player may have overlooked a possibility to checkmate his opponent, whereas another player may have made particularly effective use of material that he learned in class. Etc. etc.

Players working on lessons in Volume II should acquire the habit of recording their games. Not only is recording required for most tournament play, it also allows the student to analyze his games later with his coach.

The authors would like to acknowledge their indebtedness to those who have aided us in the preparation of *Comprehensive Chess Course.* Jonathan Berry and Indian chess enthusiast Mohan translated the two volumes, and Gordon Howe performed admirable labors as proofreader. For help with preparing the second edition, the authors are very grateful to Faneuil Adams, Dewain Barber, Svetozar Jovanovic, Bruce Pandolfini, and others who assisted in this work. Nigel Eddis, the world's leading chess photographer, took the cover photograph. For insightful advice on the new chapter, "Moving On to Expert and Master," we thank Dr. Martin Katahn. And, of course, we thank the many readers who wrote in with suggestions and corrections. Finally, we both wish to thank Lyuba Pelts, the wife of FM Pelts, who unfailingly attended to the endless small, though vital tasks involved in producing a work such as *Comprehensive Chess Course.*

Roman Pelts and Lev Alburt
New York City
August 1, 1996

Lesson One

Many of you already know the rules of play, but we shall review them briefly here for the benefit of those whose mastery of them is perhaps a bit shaky.

1. What is the "touch-move" rule?
2. Can you change a move after playing it?
3. What do the words "Kingside" and "Queenside" mean?
4. What are the relative values of the various chess pieces and pawns?
5. What is chess notation and what is its purpose?
6. How do you record a game?
7. What reward does a pawn get for reaching the last rank?
8. What other special pawn rule do you know?
9. What is the strongest move possible in a game?
10. When is a player considered to have won the game?
11. What is the name of a move which involves both the King and a Rook at the same time, and when can such a move be made?
12. What is stalemate?
13. Do we have to say "check," "checkmate," or "stalemate" during a game?
14. What happens when one of the players keeps checking his opponent endlessly?
15. Do you know the "three-time repetition of position" rule? What is it?
16. What is the 50-move rule?
17. When is a game considered to be a draw?

Answers

1. A player who touches one of his men *must* move that man. If he touches one of his opponent's men, he *must* capture it. However, if a player touches one of his own men but the man has no legal move, or if he touches one of his opponent's men but there is nothing to capture it with, then there is no penalty. If certain men are untidily placed on the board and you want to center them in their squares, you must first say "I adjust" or "j'adoube" to your opponent.

2. If a player moves a man and lets go of it with his hand, the move is considered to be completed and cannot be taken back. However, if the player is still holding on to the man after moving it, the move is not considered to be finished and the players has the right to place that man on any legally allowed square.

3. The "Kingside" is that half of the board on which the two Kings stand at the beginning of a game, while the "Queenside" is the other half of the board. See Diagram 1.

1

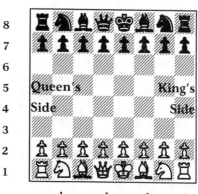

1

4. The praxis of many generations of chessplayers has shown that the men have the following relative values:

Man	Points
Queen	9
Rook	5
Bishop	3
Knight	3
Pawn	1

From these values we can see that a Knight = a Bishop = 3 pawns or that a Rook = a Knight + 2 pawns, and so on. The King is invaluable, as a game cannot continue without it.

It must always be kept in mind, however, that the exact value of a given man varies according to position on the board. Sometimes a pawn can be stronger than the entire adverse army, as a look at the crazy position in Diagram 2 will convince you.

2

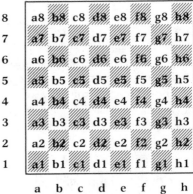

5. Chess notation is a system of symbols for designating the squares of the chessboard. It is used in order to help us to record games or positions. Let us look at the algebraic system of notation, which is what we shall be using.

The chessboard consists of 64 squares forming eight vertical lines known as files and eight horizontal lines known as ranks. The files are designated by the letters **a**, **b**, **c**, and so on to **h** (starting from White's left), and are correspondingly called the a-file, b-file, c-file, etc. The ranks are designated by the numbers from **1** to **8** (starting from White's side of the board) and are correspondingly called the 1st rank, 2nd rank, etc. For example, in the starting position (see Diagram 1) all the White pawns are on

the 2nd rank while all the Black pawns are on the 7th rank. Since each square is at the intersection of a file and a rank, it can be designated by a letter and a number.

The board with the designations of all the squares is shows from White's side in Diagram 3 and from Black's side in Diagram 4.

3

	a	b	c	d	e	f	g	h
8	a8	b8	c8	d8	e8	f8	g8	h8
7	a7	b7	c7	d7	e7	f7	g7	h7
6	a6	b6	c6	d6	e6	f6	g6	h6
5	a5	b5	c5	d5	e5	f5	g5	h5
4	a4	b4	c4	d4	e4	f4	g4	h4
3	a3	b3	c3	d3	e3	f3	g3	h3
2	a2	b2	c2	d2	e2	f2	g2	h2
1	a1	b1	c1	d1	e1	f1	g1	h1

a b c d e f g h

from White's side

4

	h	g	f	e	d	c	b	a
1	h1	g1	f1	e1	d1	c1	b1	a1
2	h2	g2	f2	e2	d2	c2	b2	a2
3	h3	g3	f3	e3	d3	c3	b3	a3
4	h4	g4	f4	e4	d4	c4	b4	a4
5	h5	g5	f5	e5	d5	c5	b5	a5
6	h6	g6	f6	e6	d6	c6	b6	a6
7	h7	g7	f7	e7	d7	c7	b7	a7
8	h8	g8	f8	e8	d8	c8	b8	a8

h g f e d c b a

from Black's side

The board can also be divided into diagonals, which are named by indicating their end squares. For example, the a1-h8 diagonal refers to the diagonal beginning with **a1** and ending with **h8**. All the squares in a given diagonal are of the same color, i.e., a diagonal can be either light-squared or dark-squared.

6. In order to record chess moves or positions, we have to know certain symbols. The major ones are given in the following table.

Main Symbols Used in Chess Notation

Symbol	Meaning
K	King
Q	Queen
R	Rook
B	Bishop
N	Knight
P	Pawn
–	moves to
x	captures
+	check
#	checkmate
0-0	castles King's side
0-0-0	castles Queen's side
?	bad move
!	good move

The symbols for designating the men and the squares allow us to record the moves of pieces and pawns. First, the symbol for the piece moved is indicated, then the symbol for the square on which the piece stood before the move, then a hyphen, and then the symbol for the square on which the piece stands after the move. If we are recording a pawn move, the symbol for the pawn (P) is left out.

Let us now go over a sample game.

Game 1

1. e2-e4
The numeral "1" indicates the number of the move, while the "e2-e4" means that the White pawn from e2 moves to e4.

1. ...   e7-e5
The three dots before the move indicate that it is Black's move. Black's King pawn moves from e7 to e5.

2. Qd1-h5?   Nb8-c6
The White Queen moves from d1 to h5. The symbol "?" indicates that the move is a poor one. The Black Knight moves from b8 to c6.

3. Bf1-c4   Ng8-f6?
The White Bishop moves from f1 to c4, while Black brings out his Knight from g8 to f6, a mistake.

4. Qh5xf7#
The Queen on h5 captured the pawn on f7. The symbol "#" means checkmate. Remember the final position, shown in Diagram 5.

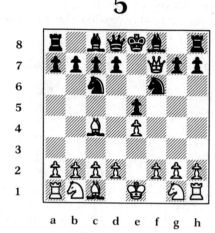

5

It occurs many times in beginners' games and is called the Scholar's Mate.

7. A pawn that reaches the last rank (8th rank for White and 1st rank for Black) must turn into a piece of its own color. Usually the strongest piece, the Queen, is chosen, but in some cases a Knight, Bishop, or Rook is chosen instead. Thus it is possible to have 9 Queens of the same color on the board at one time, or 10 Knights, and so on, if all the pawns are promoted to pieces and added to the already existing ones.

Some beginners mistakenly think that it is always good to promote a pawn to a Queen. That this is not so can be seen from Diagram 6.

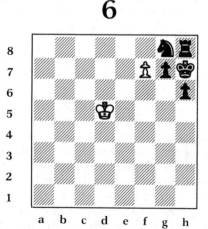

6

If White promotes his pawn to a Queen he will lose it after 1. ... Ng8-f6+, while by promoting it to a Knight (1. f7-f8N#) he can checkmate Black (see Diagram 7).

3

7

8. Another special pawn rule is the "en passant capture." This is illustrated in the position in Diagram 8, which occurred in a school tournament.

8

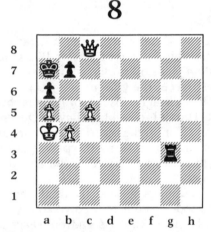

The boy playing Black moved 1. ... b7-b5 and joyfully announced "Mate!" (see Diagram 9). "No, it's your King which is mated!", replied his opponent, playing 2. a5xb6# (see Diagram 10).

9

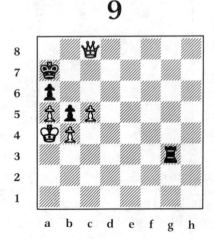

10

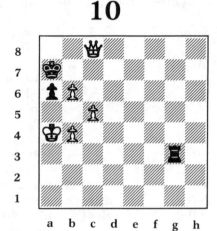

Only the tournament director's intervention settled the dispute, which had arisen because the boy with the Black pieces did not know the "en passant capture" rule. An "en passant capture" is possible when a pawn moves two squares from its starting position and ends up side by side with an enemy pawn, which can then capture it as if it had moved up not two squares, but only one. A player who wishes to capture en passant must do so on his first turn after the opposing pawn has moved up two squares.

9. The strongest move in a game is obviously a move which checkmates the opponent's King, since after that the game is finished.

11

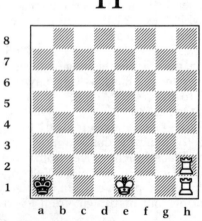

In Diagram 11, White to play mates in 1 move. This problem can be solved provided neither the White King nor the Rook on h1 has moved during the game. The solution is 1. 0-0#.

10. A game is won
  a) when one of the players checkmates the opponent's King, or
  b) when one of the players resigns, considering further resistance to be useless, or
  c) when one of the players loses on time.

11. Each players can make a simultaneous move with his King and a Rook once in a game. The move is called **castling**. A player may castle either with the King's Rook (castling short or castling K-side) or with the Queen's Rook (castling long or castling Q-side). Castling is only possible under the following conditions:
  i. Castling is not permitted if either the King or the Rook used in castling has already moved at any point in the game.
  ii. All the squares between the King and the Rook must be empty. Neither can jump over any other pieces.
  iii. The King must not be in check (castling is not allowed for the purpose of getting out of check).
  iv. The King may not move into check.
  v. The square which the King jumps over should not be under attack by any enemy man.

Now let us analyze the following game.

Game 2
Feuer–O'Kelly
Liege, 1934

1. e2-e4	e7-e5
2. Ng1-f3	Nb8-c6
3. Bf1-b5	a7-a6
4. Bb5-a4	d7-d6
5. Ba4xc6 +	b7xc6
6. d2-d4	f7-f6
7. Nb1-c3	Ra8-b8
8. Qd1-d3	Ng8-e7
9. h2-h4	h7-h5
10. Bc1-e3	

"What! It looks like he's blundered his pawn on b2!", thought Black with surprise. Finding no reason why he shouldn't, he decided to take the pawn.

10. ...	Rb8xb2?
11. d4xe5	d6xe5?

Of course he had to take on e5 with the other pawn. (11. ... fxe5). The Black player later became a grandmaster, but at the time of this

game he wasn't very strong.

12. Qd3xd8 +	Ke8xd8

See Diagram 12.

12

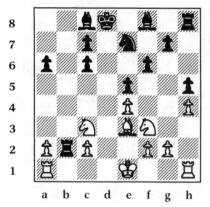

Black has lost his right to castle in this game, as his King has already moved. White, however, can castle on either side. Naturally, he chose to castle long, 13. 0-0-0 +, since that allowed him to win a Rook (see Diagram 13.)

13

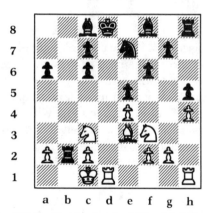

The White Rook checked Black's King and at the same time the White King attacked the Black Rook on b2. So Black resigned.

12. "Stalemate" is a position where the player whose turn it is to move is not in check but has no legal moves either with his King or with any of his other men. When a stalemate occurs, the game is considered drawn. Stalemate can arise if a player makes a thoughtless move when attempting to mate his opponent's lone King. Carelessness in winning positions is the main cause of stalemate.

14

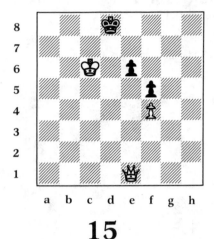

15

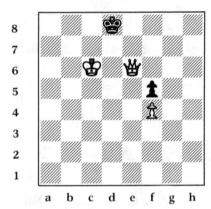

In Diagram 14, White unthinkingly played 1. Qe1xe6? and the game was drawn, since the resulting position was a stalemate (see Diagram 15). Any other move (except of course 1. Qe1-e4??) would have led to a win.

However, stalemate is not always the result of a gross blunder. Sometimes it is planned as a method of saving an otherwise lost position.

16

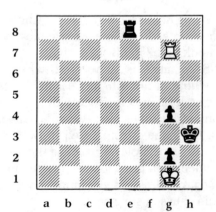

For example, in Diagram 16 Black to move could mate in two moves: 1. ... Re8-e1 + 2. Kg1-f2 g2-g1Q#. However, it was White's turn to move and he found an interesting stalemate idea. The White King has only one possible move, to f2. So White played:

1. Rg7-h7 +   **Kh3-g3**

Now the White King cannot go even to f2, since the Black King controls that square.

2. Rh7-e7!

White gives up his Rook for nothing, since once it is gone the position will be a stalemate.

2. ...   **Re8-a8**

The Black Rook tries to get away, but in vain!

3. Re7-a7!

The draw is inevitable! The White Rook keeps sacrificing itself along the 7th rank (see Diagram 17).

17

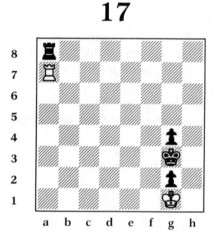

A Rook like this is called a desperado Rook.

13. It is not compulsory to announce "check," "mate," or "stalemate."

14. A series of checks from which the King cannot escape is known as "perpetual check," and the game is considered to be drawn.

18

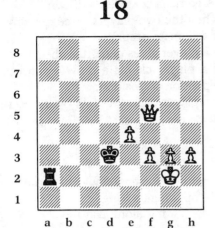

For example, in Diagram 18 Black gives perpetual check by checking the White King continuously from a2 to a1. The White King has nowhere to hide and the draw is forced. Just like stalemate, perpetual check too can be planned in advance by a player. Sometimes players even sacrifice pieces in order to obtain a draw by perpetual check.

Now let us look at a game played between two World Champions in the year 1914. White was 22-year-old Alexandre Alekhine, who became World Champion in 1927 by defeating the Cuban Jose Raoul Capablanca. Black was the reigning World Champion Emanuel Lasker, who won the title in 1894 and kept it for 27 years, until he lost it to Capablanca in 1921.

Game 3
Alekhine–Lasker

1. e2-e4	e7-e5
2. Ng1-f3	Nb8-c6
3. d2-d4	

This opening is called the "Scotch Game," because it was a favorite opening of Scottish players many years ago. The early opening up of the center does not cause Black any difficulties. By the way, do you remember what is meant by the "center" of a chess board? Right!

The center consists of the four squares d4, d5, e4, and e5.

3. ...	e5xd4
4. Nf3xd4	Ng8-f6
5. Nb1-c3	Bf8-b4
6. Nd4xc6	b7xc6
7. Bf1-d3	d7-d5
8. e4xd5	c6xd5

9. 0-0	0-0
10. Bc1-g5	Bc8-e6
11. Qd1-f3	Bb4-e7
12. Rf1-e1	h7-h6

See Diagram 19.

19

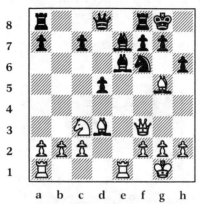

Both sides have played very well and if White had now retreated his Bishop from g5, the game would have been even. However, Alekhine was impatient to get a draw against the World Champion and so he sacrificed the Bishop for a pawn, and then his Rook on e1 for the Bishop on e6.

13. Bg5xh6	g7xh6
14. Re1xe6	f7xe6

Now the Black King is exposed and White can give perpetual check.

15. Qf3-g3 +	Kg8-h8

Not 15. ... Kg8-f7, because of 16. Qg3-g6#.

16. Qg3-g6!	

The players agreed to a draw here! See Diagram 20.

20

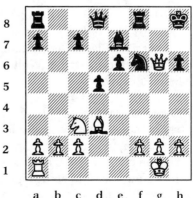

Black is up a Rook for a pawn, but he cannot avoid perpetual check. For example, 16. ... Qd8-e8 17. Qg6xh6+ Kh8-g8 18. Qh6-g5+ Kg8-h8 19. Qg5-h6+ etc.

15. If the same position with the same player to move occurs three (or more) times in a game, the game is drawn by three-time repetition of position. Incidentally, perpetual check is a case of three-time repetition of position.

21

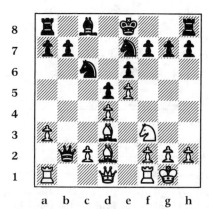

In Diagram 21, White has lost a pawn and decides that it is better to draw by three-time repetition of position than to lose the game. There followed:

1. Ra1-b1	Qb2xa3
2. Rb1-a1	Qa3-b2
3. Ra1-b1	

The first time.

3. ...	Qb2-a2
4. Rb1-a1	Qa2-b2
5. Ra1-b1	

The second time.

5. ...	Qb2-a3
6. Rb1-a1	Qa3-b2
7. Ra1-b1	

The third time. The Black Queen cannot get away from the attacks of the White Rook. White claimed a draw.

16. If 50 moves (a "move" here actually means a pair of moves, one by each side) go by with no capture or pawn move being made, either player can claim a draw. For example, a player with a King and Queen against a lone King must know how to mate within 50 moves.

17. A game is considered drawn
  a) when the two players agree to a draw;
  b) if stalemate occurs;
  c) if a player gives perpetual check;
  d) if a player claims a draw by three-time repetition of position;
  e) if a player claims a draw by the 50-move rule;

and finally,

  f) if neither side has enough material to mate the opponent's King:
   i) A King alone can never checkmate another King.
   ii) A King and Knight alone cannot checkmate a lone King.
   iii) A King and Bishop alone cannot checkmate a lone King.
   iv) A King and Bishop alone cannot checkmate a lone King and Bishop if the Bishops move on diagonals of the same color (see Diagram 22).

22

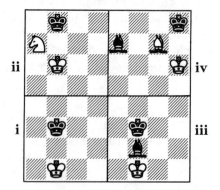

HOMEWORK
(Answers at the end)

I. Diagrams 23–30

23

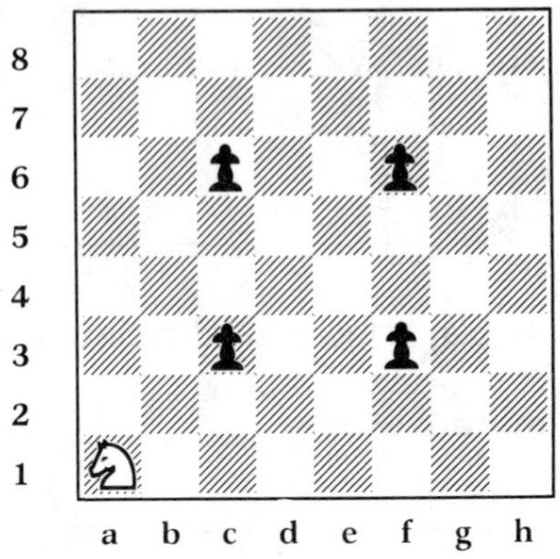

Only White moves. Write down the route that the Knight must take to visit the other three corners and then come back. In doing so, the Knight must not put itself under attack by any of the Black pawns, nor must it capture any of the pawns, nor must it land on any square more than once.

Write your answer

_____

_____

_____

24

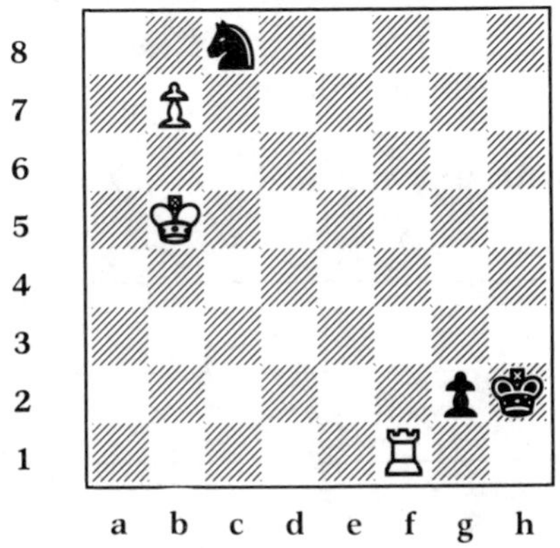

How should the game end
a)with White to move?
b)with Black to move?

Write your answer

_____

_____

_____

25

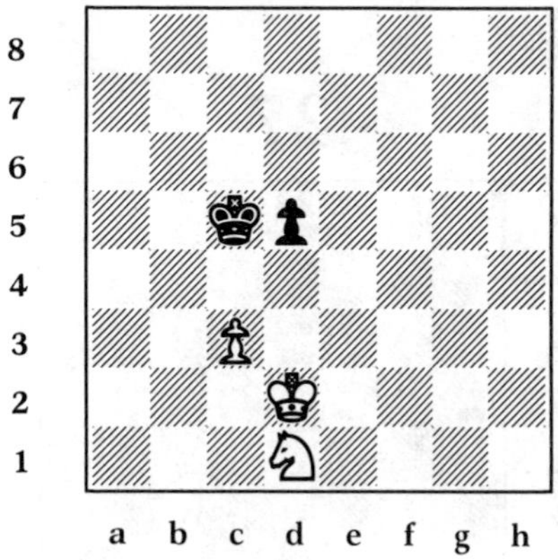

How should the game end
a)   with Black to move?
b)   with White to move?

Write your answer

_____

_____

_____

26

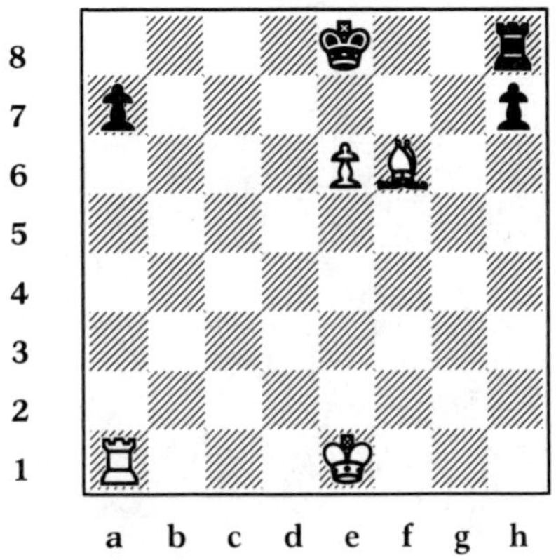

White to play and mate in two moves (the Rooks and Kings have not yet moved in the game).

Write your answer

	WHITE	BLACK
1.		
2.		
3.		

28

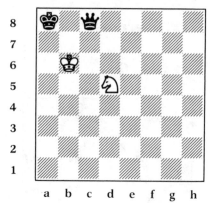

White to play. How should the game end?

Write your answer.

_____

_____

_____

27

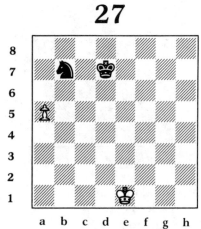

White to play and win.

Write your answer

_____

_____

_____

29

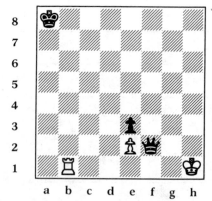

White to play and draw.

Write your answer

_____

_____

_____

30

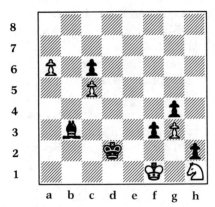

Black to play. How should the game end?

Write your answer

_____

_____

_____

II. Board Study Exercises

Write down your answers in the space below.

1. Place the board so that you are playing White. Find the squares d4, f7, and c3.
2. Looking at the board from Black's side, find the squares c6, h2, d3, and a5.

Answer questions 3–5 without looking at a board.

3. What color are the following squares: c3, h5, d6, b4?

_____

_____

4. Name all the squares making up the h2-b8 and d1-h5 diagonals.

_____

_____

5. Name the diagonals running through d5. Name the squares making up these diagonals.

_____

_____

III. Games for Analysis

Game 4

1. e2-e4	e7-e5
2. Bf1-c4	Bf8-c5
3. Qd1-f3?	Ng8-h6?

3. ... Ng8-f6 was the correct move.

4. d2-d4!	e5xd4
5. Bc1xh6	g7xh6?
6. Qf3xf7#	

See Diagram 31 for the final position.

31

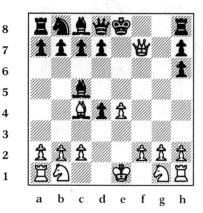

Game 5

1. e2-e4	e7-e5
2. Ng1-f3	d7-d6
3. Bf1-c4	Bc8-g4
4. c2-c3	Nb8-c6
5. Qd1-b3	Bg4xf3?

5. ... Nc6-a5! was the correct move.

6. Bc4xf7 +	Ke8-e7
7. Qb3-e6#	

See Diagram 32 for the final position.

32

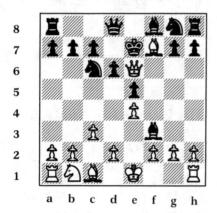

D-29

    1. Rb1-b8 + !   **Ka8-a7**

If the King takes the Rook, it's stalemate.

    2. Rb8-b7! +   **Ka7-a6**

    3. Rb7-b6 +

The desperado Rook keeps offering itself as a sacrifice. The game is a draw.

D-30

    1. ...   **Bb3-c4 +**

Or else the White pawn will Queen.

    2. Kf1-f2   **Bc4xa6**

Stalemate

II. Exercises

You can easily check your answers to the board study questions by looking at a chess-board.

SUPPLEMENTARY MATERIAL

for use at the teacher's discretion

In Diagrams 33–38 the stalemate idea is used; Diagrams 39–42 contain the perpetual check theme; Diagram 43 illustrates a three-time repetition of position; and Diagram 44 uses an en passant capture.

HOMEWORK ANSWERS
I. Diagrams 23–30

D-23
Na1-b3-c5-a6-c7-a8-b6-d7-f8-g6-h8-f7-h6-f5-g3-h1-f2-d1-e3-c2-a1. Twenty moves in all. Other routes are also possible.

D-24
  a) White to play wins with 1. b7-b8Q + ! Kh2-h3 2. Qb8xc8 + etc.

  b) Black to play wins with 1. ...g2xf1Q + 2. Kb5-c6 Nc8-e7 + and Black will win the pawn in a few moves.

D-25
  a) Black to move plays 1. ... d5-d4, exchanging off the last White pawn, after which the game is a draw!

  b) White to play should win after 1. Kd2-d3.

D-26
    1. 0-0-0!   **0-0**

On any other move White would play 2. Rd1-d8#.

    2. Rd1-g1#

D-27
1. a5-a6 Kd7-c7 2. a6-a7! and the White pawn Queens.

D-28
    1. Nd5-c7 +   **Ka8-b8**

    2. Nc7-a6 +   **Kb8-a8**

    3. Na6-c7 +

Drawn by perpetual check. If Black gives up his Queen for the Knight, it's still a draw.

33
L. Ponziani, 1769

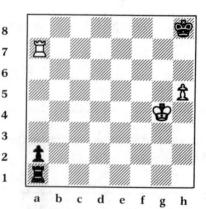

White to play and draw

    1. Kg4-g5   **Ra1-g1 +**

    2. Kg5-h6   **a2-a1Q**

    3. Ra7-a8 + !   **Qa1xa8**

Stalemate

34

L. Ponziani, 1769

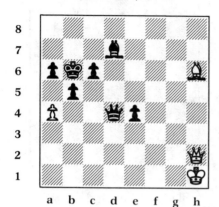

White to play and draw

1. Bh6-e3!	**Qd4xe3**
2. Qh2-f2!	**Qe3xf2**

Not 2. ... Qc5, because of 3. a4-a5 + winning the Queen.

3. a4-a5 +	**Kb6xa5**
Stalemate	

35

E. Cook

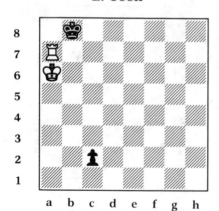

White to play and draw

1. Ra7-b7 +	**Kb8-c8**
2. Rb7-b5	**c2-c1Q**
3. Rb5-c5 + !	**Qc1xc5**
Stalemate	

36

Marshall–McClure, New York 1923

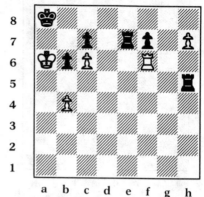

White to play and draw.

1. Rf6-h6!	**Rh5xh6**
2. h7-h8Q +	**Rh6xh8**
3. b4-b5	

and all moves by Black produce a stalemate!

37

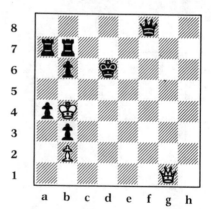

White to play and draw.

1. Qg1-c5 + !	**b6xc5**

If Black moves his King, he loses his Queen on f8.

2. Kb4-a3!	

and all moves by Black produce a stalemate.

38

H. Rinck, 1912

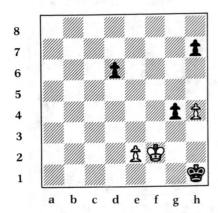

White to play and draw

1. Kf2-g3	h7-h5
2. e2-e4	Kh1-g1
3. e4-e5	d6xe5

Stalemate

Black could not play 3. ... d6-d5, as White would have won by Queening his pawn.

39

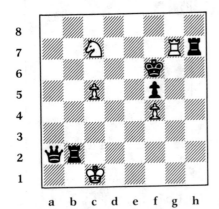

White to play and draw

1. Nc7-e8 +	Kf6-e6
2. Ne8-c7 +	Ke6-f6
3. Nc7-e8 +	

Perpetual check.

40

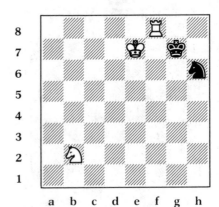

Black to play and draw

1. ...	Nh6-g8 +
2. Ke7-e8	Ng8-f6 +
3. Ke8-e7	Nf6-g8 +

Or 3. ... Nf6-d5 +, and the White King cannot escape from perpetual check without losing a Rook.

41

From a game played by A. Neuman

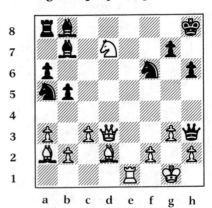

White to play and draw

1. Re1-e8 + !	Nf6xe8
2. Qd3-h7 + !	Kh8xh7
3. Nd7-f8 +	Kh7-h8
4. Nf8-g6 +	Kh8-h7
5. Ng6-f8 +	

Perpetual check.

42

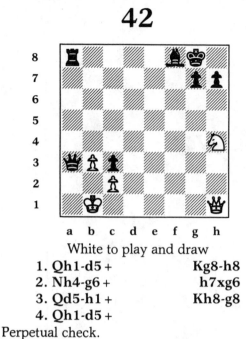

White to play and draw

1. Qh1-d5 +	Kg8-h8
2. Nh4-g6 +	h7xg6
3. Qd5-h1 +	Kh8-g8
4. Qh1-d5 +	

Perpetual check.

44

D. Ulyanov

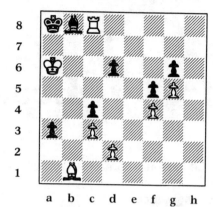

White to play and mate in 3 moves

1. Bb1-a2	d6-d5
2. d2-d4!	c4xd3
	(en passant)
3. Ba2xd5#.	

Checkmate.

43

Lipnizky (Master)–Boleslavsky (Grandmaster)
Moscow 1950

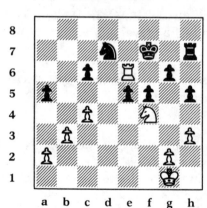

White to play and draw

1. *Re6-d6*	Kf7-e7
2. Rd6-e6 +	Ke7-f7
3. *Re6-d6*	Kf7-e7
4. Rd6-e6 +	Ke7-f7
5. *Re6-d6*	

Drawn by three-time repetition of position.

Lesson Two

A. Check Lesson 1 homework (if necessary).

B. *Review Questions:*
1. What is the most powerful move in a chess game?
2. Can a player pass his turn?
3. Which pieces can be moved before any pawn moves have been made?

Try to answer Questions 4–8 without looking at a chessboard.

4. Name the squares on which each of the White men stands at the start of a game.
5. What color (light or dark) is each of the following squares: a1, a8, h1, h8?
6. Name the squares making up the a1–h8 diagonal. What color are they?
7. Name the square where the e1-h4 and g1-a7 diagonals cross.
8. Name the square where the 4th rank crosses the h1-a8 diagonal.

45

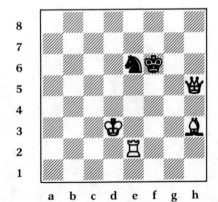

What move by the Black Knight will attack all the White pieces at the same time?

46

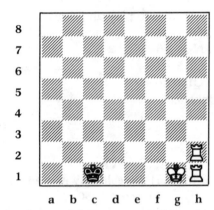

A trick puzzle! How can White checkmate Black in half a move?

Answers to Review Questions:
1. Checkmate.
2. No.
3. Knights.
4. Ra1, Nb1, Bc1, Qd1, Ke1, Bf1, Ng1, Rh1, pawns a2, b2, c2, d2, e2, f2, g2, and h2.
5. a1 and h8 are dark squares, and h1 and a8 are light squares.
6. a1, b2, c3, d4, e5 f6, g7,and h8. They are all dark squares.
7. f2.
8. e4.

D-45. 1. ... Ne6-f4 + .

D-46. White is in the middle of castling short. He has made half the move (King to g1) and by completing the move (by jumping the Rook from h1 over to f1) he will checkmate Black. The whole move is 1. 0-0#.

C. *Abbreviated Notation*

Beginners usually record their games using

16

the "full" algebraic notation, where the square on which a man stands before making a move is first indicated and then the square on which it stands after completing its move. As players become more experienced, however, they often switch over to the "abbreviated" notation, where the square from which a man starts out is omitted and only the square on which it lands is indicated. For example, 1. Nb1-c3 is written in abbreviated form as 1. Nc3. In the case of a pawn capture, the file (but not the square) from which the pawn starts out is also indicated.

47

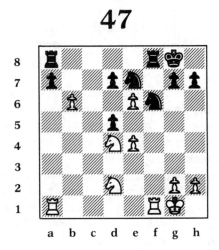

For example, the move 28. b6xa7 in Diagram 47 would be written as 28. bxa7.

Suppose now that White plays 28. Ra1-c1 in Diagram 47. This would be written in abbreviated notation as 28. Rac1. By giving the file of departure ("a") we make it clear that it is the Rook on a1 and not the Rook on f1 which moves to c1.

Sometimes in order to remove an ambiguity, we have to indicate the rank from which a piece starts out. If, for example, in Diagram 47 White plays 28. Nd4-f3, it would not be enough to write 28. Nf3, since both White Knights can go to f3. However, if we write 28. N4f3, it becomes clear that it is the Knight on the 4th rank which moves to f3.

From now on we shall be using both the full and abbreviated types of notation. The main moves in games and puzzles will be given in full notation, while in the commentaries ab-

breviated notation will be used.

Now let us analyze a game recorded in full notation. This encounter from the 1924 Paris Championship is the shortest game ever played in a major tournament.

Game 6
Gibeau–Lazard

| 1. d2-d4 | Ng8-f6 |
| 2. Nb1-d2? | |

An unfortunate move that blocks the dark-square Bishop. 2. c4 or 2. Nf3 would be better.

| 2. ... | e7-e5 |

Black hopes to set up an attack by means of this pawn sacrifice.

| 3. d4xe5 | Nf6-g4 |
| 4. h2-h3? | |

White is playing hastily, without thinking out his moves carefully. He wants to chase back the advanced enemy Knight right away even though it is not threatening anything dangerous. A possible alternative is:

4. Ngf3 Bc5 5. e3 Nc6 6. Nc4 b5 7. Ncd2 a6 8. a4, with a slightly better position for White.

| 4. ... | Ng4-e3! |

(see Diagram 48)

48

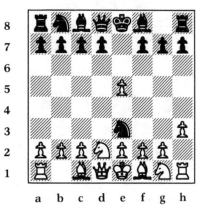

White resigns. He must lose his Queen, since if 5. fxe3, then 5. ... Qh4+ 6. g3 Qxg3 #.

Here is how this game would be recorded in abbreviated notation:

Gibeau–Lazard
(Paris, 1924)

1. d4	Nf6
2. Nd2?	e5
3. dxe5	Ng4
4. h3?	Ne3!
White resigns	
	0–1

Some Chess Terms and Concepts

Let us look at some frequently used chess terms.

Any arrangement of pieces and pawns on the chessboard is called a **POSITION**.

Pieces and pawns are known as **MATERIAL**.

At the start of a game, therefore, the two opponents are in a state of **MATERIAL EQUALITY**.

If one player has extra material (even if it is only a pawn) or material of greater value (*e.g.* a Queen for his opponent's Rook), he is said to have a **MATERIAL ADVANTAGE**.

49

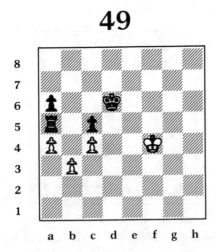

Diagram 49 shows another kind of advantage. Black is up a Rook for only a pawn, but the Rook is trapped — it cannot make any moves without being captured. As a result, it is White who has chances of winning. In positions like this we say that White has a **POSI-**

TIONAL ADVANTAGE. That is, his pieces and pawns are better placed, and in Diagram 49 that more than makes up for Black's **MATERIAL SUPERIORITY** (another term for ''material advantage'').

Queens and Rooks are called **MAJOR PIECES**, while Bishops and Knights are known as **MINOR PIECES**.

A player who captures a Rook in exchange for a minor piece is said to **WIN THE EXCHANGE**, and his opponent is said to **LOSE THE EXCHANGE**.

Voluntarily giving up material in order to achieve some goal is called a **SACRIFICE**.

Thus, if a player voluntarily gives up a Rook for a minor piece (Knight or Bishop), he is said to **SACRIFICE THE EXCHANGE**.

It is worthwhile to sacrifice almost all your material if you can checkmate your opponent's King with what you have left.

Virtually every game contains **THREATS**. A **THREAT** is an intention to make a move that is unpleasant for the opponent. For example, if you make a move which opens up the possibility of checkmating the enemy King the next move, you are threatening checkmate. Similarly, if you check the enemy King, that is a threat, since you intend to capture the King next move. A player can also threaten to win material or occupy some important square with one of his men.

Many chess terms originated in military usage. Examples are **ATTACK**, which is a combination of aggressive actions, and **COUNTERATTACK**, which is an attack unleashed by a player in reply to his opponent's attack.

50

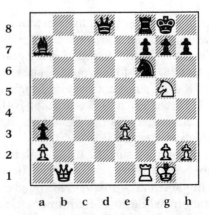

In Diagram 50, White played 1. Rf1xf6 — an **EXCHANGE SACRIFICE** with the **THREAT** of 2. Qxh7 #. White is thus **ATTACKING** the Black King. Black replied with a **COUNTERATTACK**: 1. ... Ba7xe3+; 2. Kg1-h1 Be3xg5. Black has repulsed White's attack and won a pawn. In this case, Black's **COUNTERATTACK** proved stronger than White's **ATTACK**.

Attack and Defense. Trades.

Sometimes, as for example in the "Scholar's Mate", a direct attack on the King brings a game to a rapid finish even before any men have been captured by either side. However, this does not happen very often. Usually each player tries to eliminate the opponent's men and starts a mating attack only when the enemy King has lost most of its army.

To eliminate an enemy man, you must first **ATTACK** it. This is a different meaning of the word "attack." Here it means to "threaten to capture."

An attack can be one-way or mutual. A pawn that attacks an enemy pawn, Bishop, Queen, or King is itself under attack by the enemy man. These are cases of mutual attack. On the other hand, a pawn that attacks a Knight or Rook is not itself under attack from the enemy man. These are examples of one-way attack.

When attacking, defending, or exchanging men, you must take into account the relative worth of the men involved. For example, let us analyze the position in Diagram 51.

White decided to attack the pawn on a7 by playing 1. Ra1, and Black replied with 1. ... Ra8, defending the pawn. White could now capture the a7 pawn with 2. Rxa7, but after the reply 2. ... Rxa7 White would have lost a Rook for only a pawn. So White played 2. Rea2. Now the pawn is attacked twice but defended only once (see Diagram 52).

52

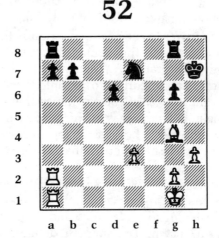

If Black does not defend it again, White could continue with 3. Rxa7 Rxa7 4. Rxa7, and Black has lost a pawn. Black could strengthen the pawn's defense by playing 2. ... Nc8, but then after 3. Bxc8 Rgxc8 (an equal trade) 4. Rxa7 Rxa7 5. Rxa7 Black still winds up losing the pawn.

Coming back to Diagram 51, let us see what might happen if Black replies to 1. Ra1 with 1. ... Nc6. White could then continue with 2. Rea2 (see Diagram 53).

51

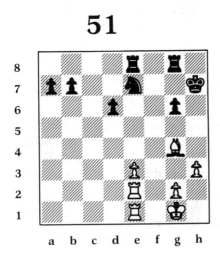

53

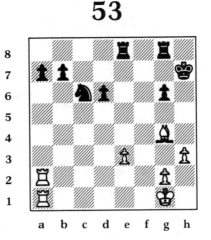

Now the a7 pawn is attacked twice but defended only by the Knight on c6. Does this mean that White is threatening to capture the pawn? Let's figure it out:

3. Rxa7 Nxa7 4. Rxa7.

White has lost a Rook in return for a Knight and a pawn (or, in other words, he has lost the Exchange for a pawn). Since we know that a Rook is worth a Knight and two pawns, it is clear that the captures have resulted in White losing about a pawn's worth of material.

So the answer to the above question is that White was not really threatening to capture the a7 pawn in Diagram 53. When you attack an enemy man, it is important to take into account not only the *number* of your own men that are attacking it, but also the value of these men. It is not worthwhile to begin attacking an enemy man with a piece of your own that is more valuable than the defender.

All the same, 1. ... Nc6 in Diagram 51 is not a good defense against 1. Ra1. White will play 2. Bf3, threatening to trade on c6 and then capture the a7 pawn. The simplest defense for Black is 1. ... a6. Now White could pile up on the a-pawn with his Bishop and other Rook, but even then capturing the pawn would not be worth it, since White would get only two pawns for his Bishop. Thus it is pointless to use pieces to attack a pawn that is defended by another pawn.

Here is another example.

Game 7

1. e2-e4	**e7-e5**
2. Ng1-f3	

The Knight attacks the pawn on e5.

2. ...	**d7-d6**

Black defends the pawn on e5 with a pawn on d6, so that now it will be useless for White to attack the e-pawn with pieces alone. So White played:

3. d2-d4

White threatens to win the pawn on e5, which is now attacked twice and defended only once. So Black defends the pawn a second time with:

3. ...	**Nb8-c6**

(see Diagram 54)

54

Now 4. d4xe5 Nc6xe5 5. Nf3xe5 d6xe5 6. Qdxd8 + Ke8xd8 would only be an equal trade of a White pawn, Knight, and Queen for the same Black men, although the resulting position, show in Diagram 55, is slightly better for White as Black has lost the right to castle.

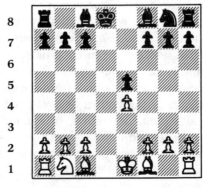

55

Now let us look at the next example.

Game 8

1. e2-e4	**e7-e5**
2. Ng1-f3	**Nb8-c6**

Black defends the pawn on e5, which the Knight on f3 was threatening to capture.

3. Bf1-c4

The Bishop attacks the pawn on f7, which, however, is defended by the Black King.

3. ...	**Bf8-c5**

This attack on the f2 pawn is also not dangerous for the time being.

4. d2-d3	**Ng8-f6**
5. Nf3-g5?	

(see Diagram 56)

56

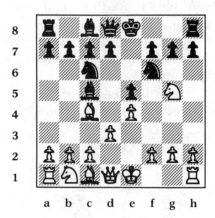

White increases the pressure on the f7 pawn and threatens to take it with his Bishop or Knight. So Black must defend the pawn again. 5. ... Qe7, although it defends the pawn a second time, will not do, as you will see from the following variation:

6. Bxf7 + Qxf7 7. Nxf7 Kxf7
(see Diagram 57)

57

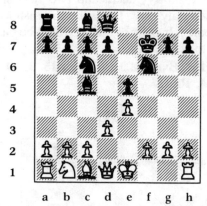

White has lost two minor pieces worth a total of six points but in return has gained Black's Queen and a pawn, worth a total of ten points, so that Black has ended up losing four points worth of material

Let us go back to Diagram 56. Another way for Black to defend the f7 pawn is with 5. ... Rf8. Now after 6. Nxf7 Rxf7 7. Bxf7 + Kxf7 White has given up a Bishop and a Knight (6 points) for a Rook and a pawn (6 points). That is, an equal trade has taken place.

58

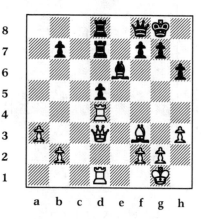

In the resulting position, shown in Diagram 58, White and Black are materially equal, but Black has a positional advantage because he has developed (i.e., brought out) three minor pieces while all of White's pieces are still sitting at home.

In spite of this, 5. ... Rf8 is a bad move, because White does not have to capture the pawn on f7 but can instead play 6. 0-0, while Black has lost the right to castle Kingside and will have difficulty in transferring his King to a safe spot.

The correct move in Diagram 56 is 5. ... 0-0!, castling and at the same time re-defending the f7 pawn.

In playing 5. Nf3-g5? White counted on Black making a mistake. The correct defence by Black, 5. ... 0-0!, however, shows up White's move to have just been a time-wasting error.

Now let us look at Diagram 59.

59

The Black pawn on d5 is attacked four times (by the Bishop, Queen, and two Rooks) and defended only three times (by the Bishop and two Rooks). In spite of that, it would be bad for White to capture it:

1. Bxd5? Bxd5 2. Rxd5 Rxd5 3. Qxd5? Rxd5 4. Rxd5

60

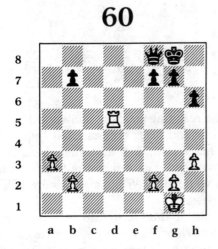

The result is shown in Diagram 60. White has lost his Queen (9 points) for a Rook (5 points) and a pawn (1 point). That is, White has lost 9 − (5 + 1), or 3, points worth of material. This happened because the White Queen was the third attacker and the Black pawn was defended three times.

Let us change Diagram 59 just a bit by shifting the White Queen from d3 to b5. The result is shown in Diagram 61.

61

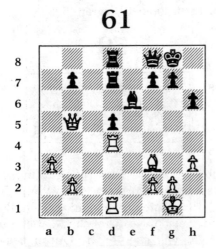

White is still attacking the d5 pawn four times and Black is still defending it three times.

However, now White can win the pawn:

1. Bxd5 Bxd5 2. Rxd5 Rxd5 *3. Rxd5*

This is the difference! In the previous example White was unable to capture with his Rook on the third move and instead captured with his Queen. Now, however, after

3. ... Rxd5 4. Qxd5

White is a pawn up (see Diagram 62).

62

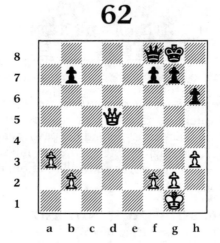

Let us follow the thought processes of a chessplayer faced with the problem of whether or not to capture the Black pawn on d5 in Diagram 61:

"I'm attacking it four times and he's defending it only three times. Now let's check the value of the attackers and defenders. I have two Rooks and a Bishop attacking the pawn and he also has two Rooks and a Bishop defending it. But in addition I have my Queen hitting the pawn, and, what's more important, I can use the Queen to make the final capture and thus hold on to it."

Only after thinking things out like this will the player make the move 1. Bxd5.

A player must learn not only to see his opponent's threats but also to take proper defensive measures against them and in addition create threats of his own. In his desire to create threats, however, a player should avoid attacking this opponent's men aimlessly and at random. Rather, he should attack a man only when he sees that he can gain some advantage by doing so. Otherwise he will just be wasting time to the detriment of his position.

In conclusion, let us see how we can defend against the "Scholar's Mate."

Game 9

1. e2-e4	**e7-e5**
2. Qd1-h5?	**Nb8-c6**

Defending the pawn on e5.

3. Bf1-c4

What is White's threat? *(4. Qxf7#)*

3. ...	**g7-g6**

Defending f7 and simultaneously attacking the Queen.

4. Qh5-f3?

Does White threaten anything now? *(5. Qxf7#)*

44. ...	**Ng8-f6**

The best defense. Black develops a piece and defends against mate at the same time.

5. Qf3-b3?

White is stubborn. He attacks the f7 pawn, which is defended only once, a second time. However, he is no longer threatening mate (see Diagram 63).

63

5. ...	**Nc6-d4!**

Black does not defend the f7 pawn but rather *counterattacks* by threatening the White Queen.

6. Qb3-c3

Only now does White realise that 6. Bxf7+ would lose a piece after 6. ... Ke7 7. Qc4 b5!.

6. ...	**d7-d5!**

Black could have captured the pawn on e4 but he decides that it is more expedient to open up a path for his light-square Bishop and quickly bring it into play.

7. e4xd5	**Bc8-f5**

What does Black threaten? *(8. ... Nxc2+; the pawn on c2 is now attacked by two Black pieces and defended only once).*

8. d2-d3

See Diagram 64.

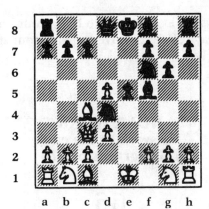

64

How can Black win the White Queen now?

8. ...	**Bf8-b4!**

Black sacrifices a Bishop!

9. Qc3xb4

There is nothing better, since if 9. Bb5+, then 9. ... Bd7 10. Bxd7+ Qxd7 leaves White with the same problem. Who can find Black's winning move now?

9. ...	**Nd4xc2+!**

See Diagram 65.

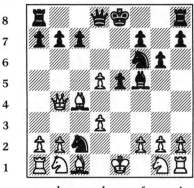

65

White resigns. The Black Knight is simultaneously attacking the White King (check), the White Queen, and a White Rook. The King must move out of check, after which the Knight will capture the Queen, leaving White with only a Bishop for a Queen, that is a material disadvantage of six points.

White lost quickly because he made more

than half his moves with his Queen (the most valuable piece). This enabled Black to bring his minor pieces into play with gain of time by attacking White's Queen or creating various threats.

Conclusion: Do not rush to bring your Queen into play before you have prepared your attack properly.

HOMEWORK
(Answers at the end)
I. Diagrams 66–73

66

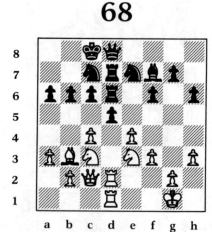

Black to play will pile up on the e5 pawn. Can White defend it?

_____

_____

_____

67

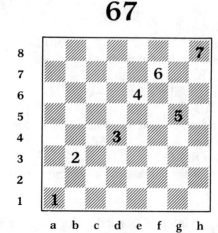

Name in order the squares marked 1 to 7. First do this with the help of the letters and numbers printed on the edges of the diagram, then cover up the rank numbers on the left edge with a piece of paper and repeat the exercise, and finally cover up both the rank numbers and the letters indicating the files and do the exercise once more.

68

Can White to play win the pawn on d5?

_____

_____

_____

69

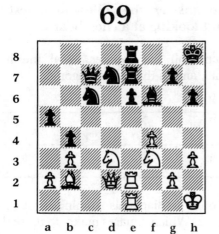

Will Black lose his e-pawn if he plays 1. ...
e6-e5?

_____

_____

_____

70

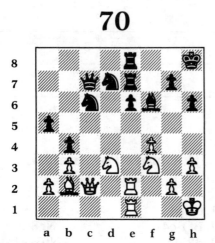

What is the difference between this position
and Diagram 69? Is 1. ... e6-e5 a good move for
Black in this changed position?

_____

_____

_____

71

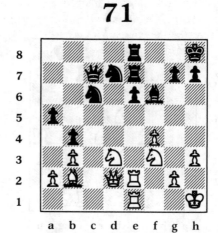

Same question as for Diagram 70.

_____

_____

_____

72

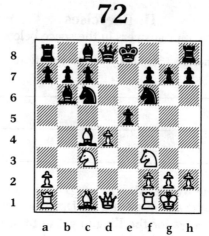

Can White to play hinder Black from
castling?

_____

_____

_____

73

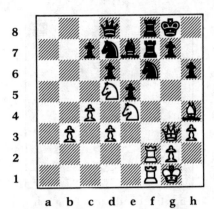

Can White to play win material?

_____

_____

_____

II. Exercises

Write your answers in the space below.

1. Change 1. bxc8N+ to full notation.

_____

_____

_____

2. The White King is on g1 and there are White pawns on g2 and f2. Describe two different ways for the King to get to f3 in three moves.

_____

_____

_____

Try to answer the following questions without looking at a chessboard.

3. Name all the squares in a) the h1-a8 diagonal, and b) the a1-h8 diagonal.

_____

_____

_____

4. Name the diagonals running through the square b2. Which squares make up these diagonals?

_____

_____

_____

5. At which square does the 2nd rank cross the c1-a3 diagonal?

_____

_____

_____

III. Games For Analysis
Game 10

1. e2-e4	e7-e5
2. Bf1-c4	Ng8-f6
3. d2-d4	Nf6xe4
4. d4xe5	c7-c6
5. Ng1-e2	Ne4xf2
6. 0-0!	

Black had counted on 6. Kxf2, after which 6. ... Qh4+ would win back the piece.

| 6. ... | Nf2xd1? |

6. ... Bc5! was necessary.

| 7. Bc4xf7+ | Ke8-e7 |
| 8. Bc1-g5# | |

See Diagram 74 for final position.

74

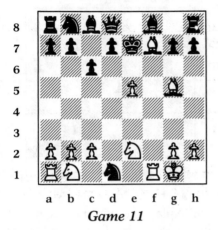

Game 11

1. e2-e4	e7-e5
2. Ng1-f3	Nb8-c6
3. Bf1-c4	Bf8-c5
4. c2-c3	Ng8-f6
5. d2-d4	Bc5-b6?

5. ... exd4 was correct.

6. d4xe5	Nf6xe4

6. ... Ng4 was better.

7. Qd1-d5	Ne4xf2?
8. Qd5xf7#	

Of course, Black would have done better to give up the Knight than to get mated. See Diagram 75 for the final position.

75

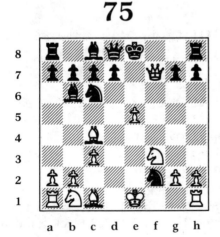

D-66 Yes, because White can match a defender for each of Black's three attackers.

D-67 a1, b3, d4, e6, g5, f7, h8.

D-68 Yes. The pawn on d5 is attacked seven times and also defended seven times. However, the preliminary exchanges will open up the c-file, after which the Black Knight on c7 will not be able to move as it must shield its King against the White Queen. So the number of Black defenders will be reduced by one and White will win the pawn.

D-69 No. The pawn on e5 will be attacked six times and defended six times as well. In addition, the defenders and attackers are of equal value. Thus, Black can safely play 1. ... e6-e5.

D-70 No. This position differs from Diagram 69 in that the White Queen is on c2 instead of d2. This change is enough to make 1. ... e6-e5 a bad move, since after the preliminary exchanges on e5, White can exchange Queens by Qxc7. As a result, one of the defending pieces will be eliminated and the attackers will outnumber the defenders.

D-71 No. This position differs from Diagram 69 in that Black's h-pawn is on its home square instead of on h6. As a result of this seemingly insignificant change, Black cannot play 1. ... e6-e5. The sequence of exchanges on e5 would result in the disappearance of all the minor pieces and Rooks and conclude with the Black Queen capturing on e5 (7. ... Qxe5). At that point, however, the Black King's fate would be sealed as White would play 8. Qd2-d8 + and mate next move. If the pawn were on h6, the King would have an escape hole and be safe.

D-72 In this position from the game Morphy–Stanley, New York 1857, White played 1. Bc1-a3!, fixing the Black King in the center, and later worked up a strong attack.

D-73 No. The Knight on f6 is attacked 5 times and defended 5 times as well (the pawn on g7 cannot be counted a defender since it shields the King against the White Queen). So the defense is adequate.

II. Answers to the Exercises

1. 1. bxc8N + , indicating a pawn promoting to a Knight, would be described in full algebraic notation by 1. b7xc8N + .

2. a) Kf1-e2-f3; b) Kh2-g3-f3.

You can check the answers to the remaining questions easily by looking at a chessboard.

SUPPLEMENTARY MATERIAL

for use at the teacher's discretion

Positions 76–81 illustrate the theme of "Attack and Defense."

76

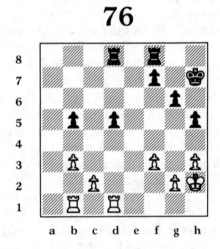

White to play and win a pawn.

   1. Rd1-d4!   **Rd8-d6**
   2. Rb1-d1   **Rf8-d8**

The two attackers are matched by the two defenders, but White has a third attacker in reserve.

   3. c2-c4!   **b5xc4**
   4. b3xc4

And White wins the pawn on d5.

77

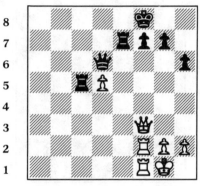

Can White play and win the pawn on f7? *No. Although White has three attackers against only two defenders, the Queen is the first attacker and will be captured by the Black Rook:*

   1. Qf3xf7 +   **Re7xf7**
   2. Rf2xf7 +   **Kf8-g8**

And White has lost his Queen for a Rook and a pawn, a material disadvantage of $9 - (5 + 1) = 3$ points.

78

White to play and win a pawn.

   1. Ra1-a7!   **Rf8-c8**
   2. Re1-c1

And Black cannot defend the c7 pawn a second time. Note that 1. Rec1 would not win since after 1. ... Rb7 2. Rc3 Black can defend the pawn a second time by 2. ... Rc8.

79

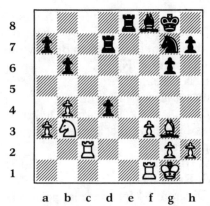

Can White play and win the pawn on d4?

No. White can attack the pawn four times, but Black has four defenders of the same value as White's attackers:

1. Bg3-f2	Ng7-e6
2. Rc2-d2	Bf8-g7
3. Rf1-d1	Re8-d8

80

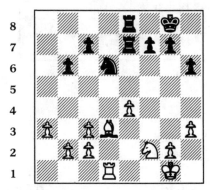

Can Black play and win the pawn on e4?

No. The attacking pieces are worth more than the defenders, and Black would lose the Exchange for a pawn (i.e., a loss of one point.):

1. ...	Nd6xe4
2. Bd3xe4	Re7xe4
3. Nf2xe4	Re8xe4

81

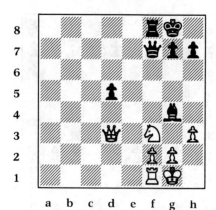

Can Black move and win a pawn?

Yes. The White Knight is attacked three times by Black and defended only twice:

1. ...	Bg4xf3
2. g2xf3	Qf7xf3
3. Qd3xf3	Rf8xf3

And Black has won a pawn.

Examples of Games with Opening Mistakes

Game 12

1. e2-e4	b7-b6
2. Bf1-c4	Bc8-b7
3. Qd1-f3?	

3. d3 is better.

3. ...	Ng8-f6
4. Ng1-h3	Bb7xe4?

4. ... e6 is better.

5. Nh3-g5?	

White should win back the pawn by 5. Bxf7+ Kxf7 6. Ng5+ Ke8 7. Nxe4.

5. ...	Be4xf3?

5. ... d5 is necessary.

6. Bc4xf7#	

See Diagram 82 for the final position.

82

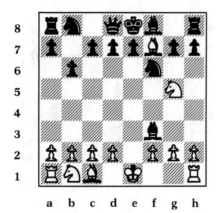

Game 13

1. d2-d4	f7-f5
2. Bc1-g5	h7-h6
3. Bg5-h4	

White tempts his opponent to open up the Black King's position.

3. ...	g7-g5
4. Bh4-g3	f5-f4?

4. ... Nf6 is correct.

5. e2-e3	h6-h5

Black defends against the threat of 6. Qh5#.

6. Bf1-d3	Rh8-h6?

Black has to play instead 6. ... Bg7 7. exf4 h4.

7. Qd1xh5 + !	Rh6xh5
8. Bd3-g6#	

See Diagram 83 for the final position.

83

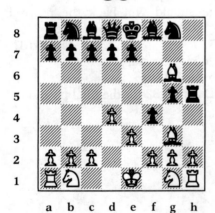

Game 14

1. e2-e4	e7-e5
2. Bf1-c4	Qd8-f6?
3. Ng1-f3	Qf6-g6?

It is bad play to move only your Queen in the opening.

4. 0-0!	Qg6xe4?
5. Bc4xf7 + !	Ke8-d8

5. ... Kxf7 would be bad as Black would lose his Queen after 6. Ng5 + .

6. Nf3xe5!	

White sacrifices a Knight.

6. ...	Qe4xe5?

It was high time Black started bring out his other pieces.

7. Rf1-e1	Qe5-f6?
8. Re1-e8#	

See Diagram 84 for the final position.

84

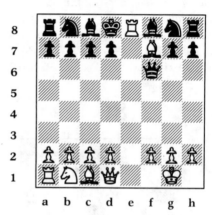

Game 15

1. e2-e3	

1. e4 is better.

1. ...	e7-e5
2. Qd1-f3?	d7-d5
3. Nb1-c3	e5-e4
4. Qf3-f4?	

A gross blunder, instead of which White should have retreated his Queen (4. Qd1).

4. ...	Bf8-d6!

85

White resigns, as he cannot save his Queen.

Lesson Three

A. Check Lesson 2 homework (if necessary).

B. *Review Questions*
1. What difference, if any, is there between an attack and a counterattack?
2. Can a player have a positional advantage even if the two sides have equal material?
3. Which pieces are called minor pieces and which are called major pieces?
4. What is meant by a sacrifice?
5. What does the phrase "sacrifice the Exchange" mean?
6. Without looking at a chessboard, name all the squares in the g1-a7 diagonal. Are they light or dark squares?

87

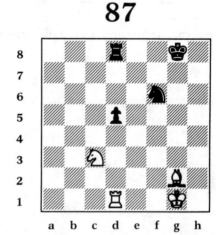

Is the Black pawn on d5 sufficiently defended?

86

Is the Black pawn on d5 sufficiently defended?

88

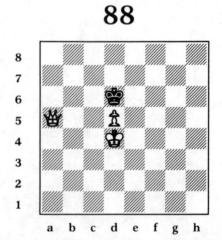

How can White checkmate Black in one move?

89

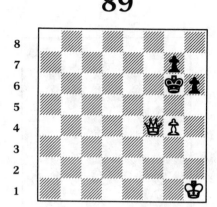

How can White checkmate Black in one move?

Answers to Review Questions:

1. A counterattack is an attack undertaken by a player in reply to his opponent's attack.

2. Yes. A **positional advantage** is a better *arrangement* of pawns and pieces (material) and can occur even when the two sides have equal material.

3. The Bishops and Knights are the **minor pieces** and the Queen and Rooks are the **major pieces.**

4. A **sacrifice** is when a player voluntarily gives up material in order to achieve some goal.

5. The difference in value between a Rook and a minor piece is known as the **Exchange.** So to **sacrifice the Exchange** means to voluntarily give up a Rook for a Bishop or a Knight.

6. g1, f2, e3, d4, c5, b6, a7 (all are dark squares.)

D-86 The pawn is attacked by two pieces and defended by only one. So it is not adequately defended and needs additional protection.

D-87 The two defenders are matched by two attackers of corresponding value, but White has a third attacker as well. So the pawn is not adequately defended and needs additional protection.

D-88 1. Qa5-d8#.

D-89 1. Qf4-f5#.

More Symbols and Terms

We are already acquainted with a number of symbols that help us to record and analyse chess games. Now here are some more useful symbols.

Symbols	Meaning
!!	excellent (beautiful) move
??	gross blunder
?!	risky (dubious) move
u	any move
=	White and Black have equal positions
+ / −	White's position is better
− / +	Black's position is better

And now let us get acquainted with a few more chess terms and concepts. You will sometimes come across expressions such as "White has a **forced** win," "an exchange of pieces is **forced,**" "the pawn queens **by force,**" "Black **forced** a draw," etc. In chess, to say that something is **forced** means that it cannot be avoided by one of the players if his opponent wants it.

90

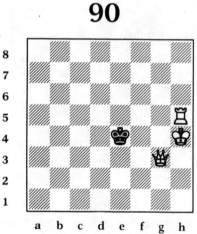

For example, in Diagram 90, we say that White has a forced mate in five moves. That means that Black cannot avoid getting checkmated in five moves or less no matter what he does:

    1. Rh5-e5 +   Ke4-d4

    2. Qg3-e3 +   Kd4-c4

        (see Diagram 91)

91

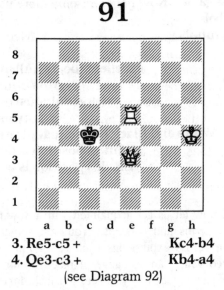

| | | | | | | | |
|a|b|c|d|e|f|g|h|

3. Re5-c5 +   Kc4-b4
4. Qe3-c3 +   Kb4-a4

(see Diagram 92)

92

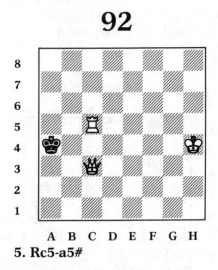

| | | | | | | | |
|A|B|C|D|E|F|G|H|

5. Rc5-a5#

You can see that Black cannot avoid the above series of five moves. Such a series of moves in which one player cannot avoid is known as a **forced variation**, in this case a five-move forced variation.

A **variation** is a series of moves united by a common idea. In Diagram 90, White's idea was to drive the Black King to the edge of the board and checkmate it.

A **combination** is a forced variation containing a sacrifice and permitting the achievement of some **aim** desired by the player who makes the combination. The **aim** of a combination can be to mate the opponent's King, obtain a draw, win material, improve your position, etc.

93

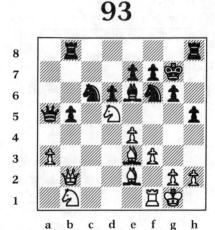

| | | | | | | | |
|a|b|c|d|e|f|g|h|

Diagram 93, from the game Steinberg–Makarov, Kiev 1956, shows an example of a combination. White had sacrificed a pawn and then an Exchange for the attack, but after a while it became clear that Black had defended successfully while at the same time retaining his material advantage. Realizing that he was more likely to lose than to win, White decided to force a draw in the position of Diagram 93 by means of a **combination:**

1. Nd5xe7!

White sacrifices the Knight with the **idea** of eliminating the pawn that defends Black's Knight on f6.

1. ...   Nc6xe7
2. Qb2xf6 + !

Now White sacrifices his Queen with the idea of drawing the Black King out of his shelter.

2. ...   Kxf6

(see Diagram 94)

94

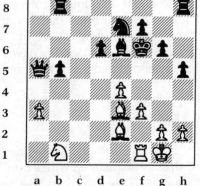

| | | | | | | | |
|a|b|c|d|e|f|g|h|

3. Be3-d4 +

And now White forces a draw by a perpetual check that Black cannot avoid!

3. ...	Kf6-g5
4. Bd4-e3 +	Kg5-h4
5. Be3-f2 +	Kh4-g5
6. Bf2-e3 +	

Draw

Another commonly used chess term is **Zugzwang**. A player is said to be in **Zugzwang** if it is his turn to move and, although he is not threatened with anything, any move that he makes will lead to a loss or to a worsening of his position.

95

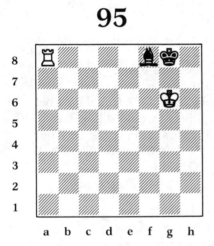

Diagram 95 is an example. Black to play loses because he is in **Zugzwang.** If he could stay put without making any moves he would not lose, but since the rules of chess do not allow a player to pass his turn Black must make the only move available to him, 1. ... Kg8-h8, although it leaves his Bishop undefended and allows White to checkmate him with 2. Ra8xf8#.

Let us examine the position again, but this time with White to move. We observe that Black, if it were his turn to play, would be in Zugzwang. Therefore White must somehow transfer his turn to Black, while conserving the elements of the position that make a Zugzwang possible. White can achieve this by making a **waiting move** with his Rook along the 8th rank, for example 1. Ra8-c8. Now Black is in Zugzwang and after the forced move 1. ... Kg8-h8 he is mated by 2. Rxc8xf8#.

A chess game can be divided into three stages: the opening (the starting moves of a game), the middlegame, and the endgame. In this section we shall discuss the opening.

All that a beginner needs to know about the opening is the basic principles of piece development that will help him to choose the right moves in the starting stages of a game. Here is a list of these principles:

1. It is best for White to start a game with 1. e2-e4 or 1. d2-d4, opening up a pathway for a Bishop and the Queen and attacking important **central squares.** Black should reply correspondingly with 1. ... e7-e5 or 1. ... d7-d5.

2. From the very first moves you should fight for control of the center (the d4, d5, e4, and e5 squares). Pieces are much stronger in the center of the board than on an edge. For example, a Knight controls (i.e., attacks) eight squares from the center, four squares from an edge, and only two squares when it has been driven into a corner.

3. The main opening principle is **rapid development** of your pieces. What this means is that you should bring your pieces into play as quickly as possible. Begin by developing your Kingside minor pieces (Knight and Bishop). This clears the way for Kingside castling, which enables you to put your King in safety and develop your Rook at the same time. After castling, bring out your Queenside pieces.

The reason for developing rapidly is that the player who succeeds in bringing his pieces into play before his opponent can obviously start attacking first and will have better chances of making effective combinations and winning the game.

A great master at exploiting advantages in development was the brilliant American chess-player Paul Morphy. Before examining examples of his play, let us first take a brief look at some highlights of Morphy's chess career, one of the most remarkable in the annals of chess.

Morphy learned to play chess at the age of ten and within just two years became the strongest player in his hometown of New Orleans. in 1857, at the age of twenty, he easily brushed aside all opposition in winning the First American Chess Congress and was on the path to becoming a chess celebrity. Not finding worthy opponents in America, Morphy went to Europe in 1858 and played a number of matches in London and then Paris. The fantastic ease with which he defeated the strongest players of the day earned him an unequalled reputation. In 1859 Morphy returned to America and, to everyone's surprise, never took part in any more tournaments.

Now let us examine one of Morphy's brilliant games. This game was played under extremely odd circumstances. The date was October 1859, and the place was the Grand Opera in Paris. the boxes and stalls were occupied by the cream of Parisian society, the "beau monde", who had come to watch a performance of the opera *The Barber of Seville*. Among these spectators were two aristocrats, the well-known Duke of Brunswick and the little-known Count Isouard. They were both chess amateurs, and by the standards of those days they did not play too badly. By a coincidence, another person who had come to the opera that night was none other than Paul Morphy, who played excellent chess — by the standards of *any* period. During the interval the Count and the Duke invited Morphy to their box and suggested a game of chess. Morphy agreed. Here is the immortal game that was played.

Game 16

White: Paul Morphy
Black: Count Isouard and the Duke of
Brunswick (in consultation)

1. e2-e4	e7-e5
2. Ng1-f3	d7-d6
3. d2-d4	Bc8-g4?

3. ... Nf6 or 3. ... Nd7 are the correct moves.

4. d4xe5	Bg4xf3

After 4. ... dxe5 White would win a pawn by 5. Qxd8+ Kxd8 6. Nxe5.

4. Qd1xf3	d6xe5

(see Diagram 96)

96

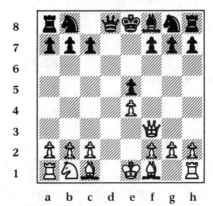

The Black Bishop made two moves and was exchanged for the White Knight, which had only made one. As a result, White has gained a development advantage over his opponent.

6. Bf1-c4

What is White threatening? *(Qxf7#.)*

6. ...	**Ng8-f6**

Black defends against the mate but has not noticed the other threat created by Morphy's last move. 6. ... Qd7 would be a better move, although Black would still be faced with a difficult defense after the possible White moves 7. Qb3, 8. Nc3, 9. 0-0, and 10. Rfd1.

7. Qf3-b3

(see Diagram 97)

97

White attacks two Black pawns at the same time. The Queen attacks the pawn on b7, while the Bishop, supported by the Queen, threatens the pawn on f7. Black cannot defend both of them.

7. ...	**Qd8-e7**

Relatively the best. Although he must lose a

pawn, Black wants to at least force an exchange of Queens after 8. Qxb7 Qb4+ and thereby hinder White's attack.

Why would 7. ... Qd7 8. Qb7 Qc6 be bad? *(Because of 9. Bb5 winning Black's Queen).*

What would happen if Black played 7. ... Nxe4? *(8. Bxf7+ Kd7 9. Qe6#).*

8. Nb1-c3!

With this move Morphy emphasizes that it is more important in the opening to develop your pieces than to capture enemy pawns.

8. ...	c7-c6

In order to defend his pawn, Black is forced to make yet another pawn move instead of developing his pieces.

8. Bc1-g5

White has now completed the development of his minor pieces.

9. ...	b7-b5?

Black expects the White Bishop to retreat, after which he could play ... Nbd7 and gradually develop his pieces. But 9. ... Qc7 would be better. See Diagram 98.

98

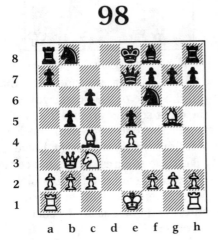

10. Nc3xb5!!

An important moment in the game. Morphy sacrifices the Knight in order to open up lines along which his other pieces can attack the Black King. This sacrifice is not an accident, but rather a manifestation of one of the principles which govern chess struggles. According to this principle, the player who has developed faster than his opponent must strive to open up lines since his pieces are ready to seize control of them. Conversely, a player who is behind in development should avoid moves that lead to

the opening of lines since his pieces are not ready to use them and they will be taken over by the opponent's pieces.

10. ...	c6xb5
11. Bc4x b5 +	Nb8-d7
12. 0-0-0	

By castling long White enables the Queen's Rook to immediately enter the struggle along the d-file. What is White's threat now? *(13. Bxd7+, and Black cannot recapture with 13. ... Nxd7 since he would lose his Queen.)*

12. ...	Ra8-d8

Why doesn't Black play 12. ... Qb4? *(Because of 13. Bxf6 Qxb3 14. Bxd7#, or 13. Bxf6 gxf6 14. Bxd7+, winning back the piece and maintaining a devastating attack.)* See Diagram 99.

99

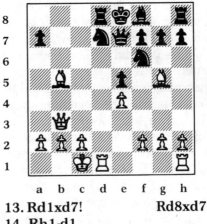

13. Rd1xd7!	Rd8xd7
14. Rh1-d1	

White sacrificed the Exchange in order to eliminate the important defensive Knight and now brings up fresh reserves in the form of the h1 Rook. Black on the other hand has conducted the opening so poorly that neither his Rook on h8 nor his Bishop on f8 can help him in his defense.

14. ...	Qe7-e6

Why is 14. ... Qb4 no good? *(Because of 15. Bxf6 followed by 16. Bxd7+.)*

15. Bb5xd7 +	Nf6xd7

See Diagram 100

100

Find the combination which Morphy made to checkmate Black in two moves.

    16. Qb3-b8 + !!   **Nd7xb8**
    17. Rd1-d8#

A brilliant finish!

If it weren't for this game, nobody in the world would have heard of Count Isouard. As it is, however, his name is known to millions of chess lovers. Thus did a genius make the Count immortal!

We learned earlier on that it is bad to bring out your Queen at the beginning of a game. How is it then that Morphy "violated" this principle and still won a beautiful game? The reason is that Morphy rapidly developed *all* his pieces. As for his Queen, it was safe because the Black pieces were not in a position to attack it. There was good co-operation among all of White's pieces (i.e., they helped one another) and White was even able to sacrifice the Queen in order to checkmate Black.

So Morphy did not really break any opening rules. We must keep in mind furthermore that exceptions to the rules are possible and that everything depends on the actual situation on the board.

The Endgame
Checkmate with Queen and Rook

Checkmate in the opening is possible only as the result of a gross blunder by one of the players and occurs rarely among strong chessplayers. Nor is it possible in every game to checkmate your opponent in the middlegame, when there are still a lot of pieces on the board. Thus games are often in fact decided only in the endgame, when the number of pieces on the board has been considerably reduced as a result of exchanges.

The main goal of a player in the endgame is generally not an immediate checkmate, as there are usually too few pieces left to organize a mating attack. Rather, the player strives first of all to queen a pawn, after which checkmating the opponent will not be difficult.

To begin with, however, here is a very simple endgame where White already has a Queen, along with a Rook and his King, while Black has only his King (see Diagram 101).

101

In order to checkmate a lone King that is away from the edge of the board, you have to control the eight squares around it as well as a ninth square: the one on which the King is standing. If the King is on an edge, however, it has only 5 escape squares, while in a corner it has only 3 escape squares. So it is obviously easier to checkmate a King on an edge than one in the center, and even easier to checkmate a King in a corner.

A Queen and a Rook can checkmate a lone enemy King without the help of their own King by driving it over to an edge. In Diagrams 90–92 we saw a commonly occurring type of mate with Queen and Rook against King, but now let us look at the main mating method, known as "row-by-row mating."

102

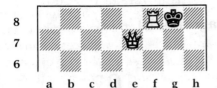

Diagram 102 shows the typical pattern resulting from "row-by-row mating." (We call the situation in Diagram 102 a pattern rather than a position because a real position always has two Kings, while in Diagram 102 the White King has been left out as not being relevant to what we want to illustrate). The idea of this mating pattern is simple: one piece controls the back row, where the enemy King stands, and the other piece controls the second-last row, cutting off the King's escape.

Now let us return to Diagram 101 and try to drive the Black King over to an edge.

1. Rc1-c4

The Rook takes control of the 4th rank and cuts the King off from half the board.

1. ...   **Ke5-d5**

The King attacks the White Rook. See Diagram 103.

103

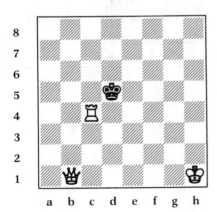

2. Qb1-b5 +

The Queen takes control of the 5th rank and at the same time protects the Rook.

2. ...   **Kd5-d6**

Since White controls the 4th and 5th ranks, the Black King is forced to retreat to the 6th rank. See Diagram 104.

104

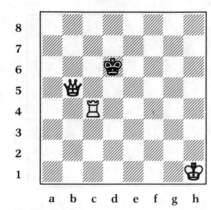

3. Rc4-c6 +

The White Queen having cut the Black King off from the 5th rank, the White Rook now takes control of the 6th rank.

3. ...   **Kd6-d7**

Since the Rook now guards the 6th rank, the Queen is able to move over to the 7th rank.

4. ...   **Kd7-d8**

The end of the road.

5. Rc6-c8#

See Diagram 105.

105

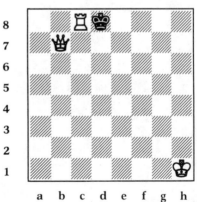

This way of mating is called the row-by-row method because the Queen and Rook in turn cut the King off from one row after another until they have driven it to the edge row (file or rank), where they can checkmate it. The Queen and the Rook are arranged in such a way that the Rook is always defended by the Queen. Thus the two pieces help each other and their joint efforts are enough to checkmate the opposing King. This is an example of good **piece co-operation.**

106

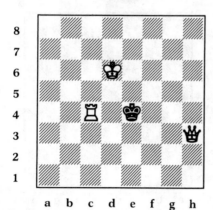

Diagram 106 shows another example. The Black King has been checkmated in the center of the board thanks to the fine co-operation of all the White pieces (including the King). The White King controls d5 and e5, the Rook guards the 4th rank and attacks the Black King, and the Queen controls the 3rd rank and f5.

HOMEWORK
(Answers at the end)

I. Diagrams 107–112

107

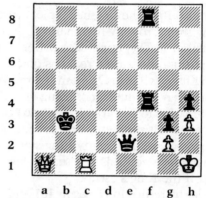

White to play and mate in six moves.

	WHITE	BLACK
1.		
2.		
3.		
4.		
5.		
6.		

108

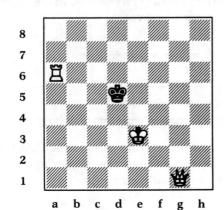

White to play and mate in two moves.

	WHITE	BLACK
1.		
2.		

110

White to play and mate in two moves.

	WHITE	BLACK
1.		
2.		

109

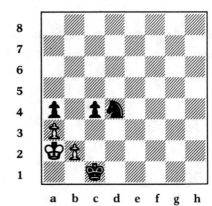

White to play and mate in two moves.

	WHITE	BLACK
1.		
2.		

111

Black to play and mate in two moves.

	WHITE	BLACK
1.		
2.		

112

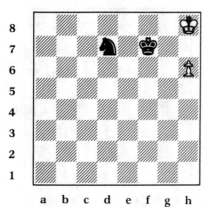

Black to play and mate in two moves.

WHITE	BLACK
1.	
2.	

II. Board Study Exercises

Write down your answers in the spaces below.

1. Place eight Queens of the same color on an empty board in such a way that none of them defends any of the others.

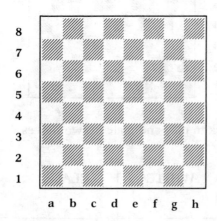

_____

_____

_____

2. Find any one of the paths in which a Black King on f8 can reach a4 in the shortest number of moves. Write it down in chess notation.

_____

_____

_____

3. Suppose you are playing Black. Name the square where the fourth row (counting from your side) crosses the fourth file (counting from your left).

_____

_____

_____

4. Write down any one of the paths in which a Knight on a8 can reach b7 in the shortest number of moves.

_____

_____

_____

5. Record one of your games in full algebraic notation and then play it over to check if you recorded it correctly.

SCORESHEET

Date: _____ 19 _____

WHITE: _____

BLACK: _____

WHITE	BLACK		WHITE	BLACK
1.			21.	
2.			22.	
3.			23.	
4.			24.	
5.			25.	
6.			26.	
7.			27.	
8.			28.	
9.			29.	
10.			30.	
11.			31.	
12.			32.	
13.			33.	
14.			34.	
15.			35.	
16.			36.	
17.			37.	
18.			38.	
19.			39.	
20.			40.	

RESULT:

WHITE WON   DRAW   BLACK WON

43

III. Games for Analysis

Game 17
Spielman–Flamberg, Mannheim, 1917

1.	e2-e4	e7-e5
2.	Nb1-c3	Ng8-f6
3.	f2-f4	

White plays a **Gambit**. A gambit is an opening in which a player sacrifices a pawn or a piece in order to develop very quickly.

3.	...	d7-d5!

The right move, counterattacking in the center.

4.	f4xe5	Nf6xe4

Threatening 5. ... Qh4+, and if 6. g3, then 6. ... Nxg3.

5.	Ng1-f3	Bc8-g4
6.	Qd1-e2	

White sets up two threats. One is to win a pawn by 7. Nxe4, and the other is play 7. Qb5+ and then take the pawn on b7.

6.	...	Ne4-c5?

Black should exchange Knights, complete his development and castle on the Kingside.

7.	d2-d4!	

Sacrificing a pawn.

7.	...	Bg4xf3
8.	Qe2xf3	Qd8-h4+
9.	g2-g3	Qh4xd4

Black has won a pawn, but at great cost. White's Queen has occupied an attacking position and the other White pieces are ready to enter the fray without loss of time.

10.	Bc1-e3!	Qd4xe5

Black wins a second pawn, but gets even farther behind in development.

11.	0-0-0!	c7-c6

White has developed his Queen, a Knight, a Bishop, and a Rook, while Black has managed to bring out only his Queen and a Knight, and even they occupy poor positions. Such disregard for development cannot remain unpunished.

12.	Nc3xd5!	

When you have more pieces active, you must act energetically so as not to give your opponent a breather.

12.	...	c6xd5
13.	Rd1xd5	Qe5-e6
14.	Bf1-c4	Qe6-e4

White was threatening 15. Rxc5 or 15. Rd8+.

15.	Be3xc5!	

See Diagram 113.

113

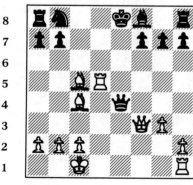

White sacrifices his Queen. Black resigns, because if 15. ... Qxf3, then 16. Re1+ Be7 17. Rxe7+ Kf8 18. Rd8#.

Rudolf Spielmann, who commanded the White army in this brilliant game, was a famous Austrian grandmaster.

HOMEWORK ANSWERS
I. Diagrams 107–112

D-107

1.	Rc1-c3+	Kb3-b4
2.	Qa1-a3+	Kb4-b5
3.	Rc3-c5+	Kb5-b6
4.	Qa3-a5+	Kb6-b7
5.	Rc5-c7+	Kb7-b8
6.	Qa5-a7#	

D-108 (by G. Carpenter)

1.	Qf3-h3	

Black is in Zugzwang. He is forced to play

1.	...	Kd4-e4

And give up control over c4, allowing

2.	Rc2-c4#	

D-109

Solution 1:

1.	Ke3-d3	Kd5-e5
2.	Qg1-g5#	

Solution 2:

1.	Qg1-c1	

Black is in Zugzwang and must give up control over c5.

        1. ...   **Kd5-e5**
        2. Qc1-c5#

D-110 (by P. Morphy)
        1. Rh1-h6

Black is in Zugzwang. If he did not have to move, White could not checkmate him, but since he must move, he loses:

a)   1. ... g7xh6 2. g6-g7#
b)   1. ... Bg8-anywhere 2. Rh6xh7#

D-111
        1. ...   **Nd4-c2**
Zugzwang.
        2. b2-b4   **c4xb3#**

C-112
        1. ...   **Nd7-f8**
Zugzwang.
        2. h6-h7   **Nf8-g6#**

II. Exercises

1. See Diagram 114. Ninety-two solutions to this problem were already known more than a hundred years ago.

114

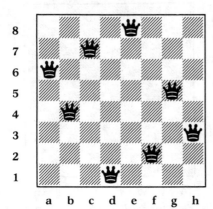

2. Kf8-e7-d6-c5-b4-a4 (five moves).
3. e5.
4. Na8-c7-b5-d6-b7 (4 moves).

SUPPLEMENTARY MATERIAL

for use at the teacher's discretion

In Diagrams 115–120 White wins by putting Black in Zugzwang.

115

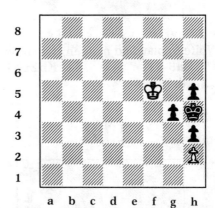

White to play and mate in two moves.
        1. Kf5-f4   **g4-g3**
        2. h2xg3#

116

G. Greco, 1624

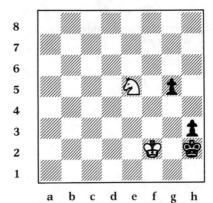

White to play and mate in three moves.
        1. Ne5-g4 +   **Kh2-h1**
        2. Kf2-f1   **h3-h2**
        3. Ng4-f2#

117

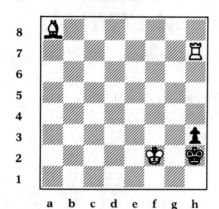

White to play and mate in two moves.
1. Ba8-h1   Kh2xh1
2. Rh7xh3#

118

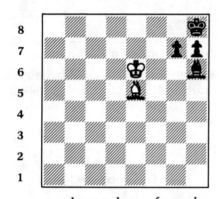

White to play and mate in two moves.
1. Ke6-f7   Bh6-any
2. Be5xg7#

119

M. Yudovich

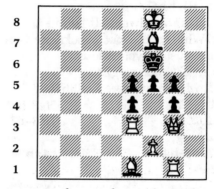

White to play and mate in two moves.
1. f2-f4   ...
  a)/... e4xf3   2. Qg3xe5#
  b)/... e5xf4   2. Be1-c3#
  c)/... g4xf3   2. Qg3xg5#
  d)/... g5xf4   2. Qg3-h4#

120

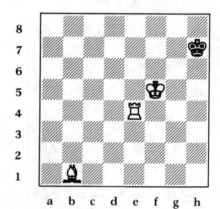

White to play and mate in two moves.
1. Kf5-f6 ...
  a)/... Kh7-h8 2. Re4-e8#
  b)/... Kh7-g8 2. Re4-e8#
  c)/... Kh7-h6 2. Re4-h4#

Game 18
Four Knights Game
**H. Dickson–H. N. Pillsbury, New Orleans
1900**

1. e2-e4	e7-e5
2. Ng1-f3	Nb8-c6
3. Nb1-c3	Ng8-f6
4. Bf1-b5	Bf8-c5
5. 0-0	0-0

H. N. Pillsbury, who played Black in this game, was an outstanding American grandmaster and one of the strongest players in the world in the late 1800s and early 1900s. This game was played in what is known as a simultaneous blindfold exhibition. That is, Pillsbury was blindfolded and was playing many games against different opponents (who were not blindfolded!) at the same time.

6. Nf3xe5	Qd8-e7

After 6. ... Nxe5 7. d4 White would win back his piece with a good game.

7. Ne5xc6?	

Trying to hang on to his extra pawn, White makes poor moves. He should instead play 7. Nf3 Nxe4 8. d4, when the Black Queen will come under fire along the open e-file.

7. ...	d7xc6
8. Bb5-d3??	

He had to play instead 8. Bc4 Nxe4 9. d3, giving up the pawn but completing his development.

8. ...	Qe7-e5
9. h2-h3	

The final mistake! Even now White could have averted disaster by playing 9. Be2.

9. ...	Bc8xh3!

By sacrificing the Bishop, Black exposes the White King's position.

10. g2xh3	Qe5-g3 +
11. Kg1-h1	Qg3xh3 +
12. Kh1-g1	Nf6-g4

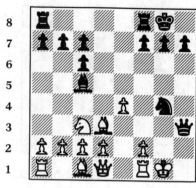

White resigns. He has to give up his Queen by 13. Qxg4 in order to avert immediate mate.

Game 19
Giuoco Piano
Greco–Amateur, Rome 1619

1. e2-e4	e7-e5
2. Ng1-f3	Nb8-c6

The Italian master Greco, White in this game, was the strongest player of his time.

3. Bf1-c4	Bf8-c5
4. c2-c3	Qd8-e7

4. ... Nf6 is played more often in this position.

5. 0-0	d7-d6
6. d2-d4	Bc5-b6
7. Bc1-g5	f7-f6?
8. Bg5-h4	g7-g5?

Black's last two moves are poor. It is more important to develop your pieces in the opening that to move pawns. 7. ... Nf6 followed by 8. ... 0-0 would be better.

9. Nf3xg5!	

White sacrifices the Knight! Only by such energetic measures can Black's incorrect play be refuted.

9. ...	f6xg5
10. Qd1-h5 +	Ke8-d7
11. Bh4xg5	Qe7-g7
12. Bc4-e6 + !	

A pretty sacrifice leading to mate.

12. ...	Kd7xe6
13. Qh5-e8 +	Qg7-e7
14. d4-d5#	

See Diagram 122 for the final position.

122

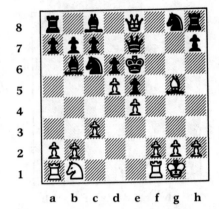

Lesson Four

A. Check Lesson 3 Homework (if necessary).

B. *Review Questions*

1. Is e2-e4 is good first move? If yes, why exactly?
2. What is the "opening"?
3. Do you know the meaning of the word "gambit"?
4. When does the endgame start?
5. What is meant by the word "forced"?
6. What is a "variation"?
7. What is a "combination"?

Try to answer questions 8–10 without looking at a chessboard.

8. What color (light or dark) is the g2 square?
9. How many moves does a Knight need to get from g4 to f5? Name these moves. Give two solutions.
10. Suppose you are playing Black. Name the square where the third row (counting from your side) crosses the a1-h8 diagonal.

Answers to Review Questions

1. 1. e2-e4 is a very good first move because it opens a path for the Queen and a Bishop. In addition, the pawn occupies a central square and controls the important squares d5 and f5.
2. The *opening* is made up of the first 10–15 moves of a game.
3. A *gambit* is an opening in which one of the players sacrifices a pawn or sometimes even a piece in order to gain an advantage in development over his opponent and to whip up a quick attack.
4. The *endgame* begins when, apart from the Kings and pawns, only a few pieces remain on the board, the rest having been exchanged off.
5. To say that something is *forced* means that it cannot be avoided.
6. A *variation* is a series of moves united by some idea. If these moves compel the opponent to make certain replies, the variation is called a *forced variation*. For example, in Diagram 123 White (to play) wins by means of a forced variation:

123

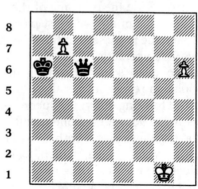

1. b7-b8N +	Ka6-b6
2. Nb8xc6	Kb6xc6
3. h6-h7	u
4. h7-h8Q	etc.

Theoretically speaking, other moves too were possible, but the moves we have given are the best for both White and Black.

7. A *combination* is a forced variation in which one or more sacrifices (of a pawn, an Exchange, or a piece) are made in order to achieve a particular aim. An example is shown in Diagram 124:

124

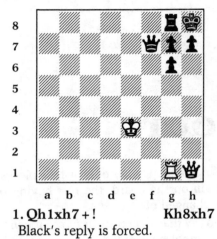

1. Qh1xh7 + !   **Kh8xh7**

Black's reply is forced.

2. Rg1-h1#

8. Light.

9. Two moves: Ng4-e3-f5 or Ng4-h6-f5.

10. f6.

Mistakes in the Opening

Every time somebody loses a game, it is because he has made some mistake. Sometimes even a mistake in the opening can be so serious as to decide the outcome of the whole game. In chess as in life we must pay for our mistakes, and the more serious the mistake the more severe the penalty.

Let us go over some opening principles whose violation results in mistakes:

1. It is bad to bring out your Queen early in the game. If you do, your opponent will be able to develop his minor pieces with gain of tempo by attacking your Queen, which, being the more valuable piece, will have to retreat.

2. Do not make passive waiting moves in the opening such a2-a3, a7-a6, h2-h3, or h7-h6. Every move should be used either to bring out a piece or to open a line (rank, file, or diagonal) for a piece.

3. Do not waste time (tempos) in the opening by unnecessarily moving the same piece several times.

4. An attack conducted with meager forces before you have completed your development and castled is premature unless your opponent has committed some gross blunder that allows you to make a combination that wins by force.

5. Do not go chasing after some small material advantage (such as a pawn) in the opening at

the cost of lagging behind in development or getting a bad position.

Now let us look at some games featuring typical opening mistakes.

Game 20

1. e2-e4	**e7-e5**
2. d2-d4	**e5xd4**
3. c2-c3	**d4xc3**
4. Bf1-c4	**c3xb2**
5. Bc1xb2	

This opening is known as the Danish Gambit. White sacrifices two pawns in order to develop his Bishops on active diagonals without loss of time.

    5. ...   **Bf8-b4 +**

A solid defense is 5. ... d5!, with the idea of giving back one (or perhaps even both) of the pawns in order to achieve full piece development. A possible variation is 6. Bxd5 Bb4 + 7. Nc3 Bxc3 + 8. Bxc3 Nf6 9. Nf3 Nxd5 10. exd5 Qe7 + 11. Kf1 0-0 12. Qd4 Qf6 13. Qxf6 gxf6 14. Bxf6 Nd7 = .

    6. Nb1-d2   **Qd8-g5?**

As you no doubt remember, it is not good to bring your Queen out early in the game. However, Black has decided that in the given position he can gain an advantage by doing so since the Queen on g5 not only defends g7 but also attacks the White pawn on g2. In addition, Black is threatening to exchange Queens by 7. ... Qxd2 + , which would be good for him since he is two pawns up. See Diagram 125.

125

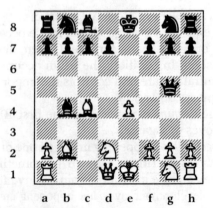

7. Ng1-f3!

White sacrifices a third pawn and continues

to rapidly bring his pieces into play.

    7. ...   **Qg5xg2**
    8. Rh1-g1   **Bb4xd2 +**
       See Diagram 126

126

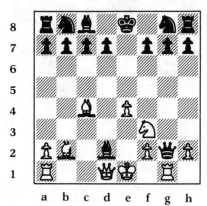

This is the position that Black had in mind when he played 6. ... Qg5. What is White to do now? If he recaptures the Bishop with his Queen he will lose his Knight, if he recaptures it with his Knight he will lose his Rook, and if he recaptures it with his King (9. Kxd2) he will lose his pawn on f2 with check.

    9. Ke1-e2!!

This move, overlooked by Black, allows White to continue with a devastating attack.

    9. ...   **Qg2-h3**
    10. Qd1xd2
       See Diagram 127.

127

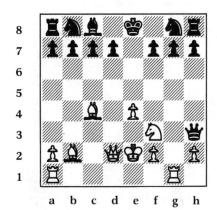

Someone who came upon this position without seeing what led up to it might be forgiven if

he thought for an instant that only White had been moving for most of the game! Black has three (!) extra pawns but has paid dearly for them. All his pieces (except the Queen) are in a deep slumber, so to speak, while all the White pieces control important files and diagonals and are ready to launch an attack. It is therefore no surprise that the struggle is over in just a few more moves.

    10. ...   **Ng8-f6**
    11. Bc4xf7 + !   **Ke8-d8**

If 11. ... Kxf7, then 12. Ng5+ wins the Queen, while if 11. ... Kf8, then 12. Ba3+ d6 13. Bxd6 + cxd6 14. Qxd6 + Kxf7 15. Ng5 again wins the Queen.

    12. Rg1xg7   **Nf6xe4**
    13. Qd2-g5 + !   **Ne4xg5**

How does White mate next move?

    14. Bb2-f6#

The final position is shown in Diagram 128.

128

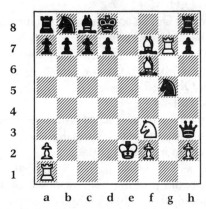

This didactic game shows how dangerous it is go to "pawn-grabbing" in the opening. As a result of his gambit, White obtained an overwhelming superiority of forces on the Kingside and in the center, and this advantage in development created excellent conditions for attaining victory.

Game 21

    1. e2-e4   **e7-e5**
    2. Ng1-f3   **f7-f6?**

A poor way of defending the pawn on e5. The pawn on f6 deprives the Knight on g8 of its natural developing square, the Black King's position becomes exposed, and White is able to work up an irresistible attack by sacrificing his

Knight. Black should instead play 2. ... Nc6, 2. ... d6, or 2. ... Nf6. (See Diagram 129 for the position after 2. ... f7-f6?).

129

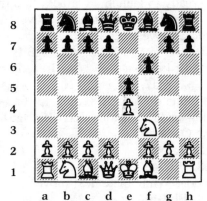

3. Nf3xe5!   **f6xe5?**

3. ... Qe7 would be better, although even then White would develop with tempo (gain of time) by 4. Nf3 Qxe4+ 5. Be2 Nc6 6. Nc3.

4. Qd1-h5+!

This early Queen sortie is justified here since White has a forced win.

4. ...   **Ke8-e7**

If 4. ... g6, then 5. Qxe5+ Qe7 6. Qxh8.

5. Qh5xe5+   **Ke7-f7**

6. Bf1-c4+

White develops his pieces with tempo (since the moves by the Black King are useless) and works up an irresistible attack.

6. ...   **Kf7-g6**

Black could prolong his resistance by 6. ... d5, although after 7. Bxd5+ Kg6 (f5 is now controlled by the Bishop on c8) 8. h4 h6 9. Bxb7! Bd6 (if 9. ... Bxb7, then 10. Qf5#) 10. Qa5 Nc6 11. Bxc6 White has four (!) extra pawns.

7. Qe5-f5+   **Kg6-h6**

How should White continue his attack?

8. d2-d4+

The Bishop on c1 enters the fray with tempo.

8. ...   **g7-g5**

How can White bring up fresh reserves now?

9. h2-h4!

The h-pawn and the Rook on h1 join the attack.

9. ...   **d7-d5**

10. Qf5-f7   **d5xc4**

How can White mate next move?

11. h4xg5#

130

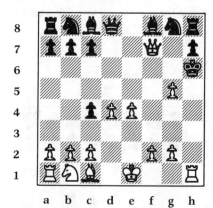

All the Black pieces looked on idly from their home squares while their King perished.

The Endgame Mate
With Two Rooks Against a King

You already know how to mate a lone King with a Queen and a Rook using the *row-by-row* method. Two Rooks too can, without the help of their own King, mate the opposing King by using the same method. The mating pattern (see Diagram 131) is also almost the same.

131

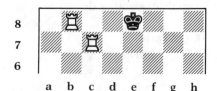

Now let us look at Diagram 132.

132

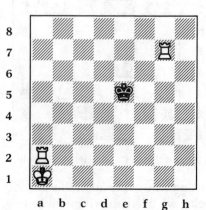

The Black King must be driven to an edge, preferably the nearest one. So let us try to drive it to the h-file. To do that, we must first prevent the King from escaping to the Queenside.

1. Rg7-d7

The Rook controls the d-file and cuts the King off from the Queenside.

1. ...   **Ke5-e6**

See Diagram 133.

133

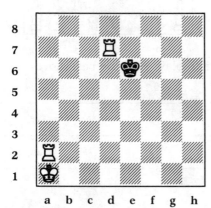

The King attacks the Rook. White moves the Rook far away, to the first rank (not to the second, where it would interfere with the other Rook). Now one Rook will be acting along the first rank and the other along the second.

2. Rd7-d1   **Ke6-e5**

Next White forces the Black King to abandon the e-file.

3. Ra2-e2 +   **Ke5-f4**
4. Rd1-f1 +

The persecution continues.

4. ...   **Kf4-g3**

See Diagram 134

134

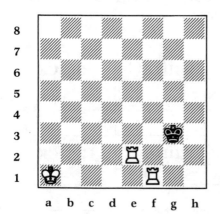

The Rook on f1 controls the f-file and White would now like to take over the g-file with the Rook from e2. However, the Rook cannot give a check immediately on g2, as it would be captured by the Black King. So White moves the Rook as far away as possible, to the other end of the board. We can now see the difference between mating a lone King with two Rooks and mating it with a Queen and a Rook. If the Rook on f1 were a Queen, the Rook on e2 would not have to run away to the other end of the board but could instead go to g2 (5. Rg2 +), since it would be supported by the Queen.

5. Re2-e8   **Kg3-g2**

Attacking the Rook on f1, which must also be moved as far away as possible, but not to the 8th rank, where it would interfere with the other Rook. So now the Rooks will be acting along the 7th and 8th ranks.

6. Rf1-f7   **Kg2-g3**
7. Re8-g8 +   **Kg3-h4**
8. Rf7-h7#

135

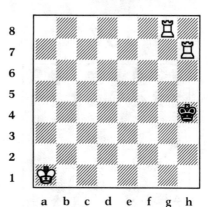

The final position is shown in Diagram 135. The Black King has nowhere further to retreat, so it's checkmate!

Two Rooks can mate the opposing King in the middle of the board as well, but only if they are aided by their own King. Diagram 136 shows an example.

136

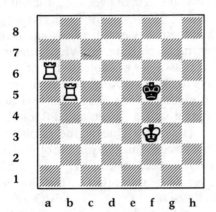

As you know, nine squares must be controlled in order to mate a King that is not on an edge. In our example, the White pieces each control a separate group of three of these nine squares, so that together they control all the nine squares, thus checkmating the Black King.

HOMEWORK
(Answers at the end)
I. Diagrams 137–142

137

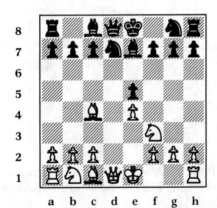

White to play. Find the best move.

_____

_____

_____

138

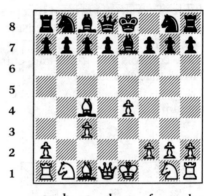

White to play. Find the best move.

_____

_____

_____

139

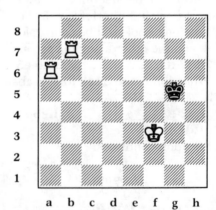

White to play. Mate in two moves. Find two solutions.

	WHITE	BLACK
1.		
2.		

	WHITE	BLACK
1.		
2.		

140

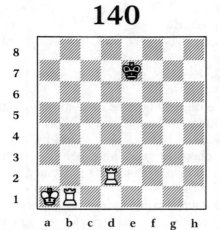

White to play. Mate in four moves. Find two methods.

	WHITE	BLACK
1.		
2.		
3.		
4.		

	WHITE	BLACK
1.		
2.		
3.		
4.		

141

White to play. Mate in two moves.

	WHITE	BLACK
1.		
2.		

142

White to play. How many moves are needed to checkmate Black? What are these moves?

WHITE	BLACK

II. Exercises

Write down your answers in the space below.

Try to answer questions 1–3 without looking at a board.

1. Can a position with White pawns on a2, a3, and b2 occur in a game?

2. How many moves will it take a Black Knight on c7 to capture a White pawn on e7?

_____

_____

_____

3. Name the diagonals running through e4. Which squares make up these diagonals?

_____

_____

_____

4. Set up several random positions with a King and two Rooks or a King, Queen and Rook against a lone King and practice checkmating the King until you can do it quickly and confidently.

5. Record one of your games in abbreviated notation and then play it over to check if you did it correctly.

III. Games With Opening Mistakes For Analysis

Game 22

1. f2-f4

This is not considered to be one of the strongest first moves since it does not open lines for the White pieces or help White's development. Furthermore, it exposes the White King's position.

    1. ...   **e7-e5**

A strong move. Black sacrifices a pawn (i.e., he is playing a gambit) but gets more than enough in return: paths are opened up for his Queen and dark-square Bishop and he can develop rapidly. 1. ... d5, freeing the way for the Queen and the light-square Bishop, would also be good.

    2. f4xe5

White loses time by capturing the pawn instead of developing. The best move would be 2. e4, with White in his turn offering Black a gambit.

    2. ...   **d7-d6**

    3. e5xd6

Bringing out a piece by 3. Nf3 would be better.

    3. ...   **Bf8xd6**

    4. Nb1-c3??

White blithely ignores the exposed position of his King. He had to play 4. Nf3.

    4. ...   **Qd8-h4 + !**

This check is good here because it has a definite follow-up that leads to victory.

    5. g2-g3   **Qh4xg3 + !**

Black sacrifices his Queen for a pawn. 5. ... Bxg3 + ! would have led to the same result also.

    6. h2xg3   **Bd6xg3#**

The final position is shown in Diagram 143.

143

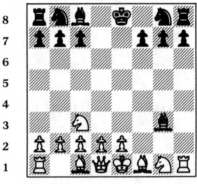

White lost quickly because he neglected the development of his pieces.

The next game also finishes very quickly.

Game 23

    1. f2-f4   **e7-e5**

    2. e2-e4

This time White plays a better move than 2. fxe5. The pawn sacrifice offered by White is called the "King's Gambit."

    2. ...   **Bf8-c5**

Black follows the very sensible policy of developing his pieces instead of grabbing a pawn. Also, he correctly avoids 2. ... Qh4 + . Beginners love to check whenever they can, but checks are often useless or even harmful. For example, White would reply to 2. ... Qh4 + with 3. g3. The attacked Queen would have to retreat and Black would just have lost time.

3. f4xe5?

White should have followed Black's example and developed a piece with 3. Nf3.

    3. ...   **Qd8-h4 + !**

Now this check is good!

    4. Ke1-e2   **Qh4xe4#**

See Diagram 144 for the final position.

144

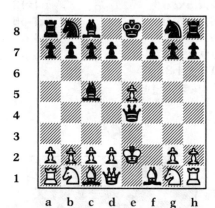

White could have avoided checkmate by playing 4. g3, but after 4. ... Qxe4 + he would have lost a Rook. In this game too White got carried away by the idea of winning a pawn and neglected his development.

Answers to the Homework
I. Diagrams 137–142

D-137

    1. Qd1-d5   **Ng8-h6**

    2. Bc1xh6   **0-0**

3. Qxf7 was threatened.

    3. Bh6-e3

And so on. The diagram position arose after the opening moves 1. e4 e5 2. Nf3 d6 3. Bc4 Nd7 4. d4 Be7? 5. dxe5 dxe5??.

D-138   The solution is exactly the same as for D-137, although this position arose from a different opening (1. e4 e5 2. d4 exd4 3. Bc4 Bb4 + 4. c3 dxc3 5. bxc3 Be7??).

D-139

Solution a):

    1. Rb7-b5 +   **Kg5-h4**

    2. Ra6-h6#

Solution b):

    Rb7-h7

Zugzwang.

    1. ...   **Kg5-f5**

    2. Rh7-h5#

D-140

Solution a):

    1. Rb1-e1 +   **Ke7-f6**

    2. Rd2-f2 +   **Kf6-g5**

    3. Re1-g1 +   **Kg5-h4**

    4. Rf2-h2#

Solution b):

    1. Rb1-b6   **Ke7-f7**

    2. Rd2-d7 +   **Kf7-e8**

    3. Rd7-a7   **Ke8-d8**

    4. Rb6-b8#

D-141

    1. Qc2-xh7 + !   **Kh8xh7**

    2. Ra2-h2#

D-142   Black can be mated in seven moves. There are many ways of doing this. Here is one:

    1. Ra1-a4   **Ke5-d5**

    2. Rb1-b5 +   **Kd5-c6**

    3. Rb5-h5

As far away from the King as possible.

    3. ...   **Kc6-b6**

    4. Ra4-g4

So that the Rooks don't get in each other's way.

    4. ...   **Kb6-c6**

    5. Rg4-g6 +   **Kc6-d7**

    6. Rh5-h7 +   **Kd7-e8**

    7. Rg6-g8#

II. Exercises

1.   No. Such a position is impossible because the only ways a pawn can get to a3 are either by advancing from a2 or by capturing from b2, but both these pawns are still on their home squares.

2.   Two moves: 1. ... Nc7-d5 2, ... Nd5xe7.

3.   You can easily check the answers your selves by looking at a chessboard.

SUPPLEMENTARY MATERIAL

for use at the teacher's discretion

Positions 145 and 146 illustrate opening mistakes and Diagrams 147–150 demonstrate the linear mate idea.

145

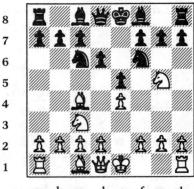

Black to play. What is White's threat and how can Black defend against it? This position arose after the following opening moves:

1. e2-e4	e7-e5
2. Ng1-f3	Nb8-c6
3. Bf1-c4	Ng8-f6
4. Nb1-c3	d7-d6?
5. Nf3-g5	

White threatens 6. Ng5xf7. Black is forced to give up a pawn, whether by 6. ... Bc8-e6 (defended once, attacked, twice), 6. ... d6-d5 (defended twice, attacked three times), or 6. ... Bc8-g4 7. Bc4xf7+ Ke8-d7 8. f2-f3.

146

From the game Petrosian–Ree, Beverwijk 1971. White to play and win a piece. This position arose after the following opening moves:

1. c2-c4	e7-e5
2. Nb1-c3	Nb8-c6
3. Ng1-f3	Ng8-f6
4. e2-e3	Bf8-b4
5. Nc3-d5	Nf6xd5?
6. c4xd5	e5-e4??

White now wins by:

7. d5xc6	e4xf3
8. Qd1-b3!	a7-a5
9. a2-a3!	Bb4-d6
10. c6xb7	Bc8-b7
11. Qb3xb7	

with an extra piece.

147

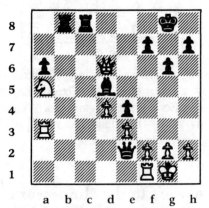

From the game Goglidze–Botvinnik, Moscow 1935. Black to play mates in three moves.

1. ...	Qe2xf1 + !
2. Kg1xf1	Rb8-b1 +
3. Kf1-e2	Rc8-c2#

148

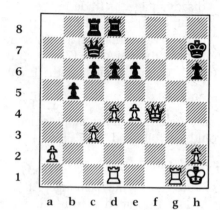

From the game Schlechter–Tarrasch, Cologne 1911. Black resigned after 1. Rd1-d3. Why?

Because he had no good defense against the threat of 2. Qxh6+ Kxh6 3. Rh3#.

149

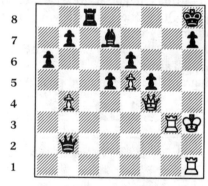

From the game Pillsbury–Maroczy, Paris 1900. White to play wins

1. Qf4-h6

Threatening 2. Qg7# or 2. Qf6#.

1. ...	Qb2xe5
2. Qh6xh7+!!	Kh8xh7
3. Kh3-g2#	

150

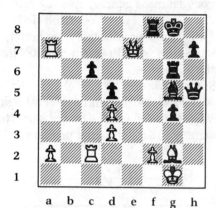

From the game Budrich–Gumprich, Berlin 1950. White to play wins.

1. Bg2xd5+!

To clear the c-file.

1. ...	c6xd5
2. Qe7xf8+!	Kg8xf8
3. Rc2-c8+	Bg5-d8
4. Rc8xd8#	

Sample Games
Containing Opening Mistakes

Game 24
Three Knights Opening
Reti–Dunkelblum, Vienna, 1914

1. e2-e4	e7-e5
2. Ng1-f3	Nb8-c6
3. Nb1-c3	Bf8-c5?!

This "active" move is not very good as it allows White to gain an advantage in the center by means of a temporary sacrifice.

4. Nf3xe5!	Nc6xe5
5. d2-d4	Bc5xd4?

Better would be 5. ... Bd6 6. dxe5 Bxe5.

| 6. Qd1xd4 | Qd8-f6? |

It would be better to defend the Knight by 6. ... d6, when 7. f4 would be dangerous for White because of 7. ... Qh4+ 8. g3 Nf3+. In bringing his Queen out to f6, Black has been tempted by the chance to threaten to win White's Queen by 7. ... Nf3+.

7. Nc3-b5!

The more stereotyped reply 7. Be3, developing a piece, would also have given White an advantage, but in this particular position the talented grandmaster Richard Reti realizes that he can better exploit Black's opening mistakes by moving his Knight a second time before completing his development, although such a move goes against a general opening principle.

7. ...   Ke8-d8?!

7. ... c6 would undoubtedly be better, but Black's position would remain difficult in any case after 8. Nd6+.

8. Qd4-c5!

Black resigns, as he cannot defend against both 9. Qf8# and 9. Qxc7+ at the same time. See Diagram 151 for the final position.

151

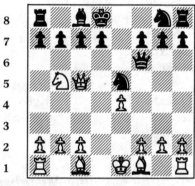

This game shows us that while as a rule we must play in accordance with the major opening principles, exceptions to these rules are sometimes possible.

Game 25

1. e2-e4	e7-e5
2. Ng1-f3	Nb8-c6
3. Bf1-c4	Bf8-c5

Both sides have played well in bringing out their Bishops to strong positions. This opening is called the Giuoco Piano.

4. d2-d3

Opening a path for the other Bishop.

4. ...   Ng8-e7?

A poor move. The Knight would be better placed on f6.

5. Nf3-g5!

Attacking the pawn on f7 a second time.

5. ...   0-0?

After this mistake, Black can no longer save himself. He should instead defend with 5. ... d5.

6. Qd1-h5!

If White plays 6. Nxf7 instead, then after 6. ... Rxf7 7. Bxf7+ Kxf7 he will have given up a

Bishop and a Knight in return for a Rook and a pawn, a disadvantageous trade in the opening stages of a game. After 6. Qd1-h5!, on the other hand, White threatens mate on h7 and simultaneously attacks the pawn on f7 a third time. Black cannot defend against both threats at once.

6. ...   h7-h6

The only defense against mate, since 6. ... Re8 would be followed by 7. Bxf7+ Kf8 8. Nxh7#.

7. Ng5xf7   Rf8xf7

Black has to give up the Exchange. After 7. ... Qe8 he would be mated in three moves: 8. Nxh6++ (double check) Kh8 9. Nf7++ (another double check!) Kg8 10. Qh8#.

8. Bc4xf7+   Kg8-f8

If 8. ... Kh8, then 9. Bxh6 gxh6 10. Qxh6#.

9. Bf7-b3   Qd8-e8

White was threatening to mate with the Queen on f7.

10. Qh5xh6

Instead of this Queen sacrifice, White could also play 10. Qf3+ Nf5 11. Qxf5, with an extra Rook and an easy win.

10. ...   g7xh6?

11. Bc1xh6#

See Diagram 152 for the final position.

152

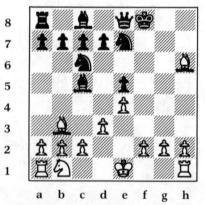

Instead of capturing the Queen, Black could have played 10. ... Ng8, which would have been followed by 11. Qh8 Ne7 12. Bg5 d5 13. Bxe7 Qxe7 14. Bxd5 Be6 15. Bxe6 Qxe6. In order to exploit his material advantage of an Exchange and three pawns, White should now strive to simplify the game by exchanging the Queens and other pieces and going into an endgame.

Lesson Five

A. Check Lesson 4 Homework (as necessary).

B. *Review Questions*

1. What is the difference between an opening and a gambit?
2. What does "Zugzwang" mean?
3. If a pawn moves from e2 to e3, and then the next move from e3 to e4, can a Black pawn on d4 capture it en passant?

Try to answer questions 4-6 without looking at a board.

4. Name the squares on which Black's Bishops stand at the start of a game. What color (light or dark) are they?
5. On which square does White's Queen stand at the start of the game? Is it a light or dark square?
6. At what square do the a3-f8 and e1-a5 diagonals cross? What color (light or dark) is it?

Answer the next questions directly from diagrams, without setting up the men on a board.

153

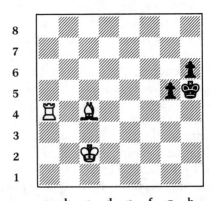

White to play and mate in one move.

154

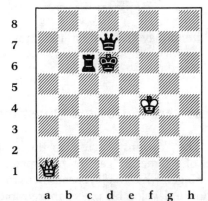

White to play and mate in one move.

155

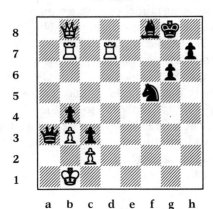

White to play and mate in two moves.

156

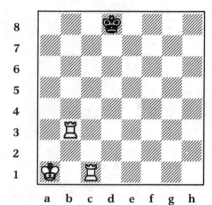

White to play and mate in two moves.

Answers to Review Questions

1. The "opening" refers to the first few moves of a game. A "gambit" is a special kind of opening in which a player sacrifices material in order to develop his pieces more rapidly.

2. A player is said to be in "Zugzwang" when all the moves available to him will worsen his position but he is forced to make one of them anyway because you are not allowed to pass your turn in chess. An example is shown in Diagram 156 (for solution see No. 10 below).

3. No. A Black pawn on d4 can capture a White e-pawn en passant only when the latter goes to e4 in a single move, i.e., e2-e4. Furthermore, if Black wants to take en passant (... d4xe3), he can only do so on the move with which he replies to White's e2-e4 — on succeeding turns the pawn on e4 will be safe from en passant captures.

4. c8 (light) and f8 (dark).

5. d1 (light.

6. b4 (dark).

D-153: 1. Bc4-f7#.

D-154: 1. Qa1-e5#.

D-155: 1. Qb8xf8 + Kg8xf8 2. Rb7-b8#.

D-156:

   1. Rb3-b7

Black is now in Zugzwang.

   1. ...   Kd8-e8

A forced King move that loses control of c8, allowing the White Rook to occupy it.

   2. Rc1-c8#

Opening Traps

Many battles in the history of warfare have been won as a result of some cunning stratagem. Similarly, chess battles too are often decided when we catch our opponent in a trap or when we ourselves fall into a trap.

What exactly is a trap? Simply put, a trap is an *enticement to make a mistake.* It is a cunning move containing some hidden, disguised threat which the trap-setter hopes his opponent will overlook. A regular characteristic of a trap is that it entices the opponent to make some tempting, natural, and apparently advantageous move or variation which, however, will meet with an unexpected refutation. Every chessplayer has at one time or another fallen into traps, even the World Champions.

Traps can be good or bad. **A trap is bad (or unsound) if it is a risky gamble** that will give you an advantage if your opponent falls into it but that will rebound to your disadvantage if your opponent sees and avoids it. That is, an unsound trap is based **only on the hope that the opponent will make a mistake.**

A trap is good (or sound) if there is no risk associated with it. If your opponent makes a mistake and falls into the trap, so much the better, but even if he sees and avoids your clever ruse, your position must not suffer. A sound trap will take into account the opponent's best replies and make sure they are not harmful.

Let us now look at some games whose outcomes were decided by a trap.

We will begin with an old trap which occurred in a game played in Paris in 1787. The 85-year-old chess master de Kermur sire de Legal was playing White, while the commander of the Black army was a weak chessplayer called Saint-Brie. Legal had been the strongest chessplayer in Paris for many years, until he acquired a talented pupil by the name of Francois Andre Danican Philidor who one fine day started winning from his teacher. Philidor later became not only the strongest chessplayer in the world but also a famous musician and composer. Legal, although overtaken by Philidor, nevertheless remained the second-best player in Paris right to the end of his life. In our days, too, pupils often start defeating their teachers. Right?

Game 26
Legal–Saint-Brie

1. e2-e4	e7-e5
2. Ng1-f3	d7-d6

This opening is called Philidor's Defense. That's right! The same Philidor who was Legal's pupil!

3. Bf1-c4	Nb8-c6
4. Nb1-c3	Bc8-g4

See Diagram 157.

157

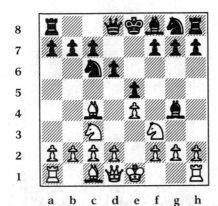

Until now both sides have played well. At this point, however, Legal touched the Knight on f3 and then quickly took his hand away, whereupon his opponent reminded him about the "touch-move" rule. The many onlookers confirmed that Legal had in fact touched the Knight and they too insisted that he move it. Legal agreed, but he said he wanted to think a bit more about where to move it, and finally he played:

5. Nf3xe5?!

The Chevalier Saint-Brie immediately snapped up the Queen, thinking that White was giving it up just like that.

5. ...   Bg4xd1??

This is the move that White's highly risky trap was based on. But if Black had thought the position over carefully, he would have realized that the Queen could not be taken but that the simple 5. ... Nxe5, on the other hand, would leave Black a piece up.

6. Bc4xf7 +	Ke8-e7
7. Nc3xd5#	

158

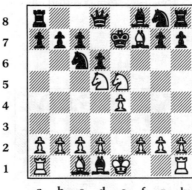

Nobody knows today whether Legal's touching the Knight really was accidental or whether it was just a ploy calculated to catch an inexperienced opponent in a pretty trap that Legal, although he knew it was unsound, was unable to resist playing.

Although the trap worked in this case, you would do well not to set such traps. Don't forget, if Black had seen through the trap, he could have won a piece.

This mate became known as "Legal's Mate", and it has been repeated many times since then in a variety of forms.

The idea of Legal's mate continues up to the present day to form the basis of threats or traps even in the games of strong players. Here is an example.

Game 27
Cheron–Jeanlose, Leysin 1929

This game was played in a "simultaneous exhibition" — Andre Cheron, many times champion of France, was playing many games at the same time against different opponents.

1. e2-e4	e7-e5
2. Ng1-f3	Nb8-c6
3. Bf1-c4	d7-d6
4. Nb1-c3	Bc8-g4

The position in which Legal set an unsound trap with 5. Nxe5.

5. h2-h3!!

The temptation to follow Legal might be great, but logic is more important! However, the move 5. h2-h3 too sets a cunning trap.

5. ...   Bg4-h5?

After 5. ... Bxf3 6. Qxf3 Nf6 (defending

against 7. Qxf7#) 7. d3 White's position would be better but it would still be a hard fight. See Diagram 159 for the position after 5. ... Bg4-h5?.

159

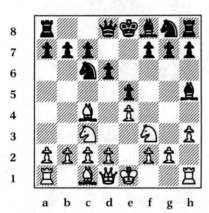

6. Nf3xe5!

Now this Legal-style Queen sacrifice is absolutely sound.

    6. ...   **Bh5xd1??**

Black should resign himself to the loss of a pawn by 6. ... Nxe5 7. Qxh5 Nxc4 8. Qb5+ c6 9. Qxc4 (or 6. ... dxe5 7. Qxh5).

    7. Bc4xf7 +   **Ke8-e7**
    8. Nc3-d5#

See Diagram 160 for the final position.

160

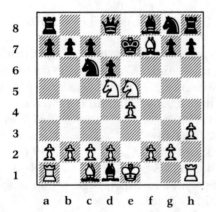

The trap in this game not only worked but, unlike Legal's trap, it was also sound. Even world champions are not averse to setting such traps!

You should make a study of both "good" and "bad" traps — the good ones so that you can use them, and the bad ones so that you can avoid them.

Let us now look at another very popular trap.

Game 28
Mullok–Kostic, Cologne 1912
    1. e2-e4   **e7-e5**
    2. Ng1-f3   **Nb8-c6**
    3. Bf1-c4   **Nc6-d4?!**
See Diagram 161.

161

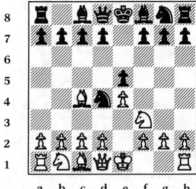

Black sets an unsound trap! White could now gain a development advantage over Black by playing 4. c3 Nxf3+ 5. Qxf3, while even the simple 4. d3 or 4. Nxd4 would give White the better game. Of course, Grandmaster Kostic realized that 3. ... Nc6-d4?! was far from the best move, but he counted on his weak opponent being tempted by the pawn that Black leaves undefended.

    4. Nf3xe5?

The first step toward disaster. The Black pawn on e5 was a "poisoned pawn."

    4. ...   **Qd8-g5!**
See Diagram 162.

162

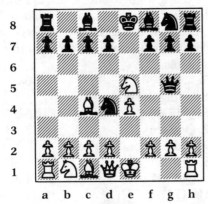

The Queen simultaneously attacks the Knight and the pawn on g2. White, however, can hardly believe his eyes and thinks, *"How can a grandmaster make such blunders? I can take his pawn on f7 with my Knight and fork his Queen and Rook!"* ("Fork" means to "simultaneously attack").

5. Ne5xf7??

And this is the second and final step towards disaster. The trap has clapped shut! Why would 5. Ng4 be a bad move?

(Because of 5. ... d5, winning the Knight or the Bishop).

White could still have saved the game by playing 5. Bxf7+ Kd8 6. 0-0 Qxe5 7. c3 followed by 8. d4. In return for his piece he would then have two pawns and chances of working up an attack against the Black King stranded in the center. In such cases White is said to have compensation for his lost piece.

5. ...   **Qg5xg2**

6. Rh1-f1

If White played 6. Nxh8, how would Black reply?

(6. ... Qxh1+ 7. Bf1 Qxe4+ 8. Be2 Nxc2+ 9. Qxc2 and Black wins the Queen. If 9. Kf1, then 9. ... Qh1#).

6. ...   **Qg2xe4 +**

7. Bc4-e2?

It's better to lose the Queen by 7. Qe2 than to get mated.

7. ...   **Nd4-f3#**

See Diagram 163.

163

White's King is completely surrounded by its own men but none of them can help. Such a mate is called a "smothered mate."

The trap in this game was pretty but unsound — it was based entirely on the presumption that the opponent would blunder.

How can you safeguard yourself from falling into a trap? Chess abounds in innumerable traps, so it is obviously impossible to memorize them all, but in spite of that strong players very rarely get taken in by them. The reason is that they follow the "major principles of piece development," the very ones that you have studied in previous lessons.

The most important thing is to always play carefully and never capture enemy pawns and pieces (even the Queen) without first thinking it over and making sure there's no trap.

Mating with a Queen in the Endgame

You already have some experience in mating a lone King and know that you must first drive it to one of the edges of the board. The Queen, the strongest chess piece, can do this all by itself, without the help of its King. Let us look at the position in Diagram 164.

164

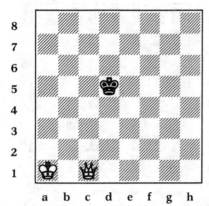

The best method is to chase the King to the nearest corner, which in our example is a8. However, if the King voluntarily heads for another corner (h8), we can mate it there as well.

1. Qc1-f4

The Queen controls the fourth rank and the f-file, cutting off several of the Black King's escape routes.

    1. ...   **Kd5-e6**

    2. Qf4-g5

The Black King having given up the fifth rank, the White Queen immediately occupies it.

    2. ...   **Ke6-d6**

    3. Qg5-f5

Now the Black King is cut off from the f-file.

    3. ...   **Kd6-c6**

    4. Qf5-e5   **Kc6-b6**

    5. Qe5-d5

See Diagram 165.

165

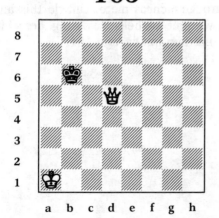

Note the technique: the Queen does its job without giving a single check, always staying a Knight's move away from the Black King, which, unable to attack the Queen, is constantly forced to give way and lose control over more squares.

    5. ...   **Kb6-c7**

Abandoning the 6th rank.

    6. Qd5-e6   **Kc7-b7**

    7. Qe6-d6   **Kb7-c8**

Leaving the second last rank.

    8. Qd6-e7   **Kc8-b8**

    9. Qe7-d7   **Kb8-a8**

    10. Qd7-c7???

See Diagram 166.

166

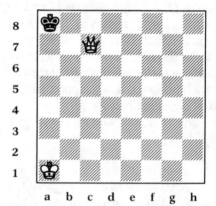

Oh, no! What have we done? The Black King is laughing and the White King is crying. And no wonder: it's stalemate, the game's a draw!

White's last move was a **gross blunder**, but beginners often fall into this trap.

In a real game, you cannot take back moves, but here let's take back our terrible last move so that you can learn how to checkmate (rather than stalemate)! See Diagram 167.

167

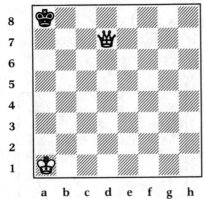

In driving the King into the corner, you have to be very careful and not make hasty moves. Leave the enemy King **two** squares on which it can move (in this case a8 and b8) and begin moving up your own King.

10. Ka1-a2	Ka8-b8
11. Ka2-a3	Kb8-a8
12. Ka3-a4	Ka8-b8
13. Ka4-a5	Kb8-a8
14. Ka5-b6	Ka8-b8

See Diagram 168.

168

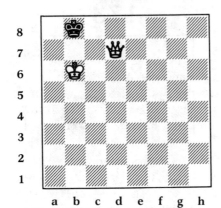

Now the White King controls a7, b7, and c7 and allows the Queen to deliver a fatal check (mate!) to the Black King.

15. Qd7-b7#
See Diagram 169 for the final position.

169

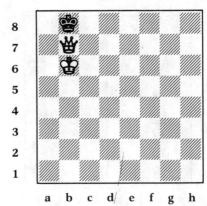

Did White have other ways of mating in one move in Diagram 168?
(Yes. 15. Qd8# and 15. Qe8#.)

We pushed back the enemy King using only our Queen. This is the easiest method for beginners. If we bring our King into play right from the start the joint action of the King and Queen will allow mate to be given more quickly. In that case, however, we must play even more carefully because stalemate can occur more often.

With correct play, a Queen and King can mate a lone enemy King within 10-15 moves. However, if you make a lot of mistakes you will run the risk of not winning the game because of the 50-move rule. Do you remember this rule?
(If 50 consecutive moves go by with no man captured and no pawns moved, then the game is a draw!)

So when mating a lone King, you have to make sure you do it within 50 moves.

Now here are a number of frequently encountered standard positions in which a Queen and King mate a lone enemy King. Remember these positions!

See Diagrams 170 and 171.

170

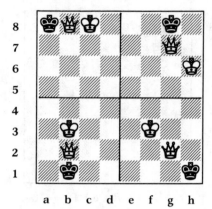

171

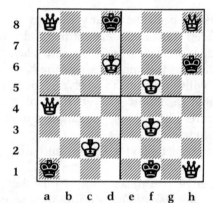

A different position is shown in each quarter-diagram. In the positions in Diagram 170, the Queen, defended by its own King, mates the enemy King from an adjoining square, while in the positions in Diagram 171, the Queen mates the enemy King from afar, while its own King takes away flight squares.

HOMEWORK
(Answers at the end)

I. Diagrams 172-177

172

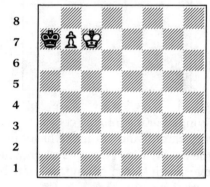

White to play. Mate in two moves.

	WHITE	BLACK
1.		
2.		

173

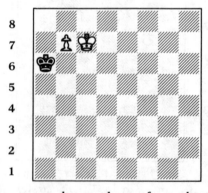

White to play. Mate in three moves.

	WHITE	BLACK
1.		
2.		
3.		

174

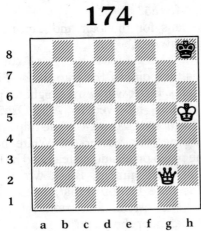

White to play. Mate in two moves.

WHITE	BLACK
1.	
2.	

176

White to play. Mate in two moves.

WHITE	BLACK
1.	
2.	

175

White to play. Mate in two moves.

WHITE	BLACK
1.	
2.	

177

White to play. Mate in four moves.

WHITE	BLACK
1.	
2.	
3.	
4.	

II. Exercises

1. Write down the position after the moves 1. e4 e5 2. Nf3 Nc6 3. Bc4 Nf6. First write down White's position, and then Black's. In giving the locations of more than one man of the same kind, (i.e., pawns, Bishops, etc.), list them in order from the a-file to the h-file. If several men of the same kind are located on the same file, then begin with the one on the lowest rank (i.e., the one nearest White's side.)

_____

_____

_____

2. Set up several random arbitrary positions with King and Queen against King and practice mating until you can do it rapidly and confidently.

Try to answer Questions 3-5 without looking at a board.

3. What color (light or dark) is f3?

4. At which square does the a3-f8 diagonal cross the d-file?

5. At which square does the h2-b8 diagonal cross the 4th rank?

III. Games Containing Opening Traps for Analysis

Game 29

1. e2-e4	e7-e5
2. Ng1-f3	Nb8-c6
3. Bf1-b5	

This opening is called the "Ruy Lopez."

3. ...	Ng8-f6
4. d2-d3	Nc6-e7?

It is against the principles of development to move the same piece twice in the opening before developing your other pieces. On top of that, the Knight is poorly placed on e7, blocking the Queen and the Bishop. In making the move, Black relies entirely on his opponent making a mistake.

5. Nf3xe5?

White falls for the bait and captures the poisoned pawn.

5. ...   c7-c6!

Here is the point of the trap. If the Bishop now retreats, Black will win a Knight for pawn by 6. ... Qa5+ followed by 7. ... Qxe5. Although it worked in this case, the trap was an unsound one. For starters, if White hadn't taken the pawn on e5 and instead had just continued his development, Black would have simply lost time. On top of that, the trap is too obvious. The ostentatious removal of the e-pawn's defender should put even a very inexperienced player on his guard.

6. Ne5-c4

Rather than lose the Knight, White decides to "give away" the Bishop.

6. ...   c6xb5??

Black is so happy at catching White in his trap that he doesn't pay any attention to White's last move and quickly snaps up the Bishop, thereby falling into a counter-trap.

7. Nc4-d6#

See Diagram 178.

178

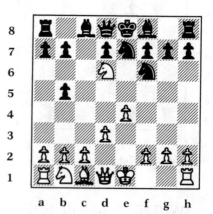

A smothered mate! Instead of greedily grabbing the Bishop, Black could have won a piece for two pawns by playing 6. ... d6 7. Ba4 b5 8. Bxb5 cxb5. While Black's trap was no good, White's trap, on the other hand, was both sound and beautiful. White had to lose a piece anyway, so he decided to "give away" the Bishop, setting a pitfall into which Black duly fell. As the old proverb says, "Don't dig a grave for somebody else, you might fall in yourself."

Game 30
Pirc Defense
Hamlisch–N.N., Vienna 1899

1. e2-e4	**d7-d6**

This defense was developed into a system and introduced into master play by the Yugoslav grandmaster Vasja Pirc.

2. d2-d4	**Nb8-d7?!**

An inaccuracy. Today Black usually plays 2. ... g6, putting off the development of the Queen's Knight.

3. Bf1-c4	**g7-g6**
4. Ng1-f3	**Bf8-g7?**

Black does not sense the danger looming over him.

5. Bc4xf7 + !!	**Ke8xf7**

5. ... Kf8 would be better, but after 6. Ng5 Black would still be in bad shape.

6. Nf3-g5 +	**Kf7-f6**

Black does not want to retreat his King to f8 or e8 because in both cases 7. Ne6 would win his Queen.

7. Qd1-f3#

See Diagram 179.

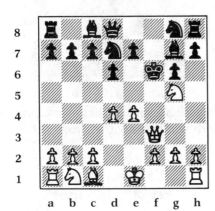

179

White played well and did not violate the principles of development. Black has only himself to blame for blundering into an opening trap.

HOMEWORK ANSWERS
I. Diagrams 172-177

D-172

1. b7-b8Q +	Ka7-a6
2. Qb8-b6#	

D-173

1. b7-b8Q	Ka6-a5
2. Qb8-b3!	

Cutting off the Black King's escape and forcing it to return to its original square because of Zugzwang.

2. ...	Ka5-a6
3. Qb3-b6#	

D-174

1. Kh5-g6!

Controlling the important squares f7, g7, and h7.

1. ...	Kh8-g8
2. Qg2-a8#	

D-175

1. Qc1-f4!

Controlling the important squares b8 and f8.

1. ...	Kc8-d8
2. Qf4-f8#	

D-176

1. Ke3-f4!

Controlling the important squares g3, g4, and g5.

a)	1. ...	Kh4-h5
	2. Qb1-h7#	
b)	1. ...	Kh4-h3
	2. Qb1-h1#	

D-177

1. Kh8-h7!

Controlling the important squares g6 and g7.

1. ...	Kf6-e7

Forced, because of Zugzwang.

2. Kh7-g6

Now the King controls the important squares f6 and f7.

2. ...	Ke7-e8

If 2. ... Kf8, then 3. Qf7#.

3. Kg6-f6

Now the Black King is again in Zugzwang. If it could stay put, it could not be mated next move, but it is forced to move onto a fatal square.

3. ...	Ke8-f8
4. Qd5-f7#	

II. Exercises

1. White: Ke1, Qd1, Ra1, Rh1, Bc1, Bc4, Nb1, Nf3, P's a2, b2, c2, d2, e4, f2, g2, h2.
Black: Ke8, Qd8, Ra8, Rh8, Bc8, Bf8, Nc6, Nf6, P's a7, b7, c7, d7, e5, f7, g7, h7.

You can easily check your answers to the other questions by looking at a chessboard.

SUPPLEMENTARY MATERIAL

for use at the teacher's discretion

Sample Games with Opening Traps

Game 31

1. e2-e4	e7-e5
2. Ng1-f3	Ng8-f6

This is Petroff's Defense, named after the first Russian chess master (1794–1867).

3. Nf3xe5	Nf6xe4?

Black must first drive the Knight away with 3. ... d6 and only then take the e-pawn.

4. Qd1-e2!

A strong move that at the same time sets a trap!

4. ...	Ne4-f6??

It is better to lose a pawn than the Queen: 4. ... d5 5. d3 Qe7 6. dxe4 Qxe5 7. exd5, or 4. ... Qe7 5. Qxe4 d6 6. d4.

5. Ne5-c6+!

See Diagram 180.

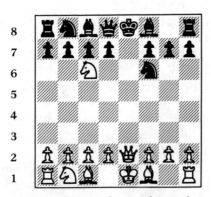

180

This is the point of the trap! The Knight attacks the enemy Queen and at the same time clears the way for its own Queen to check the enemy King. Such a check is known as a "discovered check." Black resigns, since he cannot avoid losing his Queen.

Game 32
Petroff's Defense

1. e2-e4	e7-e5
2. Ng1-f3	Ng8-f6
3. Nf3xe5	Nf6xe4?
4. Ne5xf7?	

White should play 4. Qe2 Qe7 5. Qxe4 d6 6. d4 f6 7. Nc3! dxe5 Nd5 Qd6 9. dxe5 fxe5 10. Bf4 Nc6 11. 0-0-0 with irresistible threats. Instead he plays for a trap, hoping for 4. ... Kxf7 5. Qh5+ Kf6 (or 5. ... Kg8 6. Qd5#, or 5. ... Ke7 6. Qe5+, or 5. ... g6 6. Qd5+) 6. Qf3+ Ke5 7. d4+ Kxd4, after which it is only a matter of time before Black is mated.

4. ...	Qd8-e7!

An excellent move that incidentally sets a counter-trap.

5. Nf7xh8??

It is of course better to lose a Knight by 5. Be2 than the Queen.

5. ...	Ne4-c3+!

A discovered check. See Diagram 181.

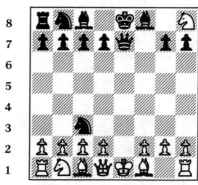

181

White resigns, since he has to lose his Queen and the Knight in the corner won't get out alive either.

Game 33
Petroff's Defense

1. e2-e4	e7-e5
2. Ng1-f3	Ng8-f6
3. Nf3xe5	Nb8-c6?

A mistake. Better would be 3. ... d6 followed by 4. ... Nxe4.

4. Ne5xc6	d7xc6
5. e4-e5?!	

5. Nc3, developing a piece, would be better.

5. ...	Nf6-e4
6. d2-d3?	

Even now it would be better to bring out the Knight, by 6. Nc3.

6. ...	Bf8-c5!

By wasting time (tempos) with unnecessary pawn moves, White has fallen into a trap.

7. d3xe4?

7. Be3 Bxe3 8. fxe3 Qh4 + 9. g3 Nxg3 would be slightly better, although White would still be in a bad state.

7. ...	Bc5xf2 + !
8. Ke1xf2	

If 8. Ke2, then 8. ... Bg4 wins the Queen.

8. ...	Qd8xd1

See Diagram 182.

182

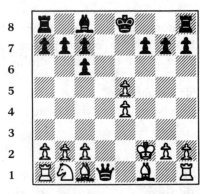

White resigns.

Game 34
Four Knights Game

1. e2-e4	e7-e5
2. Ng1-f3	Nb8-c6
3. Nb1-c3	Ng8-f6

This opening is known as the Four Knights Game.

4. Bf1-b5	Bf8-b4
5. 0-0	0-0
6. d2-d3	d7-d6

Black copies White for too long and soon falls into a trap. Here the right way to play is 6. ... Bxc3 7. bxc3 d6.

7. Bc1-g5	Bc8-g4
8. Nc3-d5	Nc6-d4
9. Nd5xb4	Nd4xb5

It's very dangerous to copy your opponent's moves for so long.

10. Nb4-d5	Nb5-d4
11. Qd1-d2	Qd8-d7
12. Bg5xf6	Bg4xf3
13. Nd5-e7 +	

Black can no longer copy and gets mated in a few moves.

13. ...	Kg8-h8
14. Bf6xg7 +	Kh8xg7
15. Qd2-g5 +	Kg7-h8
16. Qg5-f6#	

See Diagram 183 for the final position.

183

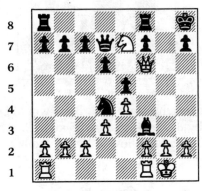

Game 35
Mieses–Equist, Nuremberg, 1895

1. e2-e4	d7-d5

This move is the Center Counter Defense.

2. e4xd5	Qd8xd5

As you can see, the disadvantage of this defense is that Black has to bring his Queen into play very early.

3. Nb1-c3	Qd5-d8

Instead of this move, which leaves White with a clear advantage in development, 3. ... Qa5 would be more active.

4. d2-d4	Nb8-c6?

A mistake, as White can easily attack the Knight with a pawn. 4. ... c6 or 4. ... Nf6 would be safer.

5. Ng1-f3	Bc8-g4?

When you are behind in development you should avoid making ambitious moves. Here, for example, 5. ... e6 could be played. White would of course have an advantage, but Black would not lose right away.

6. d4-d5	Nc6-e5?

The final mistake. Black falls into a pretty trap. Black should play 6. ... Nb8 and try to defend his very difficult position.

7. Nf3xe5!

See Diagram 184.

184

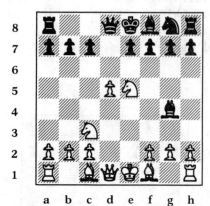

Black resigns, since 7. ... Bxd1 would be followed by 8. Bb5+ c6 9. dxc6 a6 (if 9. ... Qb6, then 10. cxb7+ followed by 11. bxa8Q+) 10. c7+ etc.

Game 36

1. d2-d4	d7-d5
2. c2-c4	d5xc4

This opening is called the Queen's Gambit Accepted.

3. e2-e3	b7-b5?

It is better not to try to hang on to the pawn and instead continue with 3. ... e6 4. Bxc4 c5!. 3. ... e5! would also be a good reply.

4. a2-a4	c7-c6?

Of course not 4. ...a6 5. axb5, and Black cannot recapture the pawn on b5 because he would lose the Rook on a8. The relatively best reply was 4. ... bxa4 5. Bxc4 e6, giving back the pawns.

5. a4xb5	c6xb5?
6. Qd1-f3!	

See Diagram 185.

185

Even a computer couldn't count all the beginners who have fallen into this trap! Black now has the choice of parting with his Rook, Knight, or Bishop. The least of the evils is to give up his Knight by 6. ... Nc6 7. Qxc6+ Bd7. Thus Black's pawn hunting has cost him a piece.

Game 37
The Queen's Gambit Declined

1. d2-d4	d7-d5
2. c2-c4	e7-e6
3. Nb1-c3	Ng8-f6

Black ignores White's pawn sacrifice and instead develops his pieces.

4. Bc1-g5	Nb8-d7

A good move that incidentally sets a trap which often catches beginners.

5. c4xd5	e6xd5
6. Nc3xd5?	

White takes the bait. He feels sure that the Knight on d5 cannot be captured.

6. ...	Nf6xd5!

A temporary Queen sacrifice that results in Black winning a piece for a pawn.

7. Bg5xd8	Bf8-b4+

An insidious check.

8. Qd1-d2	Bb4xd2+
9. Ke1xd2	Ke8xd8

See Diagram 186.

186

White's position is lost.

Game 38

1. d2-d4	d7-d5
2. c2-c4	e7-e5

This is the Albin Counter Gambit.

3. d4xe5	d5-d4

In return for his sacrificed pawn, Black gets a strong pawn on d4 that hinders the development of White's pieces.

4. e2-e3?

White attempts to exchange off Black's central pawn while preserving his extra material. However, it was better not to try to hold on to the extra pawn but rather develop his pieces by 4. Nf3, 5. g3, 6. Bg2, 7. 0-0, etc.

4. ...	Bf8-b4+
5. Bc1-d2	d4xe3!

A devious trap. Black sacrifices the Bishop.

6. Bd2xb4?

White decides that he can safely accept the "gift." However, 6. fxe3 must be played, although it results in doubled pawns.

6. ...	e3xf2+
7. Ke1-e2	

White cannot recapture the pawn on f2 because his Queen would be left undefended and Black would win it by 7. ... Qxd1. But now White is in for a surprise.

7. ...	f2xg1N+!

See Diagram 187.

187

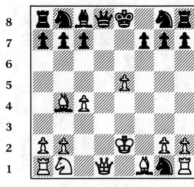

This is the point of the trap! A rare situation! A Black pawn reaches the first rank, captures a White Knight, itself becomes a Knight, and delivers a fatal check to the White King, causing White to resign immediately. It would be much less effective to promote the pawn to a Queen, since after 7. ... fxg1Q White would have time to exchange Queens by 8. Qxd8+ and after 8. ... Kxd8 capture the newborn Queen with his Rook. In Diagram 187, if the White Rook takes the Knight, 8. ... Bg4+ is decisive, while 8. Ke1 is met by 8. ... Qh4+ with a devastating attack.

Game 39
Caro-Kann Defense
Keres–Arlamovskii
Szczawno-Zdroj 1950

1. e2-e4	c7-c6

Black prepares ... d7-d5. This defense was invented in the 19th century by the German chessplayers Caro and Kann.

2. Nb1-c3	d7-d5
3. Ng1-f3	d5xe4
4. Nc3xe4	Ng8-f6
5. Qd1-e2	

A good move. Grandmaster Keres defends the Knight and prepares to castle on the Queenside. The light-square Bishop will be developed on g2.

5. ...	Nb8-d7??

The master playing Black was afraid of the move 6. Nxf6 and decided to defend the Knight on f6 with his other Knight. He made his move instaneously and was duly punished with the utmost severity.

6. Ne4-d6#

A smothered mate. See Diagram 188.

188

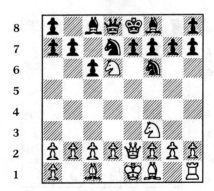

Black fell into a "children's" trap that has caught many chessplayers of varying strengths.

Game 40
Sicilian Defense
Fischer–Reshevsky, USA 1959

At the time of this game Fischer was 15 years old.

1. e2-e4	c7-c5

The Sicilian Defense. One of the most popular openings today, it got its name more than 500 years ago.

2. Ng1-f3	Nb8-c6
3. d2-d4	

White is played by the brilliant American chessplayer Robert Fischer, who won the World Championship in 1972.

3. ...	c5xd4
4. Nf3xd4	g7-g6
5. Nb1-c3	Bf8-g7

The player of the Black pieces is no beginner either but rather the well-known grandmaster Samuel Reshevsky, a former child prodigy who at the age of eight was already touring many European cities, giving simultaneous exhibitions on 20-25 boards against adult opponents.

6. Bc1-e3	Ng8-f6
7. Bf1-c4	0-0
8. Bc4-b3	Nc6-a5?

Until now both grandmasters have played very well, but here Reshevsky blunders and falls into a subtle opening trap. The right moves are 8. ... Qa5 or 8. ... d6.

9. e4-e5!	Nf6-e8

After 9. ... Nxb3 10. exf6 Nxa1 11. fxg7 White

has a clear advantage.

10. Bb3xf7+!	Rf8xf7
11. Nd4-e6!	

See Diagram 189.

189

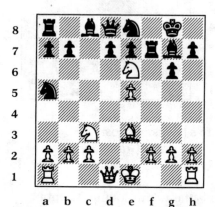

Black could resign here as his position is hopeless. Nor would 10. ... Kxf7 have saved him since White wins after 11. Ne6 Kxe6 12. Qd5+ Kf5 13. g4+ Kxg4 14. Rg1+ Kh5 15. Qd1+. No one is immune to mistakes!

Lesson Six

A. Check Lesson 5 homework (as necessary).

B. *Review Questions*

1. How many squares are there on a chessboard?
2. Can you castle if your Rook is under attack?
3. Is it a good idea to set a trap whose worth depends entirely on your opponent blundering?

Try to answer Questions 4-6 without looking at a chessboard.

4. On what squares do the Black Rooks stand at the start of a game? What color (light or dark) are these squares?
5. How many different moves can White make in the starting position?
6. At which square does the h1-a8 diagonal cross the third rank and what color (light or dark) is it?

Answer the next questions directly from the Diagrams, without setting up the men on a board.

Black to play and mate in two moves.

191

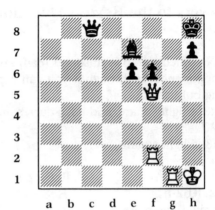

White to play and mate in two moves.

192

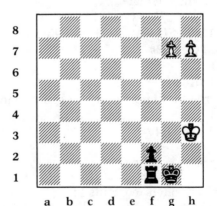

White to play and mate in two moves.

190

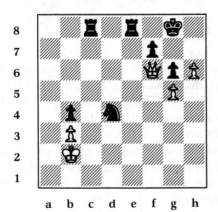

77

193

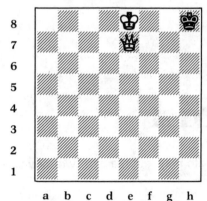

White to play and mate in two moves.

Answers to the Review Questions

1. 64.
2. Yes.
3. No. Such a trap is unsound (bad) and if your opponent sees through it you can expect nothing but trouble.
4. a8, a light square, and h8, a dark square.
5. 20.
6. f3, a light square.

D-190

1. ...	Rc8-c2 +
2. Kb2-b1	Re8-e1#

A straight-line mate.

D-191

1. Qf5xh7 +	Kh8xh7
2. Rf2-h2#	

A straight-line mate.

D-192

1. g7-g8Q +	Kg1-h1
2. Qg8-g2#	

D-193

1. Ke8-f7!

Controls the important squares g6, g7 and g8.

1. ...	Kh8-h7
2. Qe7-h4#	

The Concept of Planning

There are often moments in a person's life when he has to choose a course of action that will enable him to make best use of his abilities. At the same time, he must also find ways of overcoming any obstacles that may hinder his progress along his chosen path. He achieves all this by working out a definite plan. You can-

not always hit upon the correct plan at first shot — mistakes sometimes occur. One of the very useful things that a chessplayer learns is the art of making appropriate plans.

During a game, a player sets certain goals for himself: to win the game, to checkmate the opponent, to avoid losing, etc. He must then form a plan of play which charts out what he has to do in order to achieve these goals.

A plan indicates the main channels along which a player chooses to direct the course of the game. For example, he can make a plan to attack the enemy King or a plan to carry out a Queenside attack.

Now let us analyze the position in Diagram 194.

194

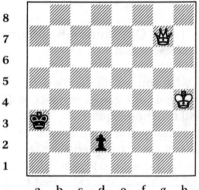

It is White's turn to play. His goal is to first eliminate the dangerous Black pawn on d2 and then checkmate the Black King. Let us form a plan of play to achieve this goal. First, we must control the d1 square, or else the pawn will promote to a Queen. Can we control d1 and at the same time attack the pawn on d2? Yes, from either of two squares — d4 and d7. So we can play, for example, 1. Qg7-d4 and the next move capture the pawn. With that, the first part of our goal has been achieved. Now let us form a further plan consisting of two stages: 1) driving the Black King to one of the board's edges, and 2) moving in with the White King, and with its help, mating the Black one. You already know how to do this.

Plans are important! Former world champion Emanuel Lasker used to say that is better to follow even a bad plan than to play without any plan at all.

Exploiting a Large Material Advantage

Who among us has not had the experience of being one or two pieces up but then drawing or even losing as a result of not finding the correct plan! Two methods of play can be recommended for exploiting a large material advantage:

1. Exchange off pieces and transpose into a winning endgame, or
2. Use your superior force to land an attack on the enemy King.

The main method is exchanging off pieces, because simplifying the position makes it easier to exploit a material advantage. Let us look at some examples.

195

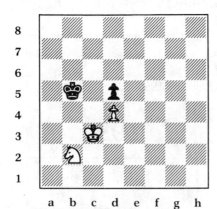

In Diagram 195, it is White's turn to move. He is up a Knight and should, of course, win. But the question is, how?

Let us form a plan:

1. Win the Black pawn.
2. Promote the White pawn to a Queen.
3. Drive the Black King to an edge.
4. Mate the Black King by the combined action of the White King and Queen (and possibly also the Knight).

Let us put this plan into action:

| 1. Nb2-d1 | Kb5-c6 |
| 2. Nd1-e3 | |

The Knight attacks the Black pawn. It would not have been as good to play 1. Nd3 followed by 2. Nb4 since the Knight would then block the path of its own King.

| 2. ... | Kc6-d6 |

Continuing to defend the pawn.

3. Kc3-b4

The King sets off towards the Black pawn in order to attack it a second time.

| 3. ... | Kd6-c6 |
| 4. Kb4-a5 | |

The White King pushes back the Black King by making use of Zugzwang.

| 4. ... | Kc6-d6 |

Because of Zugzwang, the King is forced to give up control of b5 and b6.

| 5. Ka5-b6 | Kd6-e6 |

Now Zugzwang forces the Black King to give up c5 and c6.

| 6. Kb6-c6 | Ke6-e7 |
| 7. Ne3xd5 + | |

Now the Knight and King will help the pawn to queen. See Diagram 196.

196

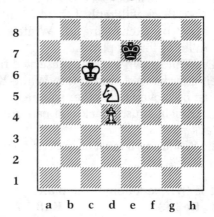

| 7. ... | Ke7-d8 |
| 8. Nd5-b6 | |

The Knight controls c8 and frees the way for the pawn.

| 8. ... | Kd8-e7 |
| 9. Kc6-c7! | |

Now the King controls the important squares d6, d7, and d8, thereby clearing the way for the pawn to queen.

9. ...	Ke7-e6
10. d4-d5 +	Ke6-e7
11. d5-d6 +	u
	(any move)
12. d6-d7	u
13. d7-d8Q	

Only the last stage of our plan remains, i.e., to mate the lone Black King, but you already know how to do this by yourself.

197

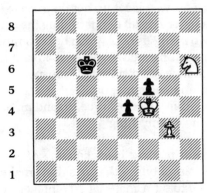

Diagram 197, with White to play, is our next example. Here too White should try to win quickly, but he must watch out for the danger of Black trying to draw by giving up his two pawns in return for the lone White pawn. For example, if White attacks the Black e-pawn by 1. Nf7, then Black will reply 1. ... f4 + and obtain a draw by exchanging off White's last pawn. So let us form a plan:

1. The White pawn must be preserved from being exchanged, and so the White King must be moved to another square.
2. The Knight must attack and capture the Black pawns.
3. The White pawn must be queened, and so on.

Here is the execution of the plan:

    1. Ke3-f3!   **Ka8-b7**

Now if 1. ... f4, then the White pawn queens by force after 2. g4.

    2. Nh8-f7   **e5-e4 +**

2. ... f4 doesn't save Black since after 3. g4 he loses both his pawns.

    3. Kf3-f4   **Kb7-c6**

    4. Nf7-h6

See Diagram 198.

198

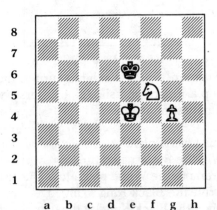

4. Kxf5 is not as good since after 4. ... e3 there is a danger of the Black pawn queening.

    4. ...   **Kc6-c5**

    5. Nh6xf5   **Kc5-d5**

    6. g3-g4

Now Black must give up his last pawn.

    6. ..   **Kd5-e6**

    7. Kf4xe4

See Diagram 199.

199

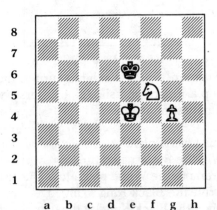

The next part of our plan is to queen the pawn with the help of the King and the Knight and then mate the lone enemy King. You can do that by yourself.

The first rule that a beginner should learn about exploiting a material advantage is to avoid all hastiness. Who among us does not remember instances where we had a large material advantage but were robbed of our victory because of just one hasty move! So remember: **Don't be hasty.**

Mating with a Rook and King against a Lone King

A Rook and King can mate a lone King only on an edge or in a corner. Diagram 200 shows four standard "Rook and King against lone King" mating positions (each quarter of the diagram shows a different position).

200

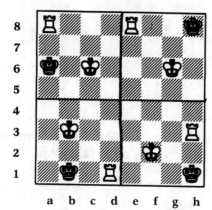

To mate a King on the edge of the board we must control all five of the squares to which it could move, and in addition a sixth square, the one on which the King stands, must be attacked by our Rook.

The Rook can control two flight squares and attack the King, while the other three squares must be controlled by our own King. When the Kings are placed such that each of them controls three of the other's flight squares, they are said to be **in opposition**. This happens when the Kings face each other with a single square between them. In Diagram 200 , for example, the Kings on b1 and b3 are in opposition, as are the Kings on a6 and c6. If the lone King is in a corner (for example, h8 or h1, as in Diagram 200), then mate is possible even without opposition.

201

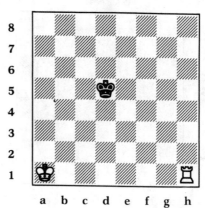

In Diagram 201, White must first of all decide which edge he wants to drive the Black King to. Let's suppose he decides to mate the Black King on the eighth rank. Then we have to form a plan:

1. Cut the Black King off from the lower half of the board.
2. Move the White King towards the center, because the Rook is much weaker than the Queen and cannot chase the enemy King to a corner or an edge by itself.
3. Drive the King into a corner by the combined action of the Rook and the King.
4. Checkmate the Black King!

Here is the execution of the plan:
  1. Rh1-h4
The Black King is cut off from the lower half of the board.

1. ...	**Kd5-e5**
2. Ka1-b2	

Only with the help of its King can the Rook push back the enemy King.

2. ...	**Ke5-d5**
3. Kb2-c3	**Kd5-e5**
4. Rh4-d4!	

202

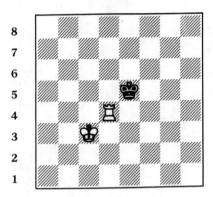

Protected by its own King, the Rook cuts the Black King off from the Queenside.

4. ...	**Ke5-f5**
5. Kc3-d3	

The King now controls e4.

5. ...	**Kf5-e5**
6. Kd3-e3!	

6. Re4+ would be a mistake because of 6. ... Kd5, and the Black King would escape to the Queenside.

6. ...	**Ke5-f5**

The Black King does not in the least want to leave the center of the board, where it is in safety, but it is forced to do so because of Zugzwang. 6. ... Ke6 would be no better because of 7. Kf4 Kf6 8. Rd6+ Ke7 9. Ke5 etc.

7. Rd4-e4	

Taking possession of the e-file.

7. ...	**Kf5-f6**

Black was again in Zugzwang. If 7. ... Kg5, then 8. Rf4 cuts the King off from the f-file.

8. Ke3-f4	

Controlling the important squares f5 and g5. Note how the White King and Rook help each other.

8. ...	**Kf6-g6**

If Black could pass his turn, he wouldn't lose. But . . . This "but" is called Zugzwang.

9. Re4-e6+!	

See Diagram 203.

203

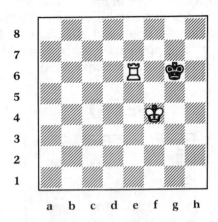

The Black King must retreat to the seventh rank, since after 9. ... Kh5 a waiting move by the Rook along the sixth rank, e.g., 10. Rf6, would again put Black in Zugzwang, forcing him to move his King into opposition by 10. ... Kh4, allowing 11. Rh6#.

9. ...	**Kg6-f7**
10. Kf4-f5	**Kf7-g7**
11. Re6-e7 +	

Forcing Black to the last rank, since 11. ... Kh6 would allow mate in two moves by 12. Rf7 (Zugzwang) Kh5 (opposition) 13. Rh7#.

11. ...	**Kg7-f8**
12. Kf5-f6	**Kf8-g8**
13. Kf6-g6!	**Kg8-f8**

See Diagram 204.

204

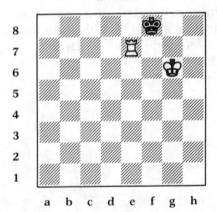

White to play and mate in two moves. Remember this method! There are six solutions. Any waiting move of the Rook along the e-file (except 14. Re8+) will put Black in Zugzwang, forcing him to play 14. ... Kf8-g8 and allow 15. Re6-e8#.

We have executed all the stages of our plan and mated Black in fifteen moves. In general, with correct play you should be able to mate with King and Rook against King in 15-20 moves starting from any position. If you do make mistakes, however, you must be very careful not to make so many as to let Black draw by the 50-move rule.

In conclusion, let us look at a short but interesting game.

Game 41
Queen's Gambit Declined
Fine–Yudovich, Moscow 1937

1. d2-d4	d7-d5
2. c2-c4	e7-e6
3. Nb1-c3	

The American grandmaster Reuben Fine, White in this game, was one of the strongest players in the world at the time.

| 3. ... | Ng8-f6 |

His opponent was the little-known Soviet master Mikhail Yudovich.

| 4. Ng1-f3 | c7-c5 |

Yudovich was of course quite excited at the prospect of playing such a fearsome opponent. He prepared for the encounter by playing over a large number of Fine's games. In one of them he noticed that Fine had won by catching his opponent in an opening trap. Yudovich found, however, that Fine's trap could be refuted by a remarkable countertrap, and so decided that in his own game with Fine he would "fall into" White's trap.

| 5. Bc1-g5 | c5xd4 |
| 6. Nf3xd4 | e6-e5 |

Yudovich thought for two or three minutes over each move, pretending that he did not know this opening very well.

7. Nd4-b5
See Diagram 205.

205

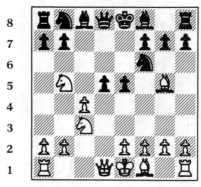

Everything is going according to Yudovich's plan. One more move , and he can "fall into" Fine's trap. Although Yudovich already had his next move figured out before the game, he pretended to think here for twenty minutes. He did not want to reply quickly, for fear that Fine would get suspicious and discover Black's idea.

| 7. ... | a7-a6 |

8. Nc3xd5?
See Diagram 206.

206

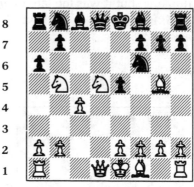

White has to play instead 8. Qa4, with a complicated game. Fine, however, glanced slyly at his opponent, thinking he had caught yet another inexperienced master in his trap, and played 8. Nc3xd5? instantaneously.

| 8. ... | a6xb5! |

207

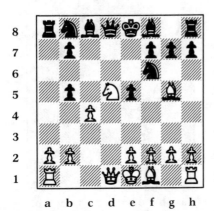

Yudovich was very excited! After all, he had managed to catch one of the world's strongest players in a trap! And, looking not at the board but at his opponent, he instantly captured the Knight. The grandmaster first recoiled from the board, and then sank into deep thought. He remembered how he had won a pretty game with this same variation after 9. Nxf6+ gxf6 10. Qxd8+ Kxd8 11. Bxf6+ Ke8 12. Bxh8 etc. This was the trap in which he had wanted to catch Yudovich. But now he saw his opponent's plan and realized that he himself had fallen into a beautifully prepared ambush. He regretted that he had made his eighth move without thinking, but it was too late now.

    9. Nd5xf6 +   **Qd8xf6!!**

See Diagram 208.

208

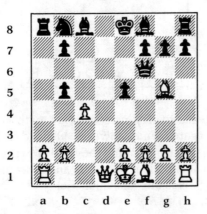

This is the "present" that Yudovich had prepared at home for the grandmaster and which he had artfully led up to. Fine had not considered this temporary Queen sacrifice in his calculations.

    10. Bg5xf6   **Bf8-b4 +**

Before capturing on f6, Black makes an in-between move, checking with his Bishop.

    11. Qd1-d2

White is forced to return the Queen.

    11. ...   **Bb4xd2 +**
    12. Ke1xd2   **g7xf6**

and Black, with a material advantage and an excellent position, quickly won.

The famous grandmaster played very well in the tournament and deservedly took first place, but in this game he was taught a good lesson! And indeed, the game was a good lesson for many amateurs as well.

HOMEWORK
(Answers at the end)

I. Diagrams 209–214.
Form a plan and find the solution.

209

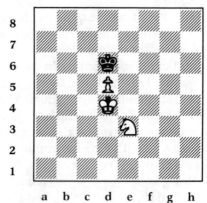

White to play and win.

_____

_____

_____

210

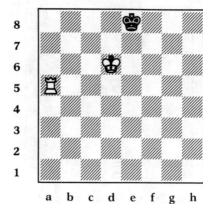

White to play. Mate in two moves.

WHITE	BLACK
1.	
2.	

212

White to play. Mate in two moves.

WHITE	BLACK
1.	
2.	

211

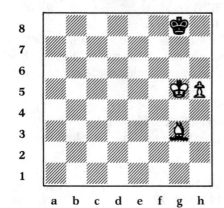

White to play and wins.

_____

_____

_____

213

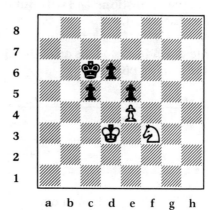

White to play and wins.

_____

_____

_____

214

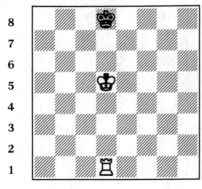

White to play. Mate in three moves.

	WHITE	BLACK
1.		
2.		
3.		

II. Exercises
Try to answer Questions 1–3 without looking at a chessboard.

1. Write down the locations of all the pieces in the starting position.

   _____

   _____

   _____

2. Which lines (rank, file, and diagonal) run through e5?

   _____

   _____

   _____

3. What color (light or dark) is e6?

   _____

4. Set up some random positions with King and Rook against King and practice mating until you can do it quickly and confidently.

5. Think up a position in which Black to play can mate in two moves.

III. Game For Analysis
Game 42
Nimzovich–Alapin, Riga 1913

1. e2-e4	e7-e6
2. d2-d4	d7-d5

This opening is called the French Defense.

| 3. Nb1-c3 | Ng8-f6 |

Aron Nimzovich, White in this game, was one of the strongest players in the world.

| 4. e4xd5 | Nf6xd5 |

It would be better to play 4. ... exd5 so as not to give White a superiority in the center.

| 5. Ng1-f3 | c7-c5 |

A loss of time. 5. ... Be7 followed by 6. ... 0-0, 7. ... b6, and 8. ... Bb7 would be better.

| 6. Nc3xd5 | Qd8xd5 |

Better would be 6. ... exd5, opening up the light-square Bishop's diagonal.

7. Bc1-e3	c5xd4
8. Nf3xd4	a7-a6
9. Bf1-e2!	

White's position is considerably better. He has brought out all his minor pieces while the master playing Black has developed only his Queen.

| 9. ... | Qd5xg2? |

Instead of this further loss of time, Black should be thinking about developing his minor pieces.

| 10. Be2-f3 | Qg2-g6 |
| 11. Qd1-d2 | e6-e5 |

Black's position is difficult, but in any case he had to start developing his pieces instead of pushing pawns.

| 12. 0-0-0!! | |

Magnificent! Nimzovich gives up his Knight for a pawn but in return all his remaining pieces rapidly enter the fray.

| 12. ... | e5xd4 |
| 13. Be3xd4 | Nb8-c6 |

Although a piece up, Black is lost. White's manifest advantage in development allows him to finish off the game with a scintillating combination.

14. Bd4-f6!

Clearing the way for the Queen. White now threatens 15. Qd8+ Nxd8 16. Rxd8#, or if 14. ... Be7, then 15. Bxc6 bxc6 16. Qd8+ Bxd8 17. Rxd8#.

14. ...	**Qg6xf6**
15. Rh1-e1+	

Black is already two pieces up but he gets mated by force.

15. ...	**Bf8-e7**

If 15. ... Be6, then 16. Qd7#; if 15. ... Ne5, then 16. Rxe5+ Qxe5 17. Qd8#; if 15. ... Qe7, then 16. Bxc6 bxc6 17. Qd8#.

16. Bf3xc6+	**Ke8-f8**

If 16. ... bxc6, then 17. Qd8#.

17. Qd2-d8+!	**Be7xd8**
18. Re1-e8#	

See Diagram 215.

215

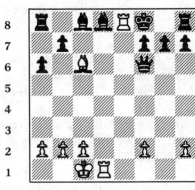

Answers to the Homework
I. Diagrams 209–214

D-209 The plan:
1. Queen the pawn.
2. Drive the Black King to an edge or corner.
3. Checkmate the Black King.

The execution of the plan:

1. Ne3-f5+	Kd6-d7
2. Kd4-e5	Kd7-c7
3. d5-d6+	Kc7-d7
4. Nf5-g7	Kd7-d8
5. Ke5-e6	Kd8-c8
6. Ke6-e7	u
	(any move)
7. d6-d7	u

8. d7-d8Q

and so on. The above variation is only one possibility; other moves also lead to the goal.

D-210 The plan:
1. Put the Black King in Zugzwang.
2. Checkmate Black.

The execution of the plan:

1. Ke5-d6!	Ke8-d8

Because of Zugzwang the King is forced to take the opposition.

2. Rf1-f8#	

D-211 The plan is similar to that for D-209. The execution:

1. Kg5-g6	Kg8-h8
2. h5-h6	Kh8-g8
3. h6-h7+	Kg8-f8
4. h7-h8Q+	

and so on. If 3. ... Kh8, then 4. Be5#. Other solutions (with different moves) are also possible.

D-212 The plan is similar to that for D-210. The execution:

1. Ra5-f5!	Ke8-d8

Because of Zugzwang the King is forced to take the opposition.

2. Rf5-f8#	

D-213 The plan:
1. Penetrate with the King to d5.
2. Transfer the Knight to c4.
3. Eliminate all the enemy pawns.
4. Queen the pawn, and so on.

The execution of the plan:

1. Kd3-c4	Kc6-c7

If 1. ... d5+, then 2. exd5+ Kd6 3. Nd2 wins.

2. Kc4-d5	Kc7-d7
3. Nf3-d2	Kd7-c7
4. Nd2-c4	Kc7-d7
5. Nc4xd6	Kd7-e7
6. Kd5xe5	Ke7-d7
7. Ke5-d5	Kd7-e7
8. Kd5xc5	Ke7-e6
9. Nd6-c4	Ke6-d7
10. Kc5-d5	Kd7-e7
11. e4-e5	Ke7-d7
12. e5-e6+	Kd7-e7
13. Nc4-e5	Ke7-d8
14. Kd5-d6	Kd8-e8
15. Ne5-c6	

Careful! 15. e7?? is stalemate.

15. ...	Ke8-f8
16. Kd6-d7	u

17. e6-e7   u
18. e7-e8Q

and so on. Other solutions (with different moves) are also possible.

D-214 The plan:
1. Take the opposition and confine the King to the eighth rank.
2. Put Black in Zugzwang.
3. Checkmate Black.

The execution of the plan:

    1. Kd5-d6

and now a)

    1. ...   **Kd8-e8**
    2. Rd1-f1

Putting Black in Zugzwang.

    2. ...   **Ke8-d8**
    3. f1-f8#

or b)

    1. ...   **Kd8-c8**
    2. Rd1-b1

Putting Black in Zugzwang.

    2. ...   **Kc8-d8**
    3. Rb1-b8#

II. Exercises

1. White: Ke1, Qd1, Ra1, Rh1, Bc1, Bf1, Nb1, Ng1, P's a2, b2, c2, d2, e2, f2, g2, h2.
Black: Ke8, Qd8, Ra8, Rh8, Bc8 Bf8, Nb8, Ng8, P's a7, b7, c7, d7, e7, f7, g7, h7.

2. Four lines pass through e5: a) the fifth rank; b) the e-file; c) the h2-b8 diagonal; and d) the a1-h8 diagonal.

3. Light.

SUPPLEMENTARY MATERIAL

for use at the teacher's discretion

Positions 216–221 deal with the theme "Plan for exploiting a large material advantage." Positions 222–227 illustrate the combined action of a King and a Rook against a lone King.

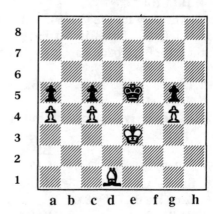

White to play and win. The plan:
1. Put Black in Zugzwang.
2. Win the pawn on c5 or the one on g5.
3. Queen the c-pawn or the g-pawn, and so on.

The execution:

    1. Bd1-f3

With the Kings facing one another in opposition, any Bishop move puts the Black King in Zugzwang.

    1. ...   **Ke5-d6**

Taking the opposition and barring the White King's access to the Black pawns.

    2. Ke3-e4   **Kd6-e6**
    3. Bf3-h1

This waiting move with the Bishop makes it Black's turn to move, but Black does not have any good moves.

    3. ...   **Ke6-e7**

Losing control over the important squares d5, e5, and f5.

    4. Ke4-f5

4. Kd5 would also win.

    4. ...   **Ke7-f7**
    5. Kf5xg5   **Kf7-g7**
    6. Kg5-f5   **Kg7-f7**
    7. g4-g5   **Kf7-g7**
    8. g5-g6   **Kg7-g8**
    9. Kf5-f6   **Kg8-f8**
    10. g6-g7 +   **Kf8-g8**
    11. Bh1-d5 +

White must be careful: 11. Kg6 or 11. Be4 is stalemate.

    11. ...   **Kg8-h7**
    12. g7-g8Q +   **Kh7-h6**
    13. Qg8-h8#

Other solutions (with different moves) are also possible.

217

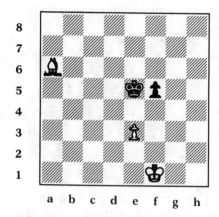

White to play and win. The plan:
1. Guard your pawn from being exchanged.
2. Win the Black pawn.
3. Queen your pawn, and so on.

The execution:

1. Ba6-b7

Controlling e4. 1. Bd3 is also possible.

1. ...	**f5-f4**

Trying to exchange off the White pawn.

2. e3-e4!

Saving the pawn from being exchanged.

2. ...	**Ke5-e6**
3. Kf1-f2	**Ke6-f6**
4. Kf2-f3	**Kf6-e5**
5. Bb7-d5	

A waiting move with the Bishop, making it Black's turn to move and thus putting Black in Zugzwang.

5. ...	**Ke5-f6**
6. Kf3xf4	**Kf6-e7**
7. Kf4-e5	

Taking the opposition and pushing back the Black King.

7. ...	**Ke7-d7**
8. Ke5-f6	

Freeing the way for the pawn and controlling e6 and e7.

8. ...	**Kd7-e8**
9. e4-e5	

and so on.

218

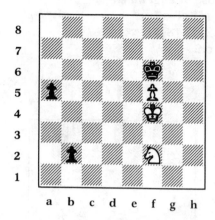

White to play and win. The plan:
1. Hold back the Black pawns.
2. Queen the f-pawn.
3. Checkmate the Black King.

The execution:

1. Nf2-e4 + !

Only with this check can White stop the Black pawns.

1. ...	**Kf6-e7**
2. Ne4-c3	

Controlling b1.

2. ...	**a5-a4**

Threatening 3. ... a3 followed by the queening of one of the pawns.

3. Nc3-b1!

Now both the critical squares, b1 and a3, are controlled by the Knight, which thus prevents the advance of both Black pawns.

3. ...	**Ke7-f6**

If 3. ... Kd6, then 4. f6 wins.

4. Nb1-a3

A waiting move that puts Black in Zugzwang by making it his turn to move.

4. ...	**Kf6-f7**
5. Kf4-e5	**Kf7-e7**

Taking the opposition.

6. f5-f6 +	**Ke7-f7**
7. Ke5-f5	**Kf7-f8**

Because of Zugzwang.

8. Kf5-e6	**Kf8-e8**

Taking the opposition.

9. f6-f7 +	**Ke8-f8**
10. Na3-b1!	

Only with this waiting move can White win. 10. Kf6? is bad because of 10. ... b1Q 11. Nxb1 a3, when 12. Nxa3 stalemates Black!

10. ...   **Kf8-g7**

Because of Zugzwang.

11. Ke6-e7   **Kg7-g6**

12. f7-f8Q

and so on.

219

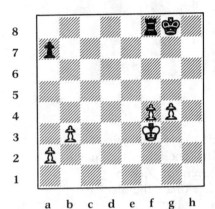

Black to play and win. The plan:

1. Attack White's Queenside pawns with the Rook.
2. Stop the advance of White's Kingside pawns.
3. If necessary, give up the a-pawn in order to eliminate all of White's pawns.
4. Checkmate with King and Rook against King.

The execution:

1. ...   **Rf8-c8**

2. f4-f5

If 2. Ke4, then 2. ... Rc2 3. Kd4 Rxa2 4. b4 Rf2 5. Kc5 Rxf4 6. b5 Rxg4 7. Kc6 Rg5 8. Kb7 Rxb5 + etc.

2. ...   **Rc8-c2**

3. g4-g5   **Rc2xa2**

4. Kf3-f4   **Ra2-b2**

5. f5-f6   **Rb1xb2**

6. g5-g6   **a7-a5**

7. Kf4-e5   **a5-a4**

8. Ke5-e6   **a4-a3**

9. Ke6-e7

Threatening 10. f7 + followed by 11. f8Q.

9. ...   **Rb3-e3 +**

and the Black pawn will go on to become a Queen!

220

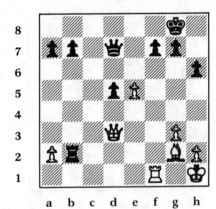

Grandmaster Schlechter–Grandmaster Marshall
Vienna 1908

White to play should win. He has a Bishop for two pawns and in addition will win Black's pawn on d5 next move. They continued as follows:

27. Qd3xd5

Being ahead in material, White tries to exchange Queens.

27. ...   **Qd7-e7**

28. Qd5-d6   **Qe7xd6**

If 28. ... Qg5, then 29. Qb8 + Kh7 30. Be4 + etc.

29. e5xd6   **Rb2-d2**

30. Bg2xb7   **Rd2xd6**

31. Kh1-g2

Bringing the King towards the center.

31. ...   **g7-g6**

32. Rf1-f2

Controlling the second rank.

32. ...   **Kg8-g7**

33. Rf2-c2

and Black resigned. If Black had played on, White should have tried to exchange Rooks and bring his King up to the center. Another good goal would be to occupy the seventh rank with the Rook so as to attack the a7 and f7 pawns.

In Diagram 220, White had an alternative way of exploiting his advantage: 27. Bxd5, threatening the pawn on f7. Then 27. ... Qh3 would not work because of 28. Bxf7 + Kh8 29. Qd8 + and 30. Qg8#. Finally, a third method of winning was shown by Tarrasch: 27. Rxf7 Qxf7 28. Bxd5 or 27. ... Kxf7 28. e6 + Qxe6 (28. ... Kxe6 29. Bh3 +) 29. Bxd5 Rb1 + 30. Kg2 Rb2 + 31. Kf3. However, such a method is not to be recommended. Try to choose the simplest means of exploiting your advantage, because it is easy to make mistakes in complicated variations.

221

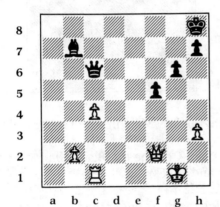

White to play. He is up an Exchange. How can he exploit his material advantage?

Black is threatening 1. ... Qh1#. The Black Queen and Bishop can cause a great deal of unpleasantness for White, since his King is exposed. Consequently, the best method for White to exploit his advantage is to exchange Queens:

1. Qf2-d4 +	Kh8-g8
2. Qd4-d5 + !	Qc6xd5
3. c4xd5	Bb7xd5

White has sacrificed a pawn but in return has managed to exchange Queens. Now the b-pawn assures him of an easy win.

4. b2-b4	Kg8-f8
5. b4-b5	Kf8-e7
6. b5-b6	Ke7-d6

If 6. ...Ke6, then 7. Rc7 h5 8. b7 Bxb7 9. Rxb7 and White must win.

7. Rc1-d1!	Kd6-c6
8. Rd1xd5!	Kc6xd5
9. b6-b7	

and the pawn will queen.

Diagrams 222–227. The theme in all these positions is the same: the confinement of the Black King by the combined action of the White pieces.

222

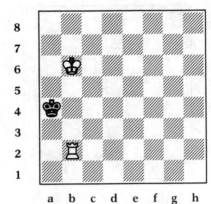

White to play. Mate in six moves.

The plan: Drive the Black King to the a1 corner and checkmate it. It is not hard to win, but there is only one way of mating in six moves:

1. Rb2-b5

Placing the Rook under the protection of its King and at the same time putting Black in Zugzwang.

1. ...   **Ka4-a3**

Black is compelled by Zugzwang to give up control over the a5 square.

2. Kb6-a5!

Attacking the a4 square.

2. ...   **Ka3-a2**

Because of Zugzwang.

3. Ka5-a4

Driving the Black King into the corner.

3. ...   **Ka2-a1**

Black was again in Zugzwang.

4. Ka4-b3!

White must be careful: 4. Ka3 would be stalemate.

4. ...   **Ka1-b1**

5. Rb5-c5

The Rook controls the c-file and keeps the King in the corner. Black is now in Zugzwang for the last time!

5. ...   **Kb1-a1**

6. Rc5-c1#

223

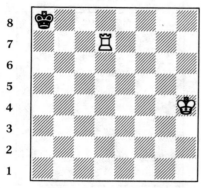

8 7 6 5 4 3 2 1

a b c d e f g h

White to play. Mate in seven moves.

The plan: Keep the Black King confined to the a8 corner and checkmate it. The idea is the same as in D-222.

1. Kh4-g5	**Ka8-b8**
2. Kg5-f6	**Kb8-c8**
3. Kf6-e7	

Defending the Rook and simultaneously attacking the d8 square.

3. ...	**Kc8-b8**

The Black King is forced to give way because of Zugzwang.

4. ...	**Ke7-d8!**

Continuing to keep the Black King in the corner.

4. ...	**Kb8-a8**

Forced because of Zugzwang.

5. Kd8-c7

White must be careful — 5. Kc8 would be stalemate.

5. ...	**Ka8-a7**
6. Rd7-d6	

The Rook controls the sixth rank and thus keeps the Black King in the corner.

6. ...	**Ka7-a8**

Again forced due to Zugzwang.

7. Rd6-a6#

224

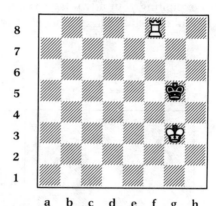

8 7 6 5 4 3 2 1

a b c d e f g h

White to play. Mate in seven moves.

The plan: Confine the Black King to the h8 corner and checkmate it.

1. Rf8-f4

Placing the Rook under the King's protection and cutting Black off from the fourth rank.

1. ...	**Kg5-g6**

If 1. ... Kh5, then 2. Rg4 Kh6 3. Kh4 Kh7 4. Kh5 Kh8 5. Kg6 Kg8 6. Rf4 Kh8 7. Rf8#. If 1. ... Kh6, then 2. Rg4 Kh5 3. Kf4 Kh6 4. Kf5 Kh5 (or 4. ... Kh7 5. Kf6 Kh8 6. Kf7 Kh7 7. Rh4#) 5. Re4 Kh6 6. Re7 Kh5 7. Rh7#.

2. Kg3-h4

Avoiding the square g4, which might be needed for the Rook.

2. ...	**Kg6-h7**

If 2. ... Kh6, then 3. Rg4 Kh7 4. Kh5 gives us a familiar position. If 2. ... Kg7, then 3. Kg5 Kh7 4. Kf6 Kh8 (or 4. ... Kg8 5. Rh4 Kf8 6. Rh8#) 5. Kf7 Kh7 6. Rh4#.

3. Kh4-g5	**Kh7-g7**
5. Rf4-f1	

A waiting move that puts Black in Zugzwang.

5. ...	**Kg7-h7**

If 4. ... Kg8, then 5. Kg6 Kh8 6. Rf8#. If 4. ... Kh8, then 5. Kg6 Kg8 6. Rf2 Kh8 7. Rf8#.

6. Kg5-f6	**Kh7-g8**

If 5. ... Kh8, then 6. Kf7 Kh7 7. Rh1#.

6. Rf1-h1	**Kg8-f8**

Forced due to Zugzwang.

7. Rh1-h8#

225

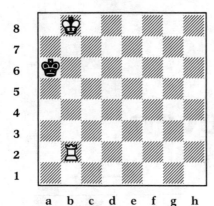

White to play. Mate in eight moves.

The plan: Confine the Black King to the a1 corner and checkmate it. We solve this problem easily by applying the method that is now familiar to us:

1. Rb2-b7	**Ka6-a5**
2. Kb8-a7!	**Ka5-a4**

The Black is continually in Zugzwang.

3. Ka7-a6	**Ka4-a3**
4. Ka6-a5	**Ka3-a2**
5. Ka5-a4	**Ka2-a1**
6. Ka4-b3	

White must be careful: 6. Ka3 would be stalemate.

6. ...	**Ka1 – b1**
7. Rb7-c7	

Putting Black into Zugzwang for the final time.

7. ...	**Kb1-a1**
8. Rc7-c1#	

226

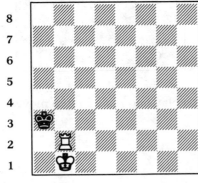

White to play. Mate in seven moves.

The plan: Confine the Black King to the a8 corner and checkmate it.

1. Kb1-c2!	**Ka3-a4**
2. Kc2-c3	**Ka4-a5**

If 2. ... Ka3, then 3. Rb4 Ka2 4. Kc2 Ka3 5. Rc4 Ka2 6. Ra4#.

3. Kc3-c4	**Ka5-a6**

If the King returns to a4 (3. ... Ka4), it will be in opposition to the White King and get checkmated by 4. Ra2#.

4. Kc4-c5	**Ka6-a7**
5. Kc5-c6	**Ka7-a8**
6. Kc6-c7	**Ka8-a7**

Unable to retreat any more, the Black King is forced to return and stand opposite its White counterpart.

7. Rb2-a2#	

227

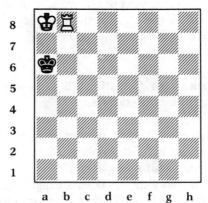

White to play. Mate in eight moves.

The plan: Drive the Black King to the a1 corner and checkmate it. By now, this problem will seem a cinch.

1. Rb8-b7

A waiting move.

1. ...	**Ka6-a5**
2. Ka8-a7	**Ka5-a4**
3. Ka7-a6	**Ka4-a3**
4. Ka6-a5	**Ka3-a2**
5. Ka5-a4	**Ka2-a1**
6. Ka4-b3	

You of course remember that 6. Ka3 can't be played, because of stalemate.

6. ...	**Ka1-b1**
7. Rb7-c7	

The final Zugzwang for Black.

7. ...	**Kb1-a1**
8. Rc7-c1#	

In all the examples the King and Rook helped each other, i.e, they co-operated well.

Lesson Seven

A. Check Lesson 6 Homework (as necessary).

B. *Review Questions*

1. How many moves are you allowed for mating if you have a Rook and King against a lone King?

2. What is meant by a "plan" in a chess game and why is it needed?

3. What is the purpose of waiting moves?

4. What is the best method of play if you have a large material advantage?

Try to answer Questions 5 & 6 without looking at a chessboard.

5. There is a White pawn on a6 and a Black one on b7. Black plays ... b7-b5. Can White capture en passant?

6. How many moves does a Knight need to get from h1 to f3? What are these moves?

Answer the next questions directly from the diagrams, without setting up the men on a board.

229

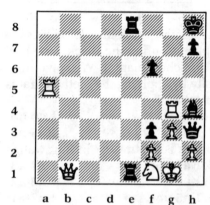

White to play and mate in two moves.

230

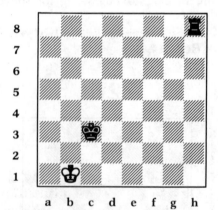

Black to play and mate in two moves.

228

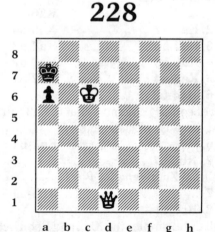

White to play and mate in two moves.

231

White to play. Who should win?

Answers to Review Questions

1. 50 moves. If you take more, the game's a draw!

2. A plan is a program of action that tells us what we have to do in order to attain the goal that we have set for ourselves.

3. Sometimes your opponent will be in Zugzwang, i.e., he will not have any good moves. In such cases you can profitably play a waiting move, which will make it your opponent's turn to play without changing the position significantly.

4. Exchanging pieces and transposing into an endgame.

5. No. White could capture en passant only if his pawn were on a5, and not on a6.

6. Four: Nh1-f2-e4-g5-f3. Other routes are also possible.

D-228

    1. Qd1-d7 +

Or 1. Qb1, or 1. Qb3.

    1. ...   **Ka7-a8**

    2. Qd7-b7#

D-229

    1. Qb1xh7 +   **Kh8xh7**

    2. Ra5-h5#

A linear mate.

D-230

    1. ...   **Rh8-a8**

Putting White into Zugzwang.

    2. Kb1-c1   **Ra8-a1#**

D-231 Black should win. He is threatening 1. ... Ra8# and the White Queen is so badly placed that it cannot help its King. The White pawn only helps Black, since without it White could win by 1. Qh1, controlling the critical square a8. But in the position as it is, the best White has is:

    1. Kg8-f8   **Ra7-a8 +**

    2. Kf8-e7   **Ra8xh8**

Black has won the Queen and in a few moves he will win the White pawn and go on to win the game.

Tactics

You already know that the **plans** that a player forms during a game answer the question of **what** must be done in order to attain a certain goal. The question of **how** to execute a plan belongs to the realm of **tactics**, which consists of combinations, exchanges, tactical themes, etc.

Tactical themes which are often encountered in positions that share certain features are known as **typical** tactical themes.

Let us now look at Diagram 232.

232

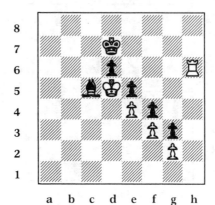

White to play and win. After

    1. Rh6-h7 +   **Kd7-d8**

    2. Kd5-e6

Black cannot prevent White from executing his plan of playing Rh7-d7 followed by Rd7xd6, giving up his Rook for the Bishop but winning all of Black's pawns in return. Here White's plan consists of exchanging his Rook for Black's Bishop and pawns, while the **tactical device** employed is the **deflection** of the Black King from the defense of the pawn on d6.

Double Attack

Games often contain opportunities for a player to win by a beautiful combination but unfortunately these opportunities frequently go by unnoticed. A knowledge of **typical tactical devices** will help in spotting combinations. Today we shall look at one of the most important of these tactical devices, known as **double attack**.

Diagrams 233 and 234 show various double attack patterns. In each of the quarter-diagrams, the double attack is carried out by a different man.

233

234

A **double attack** occurs when a piece or pawn simultaneously attacks two enemy men. Double attacks are also known as **forks**.

The most dangerous forking pieces are the Queen and the Knight, both of which attack in eight directions simultaneously.

A double attack is particularly effective when one of the pieces attacked is the King. Checking the King and simultaneously attacking another man often leads to the win of material.

Let us now look at some simple examples of double attack.

In Diagrams 235–240, White is to play and win material using the tactical device of double attack. Solve these exercises without moving the men.

235

236

237

238

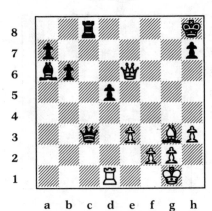

239

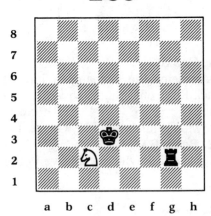

240

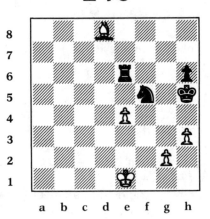

Answers

D-235 1. Kb4-b5
D-236 1. Qe4-d4 + (or 1. Qd5 +)
D-237 1. Rd8-d5 +
D-238 1. Bg3-e5 +
D-239 1. Nc2-e1 +
D-240 1. g2-g4 + Kh5-g6 2. g4xf5 +

Now here are some material-winning combinations based on the tactical device of ''double attack.'' White moves first in Diagrams 241–246.

241

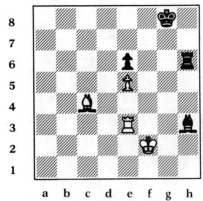

How can you win Black's Bishop?

242

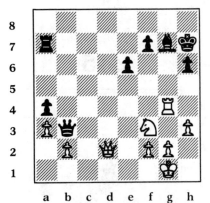

How can you win Black's Bishop?

243

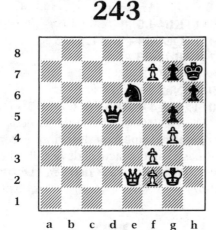

How can you win Black's Knight?

244

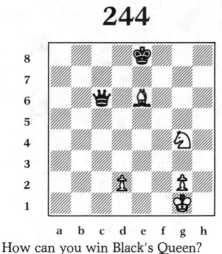

How can you win Black's Queen?

245

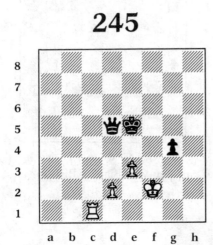

How can you win Black's Queen and draw the game?

246

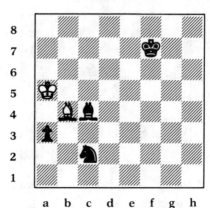

How can you win Black's pawn and draw the game?

Answers

D-241

1. Re3xh3!

By sacrificing the Exchange White decoys the Black Rook onto the h3 square.

1. ...   Rh6xh3

Otherwise White would be a piece up.

2. Bc4xe6 +

A double attack which will leave White up a Bishop.

D-242

1. Rg4xg7 + !

By giving up his Rook for the Bishop, White decoys the Black King onto g7.

1. ...   Kh7xg7

Or else 2. Qxh6# would follow.

2. Qd2-d4 +

This check wins the Rook, leaving White a Bishop up.

D-243

1. Qe2xe6!

The Queen sacrifices itself for the Knight, which controls f8.

1. ...   Qd5xe6

If 1. ... Qd8, then 2. Qf5 + and 3. f8Q etc.

2. f7-f8N + !

If the pawn promoted to a Queen the game would be a draw, but by promoting to a Knight it immediately creates a fork that will leave White a Knight up.

D-244 Black, with a material advantage, was dreaming of winning, but White made a magnificent combination and gained the victory.

1. Be6-d7+!

To decoy the Black King or Queen onto the treacherous square d7, the White Bishop sacrifices itself for the sake of a double attack. But its loss will be avenged by the Knight!

Variation a):

1. ...	**Ke8xd7**
2. Ng4-e5+	

A Knight fork.

2. ...	**Kd7-d6**
3. Ne5xc6	**Kd6xc6**

Variation b):

1. ...	**Qc6xd7**
2. Ng4-f6+	

Again a fork.

2. ...	**Ke8-e7**
3. Nf6xd7	**Ke7xd7**

White has gained three points.

In both variations, White finishes two pawns up and should win.

D-245

1. Rc1-c5!

Black has a big material advantage and felt sure of winning, but . . . . White finds a saving combination. By sacrificing the Rook, he forces the Black Queen to occupy c5.

1. ...	**Qd5xc5**

All other moves would lose.

2. d2-d4+

Forking the Queen and the King.

2. ...	**Qc5xd4**

It's better to give up the Queen for two pawns like this than for just one.

3. e3xd4+	**Ke5xd4**
4. Kf2-g3	

A draw is inevitable, as Black's last pawn will be eliminated. As a result of the combination White gained three points.

D-246 The Black pawn is threatening to queen. 1. Bc3 a2 2. Ka4 a1Q+ 3. Bxa1 Nxa1 does not save White since Black should win with his Knight and Bishop against White's lone King, although only strong and experienced players know the winning technique. However, White can save himself by a forking combination in which the King itself plays the main role.

1. Bb4xa3

The Bishop sacrifices itself for the dangerous pawn on a3 and at the same time decoys the Black Knight onto that square.

1. ...	**Nc2xa3**

If Black doesn't capture the Bishop the game should be a draw anyway.

2. Ka5-b4

Now either the Knight or the Bishop will be lost and the game will be drawn.

Note that in each of the above examples something was sacrificed in order to achieve a goal — a combination is just that.

Pawn Endgames. The Rule of the Square

We now begin the study of pawn endgames. You will often have to deal with such endgames in your games. They arise when all the pieces have been exchanged off and each side is left only with his King and some pawns.

Pawn endings demand accurate play, since a single incorrect move can change the outcome of the struggle.

Sometimes one of the players obtains an advantage of a single pawn. Is this advantage enough for victory? Should he strive to exchange off all the pieces and go into a pawn ending or should he avoid such exchanges? A player can correctly answer these questions only if he has a mastery of pawn endings.

Today we shall look at some very simple examples, in which a pawn tries to advance to the queening square without the help of its King.

247

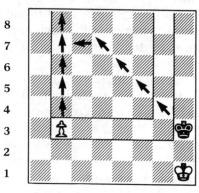

White to play wins. Black to play draws.

In Diagram 247, White to play wins and Black to play draws. With White to play we get:

1. b3-b4	**Kh3-g4**
2. b4-b5	**Kg4-f5**

The Black King approaches the White pawn along the diagonal, which is the shortest route.

3. b5-b6	Kf5-e6
4. b6-b7	Ke6-d7
5. b7-b8Q	

The Black King was unable to catch the White pawn, which has successfully queened.

Now let us look at the same position (Diagram 247) with Black to play:

1. ...	Kh3-g4
2. b3-b4	Kg4-f5
3. b4-b5	Kf5-e6
4. b5-b6	Ke6-d7
5. b6-b7	Kd7-c7

The King slightly deviates from its diagonal path because c8 is controlled by the White pawn.

6. b7-b8Q +	Kc7xb8

The Black King caught the White pawn in time and captures it.

Good chessplayers can tell in advance whether or not the King can catch the pawn in such situations. They do this by making use of the **Rule of the Square**, which states:

Draw a square one side of which is the line extending from the pawn to its queening square. If the defending King on its move can enter this square, it can catch the pawn.

When such positions occur in a game, players draw a mental picture of such squares.

Returning now to Diagram 247, we see that with **White to play** the Black King is unable to enter the smaller square b4-b8-f4-f8 and so the pawn queens, whereas with **Black to play** his King can enter the larger square b3-g8-g3-g8 and catch up with the pawn.

When applying the rule of the square to a pawn on its home square (2nd rank for a White pawn and 7th rank for a Black pawn) we must remember that the pawn can advance two squares at once on its first move. As a result we must draw the square from the third rank (for a White pawn) or the sixth rank (for a Black pawn).

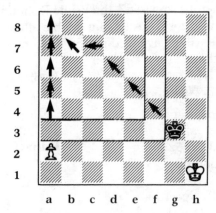

In Diagram 248, for example, White to play wins by 1. a2-a4, the Black King being unable to enter the small square a4-a8-e4-e8. Black to play, on the other hand, draws:

1. ...	Kg3-f4

The King enters the large square a3-a8-f3-f8 and catches the White pawn.

1. a2-a4	Kf4-e5
3. a4-a5	Ke5-d6
4. a5-a6	Kd6-c7
5. a6-a7	Kc7-b7
6. a7-a8Q +	Kb7xa8

The King usually chases the pawn along the diagonal because that is the shortest route. If there is some obstacle on the diagonal, the rule of the square becomes inapplicable.

For example, let us look at Diagram 249:

249

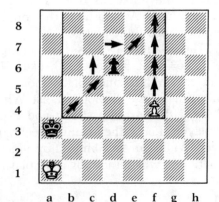

Black to play and White wins.

1. ...	Ka3-b4

The King enters the square but because there

is an obstacle (the Black pawn on d6) in its path (the a3-f8 diagonal), Black loses anyway. Nor would 1. ... d5 save Black: 2. f5 d4 3. f6 d3 4. f7 d2 5. f8Q + Kb3 6. Qf1 Kc2 7. Qb1 + Kc3 8. Ka2 and White will attack the pawn with his King, winning it and with it the game as well.

2. f4-f5	**Kb4-c5**
3. f5-f6	**Kc5-c6**

The King is forced to lose time (a tempo) in going around his own pawn.

4. f6-f7	**Kc6-d7**
5. f7-f8Q	

Black fell one move (tempo) short of drawing the game.

Now let us use our newly-acquired knowledge to make some combinations.

250

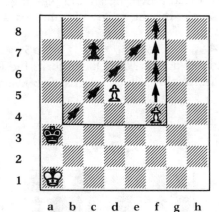

Black to play and White wins.

1. ...	**Ka3-b4**

With this move the Black King enters the square of the pawn and Black thought that the game would be drawn, but . . . .

2. d5-d6!

A combination! The White pawn sacrifices itself in order to decoy the Black pawn onto d6.

2. ...	**c7xd6**

Or else the White d-pawn would queen.

3. f4-f5

And White wins in exactly the same manner as in the previous example. The Black pawn on d6 blocks its King's path.

251

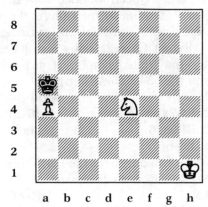

White to play wins.

1. Ne4-c3!

Otherwise the game would be drawn: 1. Nc5 Kb4 2. Kg2 Kxc5 3. a5 Kb5, and the King is in the a5-a8-d5-d8 square and easily wins the pawn.

1. ...	**Ka5-b4**

2. Kh1-g2!

A combination! The Knight is sacrificed in order to deflect the Black King from the a5-a8-d5-d8 square.

2. ...	**Kb4xc3**

Otherwise the White King will approach and, together with the Knight, will escort the pawn to its queening square.

3. a4-a5

Now the pawn cannot be stopped.

3. ...	**Kc3-b4**
4. a5-a6	**Kb4-b5**
5. a6-a7	**Kb5-b6**
6. a7-a8Q	

and so on.

252

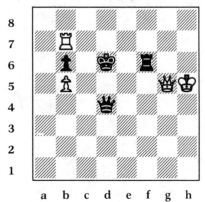

White to play wins.

1. Qg5xf6 + !

A temporary Queen sacrifice with the ultimate goal of assuring the queening of the pawn on b5. Sacrificing the Rook instead does not work: 1. Rxb6+ Qxb6 2. Qxf6+ Kc5 3. Qxb6+ Kxb6 and the White pawn is lost, as the Black King is in the b5-b8-e5-e8 square.

1. ...	Qd4xf6
2. Rb7xb6 +	Kd6-e5
3. Rb6xf6	Ke5xf6
4. b5-b6	

And the pawn queens as the Black King cannot enter the b6-b8-d6-d8 square.

4. ...	Kf6-e6
5. b6-b7	Ke6-d6
6. b7-b8Q	

and so on.

To conclude this lesson, let us look at some very short games in which a double attack decided the outcome of the struggle right in the opening.

Game 43
Combe–Hasenfuss, Folkestone 1933

1. d2-d4	c7-c5

If White replies 2. dxc5 can Black win back the pawn? Yes, with the move 2. ... Qa5+, a double attack on the King (check) and the pawn.

2. c2-c4

2. d5 would be a good move.

2. ...	c5xd4

3. Ng1-f3

White doesn't want to bring out his Queen with 3. Qxd4.

3. ...	e7-e5

Black defends the pawn on d4 and at the same time sets a trap that should be "child's play" to avoid. See Diagram 253.

253

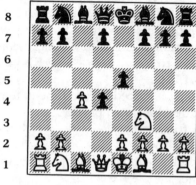

What is the trap?

4. Nf3xe5??

White falls for the bait and takes the poisoned pawn. Instead of attempting to regain the sacrificed pawn, he should play a gambit with 4. e3. But he is greedy and loses immediately.

4. ...	Qd8-a5 +

A double attack. The Queen forks the King and the Knight. White resigns. See Diagram 254.

254

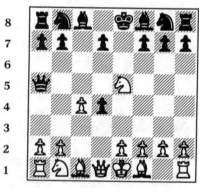

This game is the shortest ever played in the World Chess Olympics.

Game 44
French Defense

1. e2-e4	e7-e6
2. d2-d4	d7-d5
3. Nb1-c3	d5xe4
4. Nc3xe4	Ng8-f6
5. Bf1-d3	

A good move that incidentally contains a trap.

| 5. ... | Bf8-e7 |

Black sees through the trap: 5. ... Qxd4 would cost him his Queen after 6. Bb5 + .

| 6. Ng1-f3 | 0-0 |
| 7. Qd1-e2 | b7-b6? |

Until now both sides have played well but here Black overlooks a double attack of White's. He should play instead 7. ... Nbd7 followed by 8. ... b6.

| 8. Ne4xf6 + | Be7xf6 |
| 9. Qe2-e4! | |

See Diagram 255.

255

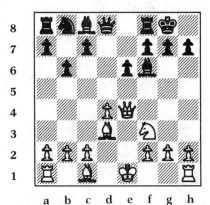

Black resigns, as he must lose his Rook. The White Queen is simultaneously threatening to mate on h7 (10. Qxh7#) and capture the Rook on a8 (10. Qxa8).

HOMEWORK
(Answers at the end)

I. The solutions to Diagrams 256–261 involve the tactical device of "double attack."

256

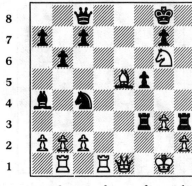

Find all the possible double attacks with White to play and with Black to play (do not move a piece to a square where it can be captured for nothing or by a less valuable man).

_____

_____

_____

257

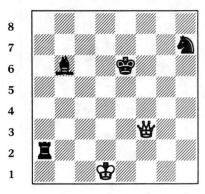

White to play. Find all the possible double attacks. Which is the best? (Do not put your Queen under attack.)

_____

_____

_____

258

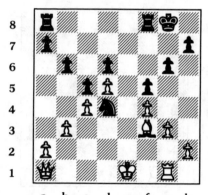

Black to play. Find the best move.

	WHITE	BLACK
1.		
2.		
3.		
4.		

260

White to play and win Black's Queen.

	WHITE	BLACK
1.		
2.		
3.		
4.		

259

Black to play and win a piece.

	WHITE	BLACK
1.		
2.		
3.		
4.		

261

White to play and win a piece.

	WHITE	BLACK
1.		
2.		
3.		
4.		

II. In Diagrams 262-267 find combinations that use the tactical device of "double attack."

262

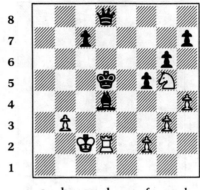

White to play and win a piece.

	WHITE	BLACK
1.		
2.		
3.		
4.		

263

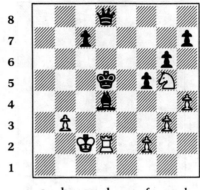

White to play and win Black's Queen.

	WHITE	BLACK
1.		
2.		
3.		
4.		

264

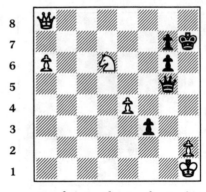

White to play and win.

	WHITE	BLACK
1.		
2.		
3.		
4.		

105

265

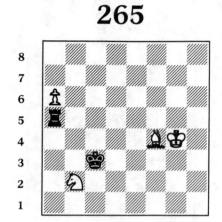

White to play and win.

	WHITE	BLACK
1.		
2.		
3.		
4.		

266

White to play and win a piece.

	WHITE	BLACK
1.		
2.		
3.		
4.		

267

What will happen if Black captures the pawn on d6?

	WHITE	BLACK
1.		
2.		
3.		
4.		

III. The solutions to Diagrams 268–273 make use of the "rule of the square."

268

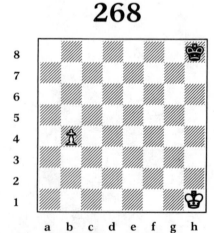

What happens if it is White to play? If it is Black to play?

269

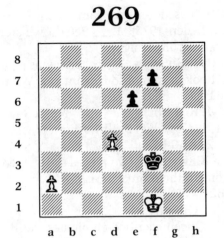

White to play. How should the game end?

	WHITE	BLACK
1.		
2.		
3.		
4.		

271

White to play and win.

	WHITE	BLACK
1.		
2.		
3.		
4.		

270

Can Black to play win?

	WHITE	BLACK
1.		
2.		
3.		
4.		

272

White to play. Queen your own pawn while stopping Black's.

	WHITE	BLACK
1.		
2.		
3.		
4.		

273

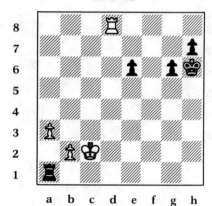

White to play and win.

	WHITE	BLACK
1.		
2.		
3.		
4.		

Answers to the Homework

D-256 With White to play: Kg1-g2; Qe1-b4; Qe1-e2; Ng6-e7+; Ng6-h4; b2-b3.

With Black to play: Qc8-e6; Qc8-e8;Rf3-e3; Ba4xc2; Nc4-e3.

D-257 Qf3-b3+ is the best move as it wins the Rook, the most valuable Black piece on the board. Other moves are: Qf3-b7; Qf3-c6+; Qf3-e4+; Qf3-h3+.

D-258 Variation a):

1. ...	Nd4-c2+
2. Ke1-d2	Nc2xa1
3. Rg1xa1	

Black has won a Queen (9 points) and lost a Knight (3 points) for a net gain of 6 points.

Variation b):

1. ...	Nd4xf3+
2. Ke1-f2	Nf3xg1
3. Kf2xg1	

In this case Black has won a Bishop (3 points) and a Rook (5 points) and lost a Knight (3 points). That is, he has won 5 points.

So we conclude that 1. ... Nc2+ is the best move, since it gains one point more than 1. Nxf3+.

D-259 (Based on the game Reti–Alekhine, Baden-Baden 1925). 1. ... Be6-d5 wins either the Rook or the Knight.

D-260 1. Rh5-d5+. This check wins a Queen for a Rook, a gain of four points for White.

D-261

1. Kc5-b6	Na7-c8+

If 1. ... Kg4, then 2. Kb7 wins a piece.

2. Kb6-b7

The King attacks two pieces simultaneously and one of them must perish.

D-262

1. Qd2xd7+!

This Queen sacrifice eliminates the Bishop defending the pawn on e6.

1. ...	Rd8xd7

2. Nf4xe6+

Now the Knight is able to capture the pawn on e6 and fork the Queen and King.

2. ...	u

3. Ne6xf8

and White is a Knight up. Black has lost four points.

D-263

1. Rd2xd4+!

This exchange sacrifice decoys the Black King onto d4.

1. ...	Kd5xd4

Otherwise the Rook would take the Queen.

2. Ng5-e6+

Our old friend the fork.

2. ...	u

3. Ne6xd8

And White is up a Knight. Black has lost a Queen and Bishop for a Rook, i.e., a total of seven points.

D-264 Black is threatening 1. ... Qg2# and apparently there is no defense. However, White is saved by an "exchanging" combination:

1. Qa8-h8+!

The Queen is sacrificed to decoy the Black King onto h8.

1. ...	Kh7xh8

2. Nd6-f7+

Again a fork.

2. ...	u

3. Nf7xg5

Now we see the idea behind the combination. White has exchanged off the dangerous Black Queen and now can win easily, since his King is within the square of the Black pawn (f1-f3-h1-h3) while the Black King hasn't the faintest hope of making it to the square of the White a-pawn (a6-a8-c6-c8).

D-265

    1. Bf4-d2 + !

A fine Bishop sacrifice that decoys the Black King onto d2.

    1. ...   **Kc3xd2**

If 1. ... Kxb2, then White plays 2. Bxa5 followed by queening the pawn.

    2. Nb2-c4 +

A fork. It is not for nothing that chessplayers consider horses to be dangerous beasts.

    2. ...   **u**

    3. Nc4xa5

and the a-pawn will queen as the Black King cannot enter the a6-a8-c6-c8 square.

D-266

    1. Rc1xc2!

An exchange sacrifice to decoy the Black Rook onto c2.

    1. ...   **Rd2xc2**

Or else White will remain a Bishop up.

    2. Bh3-f5 +

A check winning the Rook. White will be up a Bishop.

D-267 (From Ljublinskii–Kamyshov, Moscow 1949).

    1. ...   **Kd7xd6?**

was followed by

    2. Rb1-d1 +   **Kd6-e7**
    3. Rd1xd8!   **Ke7xd8**
    4. Be3xb6 +

A check winning the Rook. Black resigns, as he has lost a piece.

D-268 White wins in both cases as the Black King cannot make it in time to the b4-b8-f4-f8 square and the White pawn will queen.

D-269 White should win:

    1. d4-d5!

The pawn is sacrificed in order to establish a Black pawn in the Black King's path. 1. a4 would not work because of 1. ... Ke4 2. a5 Kd5, when the Black King, having entered the a5-a8-d5-d8 square, can stop the a-pawn.

    1. ...   **e6xd5**

Otherwise the d-pawn would queen.

    2. a2-a4   **Kf3-e4**

It doesn't help to move 2. ... d4 3. a5 d3, because of 4. Ke1! and the White King can easily stop Black's pawn. At the same time, the

Black King cannot stop the White pawn on the a-file.

    3. a4-a5   **Ke4-e5**

The King is forced to lose a decisive move (tempo) in going around its own pawn.

    4. a5-a6   **Ke5-d6**
    5. a6-a7   **Kd6-c7**
    6. a7-a8Q

Black was just one move short of catching the pawn.

D-270 Yes.

    1. ...   **Ba1-e5!**

The Bishop is sacrificed in order to deflect the White King from the c1-c4-f1-f4 square.

    2. Ke4xe5

Otherwise Black will bring his King up to accompany the pawn and win easily

    2. ...   **f4-f3**

and the pawn will queen.

D-271

    1. Nc4-b2!

Only this Knight sacrifice wins. 1. Ne5 would be met by the double attack 1. ... Kd4, winning the pawn.

    1. ...   **Kc3xb2**

Or else the White King will come up to help the pawn queen.

    2. d3-d4

and White wins, since the Black King cannot stop the pawn.

D-272

    1. Kf1-g2!

1. a4 would be a mistake because of 1. ... g2 +, winning for Black (the Bishop can easily stop the a-pawn). So White first keeps the Bishop out of play. Even though it now becomes Black's turn to play, his King still cannot make it in time to the square of the pawn.

    1. ...   **h6-h5**

The only chance.

    2. a2-a4   **h5-h4**
    3. a4-a5   **h4-h3 + !**

Black offers a pawn in an attempt to free his trapped Bishop.

    4. Kg2-h1!!

White ignores the pawn on h3. 4. Kxh3 would allow Black to win by 4. ... Bg1, but as it is the Bishop still cannot break loose.

    4. ...   **g7-g5**

Yet another pawn hurries to the aid of the Bishop.

5. a5-a6	g5-g4
6. a6-a7	g3-g2 + !

Black gives up his Bishop in a final attempt to save the game.

7. Kh1xh2	g4-g3 + !

The pawns on g3 and h3 are under attack now, but they are both "poisoned pawns." If the King captures either of them, the pawn on g2 will queen.

8. Kh2-g1!!

The Black pawns have been stopped!

8. ...	h3-h2 +
9. Kg1xg2	Kh8-g7
10. a7-a8Q	

and so on.

The White King successfully coped with a Black Bishop and three (!) Black pawns while nothing could hold back the White a-pawn. This happened because the Bishop was caught in a disastrous situation and the Black King was too far away from both the Bishop and the White pawn.

D-273 (From Petrosian–Taimanov, Moscow 1957). The future world champion played **1. Rd8-d1** and Black resigned. 1. ... Ra2 is no good because 2. Kb3 snares the Rook. If 1. ... Rxd1, then 2. Kxd1 and the Black King cannot reach the square of the a-pawn (a3-a8-f3-f8), while the White King can easily stop any of the Black pawns.

SUPPLEMENTARY MATERIAL

for use at the teacher's discretion

Defending Against a Double Attack

274

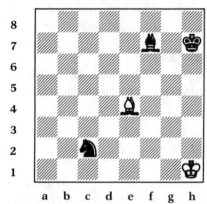

Black to play. White's Bishop is forking the King and the Knight. Can Black save his piece?

Yes, he can, by using a tactical device known as **defending against a check by interposition**:

1. ...	Bf7-g6

Now both the King and the Knight are protected.

2. Be4xc2	Bg6xc2

Pieces of equal value have been traded.

275

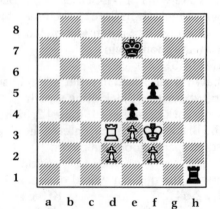

White to play. The Black pawn on e4 is forking the King and the Rook. Does White have to lose a Rook?

No. White can save himself by using a tactical device known as **counterattacking**:

    1. Kf3-g2!

The King gets out of check and at the same time attacks Black's Rook.

    1. ...   **e4xd3**

    2. Kg2xh1

White has lost nothing. All that has occurred is a trade of Rooks.

277

276

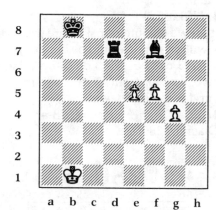

White to play.

    1. e5-e6

The pawn forks the Rook and the Bishop. Can Black avoid losing a piece?

Yes, by using the tactical device known as **in-between check**:

    1. ...   **Rd7-b7 +**

Black moves away one of his attacked pieces with check. White has no time to capture the other piece because he must first save his King. Note that the in-between check 1. ... Rd1+ would not work because of the counterattack 2. Kc2, when White would win a piece after all.

    2. u   **Bf7-e8**

Black has saved his piece.

Black to play. The White Rook is forking two Black pieces. Can Black save them?

Yes, by using the tactical device known as **defending one attacked piece with the other attacked piece**:

    1. ...   **Bb4-d6**

The defenses 1. ... Nc6 and 1. ... Na6 would be insufficient since after the new fork 2. Rb6! Black would lose a piece after all.

    2. Rb4-b6   **Bd6-e5**

    3. Rb6-b5   **Kg7-f6**

with an equal position.

278

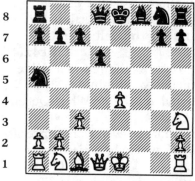

Can either White or Black to play win material? White to play wins a piece:

    1. Qd1-h5 +

A check winning the Knight on a5. 1. Qa4 + also simultaneously attacks the King and the Knight, but would not win a piece. Black could defend in two ways: a) 1. ... Nc6 (one attacked piece protects the other) or b) 1. ... c6 (the pawn covers the check and at the same time opens a diagonal along which the Queen defends the Knight).

Black to play cannot win material in spite of the fact that he can make a triple attack!

    1. ...   **Qd8-h4 +**

The Queen simultaneously attacks the King, the Knight, and the e-pawn.

    2. Nh3-f2!

One attacked piece protects the two other attacked men: the Knight moves away from the attack and at the same time covers the check and defends the e-pawn.

279

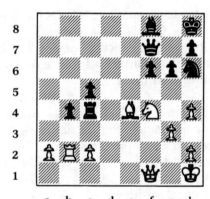

White to play. Is 1. Be4-d5 a good move?

No. Although the Bishop forks two Black pieces, the move is still a blunder. Black can win a piece by using the tactical device known as **eliminating the defender**:

    1. ...   **Rc4xf4!!**

With this exchange sacrifice Black simultaneously eliminates the Bishop's defender and attacks the White Queen.

    2. Qf1xf4

2. Bxf7 would be even worse since after 2. ... Rxf1 + Black would be a piece up.

    2. ...   **Qf7xd5 +**

As a result of his combination Black has won a Knight and a Bishop (6 points) for a Rook (5 points), i.e., he has gained one point.

You are now acquainted with the major ways of defending against double attacks. There are, however, other methods as well, and you will be introduced to them later on.

Sample Games Containing The Theme of Double Attack

Game 45
Sicilian Defense

    1. e2-e4   **c7-c5**
    2. d2-d4   **c5xd4**
    3. Ng1-f3

White could win back his pawn by 3. Qxd4, but he does not want to bring his Queen out so early. He expects that the Black pawn cannot be defended in any case.

    3. ...   **e7-e5**

Black defends the d-pawn and sets a trap at the same time.

    4. Nf3xe5??

How often we fall into traps! White thinks that the e-pawn is a gift. It would be better to play a gambit: 4. c3 dxc3 5. Nxc3 d6 6. Bc4, and the aggressive development of the White pieces makes up for the lost pawn.

    4. ...   **Qd8-a5 +!**

See Diagram 280.

280

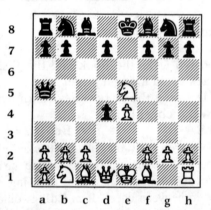

This simple Queen check was overlooked by White in his calculations when he made his last move. Black will capture the Knight on e5 and have excellent chances of winning the game.

Game 46
Vitalii Kozlov (age 12)–Kolya Petuhov (age 14)
Schoolchildren's Tournament, USSR 1974

    1. d2-d4   **Ng8-f6**
    2. Bc1-g5   **c7-c6**

A fairly good move that at the same time sets a trap.

3. e2-e3??

Who sees the strongest reply for Black? White has not noticed a double attack and pays with a piece. Instead 3. Nf3 would lead to an even game.

   3. ...   **Qd8-a5 + !**

Of course, this is the strongest move. A check winning the Bishop. See Diagram 281.

281

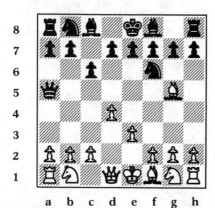

White resigned, but it would make sense for a beginner to fight on in such a situation since his opponent might in turn make a blunder.

Can Black be said to have made a **combination** in this game? *No. A combination has to contain a sacrifice. Black's move 3. ... Qa5 + is a* **tactical device** *known as* **double attack.**

Game 47
Ruy Lopez

 1. e2-e4   **e7-e5**
 2. Ng1-f3   **Nb8-c6**
 3. Bf1-b5

This move initiates the most popular opening of our times, the Ruy Lopez, named after a Spaniard in whose hands it was a fearful weapon some 400 years ago.

   3. ...   **a7-a6**

Black often makes this move, which involves a temporary pawn sacrifice.

 4. Bb5xc6   **d7xc6**

Black could also reply 4. ... bxc6, e.g. 5. Nxe5 Qg5 (attacking both the Knight and the pawn on g2) 6. Ng4 d5! (a fresh double attack, this time on the Knight on g4 and the pawn on e4) 7. Ne3 dxe4.

  5. Nf3xe5?!

White is in a hurry to win a pawn. He would

do better to continue his development by 5. 0-0 or 5. Nc3.

   5. ...   **Qd8-d4!**

A double attack allowing Black to win back his pawn. Also possible is 5. ... Qg5 (again a double attack) 6. d4 Qxg2. Not as good, however, would be 5. ... Qe7 6. d4 f6 7. Nf3 Qxe4 + 8. Be3, when Black is behind in development.

 6. Ne5-f3   **Qd4xe4 +**
 7. Qd1-e2   **Qe4xe2 +**
 8. Ke1xe2

See Diagram 282.

282

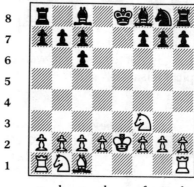

Black's position is preferable. White has lost the right to castle while Black can rapidly bring out his pieces and castle on the Queenside.

Game 48
Fima Rokhman (age 11)–Dima Shapiro (age 12)
Schoolchildren's Tournament, USSR 1972

 1. c2-c4   **d7-d5**
 2. c4xd5   **Ng8-f6**

Black could play 2. ... Qxd5 but he doesn't want to bring his Queen out so early and plans to capture the pawn with his Knight.

 3. e2-e4

White decides to defend the pawn, at the same time setting a "childishly simple" trap.

   3. ...   **Nf6xe4??**

Black can blame only himself for playing so carelessly. He grabs the pawn without noticing White's simple reply. Instead, Black should play a gambit, i.e., sacrifice a pawn in return for good play. For example: 3. ... c6 4. dxc6 Nxc6.

4. Qd1-a4 + !

A check winning the Knight. See Diagram 283.

283

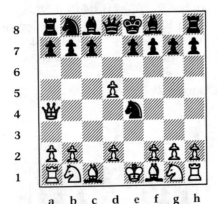

Black resigns. Of course *you* won't make such "typical mistakes," right?

Game 49

1. e2-e4	e7-e5
2. Ng1-f3	Nb8-c6
3. Bf1-e2	

A passive move. 3. Bc4 or 3. Bb5 would be better.

3. ...	Bf8-c5
4. 0-0	d7-d6
5. c2-c3	

Preparing 6. d4.

5. ...	Bc8-e6?

A blunder that costs a piece. 5. ... Bg4 or 5. ... Nf6 would be better.

6. d2-d4

Before making this move, White had to count how many times the pawn would be attacked by the Black men and how many times it would be defended.

6. ...	Bc5-b6

Black cannot win the pawn on d4 because the three attackers do not outnumber the three defenders.

7. d4-d5!

See Diagram 284.

284

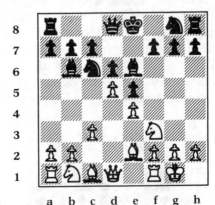

A fork which wins a piece. This is what Black overlooked when playing 5. ... Be6?. Now Black's affairs are in a bad way.

Game 50

1. e2-e4	e7-e5
2. Ng1-f3	Ng8-f6
3. d2-d3	

White defends his pawn on e4 and plans to capture the Black pawn on e5, but the move is passive and blocks the light-square Bishop. More active possibilities are 3. d4 or 3. Nxe5 d6 4. Nf3 Nxe4 5. d4.

3. ...	c7-c6

An interesting move that prepares 4. ... d5 and at the same time indirectly defends the pawn on e5.

4. Nb1-c3

White sees through Black's *first* trap: 4. Nxe5 would be bad because of 4. ... Qa5 + winning the Knight on e5.

4. ...	d7-d5!

Black again offers the pawn on e5, but seizes the center.

5. Nf3xe5?

Black's *second* trap catches White! If White wants to win the e-pawn, he should play the following line, although Black gets enough compensation for the pawn: 5. exd5 cxd5 6. Nxe5 d4 7. Qe2! (an in-between move with the Queen that prevents 7. ... dxc3 since the discovered check 8. Nc6 + would win Black's Queen) 7. ... Be7 8. Nd1 (now the Knight on e5 is defended by the Queen and White does not have to fear the double attack 8. ... Qa5 +).

5. ...	d5-d4!

This is the move the White underestimated in his calculations.

6. Nc3-e2   **Qd8-a5 +**

The same old check winning a Knight that occurs in so many games! See Diagram 285.

285

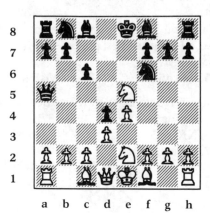

Game 51
Queen's Gambit Declined
1. d2-d4   **d7-d5**
2. c2-c4

White sacrifices a pawn for quick development.

2. ...   **Ng8-f6**

Black declines the gift, but a better way of doing so would be by 2. ... e6, defending the d-pawn with another pawn.

3. c4xd5   **Nf6xd5**
4. Ng1-f3   **Nb8-c6**

A mistake. The Black Knights are now convenient targets for the White pawns. It would be better to play 4. ... e6 or 4. ... c6, controlling the central square d5.

5. e2-e4   **Nd5-f6**
6. d4-d5!

The White pawns occupy the center and chase the Black Knights away from there.

6. ...   **Nf6xe4?**

Black plays for a trap. He expects 7. dxc6 Qxd1 + 8. Kxd1 Nxf2 + 9. Ke1 Nxh1, when he would be up an Exchange and two pawns. However, it would be better to move the Knight back to its home square with 6. ... Nb8.

7. Bc1-e3!

Now the pawn on f2 is defended by the Bishop and White really threatens to capture the Knight on c6. Black has fallen into a **countertrap.**

7. ...   **Nc6-a5**

8. Qd1-a4 + !

See Diagram 286.

286

A triple attack on the King and two Knights! Black can defend the Knight on a5 with 8. ... c6 (opening a line of defence for the Queen) but he cannot save the Knight on e4. The double attack that Black planned to execute with his Knight on e4 has been forestalled by the White Queen's triple attack. White winds up with both a material advantage and a better position.

Game 52
Borbesch–Kovacs, Zurich 1948
Sicilian Defense
1. e2 e4   **c7-c5**
2. Ng1-f3   **d7-d6**
3. d2-d4   **c5xd4**
4. Qd1xd4

Much rarer than 4. Nxd4 but not at all bad.

4. ...   **Nb8-c6**
5. Bf1-b5   **Bc8-d7**
6. Bb5xc6   **b7xc6**
7. Nb1-c3   **Ng8-f6**
8. Bc1-g5   **Ra8-b8?**

Apparently a good move, for Black attacks the pawn on b2 and probably plans to meet 9. 0-0-0 with 9. ... Qb6. The thing is, however, that White does not have to defend the b-pawn at all. The correct move was 8. ... e5 with an equal game.

9. e4-e5!   **d6xe5**
10. Nf3xe5   **Rb8xb2?**

A blunder. Black overlooks a double attack. The right move is 10. ... Rb7, defending the

115

pawn on a7 and the light-square Bishop. As it is, White gets an idea based on attacking the Black Rook by castling on the Queenside.

11. Bg5xf6

Eliminating the Knight that defends the Bishop on d7.

11. ...   **g7xf6?**

Black does not sense the danger, or else he would play 11. ... exf6, opening the a3-f8 diagonal for his Bishop and intending to try and complicate the game by replying to 12. Nxd7 with the in-between move 12. ... Rb4.

12. Ne5xd7!

The only way! 12. Qxd7+ Qxd7 13. Nxd7 would be wrong because of the in-between move 13. ... Rxc2, when both White Knights would be under attack.

12. ...   **Qd8xd7**

13. Qd4xd7+

Forcing the Black King onto the d-file.

13. ...   **Ke8xd7**

14. 0-0-0+!

See Diagram 287.

287

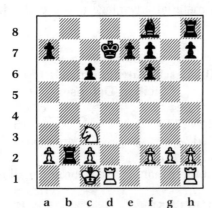

A check winning the Rook on b2. After this pretty move Black resigned right away. We have already come across a similar idea in Foyer–O'Kelly (game 2).

Game 53
Karaklajic–Fuderer, Yugoslavia 1955
Philidor's Defense

1. e2-e4	e7-e5
2. Ng1-f3	d7-d6
3. d2-d4	Nb8-d7

A good move. 3. ... Nc6 could be met with 4.

Bb5, continuing to put pressure on the pawn on e5.

4. Bf1-c4

White develops his Bishop and at the same time sets a trap. 4. Bb5 would yield nothing after the simple reply 4. ... c6.

4. ...   **Bf8-e7?**

The natural-looking move turns out to be a mistake. Black must first play 4. ... c6, and only then 5. ... Be7.

5. d4xe5   **Nd7xe5**

5. ... dxe5 would be even worse because of 6. Qd5!, winning (see lesson 4, D-137).

6. Nf3xe5   **d6xe5**

7. Qd1-h5!

288

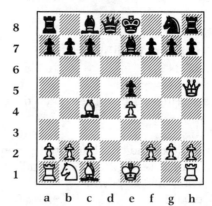

The Queen forks the pawns on e5 and f7. Black cannot defend them both and must lose one of them.

The player of the Black pieces in this game, Fuderer, was a Yugoslav master. Interestingly enough, the winner of the game, Yugoslav master Karaklajic, caught another master player, Nedeljkovic, in exacly the same opening trap in another game played five years later, also in Yugoslavia. Nor was Liberzon, who later became a grandmaster, able to avoid falling into this trap in the game he played against the master Estrin in 1958, in Moscow. As you can see, even strong chessplayers sometimes blunder!

Game 54
Imbisch–Goering, 1899
Vienna Game

1. e2-e4	e7-e5
2. Nb1-c3	Ng8-f6
3. Bf1-c4	

White would do better to play a gambit by sacrificing a pawn with 3. f4 and then quickly develop his pieces.

3. ...	Nf6xe4

A temporary piece sacrifice. 4. Nxe4 would be met by 4. ... d5, forking the Knight and Bishop and winning back the sacrificed piece with a good position.

4. Bc4xf7 +

White decides to expose the Black King's position by means of this counter-sacrifice.

4. ...	Ke8xf7
5. Nc3xe4	Nb8-c6?

Material is even, but Black could obtain a positional advantage by 5. ... d5! 6. Qf3 + Kg8 7. Ng5 Qd7! (not 7. ... Qxg5 8. Qxd5 + Be6 9. Qxe6#). Black has the better position after 7. ... Qd7! because of his strong pawn center, and he can easily drive away the White Knight from g5 by 8. ... h6.

6. Qd1-f3 +	Kf7-g8??

Here this move is a grave error indeed! The only way for Black to avoid immediate disaster is 6. ... Ke8, although even then his position is worse due to his King being stuck in the center.

7. Ne4-g5!
See Diagram 289.

289

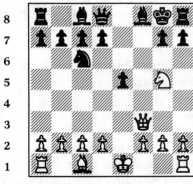

White plays the strongest move, forcing Black to capitulate immediately. There is no satisfactory defense against the double threat of 8. Qf7# and 8. Qd5#.

Lesson Eight

A. Check Lesson 7 Homework (as necessary).
B. *Review Questions*

1. How many moves does a Knight need to get from f6 to h8 and what are these moves? Try to answer this question without looking at a chessboard.
2. What is meant by a "forced variation"?
3. What is the difference between tactics and a plan?
4. What is the difference between combinations and tactical devices?

Find the solutions to questions 5–8 directly from the diagrams, without setting up the men on a board.

291

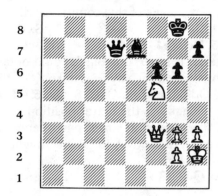

White to play. Can he win a piece?

290

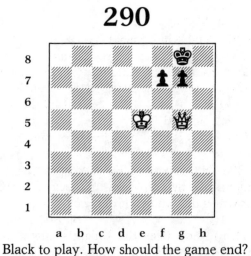

Black to play. How should the game end?

292

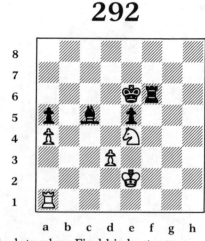

Black to play. Find his best move.

118

293

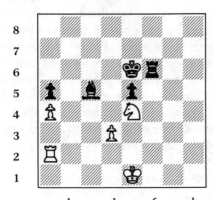

Black to play. Can he escape from the fork?

294

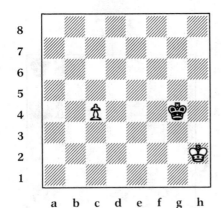

White to play. How should the game end?

295

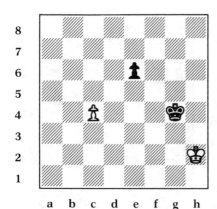

White to play. How should the game end?

Answers To the Review Questions

1. Four moves. Nf6-g8-h6-f7-h8 (other routes are also possible).

2. A **forced variation** is a series of moves united by a common purpose and which **cannot be avoided** by at least one of the players. For example, we can say that in Diagram 290 the game should finish with a forced variation.

3. A **plan** shows **what** must be done to achieve a certain goal, while **tactics** answer the question of **how** it can be done.

4. **Tactical devices** are a number of methods used in chess combat that **do not entail sacrifices of material** (pawns, pieces, Exchanges, etc.) An example is the double attack (see Diagram 290). A **combination** is a tactical device that is accompanied by the **sacrifice of material.** An example is shown in Diagram 291.

D-290 The game should be drawn:

1. ...	f7-f6 +

(A fork.)

2. Qg5xf6	g7xf6 +
3. Ke5xf6	

D-291 Yes:

1. Qf3-d5 + !

A combination with a Queen sacrifice! The Black Queen is decoyed onto d5.

1. ...	Qd7xd5
2. Nf5xe7 +	

A fork that will leave White a piece up.

2. ...	u
3. Ne7xd5	

D-292 The White Knight is forking two Black pieces but Black can use the tactical device of "counterattack," moving his Bishop to safety and at the same time attacking the White Rook:

1. ...	Bc5-d4
2. Ne4xf6	Bd4xa1

The result is just an exchange of Rooks.

D-293 In this position Black escapes from the Knight fork by employing the tactical device known as the "in-between check":

1. ...	Bc5-b4 +

The Bishop flees the Knight's attack and checks the White King. After White's reply, Black will move his Rook away from the Knight's attack.

D-294 The game should be drawn as the Black King is inside the square of the pawn (c4-c8-g4-g8):

1. c4-c5	Kg4-f5
2. c5-c6	Kf5-e6
3. c6-c7	Ke6-d7
4. c7-c8Q +	Kd7xc8

D-295 White should win. Although the Black King is inside the square of the pawn, its path is blocked by an obstacle — the Black pawn on e6:

1. c4-c5	Kg4-f5
2. c5-c6	Kf5-f6

The Black King is forced to go around the pawn.

3. c6-c7	Kf6-e7
4. c7-c8Q	

Black was one move (tempo) short of eliminating the White pawn.

Pinning

The tactical device known as **pinning** occurs in almost every game. Pinning involves three men standing in a line (diagonal, rank, or file): the **pinning** piece (Queen, Rook, or Bishop), the **pinned man** (any piece or pawn except the King) in the middle, and the man beyond the pinned man (the **shielded man**). The pinning piece is of a different color from the other two men.

296

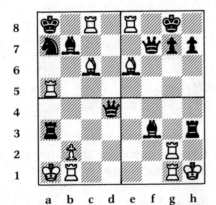

Diagram 296 shows various pinning patterns. In each quarter-diagram a different man is pinned and unable to defend its King from checkmate.

It is costly for a pinned piece to leave its post since that will expose to attack another — more valuable or undefended — piece. If this other piece is the King, as in Diagram 296, then we have what is called an **absolute pin.** That is, the pinned piece is totally paralyzed and immobilized. If, however, the other piece is **not** the King, then the pin is known as a **relative pin.** Here the pinned piece can at times, in order to achieve some specific goal, move from its post, sacrificing the more valuable piece (even the Queen) that it was pinned against. Remember Legal's Mate? (See game 26.)

Now let us look at some more examples. In Diagrams 297–302 it is White's turn to play. Find the best continuation in each case. Make use of the tactical device of pinning. Work out the solutions in your head, without moving the men about.

297

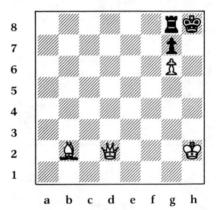

298

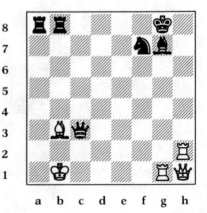

299

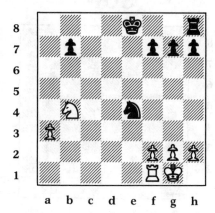

300

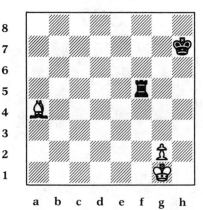

301

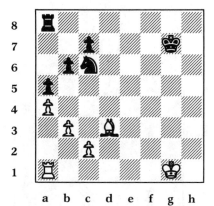

302

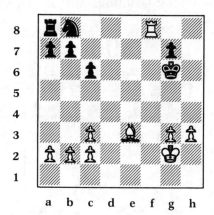

Answers

D-297 1. Qd2-h6#

White makes use of a pin. The Black pawn cannot capture the Queen because it is pinned against its King by the White Bishop.

D-298 1. Rh2-h8#

The Rook can be captured neither by the Knight, pinned against the King by the Bishop on b3, nor by the Bishop, pinned against the King by the Rook on g1.

D-299

> **1. Rf1-e1**

The Rook pins the Knight against the King along the e-file.

> **1. ...   f7-f5**

The pawn defends the Knight

> **2. f2-f3**

And the Knight must perish.

D-300

> **1. Ba4-c2**

A diagonal pin.

> **1. ...   Kh7-g6**

The King defends the Rook.

> **2. g2-g4**

Winning the rook.

D-301 1. Bd3-e4

White wins a piece. In this case the pin is **relative**, but if Black moves his Knight he will lose his Rook.

D-302 1. Be3-f4

Black loses a piece due to the relative pin of the Knight on b8. The pin is relative because the Knight has the right to move, but if it does the Rook on a8 will be lost.

Now let us try our hand at combinations

based on the tactical device of "pinning." Find the strongest continuation in Diagrams 303–308.

303

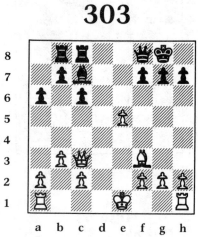

Black to play.

304

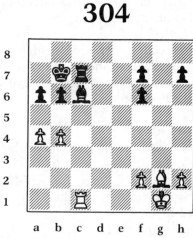

White to play.

305

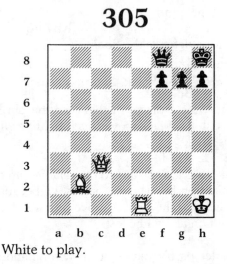

White to play.

306

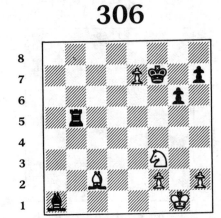

White to play, from the game Ragozin (grandmaster) – Boleslavskii (grandmaster), Moscow 1945.

307

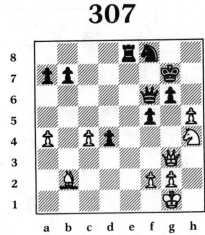

White to play, from the game Averbakh (grandmaster) – Penrose (master), London 1954.

308

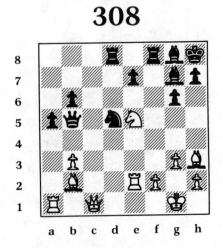

White to play, from the game Szabo (grand-master) – Donner (grandmaster), Goteborg 1945.

Answers

D-303
1. ...	Bc7xe5!

With this Bishop sacrifice Black decoys the White Queen onto the e-file.

2. Qc3xe5	

Any retreat of the Queen would lose the Rook on a1.

2. ...	Rc8-e8

Using a vertical pin, Black wins the White Queen for a net gain of two points (Queen and pawn for Rook and Bishop).

D-304
1. Rc1xc6!	

The Black Rook is decoyed onto the c6 square.

1. ...	Rc7xc6

Now the Black Rook is pinned by the White Bishop.

2. b4-b5	a6xb5
3. a4xb5	

White will win the Rook and will have made a net gain of a Bishop.

D-305
1. Qc3xg7 +!	Qf8xg7
2. Re1-e8#	

The Black Queen is diagonally pinned by the White Bishop and so cannot defend the King.

A second solution is also possible:

1. Re1-e8	Kh8-g8

If 1. ... Qxe8, then 2. Qxg7#.

2. Qc3xg7#	

The Black Queen is pinned along the rank and so cannot capture the White one.

D-306
1. e7-e8Q +	

A sacrifice to decoy the Black King onto e8.

1. ...	Kf7xe8
2. Bc2-a4	

Black resigned. Thanks to the pin, White will have won a Rook for a pawn (a net gain of four points.)

D-307
1. Bb2xd4!	

A Bishop sacrifice that Black is forced to accept, since otherwise his Queen, pinned along the diagonal, will be lost.

1. ...	Qf6xd4

The Queen has been decoyed onto d4.

2. Nh4xf5 +	

Black resigns. He will end up having lost a Queen and two pawns for a Bishop (i.e., eight points). This combination made use of two tactical devices: a Knight fork on f5 and a pin on the g6 pawn.

D-308
1. Ne5xg6 +!	

This Knight sacrifice pins the Black Bishop on g7 and exposes the Black King's position.

1. ...	h7xg6

Forced.

2. Qc1-h6 +	Bg8-h7
3. Qh6xg7#	

Endgame with King and Two Pawns versus King

A King and two pawns almost always wins against a lone King. Let us look at some examples in Diagrams 309–314.

309

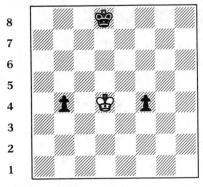

Black wins no matter who plays first.

310

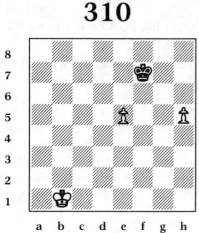

White wins no matter who moves first.

311

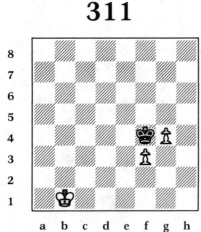

White wins no matter who moves first.

312

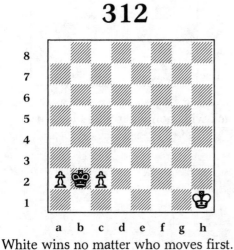

White wins no matter who moves first.

313

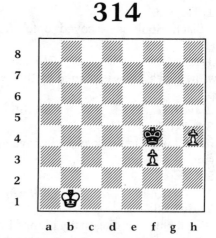

White to play wins. Black to play draws.

314

White wins no matter who moves first.

D-309 Black wins no matter who plays first:

    1. Kd4-c4

If the pawns are far removed from each other (at least three files between them) they win easily even without the help of their King.

    1. ...   **f4-f3**

    2. Kc4-d3

Capturing the b-pawn would put the White King outside the square of the f-pawn.

    2. ...   **b4-b3**

While chasing one of the pawns advancing towards its queening square, the White King is forced to leave the square of the other pawn.

    3. Kd3-c3   **f3-f2**

and so on.

D-310 White wins no matter who moves first:

    1. ...   **Kf7-e6**

    2. h5-h6

If the pawns are separated by two files and

are both on the opponent's half of the board, they can always win without the help of their King.

2. ...   **Ke6-f7**

2. ... Kxe5 would lose because of 3. h7, and the Black King cannot reach the square of the h-pawn.

3. h6-h7   **Kf7-g7**
4. e5-e6

And one of the two pawns will queen by force.

D-311 White wins no matter who moves first:

1. ...   **Kf4-g5**

The point is that the pawn on f3 is invulnerable, since capturing it would take the Black King outside the square of the g-pawn, which would then become a Queen. E.g., 1. ... Kxf3 2. g5 Kg4 3. g6 Kg5 4. g7 Kg6 5. g8Q + etc.

2. Kb1-c2

The White King approaches the pawns to help them queen.

Thus we see from this example that two pawns on neighboring squares protect each other against capture by the enemy King.

D-312 White wins no matter who moves first.

1. ...   **Kb2-c3**

Capturing either of the pawns would take the King out of the other pawn's square. E.g., 1. ... Kxa2 2. c4, and the c-pawn will queen.

2. Kh1-g2

Taking advantage of the fact that the pawns are safe from capture, the White King comes up to help them queen.

D-313 White to play wins. Black to play draws. White to play:

1. b3-b4

Controlling the c5 square and forcing the Black King to leave the square of the pawn on b5.

1. ...   **Kd5-c4**
2. b5-b6

and the pawn will queen.

Black to play:

1. ...   **Kd5-c5**
2. b5-b6   **Kc5xb6**
3. Ke7-d6   **Kb6-b5**

and Black will capture the pawn on b3 as well and draw.

D-314 White wins no matter who moves first.

1. ...   **Kf4-f5**

1. ... Kxf3 would lose because of 2. h5, and the Black King cannot reach the square of the h-pawn. At the same time, the Black King has difficulty in attacking the h-pawn, needing three moves to approach it.

2. Kb1-c2

With the pawns safe from capture, the White King has time to come to their aid.

2. ...   **Kf5-g6**

Black now threatens to win the h-pawn by 3. ... Kh5.

3. f3-f4!   **Kg6-h5**

3. ... Kf5 would be followed by 4. h5!.

4. f4-f5!

The point. Now the h-pawn is immune from capture.

4. ...   **Kh5-h6**

The only move to stop the f-pawn from queening.

5. Kc2-d3

With the pawns safe once more, the White King can continue its journey towards them to help them queen.

5. ...   **Kh6-g7**
6. h4-h5!

Take note of this tactical device: the pawns stay abreast (i.e., on the same rank) as long as they are not under attack, but when one of them is attacked, the other advances to the same rank as the King.

6. ...   **Kg7-f6**
7. h5-h6   **Kf6-f7**
8. Kd3-e4   **Kf7-f6**
9. Ke4-f4

A waiting move.

9. ...   **Kf6-f7**
10. Kf4-g5   **Kf7-g8**
11. f5-f6   **Kg8-h8**
12. f6-f7   **Kh8-h7**

Watch out, a trap!

13. Kg5-h5!

A waiting move. 13. f8Q or 13. f8R would be stalemate. Now, however, Black is in Zugzwang and must move his King to the eighth rank.

13. ...   **Kh7-h8**
14. f7-f8Q +

And mate next move.

We thus see that pawns separated by only a single file can defend each other **indirectly**, no matter where their King might be.

Two pawns of the same color on the same file are called **doubled pawns.** While, as you saw earlier, two pawns on neighboring files can easily defend each other, doubled pawns are unable to do so and are usually easy to attack.

HOMEWORK
(Answers at the end)
I. Use the tactical device of "pinning" in the solutions to Diagrams 315–320.

315

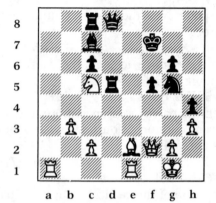

Find all the possible pins both with White to play and with Black to play.

_____

_____

_____

316

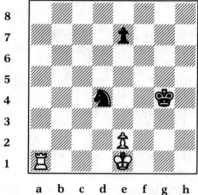

White to play. How can he win the Black Knight?

_____

_____

_____

317

White to play. How can he win the Black Knight?

_____

_____

_____

318

White to play. Find the best move.

_____

_____

_____

319

White to play and win a piece.

_____

_____

_____

320

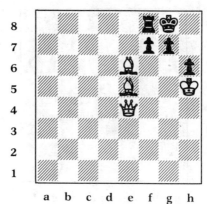

White to play and mate in two moves.

	WHITE	BLACK
1.		
2.		

II. Diagrams 321–326. In each position find a combination based on the tactical device of "pinning."

321

White to play and mate in two moves.

	WHITE	BLACK
1.		
2.		

322

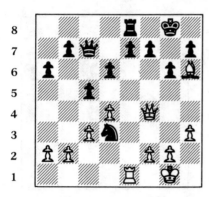

a b c d e f g h

White to play and mate in two moves.

WHITE	BLACK
1.	
2.	

323

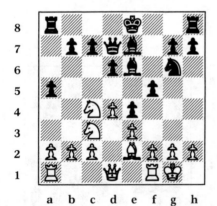

a b c d e f g h

White to play. How can he win the Exchange?

_____

_____

_____

324

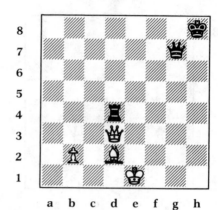

a b c d e f g h

White to play. How can he win the Exchange?

_____

_____

_____

325

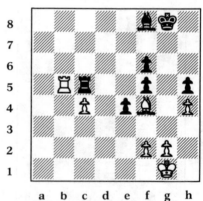

a b c d e f g h

White to play and win a piece.

_____

_____

326

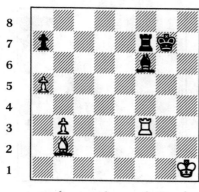

White to play and win.

_____

_____

_____

III. In Diagrams 327-332 use the "rule of the square of the pawn" to find the solutions.

327

How should the game end with White to play? With Black to play?

_____

_____

_____

328

Can Black win if it is his turn to play? And if it is White's turn?

_____

_____

_____

329

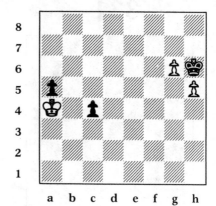

Find the draw both with White to play and with Black to play.

_____

_____

330

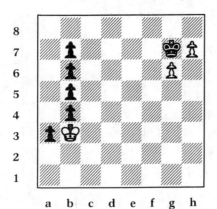

Is it possible for this position to occur? How should the game end (whether it is White or Black to play)?

_____

_____

_____

331

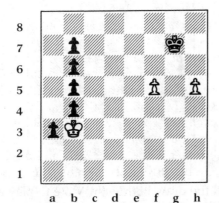

Find the draw both with White to play and with Black to play.

_____

_____

_____

332

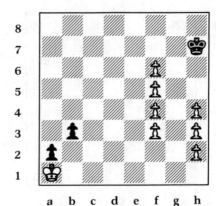

Is it possible for this position to occur? Find the draw both with White to play and with Black to play.

_____

_____

_____

Answers to the Homework

D-315 *With White to play* we can pin the Rook on d5 with **1. Be2-c4** or the Bishop on c7 with **1. Ra1-a7.**

With Black to play there are again two pins possible: **1. ... Bc7-b6**, pinning the Knight on c5, and **1. ... Rd5-d2**, pinning the Bishop on e2.

D-316

    1. Ra1-a4

A horizontal pin of the Knight.

    1. ...   **e7-e5**

    2. e2-e3

and the Knight is lost.

D-317

    1. Nc3-b5 + !   **u**

Neither the pawn on c6, pinned by the Rook, nor the Knight on d6, pinned by the Bishop, can capture the White Knight.

    2. Nb5xd6

winning the Knight.

D-318

    1. Bb5-c4!

and the Black Queen perishes because of the pin (Black ends up losing six points).

D-319

1. Rc1-c6!

The Black Bishop is pinned. White's task is to double Rooks along the c-file and at the same time keep the Black King from coming to the defense of the Bishop. Thus 1. Rc4 would not do because of 1. ... Kd6, defending the Bishop a second time.

    1. ...   **Ke5-d5**

    2. Rd1-c1

Defending the Rook on c6 and attacking the Bishop a second time. Black must lose a piece, as he cannot defend the Bishop with a second piece.

D-320

1. Qe4-g6!

This move is possible only because the pawn on f7 is pinned by the White Bishop.

    1. ...   **u**

    2. Qg6xg7#

D-321

1. Qf3xf7 + !

By sacrificing his Queen White deflects the Black Rook from the last rank and pins it.

    1. ...   **Rf8xf7**

Or else 2. Qxf8# would follow.

    2. Re1-e8#

The Black Rook is pinned and cannot cover its King.

D-322

1. Qf4-f6!

Threatening 2. Qg7#.

    1. ...   **e7xf6**

Black is forced to accept the "gift," though the pawn on e7 is pinned by the White Rook.

    2. Re1xe8#

Checkmate is worth more than the Queen!

D-323

1. Nc4-b6!

This Knight sacrifice clears the way for the White Bishop and at the same time forks the Black Queen and Rook.

    1. ...   **Qd7-d8**

It goes without saying that accepting the sacrifice by 1. ... cxb6 would be worse because of 2. Bb5, pinning and winning the Black Queen.

    2. Nb6xa8   **Qd8xa8**

and Black has lost the Exchange.

This example made use of two tactical devices: "double attack" and "pinning."

D-324

1. Qd3xd4!

Decoying the Black Queen onto d4.

    1. ...   **Qg7xd4**

Forced.

    2. Bd2-c3

A diagonal pin that dooms the Black Queen.

    2. ...   **Qd4xc3 +**

    3. b2xc3

As a result of his combination, White has exchanged the Queen and won the Exchange (a Rook for a Bishop).

D-325

1. Rb5-b8!

Pinning the Black Bishop and threatening to win it by 2. Bd6 or 2. Bh6.

    1. ...   **Kf8-f7**

Now the Black Bishop is no longer pinned by the Rook on b8 and can move. White, however, can play a combination based on a "double attack."

    2. Rb8xf8 + !   **Kf7xf8**

    3. Bf4-d6 +   **u**

    4. Bd6xc5

and White is up a Bishop.

D-326

1. Rf3xf6!

White's plan is to exchange off all the pieces and queen a pawn. To achieve his aim he makes use of the tactical device of "pinning" and the "rule of the square." It would be no good to play 1. Bxf6 Rxf6 2. Rxf6 Kxf6 3. b4 Ke6 4. b5 Kd6 5. b6 axb6 6. axb6 Kc6, and the Black King catches the pawn two moves before it can reach the queening square. White could instead try 6. a6 Kc7 7. a7 Kb7, and although again the Black King reaches the square of the a-pawn in time, the pawn is only *one* move short of queening.

    1. ...   **Rf7xf6**

    2. b3-b4!

The point! Since the Black Rook is pinned and cannot move, White does not hurry to capture it but first gains a tempo (a move, time).

    2. ...   **Kg7-f7**

Black is forced to lose a move (tempo). 2. ... a6 would not save him, because of 3. b5! axb5 4. a6 and the pawn queens by force.

    3. Bb2xf6

The Rook must be captured now or else it will run away.

3. ...	Kf7xf6
4. b4-b5	Kf6-e6
5. b5-b6	a7xb6
6. a5-a6!	

The only way! If 6. a5xb6, then 6. ... Ke6-d6 allows the Black King to reach the square of the pawn (b6-b8-d6-d8).

6. ...	Ke6-d6

Now the Black King cannot enter the square (a6-a8-c6-c8) and the pawn can queen.

7. a6-a7	Kd6-c6
8. a7-a8Q+	

and White should win. Black was just one move short of catching the pawn, the move that he had to lose because of the **pin** on his Rook.

D-327 *White to move wins.*

1. d2-d4!	Kd5-c6

1. ... Kxd4 would lose because the c-pawn would queen after 2. c6.

2. Kh8-g7	

The White King will join the pawns and help them queen.

Black to play draws:

1. ...	Kd5xc5

and the second pawn must perish too.

D-328 *Black to play wins:*

1. ...	a6-a5
2. Kd3-c4	a5-a4!
3. Kc4-c3	

If 3. Kxc5, the Black pawn cannot be stopped after 3. ... a3.

3. ...	Kh8-g7

When the pawns are safe, the King approaches.

4. Kc3-b2	

Now the pawn on a4 is in danger.

4. ...	c5-c4!
5. Kb2-a3	

If 5. Kc3, then 5. ... a3!.

5. ...	c4-c3!

The pawn on c3 indirectly defends the other pawn, as 6. Kxa4 would be followed by 6. ... c2 and the queening of the pawn.

6. Ka3-a2	Kg7-f6
7. Ka2-a3	

7. Kb1 loses immediately, as after 7. ... a3 one of the pawns must queen.

7. ...	Kf6-e5

The Black pawns are absolutely safe, but

they cannot queen without the help of their King. So the King goes to them.

If White starts in Diagram 328, he can draw easily:

1. Kd3-c4	a6-a5
2. Kc4xc5	

and since the King is in the square of the pawn (a1-a5-e1-e5) it will eliminate the second pawn too.

D-329 The game should be drawn no matter who moves first. For example:

1. Ka4-a3	

Of course, taking the pawn is a no-no since it would put the King outside the square of the other pawn.

1. ...	Kh6-g7

For the same reason the Black King too cannot capture the pawn.

2. Ka3-a4	

If 2. Kb2, then 2. ... a4 again makes the Black pawns invulnerable.

2. ...	Kg7-h6

Draw! The Kings can keep a watch on the enemy pawns but not capture them. Nor can either players push his pawns without losing. For example, if Black played 2. ... c3, he would lose after 3. Kb3.

D-330 Such a position will hardly ever occur in a game, but it is *theoretically* possible. For example, the pawn from e7 could have got to b4 by making three captures: 1. ... e7xd6, 2. ... d6xc5, 3. ... c5xb4. By continuing in this vein, we can see that Black must have made a total of six pawn captures to reach this position, and that is possible since White has lost men.

The position is a draw because the Kings can ward off the enemy pawns but cannot capture any one of them without leaving the square of another. The White King will shuttle back and forth between a2 and b3 and the Black King between g7 and h8.

D-331 This too is a draw, the only difference being that the Black King must now shuttle back and forth between f6 and f7 or h6 and h7. For example:

1. ...	Kg7-f6
2. h5-h6	Kf6-f7
3. Kb3-a2	Kf7-f6
4. Ka2-b3	

Draw.

D-332 This position is possible only theoretically and would not occur in a game. Thirteen men have disappeared from the board, and that is exactly the number of pawn captures that White had to make to get to this position.

Once again, the result should be a draw, as the Kings can stop the enemy pawns from queening but cannot capture them. For example:

| 1. h4-h5 | Kh7-h6! |

The only move. All other moves lose: e.g., after 1. ... Kg8 2. h6, Black is in Zugzwang and must let one of the White pawns queen.

| 2. h3-h4 | Kh6-h7 |

Naturally the King cannot leave the f6-f8-h6-h8 square.

| 3. f6-f7 | Kh7-g7 |
| 4. h5-h6 + | Kg7xf7 |

The pawn sacrifice has not achieved anything.

| 5. Ka1-b2 | Kf7-f6! |

Again the only move. If 5. ...Kf8, then 6. f6 Kg8 7. f5 and Black loses due to Zugzwang.

| 6. Kb2-a1 | Kf6-f7! |

Draw.

SUPPLEMENTARY MATERIAL

for use at the teacher's discretion

Fighting Against a Pin

The fewest opportunities for unpinning (escaping from a pin) occur when a piece is pinned against its King, i.e., if the pin is "absolute." The following **tactical devices** for unpinning are possible in such cases:

1. **Chasing away** the pinning piece.
2. **Interposing** a man between the pinning piece and the King.

For example, let us look at Diagram 333.

333

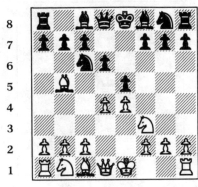

Black to play is faced with the threat of d4-d5, attacking the pinned Knight with a pawn. Black can defend by 1. ... Bc8-d7, **interposing** on the a4-e8 diagonal and thus **unpinning** the Knight.

But he can also play 1. ... Bc8-g4, since 2. d4-d5 can be parried by 2. ... a7-a6 3. Bb5-a4 b7-b5, **chasing away** the Bishop from the a4-e8 diagonal and thereby **unpinning** the Knight.

3. **Pinning** the pinning piece.

For example, let us look at Diagram 334.

334

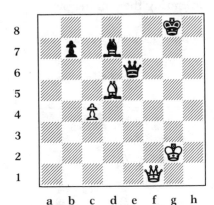

Can Black to play save his Queen?

Yes, he can, by 1. ... Bd7-c6!, pinning the White Bishop along the h1-a8 diagonal and thus saving the Black Queen.

4. Playing an **in-between check.**

For example, look at Diagram 335.

335

Can White to play win the Black Queen?

Yes. This position differs from the last one in that the White Queen is on g1, a circumstance which allows the White King to be moved away with **discovered check:**

    1. Kg2-f2 + !

The White Bishop could not capture the Black Queen because it was pinned along the h1-a8 diagonal. The King move **unpins** the Bishop and at the same time unblocks the g-file, allowing the White Queen to give an **in-between check.** The Black King must move out of check and then White can capture the Queen.

5. Eliminating the pinning piece.

For example, look at Diagram 336.

336

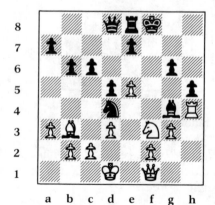

The Knight on f3 is pinned and attacked twice. How can White to play escape from the pin?

By the following combination:

    1. Rh4xg4!

Unpinning the White Knight by eliminating the pinning piece.

    1. ...   **h5xg4**

1. ... Nxf3 would be even worse because of the fork 2. Rf4 + .

    2. Nf3xd4

As a result, White has won a Knight and Bishop for a Rook (i.e., he had made a net gain of one point.)

6.   Moving the King out of the pin with the concurrent creation of strong threats.

See Diagram 337.

337

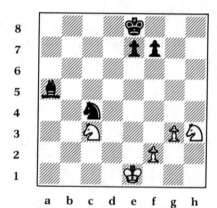

Can White to play save his piece?

Yes, he can. He must temporarily sacrifice his Knight on c3 but he can then win back a piece by making use of the idea of "double attack."

    1. Ke1-e2!

The King gets out of the pin, thereby unpinning the Knight.

    1. ...   **Ba5xc3**

Or else the Knight on c3 can run away.

    2. Ke2-d3!

Both Black pieces are under attack and one of them must perish. The net result will be that White and Black have exchanged pieces of equal value.

7.   Creating counter-threats.

See Diagram 338.

338

a b c d e f g h

Can White to play win the Black Queen?

No, because 1. Bc4-b5? can be met by the powerful counterstroke 1. ... Na5-b3+. Taking advantage of the fact that the pawn on c2 is pinned along the file, Black forks the White King and Queen. After 2. ... Nb3xd4 3. Bb5xc6+ Nd4xc6 Black will have won a piece.

If a piece is pinned not against the King but against some other piece, the pin is a **relative** one and additional methods of unpinning become possible:
1. Moving the pinned piece with check.

See Diagram 339.

339

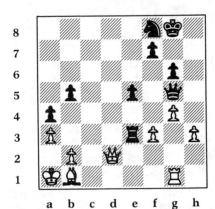

a b c d e f g h

Is 1. Rg1-e1 a good move?

No, because Black can sacrifice his Rook

with check and at the same time attack the White Queen with his own:

1. ...	Re3xa3+!
2. b2xa3	Qg5xd2

and Black has won a Queen and pawn for a Rook.

2. Moving the pinned piece with strong threats.

See Diagram 340.

340

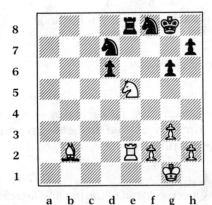

a b c d e f g h

Can White to play save his pinned Knight?

Yes.
    1. Ne5-g4!
Sacrificing the Rook against which the Knight was pinned. However, the Knight has unpinned itself with a strong threat.
    1. ...   Re8xe2?
Black's best reply is 1. ... Ne6.
    2. Ng4-h6#
Checkmate is worth more than a Rook!

3. Moving the piece shielded by the pinned piece, either with check or with strong threats.

See Diagram 341.

341

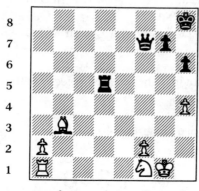

a b c d e f g h

Can Black to play unpin his Rook?

Yes, in two ways.

a)   1. ...   Qf7-g6 +

The Queen gets out of the pin and at the same time gives an **in-between check,** thereby **unpinning** the Black Rook.

b)   1. ...   Qf7-f6

The Queen gets out of the pin and attacks the White Rook.

   2. Bb3xd5   **Qf6xa1**

The net result is an exchange of Rooks.

4.   Moving the pinned piece to a square where it defends the piece it was pinned against.

   See Diagram 342.

342

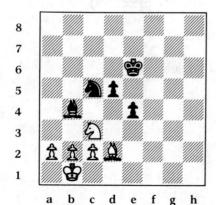

a b c d e f g h

White to play. How does he win a pawn?

1. Nc3xe4!

The Knight gets out of the pin and at the same time defends the Bishop that it was pinned against.

   1. ...   **Bb4xd2**

If 1. ... Nxe4, then 2. Bxb4.

   2. Ne4xd2

and White has won a pawn as a result of his combination.

Game 55

Center Counter Defense

1. e2-e4   d7-d5
2. e4xd5   Qd8xd5
3. Nb1-c3

This shows up the drawback of the Center Counter Defense. White brings out his Knight and attacks the Black Queen at the same time, forcing Black to lose a move (tempo) by retreating the Queen. The usual move here for Black is 3. ... Qa5, although even then it is somewhat more pleasant to be playing White.

   3. ...   Qd5-c6??

A gross blunder.

   4. Bf1-b5

Black resigns, as the pin will cost him his Queen. See Diagram 343 for the final position.

343

a b c d e f g h

Game 56
Petroff's Defense

1. e2-e4   e7-e5
2. Ng1-f3   Ng8-f6
3. Bf1-c4

White sacrifices a pawn to develop his pieces as rapidly as possible.

3. ...	Nf6xe4
4. Nb1-c3	Ne4xc3
5. d2xc3	d7-d6
6. 0-0	Bc8-g4?

He had to play 6. ... Be7 and then castle.

7. Nf3xe5!

The Knight breaks out of the pin and puts its Queen under attack. This combination is possible because the Knight creates mating threats.

7. ...	Bg4xd1

Other replies, too, lose for Black. E.g., 7 ... dxe5 8. Bxf7+ Kxf7 (if 8. ... Ke7, then 9. Bg5+) 9. Qxd8, or 7. ... Be6 8. Bxe6 fxe6 9. Qh5+ g6 (or 9. ... Ke7 10. Qf7#) 10. Nxg6 hxg6 11. Qxh8.

8. Bc4xf7+	Ke8-e7
9. Bc1-g5#	

See Diagram 344 for the final position.

344

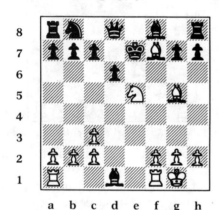

In this game too the "pin" brought nothing but disenchantment.

Game 57
Center Counter Defense

1. e2-e4	d7-d5
2. e4xd5	Ng8-f6

Black plays a gambit. He disregards the pawn and instead quickly brings out his pieces.

3. c2-c4

A dubious move. Instead of being greedy, White would do better to bring out his pieces.

3. ...	c7-c6
4. d5xc6	

Another mistake. It was not too late to get an even game with 4. d4 cxd5 5. Nc3. White, however, is very keen on having an extra pawn.

4. ...	Nb8xc6

5. d2-d3	e7-e5

Black's position is better in spite of White's extra pawn.

6. Nb1-c3	Bf8-c5
7. Bc1-g5?	

He had to develop his Kingside with 7. Be2 and castle at the first opportunity.

7. ...	0-0
8. Nc3-e4??	

A suicidal move. Legal died a very long time ago, but his idea is immortal.

8. ...	Nf6xe4!
9. Bg5xd8	

If 9. dxe4, then 9. ... Qxg5 leaves Black a piece up.

9. ...	Bc5xf2+
10. Ke1-e2	Nc6-d4#

See Diagram 345 for the final position.

345

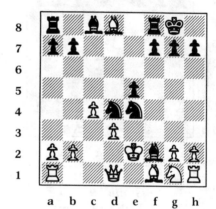

Game 58
Falkbeer–Amateur, Vienna 1847
Scotch Gambit

1. e2-e4	e7-e5
2. Ng1-f3	Nb8-c6
3. d2-d4	

This is the Scotch Game.

3. ...	e5xd4
4. Bf1-c4	

When White doesn't retake the pawn on d4, the opening becomes the Scotch Gambit.

4. ..	d7-d6
5. c2-c3	

White sacrifices a pawn but brings out his pieces quickly.

| 5. ... | d4xc3 |
| 6. Nb1xc3 | Bc8-g4 |

An unfortunate move to which the best reply is 7. Qb3. Black should have played 6. ...Nf6 or 6. ... Be6.

| 7. 0-0 | Nc6-e5?? |

He had to play 7. ... Bxf3 8. Qxf3 Ne5 9. Qe2 Nxc4 10. Qxc4 Qd7, although even in this variation White has good play for his pawn.

8. Nf3xe5!

Once again the great Legal's mate!

8. ...	Bg4xd1
9. Bc4xf7 +	Ke8-e7
10. Nc3-d5#	

See Diagram 346 for the final position.

346

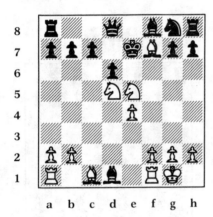

Game 59
Nimzo-Indian Defense

| 1. d2-d4 | Ng8-f6 |

The Knight controls e4 and prevents White from playing 2. e4.

| 2. c2-c4 | e7-e6 |
| 3. Nb1-c3 | |

The Knight attacks e4 and White now threatens 4. e4.

| 3. ... | Bf8-b4 |

This is the key move of the Nimzo-Indian Defense, named after the outstanding grandmaster Aron Nimzovich. The Bishop pins the Knight and thus prevents 4. e4. The Knight on c3 is paralyzed by an **absolute** pin.

4. Qd1-c2	c7-c5
5. d4xc5	Bb4xc5
6. Bc1-g5?	

Now the White Bishop pins the Black Knight, but the pin is a **relative** one since

under certain circumstances the Knight can break out of the pin even if it means exposing the Queen.

| 6. ... | Bc5xf2 + ! |

This is the combination that White did not notice. The Bishop sacrifices itself in order to decoy the White King onto f2.

| 7. Ke1xf2 | Nf6-g4 + |

The Knight breaks out of the pin with check, and at the same time the Black Queen attacks the White Bishop.

| 8. Kf2-e1 | Qd8xg5 |

See Diagram 347.

347

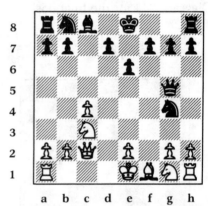

The Bishop which was pinning the Knight has perished. Black has won a pawn and has chances of winning. As you can see, pinning does not always lead to success.

Game 60

| 1. e2-e4 | c7-c6 |

This is the Caro-Kann Defense, named in honor of two 19th century German chessplayers.

| 2. d2-d4 | d7-d5 |

The White pawns have occupied the center, but Black immediately attacks them.

3. Nb1-c3	d5xe4
4. Nc3xe4	Nb8-d7
5. Bf1-c4	Ng8-f6
6. Ne4xf6 +	Nd7xf6

Now you can understand why Black played 4. ...Nbd7: in order to have the opportunity of replying here with 6. ... Nxf6.

| 7. Ng1-f3 | Bc8-g4? |

In his eagerness to pin the Knight, Black

overlooks that White can play the following combination: 8. Bxf7+! Kxf7 9. Ne5+ Ke8 10. Nxg4, and White is a pawn up with an excellent position. White saw this combination, but he wanted more.

8. Nf3-e5?

A poor trap, based solely on the possibility 8. ... Bxd1 9. Bxf7#.

8. ...   **Qd8-a5+!**

This in-between check was a surprise for White.

9. Bc1-d2   **Qa5xe5+!**

A fresh surprise and again an in-between check.

10. d4xe5   **Bg4xd1**
11. Ra1xd1   **Nf6-d5**

See Diagram 348.

348

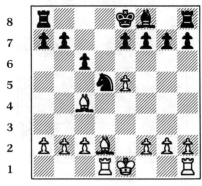

White does not have even a single extra pawn. Needless to say, he should not have let himself be tempted by an unsound trap, pretty though it might have been.

Game 61
Brikhta–Botur, Budapest 1951
Giuoco Piano

1. e2-e4   **e7-e5**
2. Ng1-f3   **Nb8-c6**
3. Bf1-c4   **Bf8-c5**

These moves constitute the Giuoco Piano, an opening which was very popular in Italy as far back as 500 years ago!

4. c2-c3

Controlling a central square and preparing to play d4.

4. ...   **Bc5-b6**

More often Black plays 4. ... Nf6, developing another piece.

5. d2-d4   **Qd8-e7**

In this particular position it is not dangerous for Black to bring out his Queen since the White pieces will find it difficult to attack it.

6. 0-0

6. d5 would be bad, since the pawn would block its own Bishop while the Black Knight would simply retreat to b8.

6. ...   **d7-d6**

Some of you might be thinking that Black could have won a pawn, but in reality he couldn't have! The reason is that 6. ... exd4 7. cxd4 Qxe4 would be followed by 8. Re1, pinning and winning the Black Queen.

7. Nf3-g5

The usual continuation is 7. h3, forestalling the pin 7. ... Bg4 and thus making the pawn on d4 more secure.

7. ...   **Ng8-h6**
8. Bc1-e3   **0-0**

After 8. ... exd4 9. cxd4 Nxd4 10. Nxf7 (if 10. Bxd4, then 10. ... Qxg5) Nxf7 11. Bxd4 White's game is more comfortable.

9. f2-f4?

A premature move. White had to play 9. h3, keeping the Black Knight out of g4.

9. ...   **e5xd4**
10. c3xd4   **Nh6-g4**
11. f4-f5

White is forced to take this desperate step since no way to defend the pawn on d4 can be seen.

11. ...   **Ng4xe3**
12. Qd1-h5

Threatening 13. Qxh7#.

12. ...   **h7-h6??**

He had to sacrifice his Queen by 12. ... Qxg5. After 13. Qxg5 Bxd4! (but not 13. ... Nxc4, because of 14. f6 g6 15. Qh6) 14. f6 Nxf1+ 15. Kxf1 Bxf6, White would have had to pay for his overly venturesome play. As it is, however, White beautifully refutes Black's gross blunder.

13. f5-f6!

Destroying Black's castled position.

13. ...   **Bc8-g4**

After 13. ... gxf6 Black would be mated in two moves: 14. Qg6+ Kh8 15. Qh7#.

14. Qh5-g6!

See Diagram 349.

349

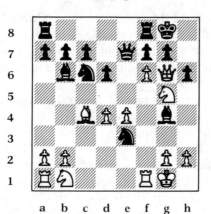

White threatens both 15. Qh7# and 15. Qxg7#. Since the pinned pawn on f7 cannot help, Black resigns.

Game 62
Steinitz–Amateur, Berlin 1863

Wilhelm Steinitz was the first official World Chess Champion, reigning from 1886 to 1894. In this game he played without his Rook on a1.

Vienna Game

1. e2-e4	e7-e5
2. Nb1-c3	Nb8-c6
3. f2-f4	

White sacrifices a pawn in order to seize the center and quickly develop his pieces.

3. ...	e5xf4
4. Ng1-f3	Bf8-b4

An unfortunate move that allows White to set up a powerful center.

5. Nc3-d5	Bb4-a5
6. Nd5xf4	d7-d6
7. c2-c3	Ba5-b6
8. d2-d4	

White has a strong pawn center while Black's Bishop has moved three times and still ended up poorly placed.

8. ...	Bc8-g4
9. Bf1-b5	

Steinitz pins the Knight and threatens to win it by 10. d5.

9. ...	Ke8-f8?

A poor method of breaking the pin. It would have been better to move the Bishop back to d7.

10. 0-0	Nc6-e5?

Black makes a "pretty" but losing move. He wants to exchange on f3 and thereby close the dangerous f-file. However, he has miscalculated. While the pawn on d4 is pinned absolutely, for it shields the King, the Knight on f3, although it too is pinned by a Bishop, nevertheless has the right to move:

11. Nf3xe5!	Bg4xd1??

How the hand itches to grab the Queen! However, Black should resist the temptation and instead play 11. ... dxe5 12. Qxg4 exf4.

12. Nf4-g6 +	h7xg6
13. Ne5xg6#	

See Diagram 350.

350

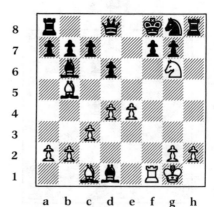

Black forgot that his pawn on f7 would be pinned by the Rook. White has few pieces left but they are working. Black, on the other hand, has many pieces, but they are sleeping.

Game 63
Alekhine–Mikulka, Paris 1928
King's Gambit

1. e2-e4	e7-e5
2. f2-f4	

This is the King's Gambit, a popular opening in the 19th century. White sacrifices a pawn in order to seize the center and rapidly mobilize his pieces.

2. ...	e5xf4

The challenge is accepted!

3. Ng1-f3	

This game was played by World Champion Alekhine in a simultaneous blindfold exhibition.

3. ...	g7-g5
4. d2-d4	h7-h6

Black could also play more aggressively with 4. ... g4, which could be met by the Knight sacrifice 5. Bc4 gxf3 6. Qxf3, with chances for both sides.

5. Nb1-c3	Bf8-g7
6. Bf1-c4	Nb8-c6
7. Nc3-d5	d7-d6

On 7. ... g4 Alekhine would have probably continued with 8. c3 (it was for this reason that he played 7. Nd5) gxf3 9. Qxf3, with an attack for the sacrificed piece.

8. c2-c3	Ng8-e7
9. 0-0	Ne7xd5
10. Bc4xd5	Nc6-e7

Being a pawn up, Black tries to exchange off the active White pieces.

11. Bd5-b3	Ne7-g6
12. g2-g3	

White tries to open the f-file and organize an attack against the pawn on f7.

12. ...	f4xg3?

12. ... g4 13. Ne1 f3, keeping the f-file closed, was worthy of consideration. The world champion would probably have sacrificed his Knight by 14. Nxf3 gxf3 15. Qxf3, with a very sharp and unclear position.

13. Nf3xg5!

With the threat of 14. Bxf7 + .

13. ...	0-0
14. Qd1-h5	

14. Nxf7 could have been met by 14. ... Qh4, with the threat of 15. ... Qxh2#.

14. ...	g3xh2 +
15. Kg1-h1!	

After 15. Kxh2 the White King would have been totally exposed, while now it is shielded and protected by the Black pawn.

15. ...	h6xg5
16. Qh5xg6	

This move is possible only because the pawn on f7 is pinned by the Bishop on b3.

16. ...	Qd8-e8?

Black defends the pawn on f7 a third time. However, a better chance would have been 16. ... d5, unpinning the pawn on f7. White cannot play 17. Bxd5 because Black would eliminate the pinning Bishop by 17. ... Qxd5 and then capture the White Queen. Instead White must reply with 17. Qh5, maintaining the attack.

17. Bc1xg5

Yet another piece joins the attack against the Black King.

17. ...	Bc8-e6

Alekhine's opponent thinks that by blocking the diagonal of the Bishop on b3 he has warded off all the threats: a retreat of the White Queen would be followed by 18. ... Bxb3 and 19. ... Qxe4 + , while after 18. Bxe6 Qxe6 the attack has been beaten off. However, he has not noticed the world champion's brilliant combination:

18. Rf1xf7!	Be6xf7?

After 18. ... Rxf7 19. Bxe6 Black would end up "only" a pawn down in an endgame: 19. ... Kf8 20. Bxf7 Qxf7 21. Qxf7 + Kxf7 22. Kxh2. As it is, however, pins by the White Bishops do him in.

19. Bg5-f6!

See Diagram 351.

351

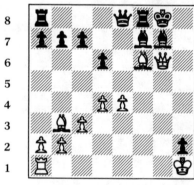

In order to counter the threat of 20. Qxg7#, Black is forced to give up his Queen by 19. ... Qxe4 + , but after 20. Qxe4 Bxf6 21. Bc2 White would have a material advantage while retaining his attack. So Black resigned.

Game 64
Sangla–Karpov, U.S.S.R. 1968

1. d2-d4	Ng8-f6

Black was played by 17-year-old Anatoly Karpov.

2. Ng1-f3	e7-e6
3. Bc1-g5	c7-c5
4. c2-c3	

An unfortunate move. White's usual con-

tinuation in this variation is 4. e3, and if 4. ...
Qb6, then 5. Nbd2, sacrificing the pawn on b2.

4. ...   c5xd4

5. c3xd4   Qd8-b6

The Queen attacks the pawn on b2 and at the
same time unpins the Knight on f6.

6. Qd1-b3   Nf6-e4

7. Bg5-f4

After 7. Qxb6 axb6 8. Bf4 Nc6 Black's position is a trifle better because his Rook controls
the a-file.

7. ...   Nb8-c6

8. e2-e3   Bf8-b4 +

9. Nb1-d2?

Of course pieces must be developed, but in
the present situation White had to interpose
the other Knight (9. Nfd2). The Knight on d2 is
pinned and attacked twice. Although it is also
defended twice, Black now removes one of the
defenders by force.

9. ...   g7-g5!

A combination based on the tactical devices
of "pinning" and "double attack."

10. Bf4xg5

After 10. Be5 f6 11. Bg3 g4 White would lose
a piece.

10. ...   Bb4xd2 +

See Diagram 352.

352

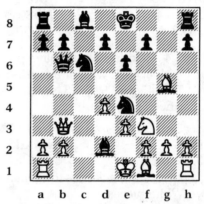

After 11. Nxd2 the Bishop on g5 would be
undefended, allowing the double attack 11. ...
Qa5, forking the Bishop on g5 and the Knight
on d2 (but not 11. ... Nxg5, because of 12. h4,
winning the Knight on g5). So White resigned.

Lesson Nine

A. Check Lesson 8 Homework (as necessary).

B. *Review Questions*

In the positions shown on Diagrams 353-358, it is White's turn to play. Find his best continuation in each case. Solve the exercises directly from the diagrams, without setting up the men on a board.

355

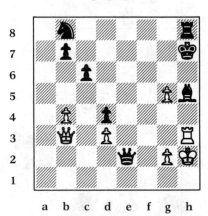

353

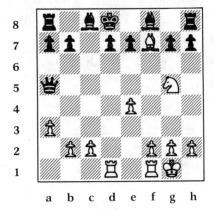

356

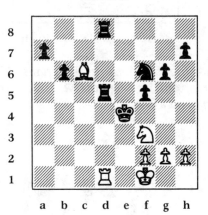

354

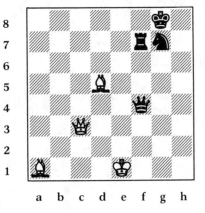

143

357

358

Find the solutions to Diagrams 359-364 directly from the diagrams, without setting up the men on a board.

359

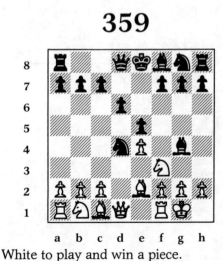

White to play and win a piece.

360

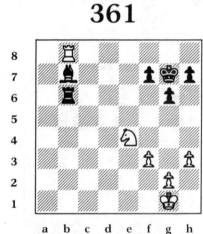

White to play. Find a combination.

361

Black to play. How can he get rid of the pin?

362

White to play. Can he save his Knight?

363

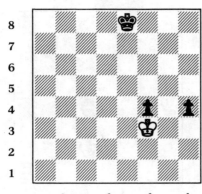

a b c d e f g h

Black to play. How should the game end?

364

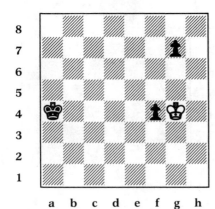

a b c d e f g h

Black to play. Can he win?

Answers to Review Questions

D-353 1. Ng5-e6#
D-354 1. Qc3xg7#
D-355 1. Qb3-f7#
D-356 1. Rd1-d4#
D-357
  1. Qc1-h6 + Kh8-g8 2. Qh6xg7#
D-358
  1. Qe5xg7 + Qg8xg7 2. Re1-e8#
D-359
  1. Nf3xd4 Bg4xe2 2. Nd4xe2!,remaining a
piece up. If 1. ... exd4, then by 2. Bxg4 White
still wins a piece.

D-360
  1. Nf3xe5!
The Legal's mate idea.

---

  1. ...   Bg4xd1
If 1. ... dxe5, then Black loses a piece after 2.
Qxg4.
    2. Bc4xf7 +   Ke8-e7
    3. Nc3-d5#

D-361
  1. ...   Rb6-b1 +
With this move Black not only gets rid of the
pin but also wins a piece.
    2. Kg1-f2   Bb7xe4
    3. Rb8xb1
If 3. fxe4, then the Rook is lost by 3. ... Rxb8.
    3. ...   Be4xb1

D-362
  1. Bg5-d2!
Only with this move can White save the
Knight. 1. Rc1 and 1. Kd2 do not work, because
of 2. ... d4, winning the Knight. After 1.
Bg5-d2!, however, the Bishop has not only
defended the Knight but also shielded the King.
    1. ...   d5-d4
    2. Nc3-e2
and so on.

D-363 Black wins after
    1. ...   h4-h3
    2. Kf3-f2
Capturing the pawn on f4 would put the
King outside the square of the pawn on h3,
which would then go on to queen.
    2. ...   Ke8-e7
    3. Kf2-g1
If the King returned to f3, the Black King
would join its pawns and help them to queen.
    3. ...   f4-f3
    4. Kg1-h2
4. Kf2 would meet with the decisive reply 4. ...
h2, followed by queening.
    4. ...   f3-f2
and so on.

D-364 Black wins after
    1. ...   g7-g5
Now White cannot touch the Black pawns.
    2. Kg4-f3
Taking the pawn on g5 would put the King
outside the square of the pawn on f4, which
would then queen.
    2. ...   Ka4-b4

The King approaches its pawns to help them queen.

The Skewer

The tactical device known as the skewer occurs very often in games. As in a pin, three pieces take part in a skewer.

365

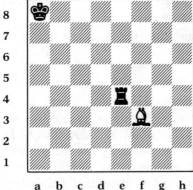

In a pin (Diagram 365), the pinned piece must shield a more valuable piece that is behind it.

366

In a skewer (Diagram 366), however, a piece, usually an important one such as the King, the Queen, or a Rook, has to move off a line when attacked by a Queen, Rook, or Bishop, leaving the piece behind it exposed to capture.

Let us look at some examples. In Diagrams 367–372 find the best continuation. Use the "skewer" tactical device. Solve the problems directly from the diagrams, without setting up the men on a board.

367

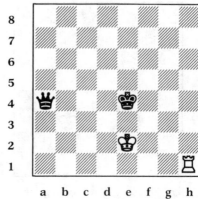

White to play.

368

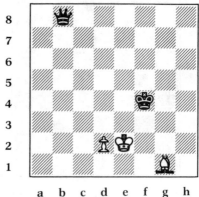

White to play.

369

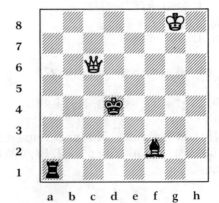

White to play.

370

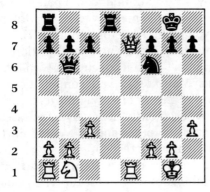

Black to play.

371

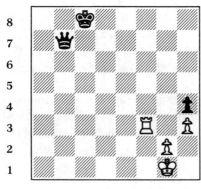

White to play.

372

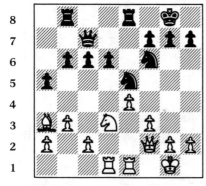

White to play.

D-367

1. Rh1-h4 +	u
2. Rh4xa4	

D-368

1. Bg1-h2 +	u
2. Bh2xb8	

D-369

1. Qc6-f6 +

(1. Qb6 + would win the Bishop but it's better to win a Rook)

1. ...	u
2. Qf6xa1	

D-370

1. ...	Rd8-e8
2. Qe7-a3	Re8xe1 +

D-371

1. Rf3-f8 +	Kc8-c7

The King is forced to occupy the same rank as the Queen, as a result of which Black will lose material.

2. Rf8-f7 +	Kc7-c6
3. Rf7xb7	Kc6xb7
4. Kg1-f2	

After capturing the pawn on h4 White will win easily.

D-372

1. Nd3xe5

The idea of this exchange is to open the d-file for the Rook on d1.

1. ...	d6xe5
2. Ba3-d6	

Now the Bishop is protected by the Rook.

2. ...	Qc7-b7
3. Bd6xb8	Re8xb8

White has won the Exchange (Rook for Bishop).

How Combinations are Created

As you already know, a combination is a forced variation containing a sacrifice and designed to achieve a definite aim (checkmate, win of material, draw in an inferior position, etc.) Combinations can occur both in attack and in defense, and in the opening as well as in the middlegame or endgame. A successfully conducted combination is a source of great pleasure to a chessplayer and remains in his memory for a long time.

However, combinations are not possible in

all positions, and no one can say *a priori* whether a given position contains a combination or not. We must learn to **find** and **create** combinations that we can use and also to **find** and **disrupt** our opponents' combinations.

Every combination consists of three elements — the situation, the idea, and the goal.

The situation is the position of certain White and Black men that warns us, "Be careful, a combination might be possible!" The possibility of a combination usually arises when a position contains some weakness such as an undefended piece, a pinned piece, an exposed King or, conversely, a smothered King, etc. A material advantage too can sometimes serve as the basis of a combination.

The idea is the method used in carrying out a combination. For example, the tactical devices of "double attack," "pinning," and "skewer" are combinational ideas.

The goal is the desired result of the combination, e.g., the win of a piece, checkmate, or stalemate.

During a game, many interesting conceptions, ideas, and combinations will occur to a player. They must be verified and the impractical ones discarded. Sometimes a player thinks along the following lines: "If it weren't for . . . , I could set up a beautiful fork", etc. Often we come to the conclusion that a combination is not possible in a given position. Sometimes, however, one of the ideas turns out to be practical and we have our combination!

Before beginning a combination, a player must have a clear picture of the **final position** in his mind.

Chessplayers usually do not memorize individual positions, but they firmly commit to memory the **ideas** behind various combinations. The reason is that a given arrangement of men on the board might not be repeated (although even that does happen sometimes!) but the ideas of the combinations are repeated time and time again. Strong players know hundreds or sometimes even thousands of **ideas.** During a game they mentally construct numerous positions that could occur in the game and in which combinations might be possible, and at the same time they try to **discover** the **ideas** of the opponent in order to **counteract** them. Sometimes just a "little"

pawn (your own or your opponent's) stands in the way of some fine combination. While analyzing some game played by world champions, you might sometimes think, "How boringly they play! Not a single combination in the whole game." Such a conclusion would be erroneous. Many ideas and combinations run through the minds of strong players during a game, but each of the two players guesses the thoughts of the other and prevents him from putting them into practice.

There are also numerous **unsound** (incorrect) combinations. These occur when a player sacrifices material without noticing some strong reply by the opponent.

It is of course always painful to lose, especially if you had a winning position. However, a player **always has only himself to blame** for his losses.

It is not the end of the world if you make mistakes, but it **is** bad if you **repeat** them. That is why every time you lose you must find out the **reason** for the loss and try not to repeat the mistake.

A player can develop his combinative abilities by **studying the various tactical devices**, by getting to know the games of masters and grandmasters, and by analysing his own games.

Now try your hand at making combinations based on the "skewer" tactical device. Set up positions 373–378 on a board and in each case find the strongest combination.

373

Black to play.

148

374

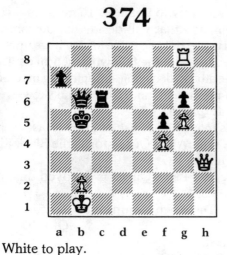

White to play.

375

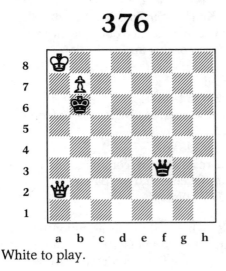

White to play.

376

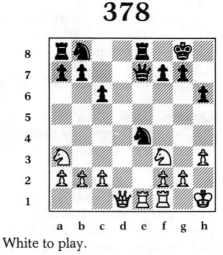

White to play.

377

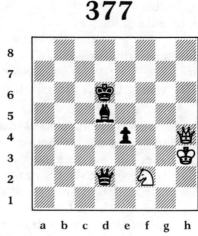

White to play.

378

White to play.

Answers

D-373 What is there in this position that suggests that a combination might be present? Well, the White King and Queen are on the same diagonal, a1-h8, and we could employ the "skewer" tactical device by playing 1. Qa1+. However, the White King would move to c4 or d3, defending the Queen. Obviously, such an approach will not bring us victory. Thinking some more, however, we are struck by the idea that it would be nice if the White King and Queen were on the same diagonal, but at some distance from each other. And then we find the combination that helps us do this:

       1. ...   **Be7-f6!**

The Bishop is sacrificed with the idea of drawing the White Queen away from the King while keeping them on the same a1-h8 diagonal.

2. Qd4xf6

Forced, because of the pin.

2. ...   **Qa8-a1 +**

Now this move wins the game.

3. u   **Qa1xf6**

Black has won a Queen for a Bishop (six points).

D-374 A look at the position shows us that the Black King and Queen are on the same file, namely the b-file. This suggests the idea of a combination. However, the skewering move 1. Qb3 + does not lead to the desired result since the Queen on b6 is defended by the King, a Rook, and a pawn. How can we **deflect** the Black Queen from b6 while keeping it on the b-file?

1. Rg8-b8!

A familiar idea! The Rook is sacrificed.

1. ...   **Qb6xb8**

Forced, because of the pin.

2. Qh3-b3 +

Now the skewer winds up the combination.

2. ...   **u**

3. Qb3xb8

White has won the Queen for a Rook (four points).

D-375 We notice here that the Black King and Queen are both on the 7th rank, a fact which tells us that under certain circumstances a combination might be possible. That is, if White could employ the skewer on the seventh rank, Black would lose his undefended Queen. We find the move 1. Qh7 +, but h7 is controlled by the Black Bishop. However, we should not let that scare us. Rather, we should count up how many points we will be sacrificing and how many we will be winning. Only after this simple calculation should we decide on our move.

1. Qh2-h7 +!

Such a sacrifice is called a **temporary** Queen sacrifice.

1. ...   **Bg6xh7**

2. Rh1xh7 +   **u**

3. Rh7xa7

As a result of the combination, White has exchanged Queens and won a Bishop (three points).

D-376 The pawn wants to queen, but it is pinned by the Black Queen and there does not

seem any way to unpin it. There is, in fact, a combination that will decide the outcome of the struggle, but to be able to play it we must be acquainted with the following tactical devices: double attack, decoying, anti-pinning methods, pawn promotion, and, finally, the skewer.

1. Qa2-b3 +

This move makes use of three ideas:

1. The White Queen **forks** the Black King and Queen.

2. The Black Queen is **decoyed** onto the b-file.

3. The pawn is **unpinned**.

1. ...   **Qf3xb3**

Forced.

2. b7-b8Q +

A move containing two ideas: queening the pawn and skewering the Black King and Queen.

2. ...   **u**

3. Qb8xb3

Naturally White decided upon the **temporary** Queen sacrifice only after visualizing the **final position**, in which he is a Queen up.

D-377 Looking at the position, we notice that the Black King and Queen are on the same file, a fact that would make the skewer possible under certain conditions. In particular, if we removed the Bishop from the board then Qd8 + would win the Black Queen. So what we have to do is to somehow **deflect** the Black Bishop from d5.

1. Nf2xe4 +!

The Knight sacrifices itself so that the combination can be carried out. The move contains two ideas: forking and deflection.

1. ...   **Bd5xe4**

Forced.

2. Qh4-d8 +!

Now the skewer decides the outcome.

2. ...   **u**

3. Qd8xd2

As a result of the combination, White has won a Queen and a pawn for a Knight $(10 - 3 = 7$ points).

D-378 What strikes our attention here is the line-up of the three Black pieces and the White Rook on the e-file. As a result, we are led to look for a combination based on the skewering idea.

1. Re1xe4!

An Exchange sacrifice with the idea of **decoying** the Black Queen onto e4.

1. ...   Qe7xe4

Or else Black would be a Knight down.

2. Rf1-e1

A skewer that wins material. Note that if there had not been a Black pawn on c6 or on f7 the Black Queen could now have defended the Rook by 2. ... Qc6 or 2. ... Qg6. Or if the Rook on e8 had been defended by another piece in addition to the Queen, White's combination would again have been impossible.

2. ...   Qe4xe1 +

With this move Black ends up losing a Queen and a Knight for two Rooks (12 – 10 = 2 points), while if the Queen had moved away, then after 3. Rxe8 + the net result would have been that a pair of Rooks had been exchanged and Black had lost a Knight (three points).

3. Nf3xe1

Endgames with King and Rook Pawn Against Lone King

An extra pawn in the endgame often makes it possible to win the game. However, there are also positions in which an extra pawn is not enough for victory. Chessplayers at all levels should have a firm knowledge of what fate awaits a given extra pawn: will it become a Queen or won't it? For this purpose, a player must know which positions are **won positions** and which ones are **drawn positions.**

The most difficult pawns to queen are the Rook pawns. Let us look at some examples. Set up each of the positions in Diagrams 379–384 on a board.

379

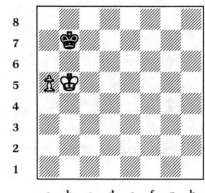

Drawn with either player to move.

380

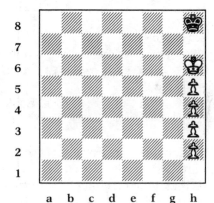

Drawn with either player to move.

381

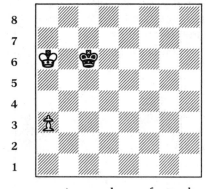

Drawn with either player to move.

382

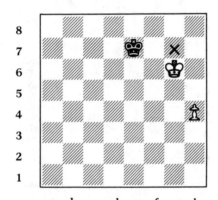

Drawn with either player to move.

383

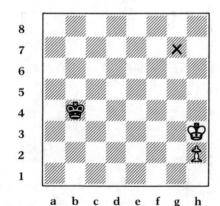

White to play wins; Black to play draws.

384

White to play wins; Black to play draws.

D-379 If the King of the weaker side is (or can get) in the way of the Rook pawn (*i.e.*, onto one of the squares in front of it), the game is always drawn.

1. a5-a6 +		Kb7-a7
2. Kb5-a5		Ka7-a8
3. Ka5-b6		Ka8-b8
4. a6-a7 +		Kb8-a8
5. Kb6-a6		Stalemate!

This is the whole point. If the weaker side's King does not lose touch with the corner square, stalemate always occurs.

D-380 You already know that by reaching the corner square in front of an enemy Rook pawn, a King can stop it from queening. In this example, Black draws in the same manner as the last one, even though here the White King is in front of its pawns.

1. Kh6-g6	Kh8-g8
2. h5-h6	Kg8-h8

Nobody can make the Black King abandon h8.

3. h4-h5	Kh8-g8
4. h3-h4	

White has four pawns on the h-file but they cannot win. It would have been better to have just a single extra pawn, but on a different file.

4. ...	Kg8-h8
5. h6-h7	Stalemate

The draw was unavoidable.

D-381 A draw also occurs when the King of the stronger side is in front of its Rook pawn but the defending (lone) King manages to lock it into the corner:

1. a3-a4	Kc6-c7

The Black King heads for a8.

2. Ka6-a7

The White King does not allow the enemy into the corner.

2. ...	Kc7-c8
3. a4-a5	Kc8-c7

The Black King stays close to the a8 corner.

4. a5-a6	Kc7-c8
5. Ka7-a8	

Or 5. Kb6 Kb8 followed by 6. ... Ka8.

5. ...	Kc8-c7
6. a6-a7	Kc7-c8

Stalemate.

D-382 No matter how many pawns there might be on the a-file, White draws in the same way as in the preceding example:

| 1. Kc2-c1 | a4-a3 |

If 1. ... Kb3, then 2. Kb1 followed by 3. Ka1.

2. Kc1-c2	Ka2-a1
3. Kc2-c1	a3-a2
4. Kc1-c2	

The White King goes back and forth between c1 and c2 and doesn't let the Black King out of the corner. As soon as Black uses up all his pawn moves, he will be stalemated!

D-383 This example shows what the stronger side must aim for in order to win.

1. Kg6-g7!

The g7 square is a **critical** square. By occupying it, the White King assures the queening of the pawn. 1. h5 would be a mistake because of 1. ... Kf8 2. h6 Kg8, when the Black King gets into the coveted corner. If 2. Kh7, then 2. ... Kf7, again with an unavoidable draw.

| 1. ... | Ke7-e6 |

The King cannot hinder the pawn from queening.

2. h4-h5

And so on. If in Diagram 383 Black moves first, he draws easily by 1. ... Ke7-f8!, controlling the critical g7 square.

D-384 We know by now that if White succeeds in occupying the critical square g7 with his King, he will win, while if the Black King manages to gain control of g7 and keep the enemy King out, the game will be a draw. The result of the game depends on whose turn it is to move. White to move succeeds in his efforts:

1. Kh3-g4	Kb4-c5
2. Kg4-g5	Kc5-d6
3. Kg5-g6	Kd6-e7
4. Kg6-g7!	

And Black cannot stop the advance of the pawn.

With Black to move, the picture is different:

1. ...	Kb4-c5
2. Kh3-g4	Kc5-d6
3. Kg4-f5	Kd6-e7
4. Kf5-g6	Ke7-*f8!*

Controlling the critical square g7.

5. Kg6-h7

If White does not play this move, the Black King will get into the corner and it will be impossible to drive it out.

5. ...	Kf8-f7
6. h2-h4	Kf7-f8
7. h4-h5	Kf8-f7
8. h5-h6	Kf7-f8

And White can only choose how to draw: stalemate the Black King or let his own King be stalemated.

HOMEWORK
(Answers at the end)

I. Diagrams 385–390. Use the skewer tactical device in the solutions.

385

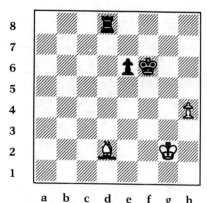

White to play and wins the Rook.

	WHITE	BLACK
1.		
2.		
3.		
4.		

386

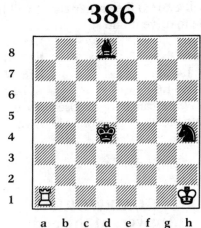

White to play and win a piece.

WHITE	BLACK
1.	
2.	
3.	
4.	

388

White to play and wins the Exchange.

WHITE	BLACK
1.	
2.	
3.	
4.	

387

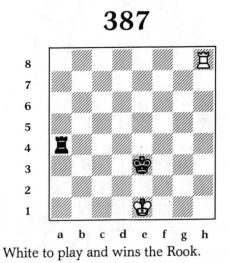

White to play and wins the Rook.

WHITE	BLACK
1.	
2.	
3.	
4.	

389

White to play. How does he win?

WHITE	BLACK
1.	
2.	
3.	
4.	

154

390

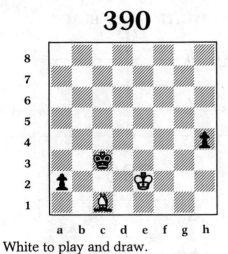

White to play and draw.

	WHITE	BLACK
1.		
2.		
3.		
4.		

II. In Diagrams 391–396 find a combination that uses the skewer tactical device.

391

How does White win? (2 solutions)

	WHITE	BLACK
1.		
2.		
3.		
4.		

	WHITE	BLACK
1.		
2.		
3.		

392

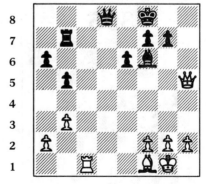

White to play and win material.

	WHITE	BLACK
1.		
2.		
3.		
4.		

393

Find a forced win for White.

394

396

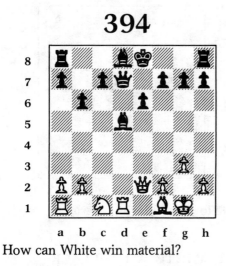

How can White win material?

Black to play and win material.

395

White to play. Can he win the Knight?

III. Diagrams 397–402 deal with Rook-pawn endgames.

397

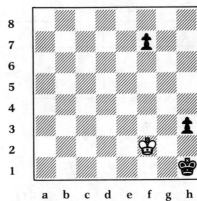

White to play and draw.

	WHITE	BLACK
1.		
2.		
3.		
4.		

398

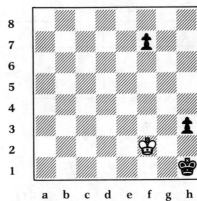

How should the game end with White to play? With Black to play?

	WHITE	BLACK
1.		
2.		
3.		
4.		

	WHITE	BLACK
1.		
2.		
3.		
4.		

399

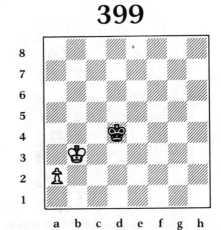

White to play. Can he win?

	WHITE	BLACK
1.		
2.		
3.		
4.		

400

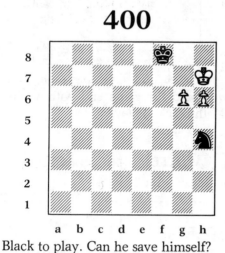

Black to play. Can he save himself?

	WHITE	BLACK
1.		
2.		
3.		
4.		

401

Can this position occur in a game? If yes, can White avoid losing if it is his turn to play?

402

Black to play and draw.

	WHITE	BLACK
1.		
2.		
3.		
4.		

Answers to the Homework

D-385 **1. Bd2-g5 +** and the Rook perishes.

D-386 **1. Ra1-d1 +**, winning the Bishop. 1. Ra4 + would be no good since the Knight is defended by the Bishop.

D-387

    1. Rh8-h3 +!

(forcing the King onto the 4th rank)

    1. ...   **any move**

    2. Rh3-h4 +

(winning the Rook.)

D-388 **1. Bd2-g5** forces the Black Queen to move, whereupon **2. Bg5-f6 +** wins the exchange.

D-389

    1. b5-b6   **h4-h3**

The Black King cannot hold back the White pawn since it is not in the pawn's square.

| 2. b6-b7 | h3-h2 |
| 3. b7-b8Q | h2-h1Q |

The Black pawn too has become a Queen, but not for long!

4. Qb8-b7 +

This check wins the Black Queen.

D-390

1. Bc1-g5!

1. Bh6 was also possible. If Black now queens his a-pawn, he will lose it immediately after 2. Bf6 +. 1. Bd2 + would lose to 1. ... Kc2.

| 1. ... | h4-h3 |
| 2. Ke2-f2 | |

The King is within the square of the h-pawn.

| 2. ... | h3-h2 |

Black sets a pretty trap.

3. Bg5-f6 + !

Only this **in-between check** allows White to draw. 3. Kg2 would lose to 3. ... h1Q + ! (decoying the King onto the first rank) 4. Kxh1 a1Q +, and White doesn't have time to play 5. Bf6 + since his King is in check.

| 3. ... | u |
| 4. Kf2-g2 | |

And the draw is unavoidable.

D-391 Black threatens 1. ... Ra1# and 1. ... Kxf4. However, White has two ways of parrying these threats.

Solution 1:

1. Rf4-a4!

Decoying the Black Rook onto the fourth rank.

| 1. ... | Ra8xa4 |

Forced, for 2. Rh3# was threatened.

2. Rh1-h3 +

Now we have the position from Diagram 387.

| 2. ... | u |
| 3. Rh3-h4 + | |

White will remain a Rook up.

Solution 2:

This is possible only if the White King and the Rook on h1 have not moved so far in this game.

1. 0-0!

Saving the King from mate and at the same time defending the Rook on f4. Now White,

with an extra Rook, should win.

D-392

1. Qd3xd4 + !

A temporary Queen sacrifice.

1. ...	Ke5xd4
2. Ba3-b2 +	u
3. Bb2xh8	

As a result of his combination, White has won a Bishop and exchanged off Queens.

D-393

1. Rc1-c8!

A Rook sacrifice to decoy the Black Queen onto c8.

| 1. ... | Qd8xc8 |

Forced.

2. Qh5-h8 +

A check that wins the Black Queen. White gains a Queen for a Rook (9 – 5 = 4 points).

D-394

1. Rd1xd5!

With this Exchange sacrifice White decoys the Black Queen onto d5.

| 1. ... | Qd7xd5 |
| 2. Bf1-g2 | Qd5-d7 |

The Queen may move to other squares, too.

3. Bg2xa8

White has exchanged Rooks and won a Bishop.

D-395 Yes.

1. Rg7xf7!

A temporary Exchange sacrifice. 1. Ra8 + with the idea of winning the Rook on h8 doesn't work because of the reply 1. ... Nd8. So White first eliminates the Knight.

1. ...	Rf2xf7
2. Ra7-a8 +	u
3. Ra8xh8	

As a result of his combination, White has exchanged Rooks and won a Knight.

D-396 From the game Sanguinetti—Fischer, 1958.

| 1. ... | Nf4xd5! |

Fischer wins a pawn, since it turns out that White cannot play 2. Qxd5 because of 2. ... Rad8, winning a Rook.

D-397 From the game Ancigin—N. Guravlev, USSR 1952.

    1. Ke3-f2!

Locking the Black King in the corner.1. Kxf3 would lose because of 1. ... Kg1 followed by the queening of the h-pawn.

    1. ...   **Kh2-h1**

Zugzwang. If it had been White's turn to move, Black would have won easily, *e.g.,* 2. Kf1 Kg3 3. Kg1 f2+ 4. Kf1 h2, etc.

    2. Kf2-f1!

Now the Black King cannot escape from the corner.

    2. ...   **f3-f2**

If 2. ... h2, then 3. Kf2 is stalemate.

    3. Kf1xf2   **Kh1-h2**

If now 3. ... h2, then 4. Kf1 is stalemate.

    4. Kf2-f1   **Kh2-g3**

    5. Kf1-g1!

The White King gets into the coveted corner, making the draw inevitable.

D-398 White to move draws after

    1. Kf2-g3!

Forcing Black to push the h-pawn, as otherwise both pawns would be lost.

    1. ...   **h3-h2**

    2. Kg3-f2!

Now the Black King is caught in the corner.

    2. ...   **f7-f5**

    3. Kf2-f1   **f5-f4**

    4. Kf1-f2   **f4-f3**

    5. Kf2-f1   **f3-f2**

    6. Kf1xf2   **Stalemate**

If Black moves first in Diagram 398, he wins easily after

    1. ...   **Kh1-h2!**

Putting White in Zugzwang: White must make some move and let the Black King out of the corner.

    2. Kf2-f1

2. Kf3 would not save White, because of 2. ... Kg1, winning.

    2. ...   **Kh2-g3**

Black, with two extra pawns, should win.

D-399 Yes!

    1. Kb3-b4!

Preventing the Black King from getting into the a8 corner.

    1. ...   **Kd4-d5**

    2. Kb4-b5!   **Kd5-d6**

    3. Kb5-b6!   **Kd6-d7**

    4. Kb6-b7!

Now the White pawn can queen.

    4. ...   **Kd7-d6**

    5. a2-a4   **Kd6-c5**

    6. a4-a5   **Kc5-b5**

    7. a5-a6

and so on.

D-400 Yes, Black can save himself, but only by means of the following Knight sacrifice:

    1. ...   **Nh4xg6!**

Otherwise White would queen his pawn after 2. g7+.

    2. Kh7xg6   **Kf8-g8**

and the draw is unavoidable.

D-401 It is theoretically possible for this position to occur but it wouldn't in practice. The Black pawns have made thirteen captures while fifteen White men have gone from the board. White draws with **1. Kg3-f2**, locking the Black King in the corner. After that, the White King shuttles back and forth between f1 and f2 until Black runs out of pawn moves and becomes stalemated. As you can see, it does not matter in this example how many extra pawns are on the f- and h-files.

D-402

    1. ...   **Kf2-e2!!**

Only thus can Black save himself. 1. ...Kg2 would lose because of 2. Kg4 Kf2 3. Kxh4 Kf3 4. Kg5, and the White King can occupy the critical square of g7 and escort the pawn to the queening square.

    2. Kf4-g4   **Ke2-e3**

    3. Kg4xh4   **Ke3-f4!**

The Black King heads for the h8 corner and at the same time restricts the White King to the h-file. When the Kings are placed like this, they are said to be **in opposition.**

    4. Kh4-h5   **Kf4-f5**

    5. Kh5-h6   **Kf5-f6**

    6. h3-h4   **Kf6-f7**

The Black King controls the critical square g7, making the draw inevitable.

SUPPLEMENTARY MATERIAL

for use at the teacher's discretion

The First Steps of the World Champions

The renowned champions began to play chess in the same way as you did. They made their very first chess moves when they were anywhere from 6 to 15 years old. They too "hung" their Queens and they too fell into "Scholar's Mates." Hard to believe? Well, let's start with Mikhail Tal, who was on the world chess throne from 1960 to 1961. Here is a game played by 9-year-old Mikhail and his brother.

Game 65
Mikhail Tal's Brother—Mikhail Tal
Riga 1945

1. e2-e4	e7-e5
2. Bf1-c4	Bf8-c5
3. Qd1-h5?	Nb8-a6??
4. Qh5xf7#	

See Diagram 403.

403

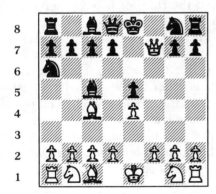

You of course know how to defend yourself against the Scholar's Mate, but Tal didn't until this game. However, he did not fall into such mates any more and fifteen years later he became the World Champion.

Boris Spassky was the World Champion from 1969 to 1972. When he was 11 years old, he played the following game:

Game 66
Boris Spassky—M. Podgaiskii, USSR 1948
Sicilian Defense

1. e2-e4	c7-c5
2. Ng1-f3	Nb8-c6
3. d2-d4	c5xd4
4. Nf3xd4	Ng8-f6
5. Nb1-c3	e7-e6
6. Bf1-e2	Bf8-b4

Pinning the Knight and threatening 7. ... Nxe4.

7. Be2-f3	Qd8-a5

Attacking the Knight on c3 a second time.

8. Nd4-b5??

He had to defend with 8. Ne2.

8. ...	Qa5xb5

See Diagram 404.

404

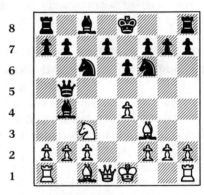

The Knight on c3 is **absolutely** pinned by the Black Bishop. As Boris Spassky recalled later, he broke into tears after Black's move and resigned the game. It is, of course, painful to give away a piece just like that, for nothing. But in every game that a player loses, he has only himself to blame!

Now take a look at a game played in a schoolchildren's tournament between two future chess stars (although they didn't know that yet).

Game 67

Viktor Korchnoi	Boris Spassky
(17 years old)	(11 years old)

Leningrad, 1948
Sicilian Defense

1. e2-e4	c7-c5
2. Ng1-f3	d7-d6
3. d2-d4	c5xd4
4. Nf3xd4	Ng8-f6
5. Nb1-c3	g7-g6
6. f2-f4	Bc8-g4

Black has played the **Dragon Variation**, but his last move is a mistake. 6. ... Nc6 is better.

7. Bf1-b5 +	Nb8-d7
8. Bb5xd7 + !	

A strong move with the aim of exploiting the poor position of the Black Bishop on g4.

8. ...	Qd8xd7

8. ... Bxd7 would be met by the unpleasant 9. e5.

9. Qd1-d3

Now 10. f5 is threatened, after which the Black Bishop might get trapped by 11. h3 and 12. g4.

9. ...	e7-e5
10. Nd4-f3	Bg4xf3
11. Qd3xf3	Qd7-g4?

Black's desire to bring about a draw by exchanging Queens leads to an immediate loss. Black could have put up resistance by 11. .. exf4 12. Bxf4 Bg7 and 13. ... 0-0

12. Nc3-d5!

See Diagram 405.

405

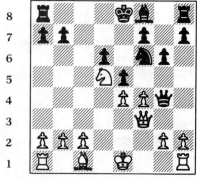

Spassky resigned, thinking that he had to lose a piece. Indeed, 13. ... Qxf3 is no good because of White's in-between checks: 14.

Nxf6+ Ke7 14. Nd5 + u 15. gxf3 and White remains a piece up. Nor would 12. ... Qh4 + save Black, because of the reply 13. g3.

However, Black can save the piece with the incredible move 12. ... Kd8!, although after 13. Qxg4 (if 13. Nxf6, then 13. ... Qh4 + followed by 14. ... Qxf6) 13. ... Nxg4 14. h3 Nh6 15. fxe5 dxe5 16. Bg5 + and 17. Bf6 White wins a pawn. As you can see, even in this line Black gets a difficult position.

World Champion Jose Raoul Capablanca reigned on the chess throne from 1921 to 1927. He learned chess at a very early age. Here is how it happened. One day, 4-year-old Jose Raoul went into his father's office and found him playing chess with a colonel. Little Capablanca's interest was aroused by the pieces moving on a board according to some rules that he did not yet know. The next day Jose Raoul again came and silently watched his father play. The third day, he suddenly saw that his father moved a Knight from a light square to another light square and that his opponent, also apparently a weak player, did not notice it. The little boy laughed and proceeded to accuse his father of cheating. The father became angry but the son immediately showed him on the board the mistake he had made. Finding it hard to believe that such a young boy could have mastered the rules of play by himself, Capablanca Senior asked his son whether he could set up the men in their starting positions. Jose Raoul not only passed this test without a mistake, but also won a game then and there against his father. A few days later, Capablanca Senior took the "Wunderkind"(child prodigy) to the chess club. One of the strongest club members agreed to play with the 4-year-old child, but insisted on giving him Queen odds. Here is what happened in that game:

Game 68
Iglesias—Capablanca (aged 4)
Havana, 1892
(White played without his Queen)

1. e2-e4	e7-e5
2. Ng1-f3	Ng8-f6
3. Nf3xe5	Nf6xe4
4. d2-d4	d7-d6
5. Ne5-f3	Bf8-e7
6. Bf1-d3	Ne4-f6

7. c2-c4	0-0
8. Nb1-c3	Nb8-c6
9. a2-a3	a7-a6
10. Bc1-d2	b7-b6
11. 0-0-0	Bc8-d7
12. Kc1-b1	

White is waiting for the child to start giving away pieces, but so far Black has been playing very well.

12. ...	Nc6-a5
13. Rd1-c1	Na5-b3
14. Rc1-c2	c7-c5
15. d4-d5	Rf8-e8
16. h2-h4	b6-b5!

Going over this game we get the impression that the players were modern experts and certainly older than four years.

17. g2-g4	Nb3-d4
18. Nf3xd4	c5xd4
19. Nc3-e4	b5xc4
20. Ne4xf6 +	Be7xf6
21. Bd3xc4	Bd7xg4
22. Bc4-d3	Bg4-f3
23. Rh1-h3	Bf3xd5
24. h4-h5	Bd5-e6
25. Rh3-g3	g7-g6
26. f2-f4	Bf6-h4
27. Rg3-g1	Kg8-h8
28. f4-f5	Be6xf5
29. Bd3xf5	g6xf5
30. Bd2-h6	Re8-g8
31. Rc2-g2	Rg8xg2
32. Rg1xg2	Qd8-f6
33. Bh6-g7 +	Qf6xg7
34. Rg2xg7	Kh8xg7
35. Kb1-c2	Kg7-f6
36. Kc2-d3	Kf6-e5
37. h5-h6	f5-f4
38. Kd3-e2	Ke5-e4

See Diagram 406.

406

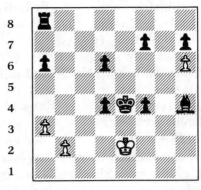

Only here did the grown-up playing White acknowledge himself vanquished. Yes, Capablanca was not considered a Wunderkind for nothing!

The brilliant American Paul Morphy was undoubtedly the strongest chessplayer of his time. His splendid combinations even today thrill chess lovers. Here is a game that Morphy played blindfolded against his uncle. This game was played on Paul Morphy's birthday.

Game 69
P. Morphy (age 12)—E. Morphy, New Orleans 1849
Giuoco Piano

1. e2-e4	e7-e5
2. Ng1-f3	Nb8-c6
3. Bf1-c4	Bf8-c5
4. c2-c3	d7-d6
5. 0-0	Ng8-f6

5. ... Bb6 or 5. ... Qe7 would be more prudent.

6. d2-d4	e5xd4
7. c3xd4	Bc5-b6
8. h2-h3	

8. Nc3 is a good move here, but Paul Morphy decides to prevent the Black Bishop from moving to g4.

8. ...	h7-h6
9. Nb1-c3	0-0
10. Bc1-e3	

Here White should retreat his other Bishop to b3.

10. ...	Rf8-e8

An unfortunate move. Black had a chance of equalizing by 10. ... Nxe4 11. Nxe4 d5.

11. d4-d5   **Bb6xe3?**

It was better to retreat the Knight to e7.

12. d5xc6   **Be3-b6**
13. e4-e5   **d6xe5**
14. Qd1-b3

White could play 14. Qxd8 Rxd8 15. Nxe5, but Paul decides to keep his Queen for the attack.

14. ...   **Re8-e7?**

He should have defended with 14. ... Be6.

15. Bc4xf7 + !

The young maestro immediately takes advantage of his opponent's hardly perceptible mistake.

15. ...   **Re7xf7**
16. Nf3xe5   **Qd8-e8**
17. c6xb7   **Bc8xb7**
18. Ra1-e1   **Bb7-a6**
19. Ne5-g6!

Black loses because of the pin on the Rook at f7.

19. ...   **Qe8-d8**
20. Re1-e7

See Diagram 407.

407

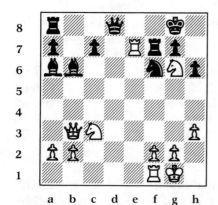

Black resigns. 20. ... Nd5 will not save him, because of 21. Nxd5 Rxe7 22. Nf6#.

The onlookers' delight at this game was indescribable.

In 1978, a 17-year-old Soviet schoolgirl called Maia Chiburdanidze became the Women's World Champion. Never before in the history of chess had there been such a young world champion. The following game shows how strong a player Maia was even at the age of twelve.

Game 70
M. Chiburdanidze—O. Andreeva
(International Master), USSR 1973
Sicilian Defense

1. e2-e4   **c7-c5**
2. c2-c3   **Ng8-f6**
3. e4-e5   **Nf6-d5**
4. d2-d4   **c5xd4**
5. c3xd4   **d7-d6**
6. Ng1-f3   **Nb8-c6**
7. Nb1-c3   **Nd5xc3**
8. b2xc3   **d6xe5?**

It was better to play 8. ... d5 or 8. ... e6, with equal chances.

9. d4-d5!   **e5-e4**

Freeing e5 for the Knight.

10. Nf3-g5

10. dxc6 Qxd1 + 11. Kxd1 exf3 would be in Black's favor.

10. ...   **Nc6-e5**
11. Ng5xe4   **Qd8-c7**

An inaccuracy. Better was 11. ... e6, undermining White's center.

12. Qd1-d4!

In this instance the Queen is splendidly placed in the center, for Black cannot attack it easily.

12. ...   **Bc8-d7**

Yet another inaccuracy. The development of the Kingside is urgently called for.

13. Bc1-a3!

Preparing the move 14. d6.

13. ...   **f7-f6**

Defending the Knight. 13. ... e6 would lose to 14. d6 Qa5 15. Bb4.

14. d5-d6   **Qc7-c6**

14. ... exd6 would be inferior, because of 15. Nxd6 + Bxd6 16. Bxd6, and White has the advantage.

15. d6xe7   **Bf8xe7**
16. Ba3xe7   **Ke8xe7**

The Black King has lost the right to castle. White's task now is to organize an attack against the King stranded in the center.

17. Qd4-b4 + !

Forcing Black to determine the position of his King.

17. ...   **Ke7-f7**

The King had four squares, but none of them guaranteed it safety. It may be that 17. ... Kd8 was the best, but Black's desire to hide her

King on the Kingside is understandable.

18. f2-f4!

White's idea is to play Bc4+, but since the Black Knight controls c4 White tries to chase the Knight away with her pawn.

18. ...   Rh8-e8

18. .., Ng6 would lose after 19. Bc4+ Be6 20. Bxe6+ Qxe6 21. f5! Qxf5 22. Nd6+. Relatively best was 18. ... Ng4, although White would still maintain a very strong attack after 19. ... 0-0-0.

19. f4xe5   Re8xe5

Black sacrificed her Knight expecting that in return she would win the White Knight, which is now pinned. However, there is a surprise in store for her.

20. 0-0-0!

Excellently played! The King goes into hiding and at the same time the White Rook attacks the Bishop.

20. ...   Re5xe4
21. Rd1xd7+!   Kf7-e8?

21. ... Qxd7 was better, although Black would still have lost a piece after 22. Qxe4.

22. Rd7-e7+!!

See Diagram 408.

408

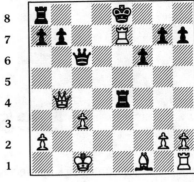

It's almost unbelievable that a 12-year-old girl could make such a move! Black resigns, since 22. ... Rxe7 would be followed by 23. Bb5, **pinning** and winning the Black Queen.

After looking at these games we can conclude that the champions possessed chess talent even in their childhood, but that they nevertheless made mistakes and were beatable. But what characterised the budding champions was above all this: even after the most unpleasant losses, they did not become disenchanted with chess or lose confidence in their abilitites. Rather, these children analyzed their mistakes and oversights with still greater energy, in order to avoid repeating them. That is what we too must learn to do!

Lesson Ten

A. Check Lesson 9 homework (as necessary).
B. *Review Questions*

Find the best continuation in Diagrams 409-420. Work directly from the diagrams, without setting up the men on a board.

409

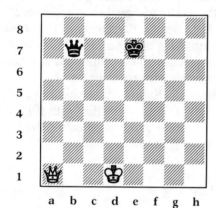

The player who moves first wins.

410

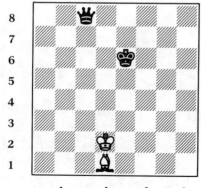

White to play.

411

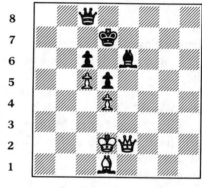

White to play.

412

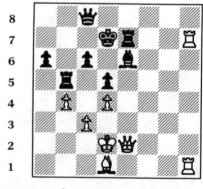

White to play.

413

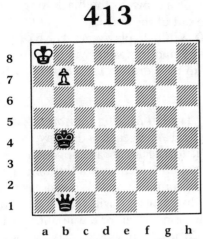

White to play.

414

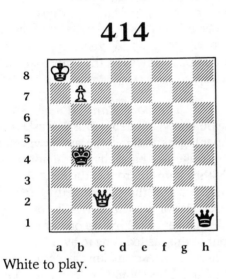

White to play.

415

White to play.

416

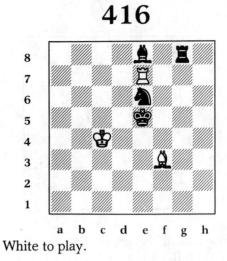

White to play.

417

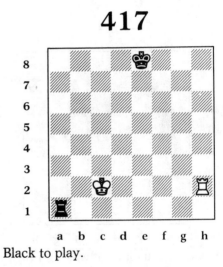

Black to play.

418

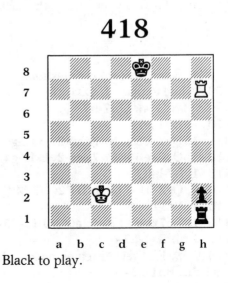

Black to play.

419

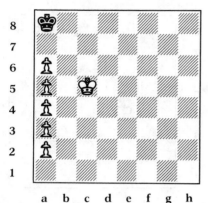

How should the game end with White to play? With Black to play?

420

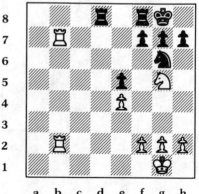

How would you play if it was your turn with White? And if it was your turn with Black?

---

should be a draw, as the Black King cannot be driven out of the corner.

D-420 White to play wins: **1. Kh7-g8 Kf6-g6 2. h6-h7** and the pawn will queen.
Black to play draws: **1. ... Kf6-f7 2. Kh7-h8 Kf7-f8.**

Typical Mating Combinations

The final aim of each of the players in a chess game is to checkmate his opponent's King. A combination which serves this aim is called a "mating combination." We can easily understand that a player will readily sacrifice any amount of material for a sound (correct) **mating combination.** Before playing the combination, the player must of course clearly visualize the **final mating position.**

There are many typical mating positions that often occur in games. A knowledge of these positions will help us to create typical mating combinations. However, they must be studied gradually.

The Back-Rank Mate

As you know, it is dangerous to waste time in the opening by making aimless pawn moves. But on the other hand, if you do not push up one of the pawns in front of the King after it has castled, you run the risk of getting mated on the back (1st or 8th) rank by your opponent's Rook or Queen. Pushing up one of the pawns in front of the castled King to avoid the danger of mate is known as "making an escape hatch" for the King. This should preferably be done in the middlegame, and the move should be tied in with the players's **plan of play.**

Answers to Review Questions
D-409 White to play: **1. Qa1-g7 +**
Black to play: **1. ... Qb7-h1 +**
D-410 1. Bd1-g4 +
D-411 1. Qe2xe6 + Kd7xe6 2. Bd1-g4 +
D-412 1. Qe2xe6 + Kd7xe6 2. Bd1-g4 +
D-413 1. b7-b8Q +
D-414 1. Qc2-b1 + Qh1xb1 2. b7-b8Q +
D-415 1. Bf3-d5 +
D-416 1. Re7xe6 +! Ke5xe6 2. Bf3-d5 +
D-417 1. ... Ra1-a2 +
D-418 1. ... Rh1-a1! (threatening **2. ... h1Q)
2. Rh7xh2 Ra1-a2 +**
D-419 1. No matter who plays first, the game

421

For example, let us look at Diagram 421, where it is White's turn to move. It would be advisable for White to make an escape hatch by playing 1. g2-g3. The g2 square is thereby freed for the King and at the same time the pawn on g3 controls f4 and h4, depriving the enemy Knight of these squares. Black can reply with 1. ... h7-h6, attacking the Knight and at the same time making an escape hatch for his King on h7. 1. ... f6?, on the other hand, would be bad because of 2. Ne6 Rd1 + (an in-between check) 3. Kg2 Rf7 4. Rb8 + Nf8 5. R2b7 Rdd7 6. Rxd7 Rxd7 7. Rxf8#, there being no escape hatch for the Black King on h7.

Sometimes a player pulls off a back-rank mate without having had to sacrifice anything, as a result of a gross blunder on the part of his opponent. Most of the time, however, the back-rank mate is the result of a combination.

Let us look at some examples. The patterns shown in Diagrams 422, 424 and 426 form the basis of the combinations in Diagrams 423, 425, and 427, respectively. Find these combinations. Solve the exercises directly from the diagrams, without setting up the men on a board. **Memorize the mating *patterns*, but not the positions of the various men in the combinations.**

423

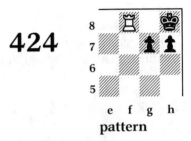

White to play mates in two moves.

424

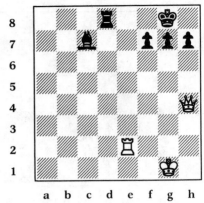

pattern

422

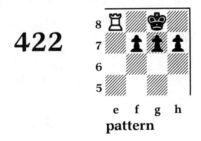

pattern

425

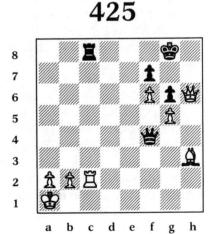

Black to play mates in two moves.

426

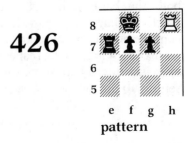

pattern

427

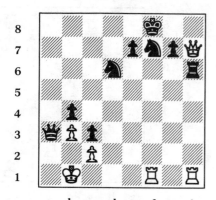

White to play mates in two moves.

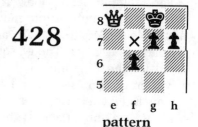

pattern

428

429

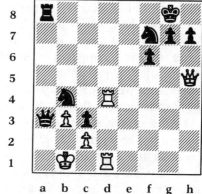

White to play and mate in three moves.

Answers

D-423

    1. Qh4xd8 + !

The Queen is sacrificed in order to eliminate the piece guarding the eighth rank.

    1. ...   **Bc7xd8**

    2. Re2-e8#

D-425

    1. ...   **Qf4-c1 +**

This kind of combination is called an **x-ray attack**, because the Rook on c8 controls c1 **through** the enemy Rook on c2.

    2. Rc2xc1

Forced. But now the Black Rook can move to c1.

    2. ...   **Rc8xc1#**

D-427

    1. Qh7-h8 + !

An x-ray attack, with the Rook on h1 attacking h8 through the Black Rook on h6.

    1. ...   **Rh6xh8**

Forced, since the Knight is pinned. Now, however, the Rook on h1 enters the fray.

    2. Rh1xh8#

In some cases the Queen is able to mate the opposing King by simultaneously controlling both the back rank and the King's escape hatch. In Diagrams 429, 431, and 433 find the combinations using the patterns shown in Diagrams 428, 430 and 432, respectively. Solve the exercises directly from the diagrams, without setting up the men on a board.

430

pattern

431

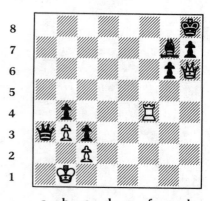

White to play and mate in two moves.

432

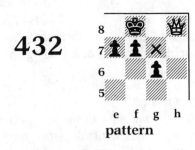

pattern

433

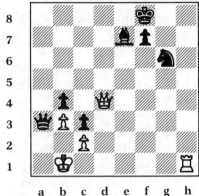

White to play and mate in two moves.

setting up the men on a board), find the combinations in Diagrams 435, 437, and 439, using the patterns in Diagrams 434, 436, and 438, respectively.

434

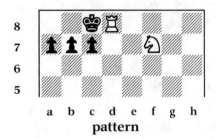

pattern

435

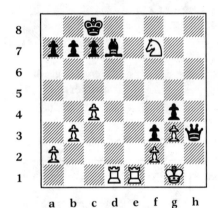

White to play and mate in two moves.

Answers

D-429
    1. Rd4-d8 + !

The idea of this Rook sacrifice is to free the h5-e8 diagonal by deflecting the Knight.
    1. ...   **Ra8xd8**

If 1. ... Nxd8, then 2. Qe8#.
    2. Rd1xd8 +   **Nf7xd8**

Forced.
    3. Qh5-e8#

D-431
    1. Rf4-f8 + !

This move is possible because the White Queen controls f8 through the Bishop on g7 (x-ray attack).
    1. ...   **Bg7xf8**
    2. Qh6xf8#

D-433
    1. Rh1-h8 +   **Ng6xh8**
    2. Qd4xh8#

Working directly from the diagrams (without

436

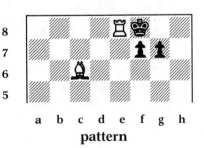

pattern

437

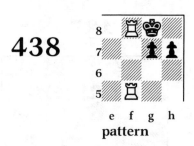

White to play and mate in two moves.

438

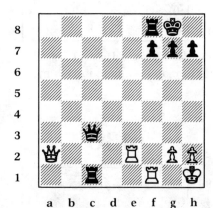

pattern

439

White to play and mate in three moves.

1. Re1-e8 + !	Bd7xe8
2. Rd1-d8#	

We achieved our goal by using the idea of **deflection**.

D-437

1. Qb5-e8 + !	

Again we make use of the x-ray attack idea. The e8 square is controlled not only by the Queen and the Bishop but also by the White Rook acting through the Black Rook on d8.

1. ...	Rd8xe8
2. Rc8xe8#	

D-439 This example makes use of two ideas: the deflection of the Black Rook from the eighth rank and the x-ray attack.

1. Qa2xf7 + !	Rf8xf7
2. Re2-e8 +	Rf7-f8
3. Re8xf8#	

Such combinations can occur even when the King has an escape hatch, provided that this escape square is controlled by an enemy man. Working directly from the diagrams (without setting up the men on a board), find the combinations in Diagrams 441, 443, and 446, using the patterns in Diagrams 440, 442, 444, and 445.

440

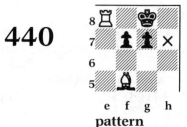

pattern

Answers

D-435 Looking at the position, we get the idea of playing the move Rd8#, but the Rook cannot jump over the Black Bishop. How can we force the Black Bishop to abandon the d-file?

441

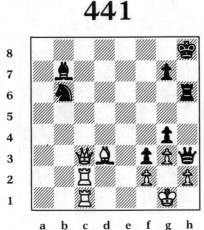

White to play and mate in three moves.

442

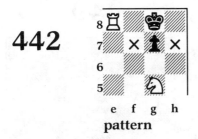

pattern

443

White to play and mate in two moves.

444

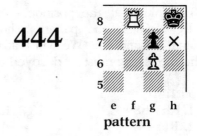

pattern

445

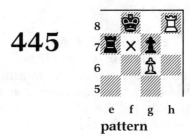

pattern

446

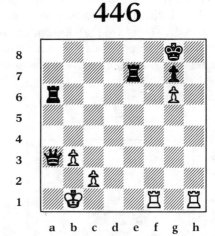

White to play and mate in two moves (two solutions).

Answers

D-441 Since the White Bishop controls the escape hatch on h7, White must break through to the eighth rank with his Rook or Queen.

    1. Qc3-c8 + !

We won't balk at sacrificing!

    1. ...   **Bb7xc8**
    2. Rc2xc8 +   **Nb6xc8**
    3. Rc1xc8#

D-443 We must first of all find the mating idea patterned in Diagram 442. Then we must decide how to **decoy** the Black King onto g8.

    1. Qh7-g8 + !   **Kf8xg8**
    2. Re1-e8#

D-446 Looking at the position, we must mentally visualize the patterns shown in Diagrams 444 and 445. We will realize then that the Black king must be **decoyed** onto h8 or f8.

Solution 1:
  1. Rh1-h8 + !   Kg8xh8
  2. Rf1-f8#

Solution 2:
  1. Rf1-f8 + !   Kg8xf8
  2. Rh1-h8#

Endgame With King and Non-Rook pawn vs. King

We shall examine positions with the pawn on any arbitrary non-Rook file (i.e., any file except the a-file and the h-file) since the results are the same for all non-Rook pawns.

A non-Rook pawn is easier to queen than a Rook pawn but here too you must have a sure knowledge of which positions are winning and which are not. Today we shall look at the positions in which the pawn can queen. You are recommended to memorize these positions.

447

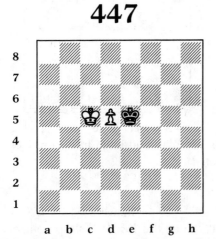

White wins no matter who moves first.

448

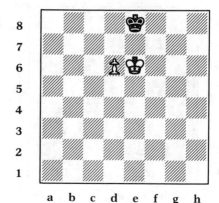

White wins only if it is Black's turn to play.

449

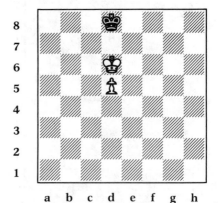

White wins no matter who moves first.

450

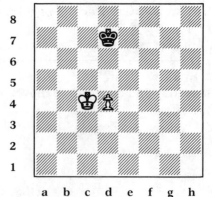

White to play wins.

174

451

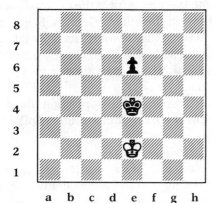

Black wins no matter who moves first.

452

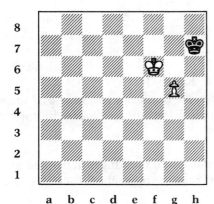

White wins no matter who moves first.

D-447 The lone King can have chances of stopping the pawn only if it is in front of the pawn. A King that is beside the pawn cannot stop it.

White to play gains a decisive advantage by:

1. d5-d6	**Ke5-e6**
2. Kc5-c6	**Ke6-f7**
3. d6-d7	**Kf7-e7**
4. Kc6-c7	

White will get a new Queen on the next move.

Black to play:

1. 1. ...	**Ke5-f6**

Trying to stop the pawn from the front by playing Kf6-e7-d7.

2. Kc5-c6

The King hurries to the c7 square, from where it will control d6, d7, and d8, the pawn's queening route.

2. ...	**Kf6-e7**
3. Kc6-c7	

Protected by the King, the pawn will become a Queen in three moves.

Conclusion: If the two Kings and the pawn are all on the same rank, and the pawn is defended, then the side with the pawn wins no matter whose turn it is to play.

D-448 This extremely important position is encountered quite often in practice. Note the position of the Kings. You will remember that when the Kings are standing across from each other with one square between them, they are said to be in **opposition.** The King which has obtained such a position after making its move (so that it is the opposing side's turn to move) is said to have **taken the opposition.** In the present example, the outcome of the struggle depends on who has the opposition. If White has the opposition, so that it is Black's turn to play, then White wins:

1. ...	**Ke8-d8**

Trying to stop the pawn.

2. d6-d7	**Kd8-c7**

Black had no other move — he was in zugzwang.

3. Ke6-e7

The pawn will queen next move.

If on the other hand Black has the opposition in Diagram 448, so that it is White's turn to move, then the game is a draw:

1. d6-d7 +

On any other move Black would reply 1. ... Kd7 and would again draw.

1. ...	**Ke8-d8**
2. Ke6-d6	

Stalemate. This time it was White who was in zugzwang. He could have avoided stalemate only by giving up his pawn, but that would of course be a draw anyway.

As you see, in this example the right to play first is advantageous neither for White nor for Black. Such a situation is known as **mutual zugzwang.**

Conclusion: If a protected pawn reaches the seventh rank **without check**, it will queen;

otherwise the game is a draw. (Of course, all the conclusions apply to Black as well, when it is Black who is trying to queen the pawn.)

D-449 When the King is in front of its own pawn, the chances of victory are considerably increased. If in addition, as in the present example, the King is on the sixth rank, then the pawn will queen by force no matter whose turn it is to move. The Kings are in opposition. This means that each King takes away three intervening squares (c7, d7, and e7 in the present case) from the other.

With Black to play, White's task is not complicated:

1. ...   **Kd8-e8**

Because of Zugzwang, Black loses control of c7.

2. Kd6-c7

Immediately occupying c7. Now the pawn will queen by force. The same thing would have happened after 1. ... Kc8, except that White would have played 2. Ke7 instead.

Let us see now what would happen with White to play:

1. Kd6-e6   **Kd8-e8!**

The Black King takes the opposition. On any other move 2. Ke7 would be decisive.

2. d5-d6!

This "reserve" tempo (move) forces Black to **yield the opposition.**

2. ...   **Ke8-d8**

3. d6-d7

The pawn has reached the seventh rank **without check**!

3. ...   **Kd8-c7**

Zugzwang occurs very frequently in pawn endings.

4. Ke6-e7

And White wins.

Conclusion: If the White King is on the sixth rank and in front of its own pawn, White is always assured of winning.

D-450

1. Kc4-d5!

Only thus! The advantage of taking the opposition is that White puts Black into zug-

zwang, forcing him to move his King to one side, and thereby assures the penetration of his own King on the other side. 1. Kc5 would be a mistake since Black would draw by taking the opposition with 1. ... Kc7!. On any other White move, Black would save himself by 1. ... Kd6.

1. ...   **Kd7-e7**

Forced to give up the opposition, Black loses control over c6. 1. ... Kc7 would be followed by 2. Ke6!.

2. Kd5-c6!

The main idea of this outflanking maneuver with the King is to chase the enemy King away from the pawn, which is thereby enabled to advance to the queening square.

2. ...   **Ke7-d8**

On 2. ... Ke6, 3. d5+ is decisive: 3. ... Ke7 4. Kc7 and the pawn queens.

3. Kc6-d6!

As you already know, if the King is on the sixth rank and in front of its pawn, the win is assured.

3. ...   **Kd8-e8**

4. Kd6-c7!

The road has been cleared for the pawn, which will become a Queen in four more moves.

Conclusion: If the King is in front of its pawn and can take the opposition, the win is assured.

D-451 White to play has to give up the opposition immediately and lose the game. For example:

1. Ke2-d2   **Ke4-f3**

Clearing the way for the pawn. 1. Kf2 would have been met by 1. ... Kd3.

2. Kd2-d3   **e6-e5**

The pawn must be brought up.

3. Kd3-d2   **e5-e4**

3. ... Kf2 would be bad because of 4. Kd3, forcing the Black King to retreat.

4. Kd2-e1   **Kf3-e3!**

If Black gets his King on the third rank and in front of his pawn, he always wins! 4. ... e3 would be a mistake allowing White to draw by taking the opposition with 5. Kf1!. For example: 5. ... e2+ 6. Ke1 Ke3 stalemate.

5. Ke1-d1   **Ke3-f2!**

On 5. Kf1 Black would have won by 5. ... Kd2. Now the pawn has obtained the green light and will queen in three moves.

With Black to move in Diagram 451, White has the opposition but must still lose, because Black can make it White's turn to play by pushing his pawn. After that, Black wins easily.

1. ...	**e6-e5!**

Regaining the opposition.

2. Ke2-f2	**Ke4-d3**
3. Kf2-f3	

3. Ke1 would also lose, because of 3. ... Ke3! 4. Kf1 Kd2! etc.

3. ...	**e5-e4 +**
4. Kf3-f2	**Kd3-d2!**

And the pawn cannot be stopped.

Conclusion: In positions where the King is in front of its pawn and there is at least one square between the King and the pawn, victory is always assured.

D-452 With Black to play, White wins easily:

1. ...	**Kh7-g8**

1. ... Kh8 would not save Black, as White wins after 2. g6 Kg8 3. g7 Kh7 4. Kf7.

2. Kf6-g6!	

Taking the opposition. 2. g6 would lead to a draw after 2. ... Kf8! 3. g7+ Kg8 4. Kg6 stalemate.

2. ...	**Kg8-h8**

If 2. ... Kf8, then the White pawn would be unstoppable after 3. Kh7.

3. Kg6-f7	**Kh8-h7**
4. g5-g6 +	**Kh7-h8**
5. g6-g7 +	**Kh8-h7**
6. g7-g8Q +	

And so on.

With White to play, a few complications arise as a result of the g-pawn being near the edge of the board.

1. Kf6-f7!	

Watch out for the trap! 1. g6 + ?? would be no good because of 1. ... Kh8! after which the draw is unavoidable in all variations:

(a) 2. Kf7 stalemate. This is possible only with a Knight (g or b) pawn.

(b) 2. g7 + Kg8 3. Kg6 is again stalemate.

(c) On any other move by the White King, Black draws with 2. ... Kg7.

1. ...	**Kh7-h8**
2. Kf7-g6!	

Again 2. g6? must be avoided because of stalemate.

2. ...	**Kh8-g8**
3. Kg6-h6!	

With the idea of controlling h7 in order to drive the Black King out of the corner.

3. ...	**Kg8-h8**

Or else 4. Kh7 would follow.

4. g5-g6	

Having completed the maneuvers with his King, White advances his pawn.

4. ...	**Kh8-g8**
5. g6-g7	**Kg8-f7**

Forced.

6. Kh6-h7	

And White wins.

Today we have looked at cases where the pawn has succeeded in forcing its way through to the queening square. The next lesson will acquaint you with examples where the pawn does not manage to do this and the game ends in a draw.

HOMEWORK
(Answers at the end)

Remember the pattern shown in each of the odd-numbered diagrams 453-463 and use it in solving the coresponding even-numbered diagrams 454-464.

453

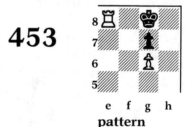

pattern

454

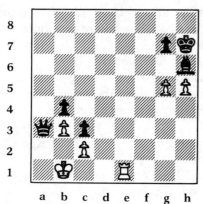

White to play and mate in two moves.

WHITE	BLACK
1.	
2.	

457

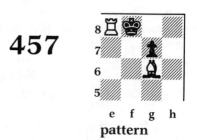

pattern

WHITE	BLACK
1.	
2.	

455

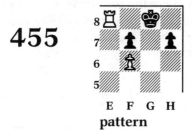

pattern

458

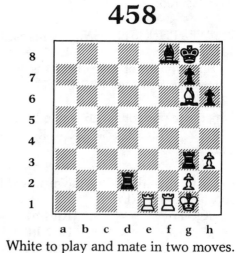

White to play and mate in two moves.

WHITE	BLACK
1.	
2.	

456

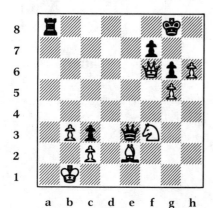

Black to play and mate in two moves.

459

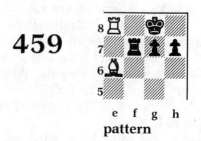

pattern

460

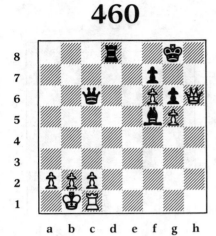

Black to play and mate in two moves.

WHITE	BLACK
1.	
2.	

461

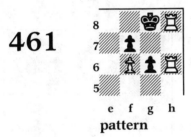

pattern

462

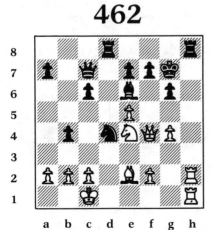

White to play and mate in three moves.

WHITE	BLACK
1.	
2.	

463

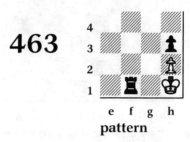

pattern

464

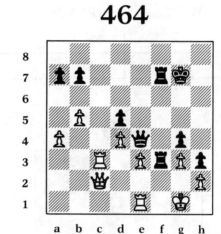

Black to play and mate in three moves.

WHITE	BLACK
1.	
2.	

II. In Diagrams 465-476 find the strongest continuation. Use the tactical device of "back-rank mate."

465

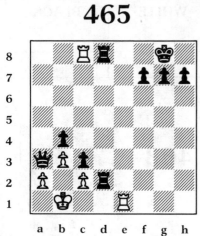

White to play and mate in two moves.

WHITE	BLACK
1.	
2.	

466

White to play and mate in two moves.

WHITE	BLACK
1.	
2.	

467

White to play and mate in three moves.

WHITE	BLACK
1.	
2.	

468

White to play and mate in three moves.

WHITE	BLACK
1.	
2.	

180

469

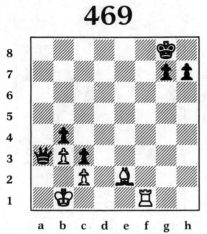

White to play and mate in two moves.

WHITE	BLACK
1.	
2.	

471

Black to play and mate in three moves.

WHITE	BLACK
1.	
2.	

470

Black to play and mate in two moves.

WHITE	BLACK
1.	
2.	

472

Black to play and mate in two moves.

WHITE	BLACK
1.	
2.	

473

White to play and mate in four moves.

	WHITE	BLACK
1.		
2.		
3.		
4.		

474

White to play and win.

	WHITE	BLACK
1.		
2.		
3.		
4.		

475

White to play and win a piece.

	WHITE	BLACK
1.		
2.		

476

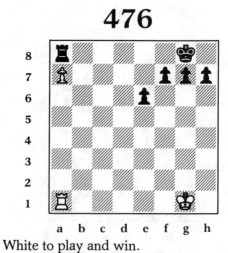

White to play and win.

	WHITE	BLACK
1.		
2.		

Diagrams 477–482 deal with endgames.

478

Either side to play. Queen the pawn.

477

Black to play and queen the pawn (two solutions).

	WHITE	BLACK
1.		
2.		

	WHITE	BLACK
1.		
2.		

	WHITE	BLACK
1.		
2.		

	WHITE	BLACK
1.		
2.		

479

White to play. Queen the pawn.

	WHITE	BLACK
1.		
2.		

480

Either side to play. Queen the pawn.

	WHITE	BLACK
1.		
2.		

	WHITE	BLACK
1.		
2.		

481

8
7
6
5
4
3
2
1

a b c d e f g h

White to play. Queen the pawn.

	WHITE	BLACK
1.		
2.		

482

8
7
6
5
4
3
2
1

a b c d e f g h

White to play. Queen the pawn.

	WHITE	BLACK
1.		
2.		

Answers

D-454
    1. g5-g6 + !
Forcing the King to retreat to the last rank.
    1. ...   **u**
    2. Re1-e8#

D-456
    1. ...   **Qe3-c1 + !**
By sacrificing his Queen, Black decoys the White King onto c1.
    2. Kb1xc1   **Ra8-a1#**

D-458 When you know the pattern, it's not hard to find the solution:
    1. Rf1xf8 + !   **Kg8xf8**
    2. Re1-e8#

D-460
    1. ...   **Qc6xc2 + !**
  Deflecting the Rook from the defense of the first rank and **pinning** it at the same time.
    2. Rc1xc2   **Rd8-d1#**

D-462 How can the Black King be forced to retreat to the eighth rank?
    1. Qf4-f6 + !!

When we've found a mating idea, we can of course sacrifice any piece in order to make the idea a reality.

1. ...	e7xf6
2. e5xf6 +	any move
3. Rh2xh8#	

D-464 The idea of the combination is to entice (decoy) the White King onto h1. But the Black Queen cannot get to h1 so long as the Black Rook is in its way. So:

| 1. ... | Rf3-f1 + !! |

Freeing the way for the Queen.

| 2. Re1xf1 | Qe4-h1 + ! |
| 3. Kg1xh1 | Rf7xf1# |

D-465

| 1. Re1-e8 + ! | |

White makes use of the "x-ray attack" tactical device — the Rook on c8 controls e8 **through** the Black Rook on d8.

| 1. ... | Rd8xe8 |
| 2. Rc8xe8# | |

D-466 We discover the idea of Re8#, but find that the Black Bishop is in the way. So:

| 1. Rc1-c8 + ! | |

White makes use of the tactical device of "line clearance."

| 1. ... | Be6xc8 |
| 2. Re1-e8# | |

D-467 The White Rooks attack e8, but the square is defended by the Black Rook and Bishop. That is, there are apparently two attackers versus two defenders. Actually, however, the White Queen also attacks e8 (an x-ray attack), and so:

| 1. Re2-e8 + | Rd8xe8 |
| 2. Re1xe8 + | Bc6xe8 |

Clearing the way for the White Queen.

| 3. Qa4xe8# | |

D-468 The White Rook and the pawn on c7 control the d8 square, but the two Black Rooks defend it. That is, there are two attackers against two defenders.

| 1. Qa6xc8 + ! | |

Eliminate one of the defenders **with check.** And not 1. Qxa8, allowing 1. ... Qh1#.

| 1. ... | Ra8xc8 |

| 2. Rd1-d8 + | Rc8xd8 |
| 3. c7xd8Q# | |

D-469 We can't play 1. Rf8 + since the King would capture the Rook. So we make use of the "driving away" tactical device:

| 1. Be2-c4 + | Kg8-h8 |

Forced.

| 2. Rf1-f8# | |

D-470

| 1. ... | Nc4-d2 + |

The King is **driven away** from the White Rook.

| 2. Kb1-a1 | Rc8xc1# |

D-471 When you have the chance to capture your opponent's Queen, don't do it instantaneously. Always take a look first to see whether you don't have a better move. In the present case, for example, the White Queen is under attack, but more important is the fact that White's back rank (the first rank) is hopelessly weak:

| 1. ... | Rb8-d8! |

A **quiet move.** White could well resign now.

| 2. Qb7xb5! | |

The last chance. Maybe Black will hastily reply with 2. ... Rd1 +, when White would win by 3. Qf1.

| 2. ... | c6xb5 |
| 3. any move | Rd8-d1# |

D-472

| 1. ... | Qa2-b1 + !! |

The "decoy" theme.

| 2. Kc1xb1 | Rd4-d1# |

D-473 Looking at the e8 square, we see that it is attacked five times by White and defended only four times by Black. Therefore:

| 1. Qe4-e8 + ! | |

1. dxc8Q + would be no good because of 1. ... Qxc8!, when Black would maintain four defenders while White would also only have four attackers instead of five.

1. ...	Nf6xe8
2. d7xe8Q +	Rc8xe8
3. Re3xe8 +	Ra8xe8
4. Re1xe8#	

D-474 This is a position from a game between two outstanding grandmasters played in Margate, 1937. Paul Keres, playing White, defeated the world champion Alexander Alekhine as follows:

1. Qd3xd7 + !

Black resigned, 1. ... Rxd7 would have been met by 2. Re8 + Rd8 3. Rxd8#.

D-475 The Black Queen is **overloaded** with duties — it must defend both the eighth rank and the Bishop.

1. Qf3xb3!

The **deflection** theme. Black loses a Bishop, since he cannot reply 1. ... Qxb3, because of 2. Rd8 + Re8 3. Rxe8#.

D-476

1. Ra1-b1!

This move is possible because Black didn't make an escape hatch for his King in good time.

1. ...   **Ra8-f8**

1. ... Rxa7 would allow 2. Rb8#. Any other Black move would also let White win by 2. Rb8.

2. Rb1-b8   **g7-g6**

Creating an escape hatch.

3. a7-a8Q   **Rf8xb8**

4. Qa8xb8 +

With a Queen for four pawns (a five-point advantage), White should win.

D-477

a)   **1. ...**   **Kd4-c3**

     2. Kc1-d1   **Kc3-b2**

And the pawn is unstoppable.

b)   **1. ...**   **Kd4-d3**

     2. Kc1-d1   **c4-c3**

     3. Kd1-c1   **c3-c2**

     4. Kc1-b2   **Kd3-d2**

And so on.

D-478

a) Black to play:

1. ...   **Kc8-c7**

Taking the opposition.

2. Kc5-d5!

Forcing Black to yield the opposition.

2. ...   **Kc7-c8**

3. Kd5-c6!   **Kc8-d8**

4. Kc6-d6!   **Kd8-e8**

5. e6-e7

And the pawn will queen.

b) White to play:

1. Kc5-c6!

Achieving the familiar winning position.

D-479

1. Kd1-c2!

1. Kd2 would lead to a draw after 1. ... Ke7 2. Kc3 Kd6 3. Kc4 Kc6, with a theoretically drawn position.

1. ...   **Kf8-e7**

2. Kc2-b3!

Now 2. Kc3 would have led to a draw.

2. ...   **Ke7-d6**

3. Kb3-a4!

3. Kc4 would only draw.

3. ...   **Kd6-c6**

4. Ka4-a5!

Four strong moves have brought White to a theoretically won position. His King is in front of the pawn and he can capture the opposition.

4. ...   **Kc6-b7**

5. Ka5-b5!   **Kb7-a7**

6. Kb5-c6   **Ka7-a8**

7. Kc6-b6!   **Ka8-b8**

8. b4-b5   **Kb8-a8**

9. Kb6-c7

And the pawn will queen in three more moves.

D-480

a) Black to play:

1. ...   **Ka8-b7**

2. a7-a8Q + !

By sacrificing the pawn, White obtains a theoretically won position.

2. ...   **Kb7xa8**

3. Kb5-a6!

Taking the opposition.

3. ...   **Ka8-b8**

4. b6-b7

And White wins.

b) White to play:

1. Kb5-c5

Another way to win is 1. Ka5 Kb7 2. a8Q + Kxa8 3. Ka6, with a familiar position. But be careful — 1. Ka6 and 1. Kc6 lead to stalemate!

1. ...   **Ka8-b7**

2. a7-a8Q + !

This is the only way to win in this position — sacrifice the pawn and then take the opposition.

2. ...   **Kb7xa8**

3. Kc5-c6

White takes the **diagonal** opposition.

3. ...   **Ka8-b8**
4. b6-b7
And so on.

D-481
      1. Bb1xd3!
White exchanges the last pair of pieces,
knowing that the pawn ending is theoretically
won for him.
      1. ...   **Ke3xd3**
      2. Kh1-h2!
2. g4 would lead to a draw since the Black
King could enter the square of the pawn by 2.
... Ke4.
      2. ...   **Kd3-e4**
      3. Kh2-g3   **Ke4-f5**
      4. Kg3-h4
And White should win (with correct play).

D-482
      1. Ba8-d5!!
The only way to save the pawn.
      1. ...   **Kc5xd5**
      2. Ka6-b5!
The King manages to come to the pawn's aid
in time.
      2. ...   **Kd5-d6**
      3. c3-c4   **Kd6-c7**
      4. Kb5-c5!
Reaching a theoretically won ending. You
already know how to play this position.

SUPPLEMENTARY MATERIAL

for use at the teacher's discretion

Defending the Back Rank
A back-rank mate is usually the result of the
rank being **insufficiently defended** against
invasion by the opponent's major pieces
(Rooks and Queen.) Often a player falls into a
back-rank mate because of **carelessness** on
his part: he **moves instantly**, thinking only
about his own aims and forgetting to take into
consideration the **ideas of his opponent**. So,
to begin with, you must pay **careful attention**
to the back rank, both your own and your opponent's. And, of course, you have to know the

methods of defending the back rank. Let us
now look at some examples.

483

Is this mate?

It's not, of course. Black has at his disposal
the simplest method of defense — that of eliminating the enemy piece which has invaded the
back rank:
      1. ...   **Bh1xa8**

484

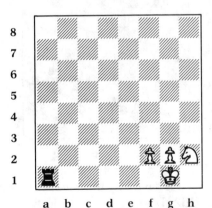

This only looks like mate, for White can play
1. Nh2-f1. The Knight not only defends the
King against the check but also creates an
"escape hatch" for the King by vacating the
square it was on (h2).

187

485

White to play. Can he checkmate Black?

No. White attacks e8 twice, but Black has it defended an equal number of times. You can see that the **defense is sufficient** if the number of defenders is **not less** than the number of attackers.

487

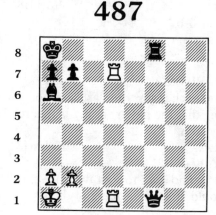

White to play. Is Black's back rank sufficiently defended?

Yes, it is. Although White appears to have two attackers against only one defender, in actual fact his Rook on d1 is **pinned** and cannot leave the first rank.

486

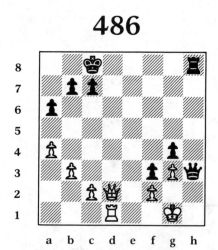

Can White to play mate Black?
No. Black is saved by the **escape hatch:**

1. Qd2-d7 +	**Kc8-b8**
2. Qd7-d8 +	**Rh8xd8**
3. Rd1xd8 +	*Kb8-a7*

488

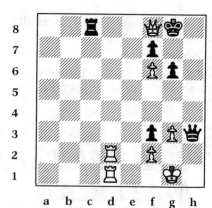

With which piece should Black capture the White Queen?

With the Rook, of course! Because otherwise:

1. ...	**Kxf8**
2. Rd8 +	**Rxd8**
3. Rxd8#	

489

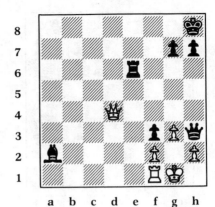

White played **1. Qa4xe8 +**. How should Black reply?

With **1. ... Re2xe8!** (maintaining two defenders on the back rank). Otherwise Black would be mated: **1. ... Rdxe8 2. Rf8 + Rxf8 3. Rxf8#.**

490

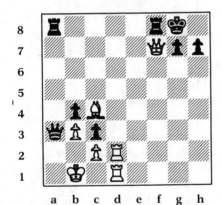

What to do? To take or not to take?

Not to take! Black wins by retreating his King into the corner, after which White cannot avoid getting mated by ... Qb2#. If, on the other hand, Black plays 1. ... Rxf7, **he** would be the one to get mated, after 2. Rd8 + Rxd8 3. Rxd8#.

491

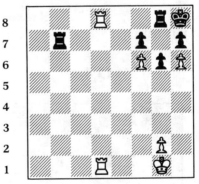

Black threatens 1. ... Qg2#. Can White save himself?

No, he cannot. Black is able to defend his back rank because of an **x-ray attack**. Namely, his Bishop controls g8 **through** the Rook on e6. For example:

| **1. Qd4-d8 +** | **Re6-e8!** |
| **2. Qd8xe8 +** | **Ba2-g8** |

And White is defenseless.

492

White threatens 1. Rxg8 + Kxg8 2. Rd8#. Is Black in a position to defend himself?

Yes — Black can save himself by using the x-ray attack motif:

| **1. ...** | **Rb7-b8!** |

The Black Rooks defend each other **through** the White Rook on d8.

| **2. Rd8xb8** | **Rg8xb8** |

493

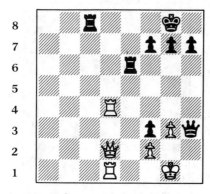

White to move. Who should win?

White loses.

1. Rd4-d8 +

does not save him because Black can make use of the x-ray attack principle.

1. ...   **Re6-e8!**

1. ... Rxd8 would lose to 2. Qxd8 + followed by mate next move.   Now, however, the Rook on c8 defends the Rook on e8 **through** the White Rook on d8.

2. Rd8xe8 +

2. Rxc8 would not save White, because of 2. ... Qg2#.

2. ...   **Rc8xe8**

White is defenseless against mate next move.

494

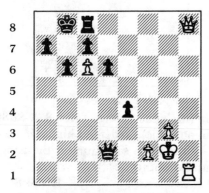

White threatens 1. Qxc8 + Kxc8 2. Rh8#. Can Black defend his back rank?

Yes, by

1. ...   **Qd2-g5!**

The only move that saves Black. It is obvious that Black cannot play 1. ... Rxh8, because of 2. Rxh8#. If now

2. Qh8xc8 +   **Kb8xc8**
3. Rh1-h8 +

then after

3. ...   **Qg5-d8**
4. Rh8xd8   **Kc8xd8**

White should lose, as Black is two pawns up in the pawn ending.

There are also other methods of defending the back rank. You will be introduced to them later on.

495

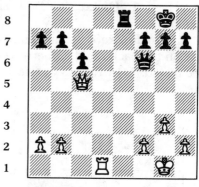

Black to move. Can he play **1. ... Qf6xb2?**

No. White wins material after:

2. Qc5-e7!

Deflecting Black's Rook from the eighth rank.

2. ...   **Re8-f8**

It doesn't help to play 2. ... Qe2 because of 3. Qxe2 Rxe2 4. Rd8 + Re8 5. Rxe8#.

3. Rd1-d8   **Qb2-b1 +**
4. Kg1-g2   **Qb1-e4 +**

Otherwise 4. ... h6 5. Rxf8 + and so on, or 4. ... Rxd8 5. Qxd8#.

5. Qe7xe4   **Rf8xd8**

Black loses his Queen for a Rook and pawn. 9 − (5 + 1) = 3 points. Instead of capturing White's pawn, Black should make an escape hatch by playing 1. ... h6 or 1. ... g6.

Sample Games
With a Back-Rank Mate

Game 71
(Schoolchildren's Tournament)
1. d2-d4   **e7-e5?**

A very dubious opening, played with the intention of **surprising the opponent.**

| 2. d4xe5 | Nb8-c6 |
| 3. Ng1-f3 | Qd8-e7 |

Black tries to win back his pawn and at the same time sets a devious **trap** for his opponent.

4. Bc1-f4?

The pawn should be defended by 4. Qd5.

| 4. ... | Qe7-b4 +! |

A triple attack! The King, Bishop, and the b-pawn are forked.

| 5. Bf4-d2 | Qb4xb2 |
| 6. Bd2-c3? | |

This Bishop is making too many moves in the opening. White has to play 6. Nc3, with an approximately equal game.

| 6. ... | Bf8-b4! |

Black visualizes the back-rank mating pattern shown in Diagram 496.

496

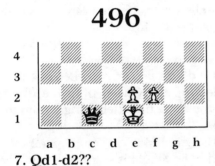

7. Qd1-d2??

The White Queen helps the enemy to put his devious plans into effect. Instead, White had to play 7. Bxb4 Qxa1 8. Bc3 Qxa2, giving up the Exchange and a pawn but avoiding mate.

| 7. ... | Bb4xc3 |
| 8. Qd2xc3? | |

It was at any rate better to give up the Rook and pawn by 8. Nxc3 Qxa1 + 9. Nd1 Qxa2.

| 8. ... | Qb2-c1# |

497

Compare the final position in Diagram 497 with the pattern in Diagram 496. White's neglect of his development was the cause of his disastrous loss in this game.

Game 72
Danish Gambit (analysis)

1. e2-e4	e7-e5
2. d2-d4	e5xd4
3. c2-c3	

A pawn sacrifice for rapid piece development.

| 3. ... | d4xc3 |
| 4. Bf1-c4 | |

In order to gain a lead in development over his opponent, White sacrifices a second pawn.

| 4. ... | c3xb2 |
| 5. Bc1xb2 | d7-d5! |

By returning one pawn, Black gets a fine game.

| 6. Bc4xd5 | Bf8-b4 + |
| 7. Ke1-f1? | |

7. Nc3 would be preferable, although even then Black would have the better position after 7. ... Bxc3 + 8. Bxc3 Nf6.

| 7. ... | Ng8-f6! |

Black espies the possibility of the back-rank mating pattern shown in Diagram 498.

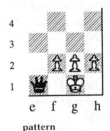
498

pattern

8. Bd5xf7+?

Nor does 8. Qa4 + work, because of 8. ... Nc6 9. Bxc6 + bxc6 10. Qxb4 Qd1 + 11. Qe1 Ba6 +! 12. Ne2 Bxe2 + 13. Kg1 Qxe1#.

(Compare with the pattern in Diagram 498.)

| 8. ... | Ke8xf7 |
| 9. Qd1-b3 + | |

White has played a faulty combination, not having seen Black's mating counterattack.

9. ...	Bc8-e6
10. Qb3xb4	Qd8-d1 +
11. Qb4-e1	Be6-c4 +
12. Ng1-e2	Bc4xe2 +
13. Kf1-g1	Qd1xe1#

499

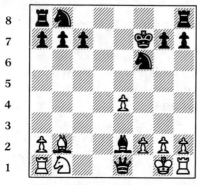

Compare the final position, shown in Diagram 499, with the back-rank mating pattern in Diagram 498.

After sacrificing a pawn in the opening, White was in too much of a hurry to get it back and miscalculated, underestimating Black's threats.

Game 73
Efimov–Bronstein, USSR 1942
King's Gambit

1. e2-e4	e7-e5
2. f2-f4	e5xf4

Black in this game was 17-year-old David Bronstein, who later went on to become one of the strongest players in the world.

3. Ng1-f3	Ng8-f6
4. e4-e5	Nf6-h5
5. Nb1-c3	d7-d6
6. Bf1-c4	d6xe5?

Better would be 6. ... Nc6 7. Qe2 Be6!, with an equal game.

7. Nf3xe5?

White could have gained an advantage by 7. Bxf7+! Kxf7 8. Nxe5+ and 9. Qxh5.

7. ...	Qd8-h4+
8. Ke1-f1	

Not much better would be 8. Ke2, because of 8. ... f3+, when the White King would be in danger.

8. ...	Bc8-e6

500

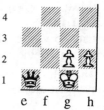

Bronstein has seen the possibility of achieving the back-rank mating pattern shown in Diagram 500 and starts to put together a combination. To begin with, he decides to deflect White's Bishop.

9. Bc4xe6?

White had to play 9. d4 and sacrifice the Exchange with 9. ...Ng3+ 10. Kg1 Nxh1 11. Kxh1.

9. ...	Nh5-g3+
10. Kf1-g1?	

The only way to offer resistance was with 10. hxg3 Qxh1+ 11. Kf2.

10. ...	Bf8-c5+!

Wins by force.

11. d2-d4	Bc5xd4+!

Deflecting the Queen from the first rank and at the same time **decoying** it onto the d4 square.

12. Qd1xd4	Ng3-e2+!

A fork! The Knight is sacrificed, but the road is cleared for the Queen.

13. Nc3xe2?

It is better to lose your Queen than to get mated.

13. ...	Qh4-e1#

501

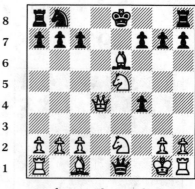

Compare the final position, shown in Diagram 501, with the back-rank mating pattern in Diagram 500. Bronstein sacrificed three (!) pieces, but achieved his aim!

Game 74
Rudnev–Kopylev, USSR 1939
English Opening

1. c2-c4

The mid-19th century English masters used to open their games with this move, hence the opening's name.

1. ...   **Ng8-f6**

2. Nb1-c3   **d7-d5**

Attacking the center.

3. c4xd5   **Nf6xd5**

4. e2-e4   **Nd5-b4**

Black sets a pretty trap: 5. d4? would be followed by 5. ... Qxd4! 6. Qxd4 Nc2+ 7. ... Nxd4, and White would be a pawn down.

5. Qd1-a4 +

An unfortunate move that allows Black to develop his pieces. 5. d3 would have been a better move.

5. ...   **Nb8-c6**

6. d2-d4?

It would have been better to drive away the dangerous Knight by playing 6. a3.

6. ...   **Bc8-d7!**

White had hoped that Black would regale himself on a pawn by playing 6. ... Qxd4, when White would get a fine game after 7. Be3, 8. Rd1 or 8. a3, etc. After the move played in the game White is in considerable difficulties. No defense is visible against the threat of 7. ... Nxd4 8. Qxb4 Nc2+ 9. ... Nxb4.

7. Bf1-b5?

It would have been better to go home with the Queen and give up the pawn: 7. Qd1 Nxd4 8. Bd3, although even then White's position would have been difficult.

7. ...   **Nc6xd4!**

Again the Knight on b4 cannot be captured.

8. Ke1-f1?

The King is so frightened of the fork that it decides to run a bit farther away from the Black Knights. However, White would have done better to first exchange Bishops and Queens and then make a move; not with his King, but with his Rook. After the King move, the master playing Black **sensed a combination.** He **mentally** removed the White Queen and the Knight on c3 from the board and placed his own Queen on d1, and saw that White would be mated as in the back-rank mating pattern in Diagram 502.

502

But for the time being, all this was only a dream.

8. ...   **Nd4xb5**

Freeing the d-file for the Queen.

9. Qa4xb4

9. Nxb5 would not save White, because of 9. ... e5 followed by 10. ... a6, winning the pinned Knight.

9. ...   **e7-e5**

This pawn move opens up the diagonal for the Bishop, which now attacks the Queen. This type of tactical device is known as a "discovered attack."

10. Qb4-c4   **Nb5xc3**

Black's dreams are gradually starting to come true. The White Queen has lost control over d1 and the Knight on c3 has already been eliminated.

11. b2xc3   **a7-a6!**

A good move that at the same time sets a trap!

12. a2-a4?

Only 12. Ke1 could have saved White.

12. ...   **Bd7-b5!!**

White placed his pawn on a4 thinking that the Black Bishop would no longer dare to occupy b5, but . . . the Bishop sacrifices himself.

13. a4xb5

Alas! This is one of those positions in which even the World Champion could not help White!

13. ...   **Qd8-d1#**

503

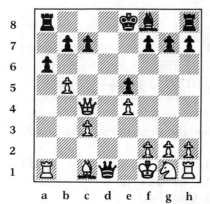

Compare the final position, shown in Diagram 503, with the back-rank mating pattern in Diagram 502. As you can see, Black's dream has come true! The tragedy in this game occurred because the White Queen went travelling in the opening, leaving the King to the mercy of his fate.

Game 75
Caro-Kann Defense

This game was played in a simultaneous exhibition given by Grandmaster Igor Zaitsev in 1970. Zaitsev was White.

1. e2-e4	c7-c6
2. d2-d4	d7-d5
3. e4xd5	c6xd5
4. c2-c4	Ng8-f6
5. Nb1-c3	Nb8-c6
6. Bc1-g5	

So far everything is understandable. Both players have been rapidly bringing out their pieces and fighting for the center.

6. ...   **Qd8-b6?**

A more reliable move would have been 6. ... e6, with the idea of developing the dark-square Bishop and then castling.

7. c4xd5	Nc6xd4

If 7. ... Qxb2, then White obtains a considerably better position after 8. Rc1.

8. Ng1-f3

Even stronger would have been 8. Be3 e5 9. dxe6 Bc5 10. Qa4+ Qc6 11. 0-0-0!.

8. ...	Nd4xf3 +
9. Qd1xf3	Qb6xb2

Finding himself in a difficult position, Black tries to complicate the struggle.

10. Ra1-c1

10. Rb1! would have been stronger. For example, 10. ... Qc2 11. Bb5 + Bd7 12. 0-0, with a huge advantage in development.

10. ...   **Bc8-d7**

11. d5-d6

It may well have been better to play 11. Be2 followed by 12. 0-0.

11. ...   **Ra8-c8?**

Black should have played 11. ... Bc6, with approximately equal chances.

After the move actually played, however, the Grandmaster espied a possibility of mating on the back rank and visualized the pattern shown in Diagram 504.

504

Foreseeing this mating position, White began to set up a combination.

12. Bf1-b5!

White needs the pawn on b7 but it is defended by the Black Queen. So White uses the tactical device of **interference**. The Bishop, by sacrificing itself, interferes with the Queen's action along the b-file.

12. ...   **Bd7xb5**

Allows a spectacular finish. However, on 12. ... Bc6 White could simply castle and remain in an overwhelming position.

13. Qf3xb7!

A double attack forking the Rook and the Bishop. While the Bishop cannot move because it is pinned, the Rook can capture the Knight that White is offering as a sacrifice.

13. ...   **Rc8xc3**

Black has a lost position even though he is up two pieces.

14. d6-d7 + !!

As a preparation for carrying out the idea of a back-rank mate, White must first entice the Black Knight onto the d7 square.

14. ...   **Nf6xd7**

14. ... Bxd7 would be no better, because of 15. Qxb2, while 14. ... Kd8 would be followed by 15. Qc8 + ! Rxc8 16. dxc8Q#.

| 15. Qb7-c8+! | Rc3xc8 |
| 16. Rc1xc8# | |

505

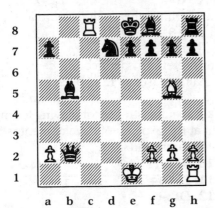

Compare the final position, shown in Diagram 505, with the back-rank mating pattern in Diagram 504.

Black played actively, but chose a faulty plan in the opening. He should have developed his Kingside and not his Queenside. The Grandmaster superbly exploited the weakness of the back rank and taught his opponent a good lesson.

Game 76
Richards–Locock, Correspondence 1975
Two Knights Defense

1. e2-e4	e7-e5
2. Ng1-f3	Nb8-c6
3. Bf1-c4	Ng8-f6

This is the starting position of the Two Knights Defense.

| 4. d2-d4 | e5xd4 |
| 5. 0-0 | |

By sacrificing a pawn, White rapidly brings his pieces into the fray.

| 5. ... | Bf8-c5 |
| 6. e4-e5 | d7-d5 |

A counterattack.

7. e5xf6	d5xc4
8. Rf1-e1 +	Bc8-e6
9. Nf3-g5	Qd8-d5

Not 9. ... Qxf6, because of 10. Nxe6 fxe6 11. Qh5 + 12. Qxc5.

| 10. Nb1-c3 | Qd5-f5 |

Of course 10. ... dxc3 would be bad because of 11. Qxd5.

| 11. g2-g4 | |

An aggressive move.

| 11. ... | Qf5-g6 |

11. ... Qxf6 is considered to be weaker because of 12. Nce4 Qe7 13. Nxe6 fxe6 14. Bg5 Qf8 15. Qe2, with a strong attack.

| 12. Nc3-e4 | |

White would get nothing from 12. fxg7 Rg8 13. Nce4 Be7!.

12. ...	Bc5-b6
13. Ng5xe6	f7xe6
14. f6-f7 + !	

Decoying the King or the Queen onto the f7 square.

| 14. ... | Qg6xf7 |

Not 14. ... Kxf7, because of 15. Ng5 + and 16. Rxe6, catching the Queen.

| 15. Ne4-g5 | Qf7-d7 |
| 16. Ng5xe6 | Nc6-e7? |

Black should have played 16. ... Kf7, removing the King from the e-file with the White Rook on it.

17. Bc1-g5	Ke8-f7
18. Qd1-f3 +	Kf7-g8
19. Bg5xe7	Qd7xe7

After this move White sensed a mating idea and came up with the back-rank mating patterns shown in Diagrams 506 and 507.

506

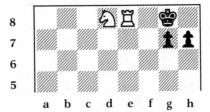

507

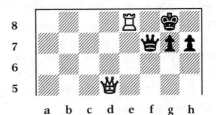

20. Qf3-d5	Qe7-f7?

A mistake. True, Black's position is bad anyway, but he could have offered more resistance with 20.... c6, although after 21. Qxc4 Qf7 22. Re4! White has a decisive attack.

21. Ne6-d8!

A spectacular stroke. 21. ... Qxd5 would be met by 22. Re8# as in Diagram 506.

21. ...	Ra8xd8
22. Qd5xd8 +	Qf7-f8
23. Qd8-d5 +	Qf8-f7
24. Re1-e8#	

508

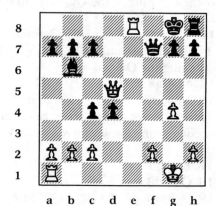

Compare the final position, shown in Diagram 508, with the back-rank mating pattern in Diagram 507.

Both sides played well in the opening, but in the middlegame Black committed an error which was brilliantly exploited by his opponent.

Game 77
Volchok–Kreslavskii, Kiev 1970
Ruy Lopez

1. e2-e4	e7-e5
2. Ng1-f3	Nb8-c6
3. Bf1-b5	a7-a6
4. Bb5xc6	d7xc6

A good move, opening up paths for the Bishop and the Queen. 4. ... bxc6 is not as good.

5. 0-0

5. Nxe5? would be unsatisfactory for White because of 5. ... Qd4 or 5. ...Qg5. In both cases Black would win back his pawn and obtain a good game.

5. ...	f7-f6

Now 6. Nxe5 was already a real threat.

6. d2-d4	Bc8-g4
7. c2-c3	

White defends his center.

7. ...	e5xd4?

A risky continuation. 7. ... Bd6 would be better.

8. c3xd4	Bg4xf3?

Black continues his faulty plan. He should instead play 8. ... Qd7.

9. Qd1xf3!

White prefers to sacrifice the center pawn rather than expose his King by 9. gxf3.

9. ...	Qd8xd4?

Black's opening strategy of playing for material gain at the expense of development is fundamentally unsound.

10. Rf1-d1	Qd4-c4
11. Bc1-f4	Qc4-f7
12. Qf3-g3	

Attacking the pawn on c7 a second time.

12. ...	Bf8-d6

In a difficult position, Black decides to return the pawn but complete his development.

13. Bf4xd6	0-0-0

Black counts on capturing the Bishop on his next move, as it is pinned and cannot move without allowing mate on the first rank. The master playing White thought for a long time here and came up with the pretty back-rank mating pattern shown in Diagram 509.

509

How did this idea arise? The starting point was the observation that if the Rook on d1 were **defended**, the Bishop would be unpinned. So the move 14. Qg4+, defending the Rook on d1, was found. Then the reply 14. ... Qd7 was discovered. And only after that did White see the amazing variation 15. Be7!! Qxg4 16. Rxd8#, as in Diagram 509. However, the immediate 14. Qg4+ would achieve nothing if

Black replied 14. ... f5!. So White first tries to deflect the pawn from f6.

14. e4-e5!

A strong move that at the same time sets an original trap whose point is overlooked by Black.

14. ...　　　　　　　**f6xe5?**

Black had to play 14. ... cxd6, although after 15. exd6 White has the advantage because of his strong passed pawn and his chances for an attack on Black's King.

15. Qg3-g4+　　　　　　**Qf7-d7**

It is difficult to suggest anything better, as Black would anyway be a piece down.

16. Bd6-e7!

Here is the surprise! A very pretty move that could well be overlooked even by a strong player.

16. ...　　　　　　　**Qd7xg4?**

It would, of course, have been better to give up the Queen by playing 16. ... Nxe7, even though Black would have still stood to lose.

17. Rd1xd8#

510

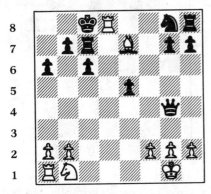

Compare the final position, shown in Diagram 510, with the back-rank mating pattern in Diagram 509.

Black did not apprehend the threat of mate in time and was duly punished.

Game 78
Adams–Torre, New Orleans 1920
Philidor's Defense

1. e2-e4	e7-e5
2. Ng1-f3	d7-d6
3. d2-d4	e5xd4

An unfortunate move that leaves White with a free game. Instead, Black could with no risk have maintained the tension in the center by 3. ... Nf6 4. dxe5 Nxe4 or 3. ... Nbd7.

4. Qd1xd4

It is usually undesirable to bring the Queen out early, but here White plans to answer 4. ... Nc6 by 5. Bb5 and then exchange the Bishop for the Knight.

4. ...	Nb8-c6
5. Bf1-b5	Bc8-d7
6. Bb5xc6	Bd7xc6
7. Nb1-c3	Ng8-f6
8. 0-0	Bf8-e7
9. Nc3-d5	Bc6xd5
10. e4xd5	0-0
11. Bc1-g5	c7-c6?

A faulty plan. Black's position is somewhat cramped, and in such situations a player should not open lines but rather try to exchange some pieces in order to increase the activity of the remaining ones. Consequently, it would have been useful here to make the move 11. ... h6, to be followed by 12. ... Nd7. Although the position then would be favorable for White, Black would nevertheless have every chance of equalizing the game.

12. c2-c4	c6xd5
13. c4xd5	Rf8-e8
14. Rf1-e1	a7-a5
15. Re1-e2	

Vacating e1 for the other Rook.

15. ...　　　　　　　**Ra8-c8?**

For many moves Black has had the opportunity of playing ... h6, attacking the Bishop and at the same time creating an escape hatch for his King. He will have occasion to regret ignoring this possibility.

16. Ra1-e1!

Now 16. ... h6 would already be too late, because of 17. Bxf6 Bxf6 18. Rxe8, winning the Queen.

16. ...　　　　　　　**Qd8-d7**

Connecting the Rooks and intending 17. ... h6 after all.

17. Bg5xf6!!

White has discovered the possibility of a back-rank mate according to the pattern shown in Diagram 511, and starts a deeply thought-out combination.

197

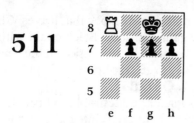

511

17. ...   Be7xf6?

Of course if Black had foreseen the further course of events, he would have played 17. ... gxf6, although even then he would have had a difficult position after 18. h3, threatening 19. Rxe7 Rxe7 20. Rxe7 Qxe7 21. Qg4+ and 22. Qxc8+, remaining a piece up. The immediate 18. Rxe7 would not work because of 18. ... Qxe7! 19. Rxe7 Rc1+ 20. Re1 Rcxe1+ 21. Nxe1 Rxe1# (compare with the back-rank mating pattern in Diagram 512.)

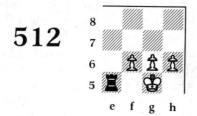

512

18. Qd4-g4!!

The start of a forcing maneuver that will result in one of the Black pieces (the Queen or the Rook on c8) being deflected from the defense of the Rook on e8.

18. ...   Qd7-b5

Declining the present, since if 18. ... Qxg4, then 19. Rxe8+ Rxe8 20. Rxe8#. Now Black is threatening to mate White according to the pattern of Diagram 512: 19. ... Qxe2 20. Rxe2 Rc1+ 21. Re1 Rcxe1+ 22. Nxe1 Rxe1#.

19. Qg4-c4!

Take me, please!

19. ...   Qb5-d7

20. Qc4-c7!

Take, me please! A most interesting situation! The undefended White Queen pursues the Black Queen, depriving it move by move of all the squares on the a4-e8 diagonal.

20. ...   Qd7-b5

21. a2-a4!

Not 21. Qxb7? Qxe2! and it's Black who now

wins: after 22. Qxc8 Qxe1+ 23. Nxe1 Rxc8 he is up a Rook (or 22. Rxe2 Rc1+ 23. Ne1 Rxe1+ 24. Rxe1 Rxe1#, as in the mating pattern of Diagram 512).

21. ...   Qb5xa4

The other variations also lose:

a)   21. ... Rxc7 22. Rxe8+ Qxe8 23. Rxe8# (pattern of Diagram 511);

b)   21. ... Qxe2 22. Rxe2 Rxe2 23. Qxc8+ Re8 24. Qxe8# (pattern of Diagram 511.);

c)   21. ... Rxe2 22. Qxc8+ Qe8 23. Qxe8+ Rxe8 24. Rxe8# (pattern of Diagram 511)

22. Re2-e4!

The chase continues!

22. ...   Qa4-b5

On 22. ... Kf8, 23. Qxd6+ etc. would be decisive, while other moves would lose because of the variations given above.

23. Qc7xb7!

The pursuit has ended. The Black Queen has nowhere left to go, and so Black resigned. The final position is shown in Diagram 513.

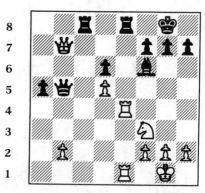

513

In this game you saw a complicated but undoubtedly one of the most beautiful combinations on the theme of back-rank mate. However, if Black had taken care in good time to make an **escape hatch** for his King, we would have been deprived of the opportunity of seeing this chef d'oeuvre.

Game 79
Alekhine (aged 16)—Kenlein,
Moscow 1908
Colle System

1. d2-d4   d7-d5

2. Ng1-f3	Ng8-f6
3. e2-e3	e7-e6
4. Bf1-d3	Nb8-d7
5. Nb1-d2	Bf8-d6

This opening is named after the Belgian master Edgar Colle.

6. e3-e4

Attacking the center and opening a pathway for the dark-square Bishop.

| 6. ... | d5xe4 |

White was threatening the fork 7. e5.

7. Nd2xe4	Nf6xe4
8. Bd3xe4	0-0
9. 0-0	

The player of the White pieces later went on to become the world champion, but at the time of this game he was only sixteen years old.

| 9. ... | f7-f5? |

Black attempts to develop an attack even before completing the development of his Queenside. The pawn on f7 defended the King and the pawn on e6. After Black's move, both e6 and the a2-g8 diagonal have become weak. 9. ... e5 would also have been bad, because of 10. dxe5 Bxe5 11. Nxe5 Nxe5 12. Bxh7+ Kxh7 13. Qh5+ followed by 14. Qxe5, and White is a pawn up. The correct move for Black was 9. ... Nf6, bringing the Knight closer to the King.

| 10. Be4-d3 | e6-e5? |

Here again 10. ... Nf6 would have been better.

11. Bc1-g5!

Decoying the Queen onto the e-file.

| 11. ... | Qd8-e8 |

Even worse would be 11. ... Be7, because of 12. Bxe7 Qxe7 13. Nxe5 Nxe5 14. Re1, with advantage to White.

| 12. d4xe5 | Nd7xe5 |
| 13. Rf1-e1 | |

Pinning the Knight and threatening to win a piece by 14. Nxe5 Bxe5 15. Bf4. At this point Alekhine sensed the possibility of the back-rank mating pattern shown in Diagram 514.

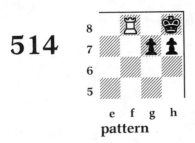

514

pattern

However, to turn this possibility into reality, Black's **help** is needed.

| 13. ... | Qe8-h5?? |

By abandoning the eighth rank, the Queen helps White to turn his plans into reality. Instead, Black must play 13. ... Nxf3+, although White will have a big advantage in development after 14. Qxf3.

14. Nf3xe5!

Preparing a combination.

| 14. ... | Qh5xg5 |

Or else Black would lose a piece.

15. Bd3-c4+

Chasing the King into the corner and clearing the d-file for the Queen.

| 15. ... | Kg8-h8 |

16. Qd1xd6!!

Alekhine could have won the exchange by 16. Nf7+ Rxf7 17. Bxf7 (17. Re8+ does not work because of 17. ... Rf8, the Rook on f8 being defended by the Bishop on d6). However, the weakness of Black's back rank allows White to win more than just the exchange. See Diagram 515 for the final position, after 16. Qd1xd6.

515

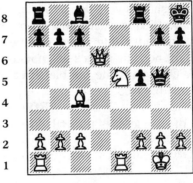

Black resigned, since after 16. ... cxd6 there would have followed 17. Nf7+, and if 17. ... Rxf7, then 18. Re8+ Rf8 19. Rxf8# — the back-rank mating pattern illustrated in Diagram 514. If instead of 17. ... Rxf7, Black plays 17. ... Kg8, he would end up a piece and a pawn down after 18. Nxg5+ (discovered check) 18. ... Kh8 19. Nf7+ Kg8 20. Nxd6+. Playing 13. ... Qh5?, Black did not notice White's combination and lost by force.

Game 80
Martinik–Dobosz, Poland 1973
Sicilian Defense

1. e2-e4	c7-c5
2. f2-f4	e7-e6
3. Ng1-f3	d7-d5
4. Bf1-b5 +	Bc8-d7
5. Bb5xd7 +	Qd8xd7
6. e4xd5	e6xd5
7. 0-0	Nb8-c6
8. d2-d4	Ng8-f6

So far both sides have played well, rapidly bringing out their pieces.

9. b2-b3?

A faulty plan. The Bishop should not abandon the important c1-h6 diagonal. Better would be 9. Ne5 Nxe5 10. fxe5, opening lines for the Bishop and the Rook.

9. ...	c5xd4
10. Bc1-b2	Bf8-c5
11. Kg1-h1	0-0
12. Nf3xd4	Nf6-g4

Threatening a fork with 13. ...Ne3.

13. Nd4xc6

White's position would be bad after 13. Qd2 too: 13. ... Rae8 14. c3 Re4, with the idea of 15. ... Rfe8.

13. ...	b7xc6
14. Qd1-f3?	

Black's Bishop is very dangerous and White should have tried to exchange it off by playing 14. Bd4. Instead White plays a move that is based on the hope that Black will not notice the **trap** 15. Qc3, with the double threat of 16. Qxg7# and 16. Qxc5.

14. ...	Rf8-e8!

Black of course sees through White's trap and makes a good developing move that at the same time sets a counter-trap based on the weakness of the first rank.

15. Qf3-c3?

Expecting only 15. ... Bf8.

15. ...	Ng4-f2 +!

The Rook is deflected from the first rank.

16. Rf1xf2

If 16. Kg1, then the White Queen is lost after 16. ... Ne4 + (discovered check).

16. ...	Bc5-d4!!

A quiet move after which White resigned. See Diagram 516 for the final position.

516

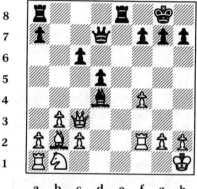

If 17. Qxd4, then after 17. ... Re1 + 18. Rf1 Rxf1 + 19. Qg1 Rxg1 + 20. Kxg1 Black has a Queen for two minor pieces, while if 17. Qd2, Black wins by 17. ... Bxb2 followed by 18. ... Bxa1, finishing a Rook ahead.

Although White managed to avoid mate in this game, the weakness of his back rank cost him a considerable amount of material.

Lesson Eleven

A. Check Lesson 10 Homework (as necessary).

B. *Review Questions*

Find the solutions to Positions 517–522 directly from the diagrams — do not set up the men on a board.

517

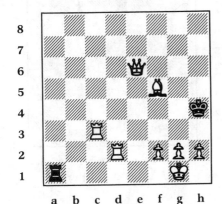

How should the game end?

518

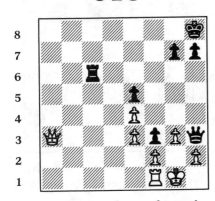

White to move. What would you play?

519

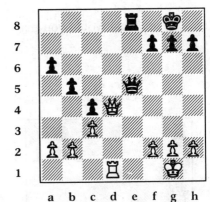

Whoever moves first wins. How?

520

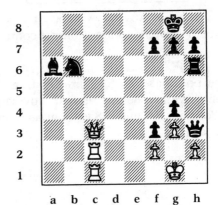

White to move. How should the game end?

521

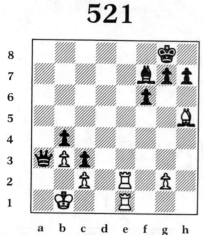

White to move. What would you play?

522

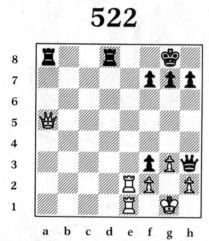

White to move. Find the strongest continuation.

Solve positions 523–526 directly from the diagrams, without setting up and moving the men. Positions 527 and 528 you can set up on a chessboard.

523

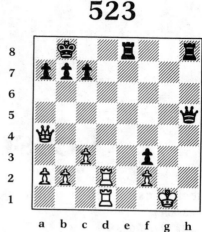

White to play. How should the game end?

524

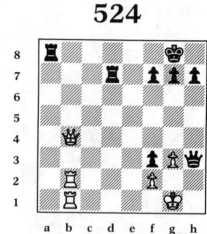

White to play. Who should win?

525

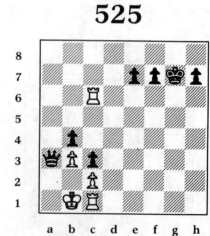

White to play and mate in two moves.

526

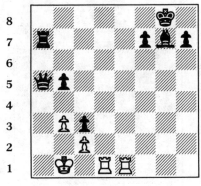

White to play and mate in three moves.

527

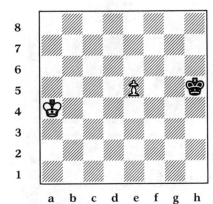

White to play. Can he win?

528

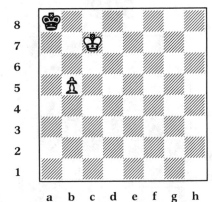

White to play and win.

D-517 White will be mated on the fourth move at the latest:

1. Bf5-b1	Ra1xb1+
2. Rc3-c1	Rb1xc1+
3. Rd2-d1	Rc1xd1+
4. Qe6-e1	Rd1xe1#

A back-rank mate.

D-518 1. Qa3-f8#

1. Qa8+ would not work because of 1. ... Rc8, parrying the check while continuing to threaten 2. ... Qg2#.

D-519 White to play wins by

1. Qd4xe5	Re8xe5
2. Rd1-d8+	Re5-e8
3. Rd8xe8#	

A back-rank mate.

Black to play wins by

1. ...	Qe5-e1+
2. Rd1xe1	Re8xe1#

A back-rank mate.

D-520 White attains victory by sacrificing his Queen:

1. Qc3-c8+!	Ba6xc8
2. Rc2xc8+	Nb6xc8
3. Rc1xc8#	

A back-rank mate.

D-521

1. Re2-e8+!	Bf7xe8
2. Re1xe8#	

A back-rank mate.

D-522

1. Qa5xd8+!

1. Qxa8 does not work because of 1. ... Qg2#.

1. ...	Ra8xd8
2. Re2-e8+	Rd8xe8
3. Re1xe8#	

A back-rank mate.

D-523 White should lose, even if he moves first. 1. Qa4xe8+ does not save him, because of 1. ... Qh5xe8!, defending the last rank against mate. Nor is there any other satisfactory defense against the threat of 1. ... Qh1#.

D-524 Black wins, since White cannot defend himself against the threat of 1. ... Qg2#. If 1. Qb4-b8+, then 1. ... Rd7-d8! (but not 1. ... Rxb8, because of 2. Rxb8+ Rd8 3. Rxd8# — a back-rank mate) 2. Qb8xd8+ (any other move would be followed by 2. ... Qg2#) 2. ... Ra8xd8 3. any move Qh3-g2#.

D-525 1. Rc1-g1 any; 2. Rc6-c8#.

D-526

1. Re1-e8 +	Bg7-f8
2. Rd1-g1 +	Kg8-h8
3. Re8-f8#	

D-527 White wins:

1. Ka4-b5	Kh5-g6
2. Kb5-c6	Kg6-f7
3. Kc6-d7	

and White will queen his pawn by force in three moves.

D-528

1. Kc7-b6!

Careful! After 1. b6 it's stalemate!

1. ...	Ka8-b8
2. Kb6-a6	Kb8-a8
3. b5-b6	Ka8-b8
4. b6-b7	Kb8-c7
5. Ka6-a7	

and White gets a Queen next move.

Typical Mating Combinations
Mate by a Major Piece (Queen or Rook) Helped by Other Men

There are many typical mating patterns, and they often serve as the basis of beautiful combinations. Let us examine the mechanisms involved in such combinations.

To begin with, look at the mating pattern shown in Diagram 529.

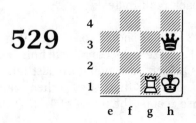

Now find the solutions to Positions 530–533.

530

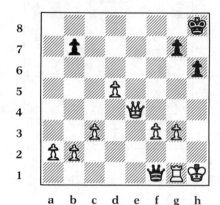

Black to play and mate on his first move.

531

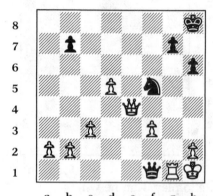

Black to play and mate in two moves.

532

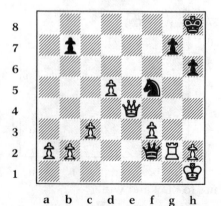

Black to play and mate in three moves.

533

Black to play and mate in four moves.

This position occurred in a game played by Adolph Anderssen, the strongest player of the mid-19th century.

Solutions to D-530 to D-533

D-530   1. ... Qf1-h3#

D-531
1. ...   Nf5-g3 +
Exposing *the White King.*
2. h2xg3   Qf1-h3#

D-532
1. ...   Qf2-f1 +
With the idea of blocking g1 with the Rook and **opening** the f1-h3 line.
2. Rg2-g1   Nf5-g3 +
3. h2xg3   Qf1-h3#

D-533
1. ...   Bh3-g2 +
Deflecting the Rook from the first rank and **freeing** h3 for the Queen.
2. Rg1xg2   Qf2-f1 +
3. Rg2-g1   Nf5-g3 +
4. h2xg3   Qf1-h3#

Thus, Black in Position 533 made a complex combination based on mating pattern 529 and using five different tactical motifs.

Let us look at some other commonly encountered mating patterns and combinations based on them.

Solve positions 535–539 by making use of the mating pattern shown in Diagram 534.

534

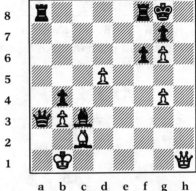

pattern

535

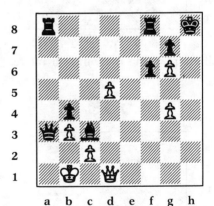

White to play and mate on his first move.

536

White to play and mate in two moves.

537

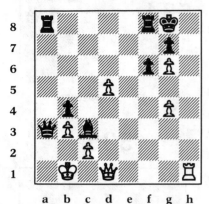

White to play and mate in three moves.

538

White to play and mate in four moves.

539

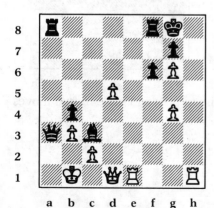

White to play and mate in five moves.

This position is based on a problem published in the year 1512 by P. Damiano, and the type of mating pattern it illustrates is known as Damiano's mate.

Solutions to D-535 to D-539

D-535 1. Qh1-h7# Damiano's mate.

D-536 1. Qd1-h1 + Kh8-g8 2. Qh1-h7# Damiano's mate.

D-537
    1. Rh1-h8 +
Deflecting the King to a square where it can be checked by the Queen, and **clearing the square** h1 for the Queen.

1. ...	Kg8xh8
2. Qd1-h1 +	Kh8-g8
3. Qh1-h7#	

Damiano's mate.

D-538
    1. Re1-h1 +.
Clearing the line for the Queen.

1. ...	Kh8-g8
2. Rh1-h8 +	Kg8xh8
3. Qd1-h1 +	Kh8-g8
4. Qh1-h7#	

Damiano's mate.

D-539
    1. Rh1-h8 +
Deflecting the King to a square where it can be checked and **clearing the square** h1 for the other Rook.

1. ...	Kg8xh8
2. Re1-h1 +	Kh8-g8
3. Rh1-h8 +	Kg8xh8
4. Qd1-h1 +	Kh8-g8
5. Qh1-h7#	

Damiano's mate.

Thus, White in the position of Diagram 539 carries out a complex combination involving three tactical motifs.

Solve positions 541–544 by making use of the mating pattern shown in Diagram 540.

540

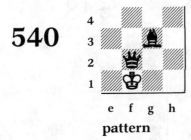

pattern

541

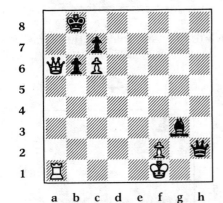

Black to play and mate on his first move.

542

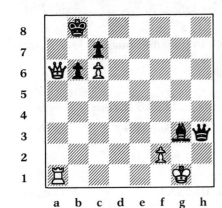

Black to play and mate in two moves.

543

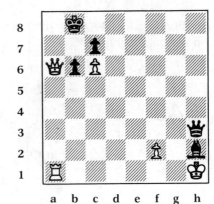

Black to play and mate in three moves.

544

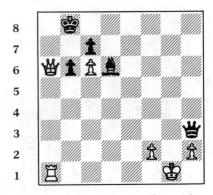

Black to play and mate in four moves.

Solutions to D-541 through D-544.

D-541   1. ... Qh2xf2#

D-542   1. ... Qh3-h2 + 2. Kg1-f1 Qh2xf2#

D-543
1. ...	Bh2-g3 +

Discovered check.
2. Kh1-g1	Qh3-h2 +
3. Kg1-f1	Qh2xf2#

D-544
1. ...	Bd6xh2 +
2. Kg1-h1	Bh2-g3 +
3. Kh1-g1	Qh3-h2 +
4. Kg1-f1	Qh2xf2#

207

The combination in Position 544 is based on the tactical motif of discovered check.

Solve positions 546–549 using the mating pattern shown in Diagram 545.

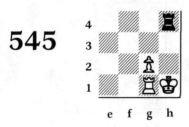

546

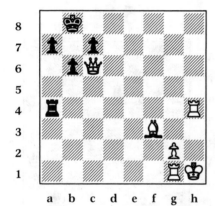

Black to play and mate on his first move.

547

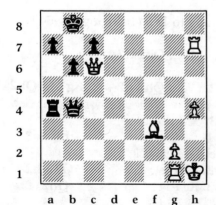

Black to play and mate in two moves.

548

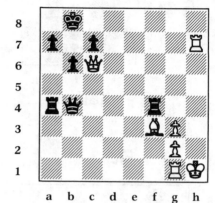

Black to play and mate in three moves.

549

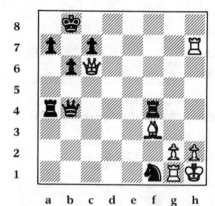

Black to play and mate in four moves.

Solutions to D-546 through D-549

D-546   1. ... Ra4xh4#

D-547
1. ...	Qb4xh4 + !
2. Rh7xh4	Ra4xh4#

D-548
1. ...	Rf4-h4 + !
2. g3xh4	Qb4xh4 + !
3. Rh7xh4	Ra4xh4#

D-549
1. ...	Nf1-g3! +

Exposing the White King.
2. h2xg3	Rf4-h4 + !
3. g3xh4	Qb4xh4 + !
4. Rh7xh4	Ra4xh4#

The combination in Position 549 works with the help of the tactical motif of **exposing the King.**

Solve Positions 551–554 using the mating pattern shown in Diagram 550.

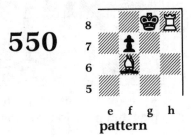

550

pattern

553

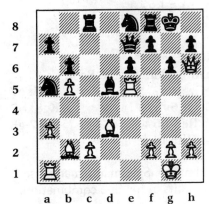

White to play and mate in three moves.

551

White to play and mate on his first move.

554

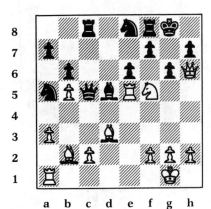

White to play and mate in four moves.

The position in Diagram 554 is from a game won by the outstanding grandmaster Rudolf Spielmann against Henschtscher in Vienna in 1929.

Solutions to D-551 through D-554
D-551   1. Rh5-h8#
D-552
     1. Re5-h5 +
Exploiting the **pin** on the g6 pawn.
     1. ...   Kh7-g8
     2. Rh5-h8#

D-553
     1. Qh6xh7 + !
Exposing the King and **decoying** it to a square where it will be checked.

552

White to play and mate in two moves.

209

```
1. ...                        Kg8xh7
2. Re5-h5 +                   Kh7-g8
3. Rh5-h8#
```

D-554
```
   1. Nf5-e7 + !
```
Clearing a line for the Rook.
```
   1. ...                        Qc5xe7
   2. Qh6xh7 + !                 Kg8xh7
   3. Re5-h5 +                   Kh7-g8
   4. Rh5-h8#
```

Grandmaster Spielmann made use of four tactical motifs in his fine combination.

Solve positions 556–559 using the mating pattern shown in Diagram 555.

557

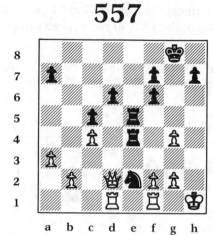

Black to play and mate in two moves.

558

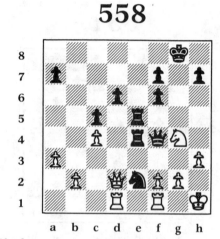

Black to play and either win a piece or mate in three moves.

555

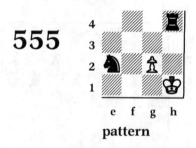

pattern

556

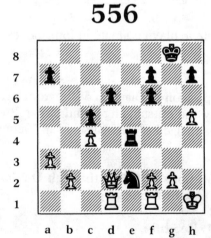

Black to play and mate on his first move.

559

Black to play and either win a piece or mate in four moves.

Position 559 occurred in the game Giuli–Henneberger played in Zurich in 1941. The mating pattern illustrated there is known as "Anastasia's mate" because the idea was first published in the novel *Anastasia and Chess* printed in 1803.

Solutions to D-556 through D-559

D-556
    1. ...   **Re4-h4#**
Anastasia's mate.
D-557
    1. ...   **Re5-h5 + !**
Clearing the line for the other Rook.
    2. g4xh5   **Re4-h4#**

D-558
    1. ...   **Qf4xg4!**
Exposing the King.
    2. h3xg4
2. f3 does not save White, because of 2. ... Ng3+ 3. Kg1 Nxf1 4. fxg4 Nxd2.
    2. ...   **Re5-h5 + !**
    3. g4xh5   **Re4-h4#**

D-559
    1. ...   **Nd4-e2 +**
Decoying the Black King onto the h-file.
    2. Kg1-h1   **Qf4xg4!**
    3. h3xg4
Or else White loses a piece.
    3. ...   **Re5-h5 + !**
    4. g4xh5   **Re4-h4#**
Black exploited three tactical motifs in this combination.

Endgames with King and non-Rook Pawn vs. King
(Continuation. For beginning, see Lesson 10)

In this lesson we shall study examples in which the pawn is unable to queen and the game ends in a draw.

560

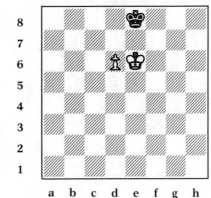

Drawn only if it is White's turn.

561

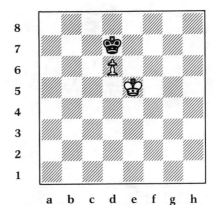

Drawn no matter who moves first.

562

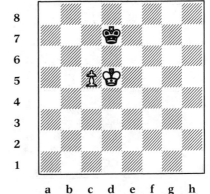

Drawn no matter who moves first.

563

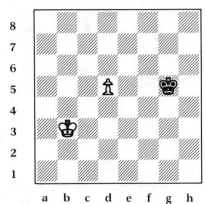

Drawn only if it is Black's turn.

564

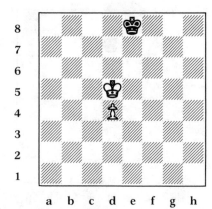

Drawn only if it is Black's turn.

565

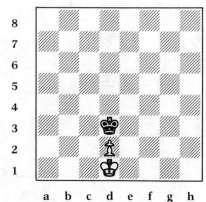

Drawn no matter who moves first.

Analysis of D-560 through D-565

D-560 The Kings are in opposition and the position is one of mutual Zugzwang: it is disadvantageous both for White and for Black to make the first move. If Black begins, he loses, since the White pawn will reach the seventh rank **without checking:**

1. ...	Ke8-d8
2. d6-d7	Kd8-c7

There is no other move. Black is thus forced to give up control over e7.

3. Ke6-e7

and White wins.

With White to play, the position is drawn, since the pawn reaches the seventh rank **with check:**

1. d6-d7 +

Or else Black will draw with 1. ... Kd7 (see the next example).

1. ...	Ke8-d8
2. Ke6-d6	stalemate

Conclusion: If the pawn, defended by its King, reaches the seventh rank with check, the game is drawn; otherwise, it will be able to queen.

D-561 This is a theoretically drawn position. However, Black has to know how to maneuver correctly with his King, since the slightest mistake will lead to a loss. The Black King should shuttle back and forth between d7 and d8 and occupy c8 or e8 **only** when by doing so it takes the opposition. For example:

1. Ke5-d5	Kd7-d8!

Waiting for White's next move. Otherwise Black would lose the opposition and the game:
a) 1. ... Ke8 2. Ke6! Kd8 3. d7 Kc7 4. Ke7 etc.; or
b) 1. ... Kc8 2. Kc6!, winning.

2. Kd5-c5

Trying to confuse the opponent.

2. ...	Kd8-d7!

Again the only move.

3. Kc5-d5	Kd7-d8!

The only way.

4. Kd5-c6	Kd8-c8!

Taking the opposition.

5. d6-d7 +	Kc8-d8
6. Kc6-d6	stalemate

If he moves first in the above example (Diagram 561), Black defends in the same way:

1. ...	Kd7-d8!
2. Ke5-d5	Kd8-d7!

and so on.

Conclusion: If the lone King can take the opposition on the eighth rank when the enemy King and pawn are on the sixth rank, the game is always drawn.

D-562 Having the opposition is not of decisive importance in this position since Black will have the opportunity of taking the opposition on the last rank, as in the previous example.

1. c5-c6 +	Kd7-c7!

1. ... Kc8 2. Kd6 Kd8!, taking the opposition, also leads to a draw. All other moves lose, since they allow White to take the opposition with the Black King on the last rank:

a) 1. ... Kd8 2. Kd6! Kc8 3. c7 Kb7 4. Kd7 any 5. c8Q;
b) 1. ... Ke8 2. Ke6! Kd8 3. Kd6!, etc.;
c) 1. ... Ke7 2. Ke5! Ke8 3. Ke6! Kd8 4. Kd6!, with a familiar position.

2. Kd5-c5	Kc7-c8!
3. Kc5-b5	Kc8-c7!
4. Kb5-c5	Kc7-c8!
5. Kc5-d6	Kc8-d8!
6. c6-c7 +	Kd8-c8
7. Kd6-c6	stalemate

Black to move draws in the following manner:

1. ...	Kd7-c7!

The only move to draw. All other moves lose:

a) 1. ... Kc8 2. Kc6! Kb8 3. Kd7 and the pawn cannot be stopped;
b) 1. ... Kd8 2. Kd6! Kc8 3. Kc6 etc.;
c) 1. ... Ke8 (or 1. ... Ke7) 2. Kc6! Kd8 3. Kb7 and the pawn will queen.

2. c5-c6	Kc7-c8!
3. Kd5-d6	Kc8-d8!
4. c6-c7 +	Kd8-c8

with a draw.

Conclusion: If the pawn is no further than the fifth rank, then the lone King draws whether it has the first move or not, provided that it is in front of the pawn and there is no more than one square separating it from the pawn.

D-563 We already know that a King can hold back an enemy pawn if it can get in **front** of the pawn, but **not from the side.** So the Black King here must try to go round to the front of the pawn:

1. ...	Kg5-f6!

1. ... Kf5 loses because of 2. Kc4 Ke5 3. Kc5, when the pawn will queen easily.

2. Kb3-c4	Kf6-e7
3. Kc4-c5	Ke7-d7!

Just in time! Now it's a draw.

4. d5-d6	Kd7-d8!
5. Kc5-c6	Kd8-c8!
6. d6-d7 +	Kc8-d8
7. Kc6-d6	stalemate

If White has the first move, he wins as follows:

1. Kb3-c4	Kg5-f6
2. Kc4-c5	Kf6-e7
3. Kc5-c6!	

The King has reached the sixth rank ahead of the pawn. This is always a win.

3. ...	Ke7-d8
4. Kc6-d6!	Kd8-c8
5. Kd6-e7	

and the pawn will queen in three more moves.

D-564 It goes without saying that White to move can win easily in a number of ways, e.g.:

1. Kd5-e6	Ke8-d8
2. Ke6-d6	Kd8-e8
3. Kd6-c7	

and the pawn will advance unhindered to its queening square.

However, Black can draw if he has the first move:

1. ...	Ke8-d7!

The saving move! Black seizes the opposition.

2. Kd5-e5	Kd7-e7!

Keeping the opposition. All other moves would lose:

a) 2. ... Kc6 3. Ke6 Kc7 4. d5 Kd8 5. Kd6! etc.;
b) 2. ... Kc7 3. Ke6 Kc6 4. d5 + Kc7 5. Ke7 and the pawn will queen;
c) on any other second move by Black, White wins easily by 3. Kd6.

3. d4-d5	

White cannot break through with his King and has to push his pawn. If 3. Kf5, Black draws by 3. ... Kf7 or 3. ... Kd6.

3. ...	**Ke7-d7!**

Again the only move. Any other move would lose to 4. Kd6.

4. d5-d6	**Kd7-d8!**

Once again the only drawing move. Black fights for the opposition. Any other move would allow White to win by 5. Ke6.

5. Ke5-d5

White tries to confuse his opponent. On 5. Ke6 Black would take the opposition by 5. ... Ke8, after which the draw is inevitable.

5. ...	**Kd8-d7!**

The only way!

6. Kd5-c5

Maybe Black will blunder?

6. ...	**Kd7-d8!**

Black maneuvers his King correctly and gets the draw.

7. Kc5-c6	**Kd8-c8!**

Black has won the opposition.

8. d6-d7 +	**Kc8-d8**
9. Kc6-d6	**stalemate**

Conclusion: If the lone King is in front of the pawn, but not on the last rank, and gets the opposition against the enemy King, the game is drawn provided that the pawn does not have any spare moves, i.e., if the enemy King is on the square directly in front of its pawn.

D-565 Finally, let us see how to fight against a pawn that is on its starting square. In Diagram 565, the Black King has occupied the square in front of the White pawn and prevents the latter from moving. However, the King cannot remain on this square forever since it will have to retreat when it is Black's turn to move. Then the pawn will be able to advance, supported by the White King, but if Black maneuvers correctly with his King, he should draw. Otherwise, he will lose. It does not matter whose turn it is in Diagram 565; let us suppose that it is White's turn:

1. Kd1-c1

A waiting move that transfers the obligation to move to Black. 1. Ke1 would also be possible.

1. ...	**Kd3-d4!**

Although in the present position it is not of crucial importance where the King moves to (except of course 1. ... Ke2, when the reply 2. d4 puts the pawn out of reach), **you should develop the habit of retreating along the file on which the pawn stands.**

2. Kc1-c2

Controlling d3.

2. ...	**Kd4-c4!**

Taking the opposition and hindering the advance of the White King. All other moves would lose, since the White King would **get the opposition in front of its pawn.**

3. d2-d3 +	**Kc4-d4**
4. Kc2-d2	**Kd4-d5**
5. Kd2-e3	**Kd5-e5!**
6. d3-d4 +	**Ke5-d5**
7. Ke3-d3	**Kd5-d6**
8. Kd3-c4	**Kd6-c6!**
9. d4-d5 +	**Kc6-d6**
10. Kc4-d4	**Kd6-d7**
11. Kd4-e5	**Kd7-e7!**
12. d5-d6 +	**Ke7-d7!**
13. Ke5-d5	**Kd7-d8!**
14. Kd5-c6	**Kd8-c8!**
15. d6-d7 +	**Kc8-d8**
16. Kc6-d6	**stalemate**

As you can see, in order to play pawn endgames well you have to know how to make use of **tactical devices** such as the **opposition, waiting move, Zugzwang,** etc. You also have to know inside out (like a multiplication table) which positions are won and which are drawn.

You have now worked through Level II (Intermediate I) of our chess training program. The next, and last, lesson will be a test. Twenty tests of equal difficulty, each containing six questions, have been prepared. Each student will pick one at random and answer all six questions on it. The test will show how well you have mastered the contents of the course.

HOMEWORK

1. Review the homework assignments of previous lessons.
2. Play often, but not more than one and a half hours a day.
3. Familiarize yourself with the typical mating patterns shown in Diagrams 566–601. These involve a major piece (Queen or Rook) assisted by other pieces and pawns.
4. Make up positions in which White (or Black) can make a two-move combination leading to these typical mating patterns.

566

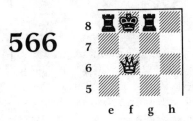

567

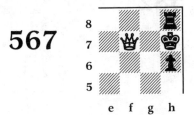

568

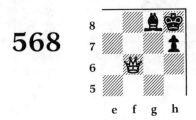

569

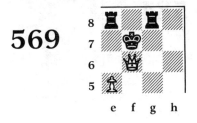

570

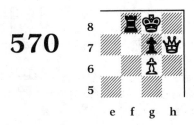

571

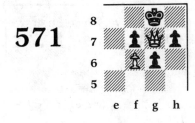

572

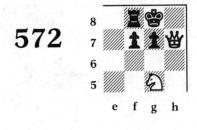

573

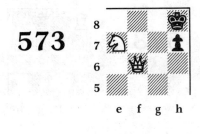

574

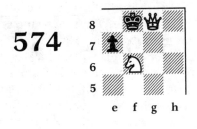

575

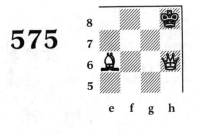

576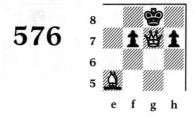

577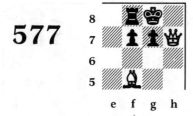

578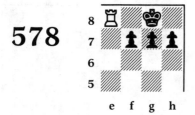

579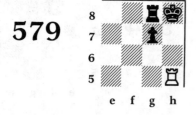

580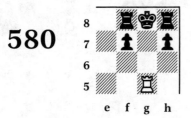

581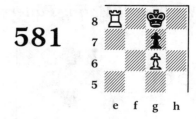

582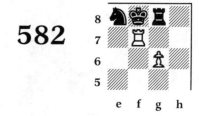

583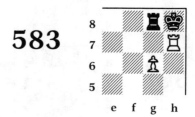

584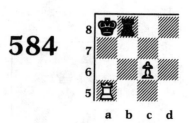

585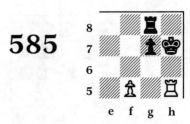

586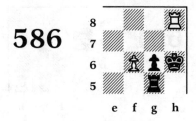

591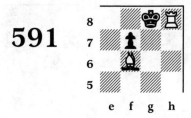

587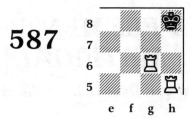

592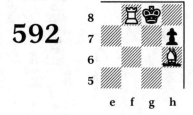

588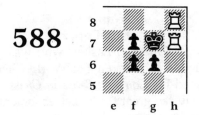

593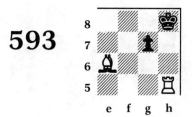

589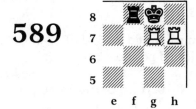

594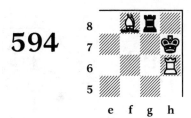

590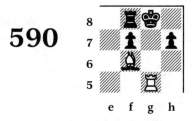

595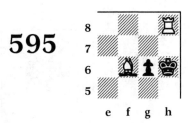

596

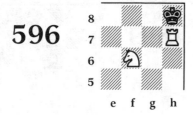

601

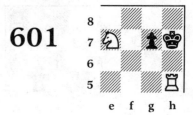

597

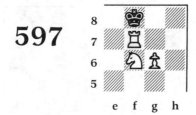

SUPPLEMENTARY MATERIAL

for use at the teacher's discretion

Sample Games Illustrating Typical Major Piece (Queen or Rook) Mating Patterns

Game 81
Ruy Lopez

In 1895 Emanuel Lasker, who was just beginning his 27-year reign as World Champion, published his *Common Sense in Chess*, a book that acquired great fame. Let us look at an interesting game from that book.

1. e2-e4	**e7-e5**
2. Ng1-f3	**Nb8-c6**
3. Bf1-b5	**Ng8-f6**
4. 0-0!	**Nf6xe4**
5. Rf1-e1	

598

Stronger would be 5. d4 Be7 6. Qe2, with a complicated position.

5. ...   **Ne4-d6**

5. ... Nf6 6. Nxe5 Be7 7. d4 0-0 8. Nc3 would be to White's advantage.

6. Nb1-c3

Since Black cannot defend the pawn on e5, White is in no rush to capture it and instead develops a piece.

6. ...   **Nd6xb5**

It was more important to block the e-file by playing 6. ... Be7.

7. Nf3xe5!

Luring Black into a clever trap. White does not hurry to capture the Knight on b5 since Black does not have time to save it. The threat is to win Black's Queen by means of the **discovered check** 8. Nxc6+.

599

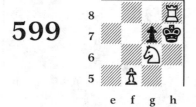

600

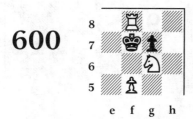

7. ...   **Nc6xe5?**

It was still not too late to play 7. ... Be7, preventing the discovered check and preparing to castle. 7. ...Nxc3 would lose after 8. Nxc6+ Be7 9. Nxe7 Nxd1 10. Ng6+ (another discovered check) 10. ... Qe7 11. Nxe7, when White remains a piece up.

8. Re1xe5+   **Bf8-e7**
9. Nc3-d5!

White could capture the Knight with his Rook or his Knight but prefers to pile up on the pinned Bishop, which cannot be defended.

9. ...   **0-0**

Trying to get his King out of danger.

10. Nd5xe7+   **Kg8-h8**

If White looks at the position closely, he can see five possible mating patterns (see Diagrams 602–606).

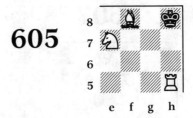

605

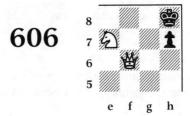

606

11. Qd1-h5!

Threatening 12. Qxh7+ Kxh7 13. Rh5# (Anastasia's mate, Diagram 602). White could also win with 11. Nxc8 Nd4 12. Ne7 Re8 13. c3, remaining a piece up.

11. ...   **g7-g6**

A pretty variation is 11. ... h6 12. d3! d6 13. Bxh6 gxh6 14. Qxh6# (Diagram 604). If instead of 13. ... gxh6, Black replied to 13. Bxh6 with 13. ...g6, then 14. Bxf8+! gxh5 15. Rxh5# (Diagram 605). White's attack is irresistible in other variations as well.

12. Qh5-h6   **d7-d6**

There is already no satisfactory defense for Black.

13. Re5-h5!

Threatening 14. Qxh7# (Diagram 603).

13. ...   **g6xh5**
14. Qh6-f6#

The mating pattern shown in Diagram 606. See Diagram 607 for the final position.

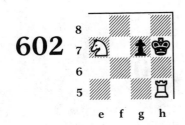

602

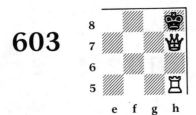

603

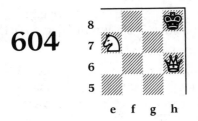

604

607

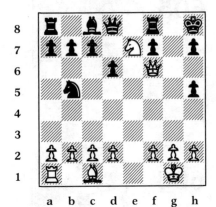

A beautiful game, made up by World Champion Lasker especially for instructional purposes.

Game 82
Giuoco Piano

Gioachino Greco, an early 17th century Italian chessplayer, left behind a manuscript containing analyses of many opening variations used in his time. This game is one of the analyses.

1. e2-e4	**e7-e5**
2. Ng1-f3	**Nb8-c6**
3. Bf1-c4	**Bf8-c5**
4. c2-c3	**Ng8-f6**

All these moves are encountered even today in the games of chessplayers of all levels.

5. Nf3-g5?

The best move is 5. d4, but 5. d3 is also possible. As you can see, 350 years ago players sometimes ignored the main principles of opening play and moved the same piece twice in the opening.

5. ...	**0-0**
6. d2-d3	**h7-h6?**

Black was not faced with any threat and should have continued his development by means of the move 6. ... d6.

7. h2-h4	**h6xg5??**

There is no rule in chess that says that capturing is obligatory! With this capture Black only furthers White's aggressive designs. 7. ... d6 should still have been played.

8. h4xg5	**Nf6-h7?**

We like to capture pieces but are not so eager to give them back! Black had to play 8. ... g6,

maintaining control over h5.

9. Qd1-h5

Various mating patterns are in the air (see Diagrams 608-610).

9. ...	**Rf8-e8**

Planning to answer 10. Qxh7+ with 10. ... Kf8. 9. ... Nxg5 would not save Black, because of 10. Qh8# (back-rank mate, Diagram 609), while any other move would run up against 10. Qxh7# (Diagram 608).

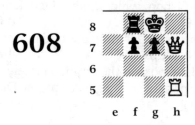

608

609

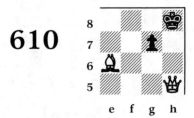

610

10. Qh5xf7+	**Kg8-h8**
11. Rh1xh7+!	**Kh8xh7**
12. Qf7-h5#	

The mating pattern of Diagram 610. The final position is shown in Diagram 611.

611

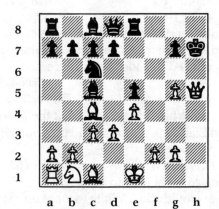

This is the famous Greco's Mate. This analysis shows the great danger of a coordinated attack by the Queen and a Rook along the open h-file.

Game 83
Reiner–Steinitz, Vienna 1860
Scotch Gambit

1. e2-e4	e7-e5
2. Ng1-f3	Nb8-c6

The Black pieces were conducted by a great player who in 1886 became the first official World Champion in chess history.

3. d2-d4	e5xd4
4. Bf1-c4	

This opening is a gambit as White strives to develop his pieces rapidly rather than recapture his pawn immediately.

4. ...	Bf8-c5

Black develops and defends the pawn at the same time. 4. ... Bb4+ would be risky due to 5. c3 dxc3 6. 0-0 cxb2 7. Bxb2, with a considerable advantage in development for White.

5. 0-0	d7-d6

5. ... Nge7 would be a mistake because of 6. Ng5 Ne5 7. Bb3 h6 8. f4 hxg5 9. fxe5, with an irresistible attack for White. Downright bad after 6. Ng5 would be 6. ... 0-0, because of 7. Qh5 h6 8. Nxf7, with a quick victory in sight.

6. c2-c3	Bc8-g4!

Black aims for a counter-attack. 6. ... dxc3 7. Nxc3 would give White good play.

7. Qd1-b3	

A fork: both the b7 pawn and the f7 pawn are attacked. This would be fine if it didn't lead to White's own King becoming exposed.

7. ...	Bg4xf3!

Ignoring White's threats.

8. Bc4xf7 +	Ke8-f8
9. Bf7xg8	Rh8xg8
10. g2xf3	

Let us evaluate the position that has arisen. By giving back the pawn, Black has achieved excellent development and has good chances for an attack against White's weakened King.

10. ...	g7-g5!

Energetically played! There is no time to protect the pawn on b7.

11. Qb3-e6	

After 11. Qxb7 Ne5 White would find it very difficult to defend his King.

11. ...	Nc6-e5
12. Qe6-f5 + ?	

Weak players love to check. But it is better to checkmate once than to check 1000 times. Here White should have played 12. Kh1 and then tried to develop his Queenside.

12. ...	Kf8-g7!

A clever move! 13. Bxg5 is to be met by 13. ... Kh8!, when the White Bishop would be caught in a dangerous pin.

13. Kg1-h1	Kg7-h8
14. Rf1-g1	

White will pay a heavy price for forgetting about his Queenside. He had to play 14. cxd4 Bxd4 15. Nc3 g4 16. Bf4, bringing out his pieces at the cost of a pawn.

14. ...	g5-g4!

Clearing the way for the Queen and anticipating the mating patterns shown in Diagrams 612 and 613.

15. f3-f4?	

The best chance was 15. Bf4. 15. fxg4 would have been met by 15. ... Qh4, threatening 16. ... Raf8.

15. ...	Ne5-f3
16. Rg1xg4	

White does not sense the danger.

16. ...	Qd8-h4!!

Take me, please! The threat is 17. ... Qxh2 mate (Diagram 612).

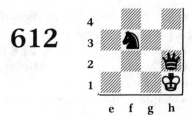

612

17. Rg4-g2

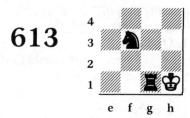

613

White doesn't like the idea of getting mated 17. Rxh4 Rg1# (Diagram 613).

17. ...   **Qh4xh2 + !**

Forcing White to accept the Queen sacrifice!

18. Rg2xh2   **Rg8-g1#**

614

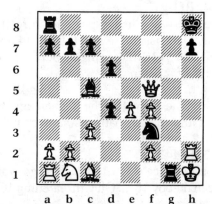

A beautifully played game by the World Champion. As for White, he got mated before he got around to making a single move with his Queenside pieces.

Game 84
Koshtenko–Lerner, Soviet Union 1962
French Defense

1. e2-e4	e7-e6
2. d2-d4	d7-d5

These moves constitute the French Defense.

3. Nb1-c3	Bf8-b4
4. Ng1-e2	

White sacrifices the pawn on e4. Former World Champion Alexander Alekhine sometimes utilized this idea with success.

4. ...	d5xe4
5. a2-a3	Bb4xc3 +

Or else White would win back the pawn on e4 and Black's 3. ... Bb4 would turn out to have been pointless.

6. Ne2xc3	Ng8-f6?

Black could hold onto the pawn with 6. ... f5, but that would allow White to whip up a strong attack after 7. f3! exf3 8. Qxf3 Qxd4 9. Qg3!. It is better to give back such pawns and instead concentrate on developing your pieces quickly. Here, for example, after 6. ... Nc6 7. Bb5 Ne7 8. Nxe4 0-0 9. c3 e5! the game is equal.

7. Bc1-g5!

White not only wins back his pawn but also pins the Knight on f6, a pin which will be very unpleasant for Black as he has already exchanged off his dark-square Bishop.

7. ...	Nb8-c6
8. Bf1-b5	

Pinning the other Knight.

8. ...	0-0

If 8. ... Bd7, then 9. Nxe4, which cannot be met by 9. ... Nxd4 because of 10. Bxf6 gxf6 11. Bxd7 + Qxd7 12. Nxf6 +, winning the Queen.

9. Bb5xc6	b7xc6
10. Nc3xe4	

White has won back his pawn and it is not obvious how Black can unpin his Knight.

10. ...	Qd8-d5

It is on this move that Black had placed his hopes. Realizing that his position is difficult, he decides to take a risk.

11. Ne4xf6 +

White sees that the Pillsbury mating pattern (Diagram 615) is a possibility and begins to prepare a combination.

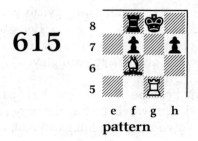

615

pattern

11. ...   **g7xf6**

Forced.

12. Bg5xf6   **Qd5xg2?**

A fatal mistake! Black has to play 12. ... Qf5, trying to chase away White's dangerous Bishop. However, he thinks that White will save his Rook with 13. Rf1, whereupon after 13. ... Ba6 it would be White who is in trouble.

13. Qd1-f3!!

Now there's a move for you! Black resigned right away. The Queen cannot be taken because of Pillsbury's mate (Diagram 615): 13. ... Qxf3 14. Rg1+ Qg4 15. Rxg4#. And after 13. ... Qg6 14. 0-0-0 Qh6+ 15. Kb1 White wins easily too. See Diagram 616 for the final position.

616

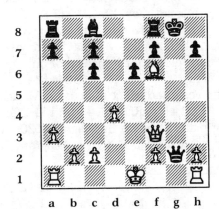

Black lost because of the dangerous pin on the f6 Knight, while the final catastrophe occurred because he did not notice Pillsbury's mate.

Game 85
(from under-13 tournament)

1. d2-d4   **Ng8-f6**

The Knight controls e4, preventing the White e-pawn from moving there.

2. Nb1-d2?

An unfortunate move that blocks the Bishop and Queen. 2. c4 or 2. Nf3 are better.

2. ...   **e7-e5**

Black sacrifices a pawn in the hopes of rapidly bringing out his pieces.

3. d4xe5   **Nf6-g4**

4. Ng1-f3   **Bf8-e7**

4. ... Nc6 would be more accurate, but Black

was tempted by the trap from the game Gibeau–Lazard (Game 6), and plays 4. ... Be7 in anticipation of the mating pattern shown in Diagram 617.

617

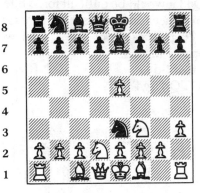

5. h2-h3??

It was this "natural" move that Black was counting on. Instead of hurrying to chase away the Knight, White could have got a good game after 5. e3 Nc6 6. Nc4 b5 7. Ncd2 a6 8. a4.

5. ...   **Ng4-e3!**

White resigned. He had not taken Black's last move into account in his earlier calculations. If 6. fxe3 (otherwise the Queen is lost), then 6. ... Bh4+ 7. Nxh4 Qxh4+ 8. g3 Qxg3# (see the mating pattern of Diagram 617). The final position is shown in Diagram 618.

618

White was routed because of his carelessness.

Game 86
Mayet–Anderssen, Berlin 1851
Ruy Lopez

1. e2-e4   **e7-e5**

2. Ng1-f3   **Nb8-c6**

Black was Adolph Anderssen, a German

master who was the strongest player in the world in the middle of the nineteenth century.

3. Bf1-b5	**Bf8-c5**
4. c2-c3	**Ng8-f6**
5. Bb5xc6?	

This exchange only helps Black to bring out his Bishop. 5. d4 is better.

5. ...	**d7xc6**
6. 0-0	**Bc8-g4**
7. h2-h3	

It would be safer to play 7. d3 followed by 8. Be3, trying to exchange off the dark-square Bishops.

7. ...	**h7-h5**

Anderssen sacrifices the Bishop in order to open the h-file. Feeling more at home in complications than his opponents, Anderssen often took risks.

8. h3xg4	**h5xg4**
9. Nf3xe5?	

When you have a material advantage you should try to exchange pieces. It was better therefore to play 9. d4 exd4 10. Nxd4.

9. ...	**g4-g3?**

It is easy to make a mistake in such sharp positions. 9. ... Nxe4! is stronger. This cannot be met by 10. Qxg4 since after 10. ... Bxf2+! 11. Rxf2 Rh1+!! 12. Kxh1 Nxf2+ 13. Kg1 Nxg4 14. Nxg4 Qd3 it would be difficult for White to develop his Queenside pieces. Even worse would be 10. Nxg4 because of 10. ... Qh4 with an unstoppable mate.

10. d2-d4	**Nf6xe4**
11. Qd1-g4?	

White sees that the mating pattern of Diagram 619 is a possibility: the move 11. Qd1-g4 is directed against the threat of 11. ...Rh1+! 12. Kxh1 Qh4+ 13. Kg1 Qh2#. However, a better defense was 11. fxg3! Nxg3 12. Re1, eliminating all of Black's threats.

11. ...	**Bc5xd4?**

Both adversaries have overlooked a typical tactical device: 11. ... gxf2+ 12. Rxf2 Rh1+! 13. Kxh1 Nxf2+ followed by 14. ... Nxg4, when White has only two minor pieces for his Queen. Anderssen was tempted by the mating pattern shown in diagram 620.

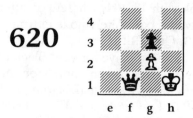

12. Qg4xe4?	

The last mistake. It was necessary to play 12. cxd4, intending to reply to 12. ... Qxd4 with 13. Qd7+, with complicated play. Black would do better to instead play 12. ... gxf2+ 13. Rxf2 Rh1+ 14. Kxh1 Nxf2+ 15. Kg1 Nxg4, winning the Queen, although now he has had to give up three minor pieces for it instead of only two.

12. ...	**Bd4xf2+!**

White resigned, since mate is unavoidable: 13. Rxf2 Qd1+ 14. Rf1 Rh1+! 15. Kxh1 Qxf1# (mating pattern shown in Diagram 620). The final game position is shown in Diagram 621.

Both players made mistakes in this game, but it was White who made the last mistake and as a result fell victim to a beautiful mate.

Game 87
Rieman–Anderssen, Germany 1876
King's Gambit

1. e2-e4   **e7-e5**

Black was played by the strongest chess-player of the mid-19th century.

2. f2-f4

This gambit was very popular in those times.

2. ...   **e5xf4**

3. Bf1-c4   **Qd8-h4 +**

4. Ke1-f1

White has lost his right to castle but in compensation he has gained the center and can develop his pieces more quickly. The game is equal.

4. ...   **d7-d5!**

Black is willing to give back the pawn in order to gain a **tempo** for developing his pieces.

5. Bc4xd5   **Ng8-f6**

6. Nb1-c3   **Bf8-b4**

7. e4-e5

The idea of this pawn sacrifice is to keep the Black King in the center and whip up an attack.

7. ...   **Bb4xc3**

8. e5xf6   **Bc3xf6**

9. Ng1-f3   **Qh4-h5**

10. Qd1-e2 +

It was for the sake of this check that White sacrificed a pawn on the seventh move.

10. ...   **Ke8-d8!**

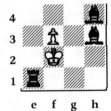

622

pattern

623

pattern

Anderssen visualizes several potential mating patterns (Diagrams 622 and 623) and begins to set up a combination. That is why he frees e8 for his Rook.

11. Qe2-c4   **Rh8-e8**

A trap! In order to see it, you don't necessarily have to be a very strong player, but all the same it is Queen sacrifices that are the most often overlooked.

12. Bd5xf7?

White had to play 12. d3, with a good game. Instead, he gets mated in five moves.

12. ...   **Qh5xf3 + !**

Exposing the King and **deflecting** the pawn on g2 from control of h3. At the same time, the Knight controlling e1 is eliminated — this tactical motif is known as "eliminating the defense." Anderssen thus makes use of three tactical motifs in one move.

13. g2xf3   **Bc8-h3 +**

14. Kf1-f2

Or 14. Kg1 Re1 + 15. Kf2 Bh4# (Mating pattern of Diagram 622).

14. ...   **Bf6-h4 +**

15. Kf2-g1   **Re8-e1 +**

16. Qc4-f1   **Re1xf1#**

The mating pattern of Diagram 623. The final position is shown in Diagram 624.

624

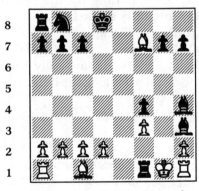

White lost because he "fell into" Black's combination.

Game 88
Sanchez–Sotolareya, Mexico 1948
Veresov's Opening

1. d2-d4	Ng8-f6
2. Bc1-g5	d7-d5
3. Nb1-c3	

These moves constitute Veresov's Opening, named after a Soviet master.

3. ...	c7-c5
4. d4xc5	

A risky move. It would be better to play 4. e3 and develop the Kingside as soon as possible.

4. ...	d5-d4
5. Bg5xf6	e7xf6

Opening a diagonal for the Bishop.

6. Nc3-e4	Bc8-f5

The opening has given Black the upper hand — he can bring out his pieces quickly.

7. Ne4-d6 +	

White decides to return the pawn in order to exchange off the dark-square Bishops.

7. ...	Bf8xd6
8. c5xd6	Qd8xd6
9. Ng1-f3	Nb8-c6

Black has completed his development and is ready to castle on either side, while the White King, on the other hand, will be stuck in the center for a long time.

10. c2-c3	

It would be better to play 10. a3, controlling the b4 square. **Opening up the position is advantageous only to the better-developed side** (in this case, Black).

10. ...	0-0-0

By castling, Black automatically brings his Rook into the attack along the d-file.

11. c3xd4?	

It would be better to play 11. Nxd4 and try to exchange Queens.

11. ...	Qd6-b4 + !

This **in-between** check was underestimated by White. Black on the other hand visualizes two mating patterns (Diagrams 625 and 626).

625

626

12. Qd1-d2	Nc6xd4!

Now White cannot play 13. Qxb4 because of 13. ... Nc2# (mating pattern of Diagram 625).

13. Ra1-c1 + ??	

White had to play 13. Nxd4 and exchange Queens.

13. ...	Nd4-c2 + !!
14. Rc1xc2 +	Bf5xc2
15. Qd2xb4	Rd8-d1#

The mating pattern of Diagram 626. The final position is shown in Diagram 627.

627

White was severely punished for not getting around to developing his Knights.

Game 89
Ezerskii–Lel'chuk, Soviet Union 1950
King's Gambit

1. e2-e4	e7-e5
2. f2-f4	

The aim of this pawn sacrifice is to develop as speedily as possible and open up the f-file for the Rook.

2. ...	Nb8-c6
3. Ng1-f3	d7-d6
4. f4xe5?	

4. d4, attacking the central pawn on e5, is better.

4. ...	Nc6xe5?

Why give up the center? After 4. ... dxe5, opening lines for the dark-square Bishop and the Queen, Black would have a fine game.

5. d2-d4	

White now has a strong pawn center.

5. ...	Ne5-g6?

Black should not lose time by retreating the Knight. It would be better to play 5. ... Nxf3+ 6. Qxf3 Qf6, trying to exchange Queens, although even then White would undoubtedly have the better position.

6. Bf1-c4	Bf8-e7
7. 0-0	Ng8-f6
8. Nb1-c3	0-0
9. Qd1-e1!	

Black was threatening 9. ... Nxe4 10. Nxe4 d5, breaking up White's pawn center. The White Queen therefore defends the pawn on e4 while at the same time trying to penetrate into the Kingside.

9. ...	Rf8-e8?

Black's desire to place his Rook on the same file as the White Queen is understandable, but the move weakens the f7 pawn. Since Black's position is cramped, a better move would be 9. ... Be6, trying to exchange Bishops. 10. d5 in reply would not be dangerous for Black, since the move would block the diagonal of White's Bishop.

10. Nf3-g5	

White immediately exploits the weakness of the f7 pawn by attacking it.

10. ...	d6-d5?

Black should admit his mistake and return his Rook to f8. He could also play 10. ... Nh8. The text move leads to an opening of lines that is favorable for White, since his pieces are the more active.

11. Nc3xd5	Nf6xd5?

Black rushes to his doom. It is better to give up a pawn than to lose the game right away. He had to defend the f7 pawn by 11. ... Be6, 11. ... Rf8, or 11. Nh8.

12. Bc4xd5	

Even simpler was 12. Nxf7

12. ...	Be7xg5
13. Bd5xf7 +	Kg8-h8
14. Bf7xe8	Bg5xc1

Around now, White started to visualize the following potential mating patterns (see Diagrams 628–631). But they can become reality only if Black plays poorly.

628

629

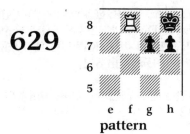

pattern

630

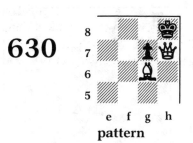

pattern

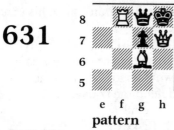

631

pattern

15. Be8xg6

Eliminating the Knight that was defending the important f8 square.

15. ...   **Bc1xb2?**

The last mistake. Better is 15. ... Bg5 followed by 16. ... Qxd4+, with some counterplay for the lost exchange. 16. Qb4 would not work for White because of 16. ... Be7, winning a Bishop.

16. Qe1-h4!!   **Qd8-g8**

16. ... Qxd4+ (or 16. ... Bxd4+) would not save Black since White can reply 17. Kh1, with a mating attack. After 16. ... Qxh4?, the mating pattern of Diagram 629 would become reality: 17. Rf8#.

17. Rf1-f8!

The Rook attacks the Queen and says, "Take me, please!" Such effrontery turned out to be too much for Black, and he resigned. The fact is that he gets mated in all variations:

a)   17. ... Qxf8 18. Qxh7# (pattern of Diagram 630);

b)   17. ... h6 18. Rxg8+ Kxg8 19. Qd8# (pattern of Diagram 628 — a back-rank mate);

c)   17. ... Bxd4+ 18. Kh1 Be6 19. Qxh7# (pattern of Diagram 631).

The final position is shown in Diagram 632.

632

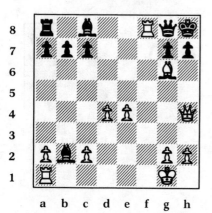

Black played actively . . . , but badly! The safety of his King should have been his primary concern.

Game 90
Gruenfeld–Torre, Baden-Baden 1925

Dutch Defense

1. d2-d4

White was an outstanding Austrian grandmaster after whom one of the most popular modern openings, the Gruenfeld Defense, is named. His opponent was a talented Mexican master.

1. ...   **e7-e6**
2. Ng1-f3   **f7-f5**

This move introduces the Dutch Defense.

3. g2-g3

This move, recommended by Gruenfeld, is often played in such positions even today.

3. ...   **Ng8-f6**
4. Bf1-g2   **d7-d5**

This variation is called the "stonewall" variation.

5. 0-0   **Bf8-d6**
6. c2-c4   **c7-c6**

If 6. ... dxc4, then White plays 7. Qa4, winning back the pawn with a good position.

7. Qd1-c2   **0-0**
8. b2-b3   **Nf6-e4**
9. Bc1-b2   **Nb8-d7**

Both players are developing rapidly. The position is about even.

10. Nf3-e5   **Qd8-f6**
11. f2-f3

After this move, Torre noticed an interesting potential mating pattern (Diagram 633) that was overlooked by White.

633

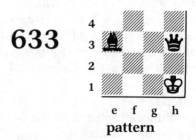

pattern

11. ...   **Nd7xe5**
12. d4xe5??

Gruenfeld could have obtained the better game by means of the **in-between** move 12.

c5!. E.g., 12. ... Bc7 13. dxe5 Bxe5 14. Bxe5 Qxe5 15. fxe5, and 15. ... Qxa1 doesn't work, because of 16. Nc3, netting the Queen. However, Gruenfeld overlooked Black's **in-between** check which immediately decides the outcome of the struggle.

| 12. ... | Bd6-c5 + ! |

The Bishop escapes from the pawn with check! 12. ... Bxe5 would not work, because of 13. Bxe5 Qxe5 14. fxe4 Qxa1 15. Nc3, and Black must lose material.

| 13. Kg1-h1 | Ne4xg3 + ! |

White resigned, since he will be mated by force: 14. hxg3 Qh6+ 15. Bh3 Qxh3# (mating pattern of Diagram 633). The final game position is shown in Diagram 634.

634

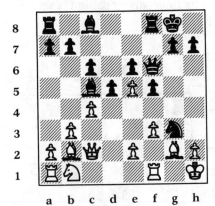

Grandmaster Gruenfeld was caught in his opponent's trap and, it goes without saying, he remembered this game for the rest of his life.

Game 91
Alekhine–Mindeno, Holland 1933

Ruy Lopez

1. e2-e4	e7-e5
2. Ng1-f3	Nb8-c6
3. Bf1-b5	

White was the reigning World Champion. This game was played during a simultaneous exhibition where Alekhine was playing many games against different opponents at the same time.

3. ...	d7-d6
4. d2-d4	e5xd4
5. Qd1xd4	

The idea behind this move is to prepare Queenside castling.

5. ...	Bc8-d7
6. Bb5xc6	Bd7xc6
7. Nb1-c3	

7. Bg5 would be premature because of 7. ... Be7! 8. Qxg7 Bf6, with a good game for Black.

7. ...	Ng8-f6
8. Bc1-g5	Bf8-e7
9. 0-0-0	0-0

Both sides have brought out all their minor pieces. They have both castled, but on different sides. White's position is preferable, as Black is cramped

| 10. h2-h4 | |

Preparing 11. Nd5 by protecting the Bishop, since 10. Nd5 would lose a piece after 10. ... Nxd5. Another possible plan for White was to play 10. Rhe1, threatening 11. e5, but Alekhine always preferred to attack the King.

| 10. ... | h7-h6 |
| 11. Nc3-d5! | h6xg5? |

Accepting the sacrifice leads to defeat. Black should have played 11. ... Nxd5 12. exd5 Bd7.

| 12. Nd5xe7 + ! | |

12. hxg5 would be followed by 12. .. Nxd5 13. exd5 Bxg5 + .

12. ...	Qd8xe7
13. h4xg5	Nf6xe4
14. Rh1-h5	

Black has an extra Bishop but his position is lost, since White's attack along the h-file cannot be parried. The World Champion visualized five potential mating patterns at this point (see Diagrams 635–639) and began to set up a brilliant combination.

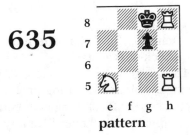

pattern

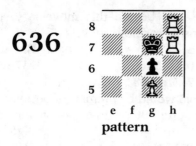

636

pattern

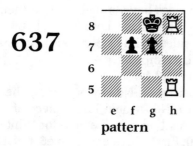

637

pattern

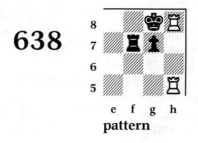

638

pattern

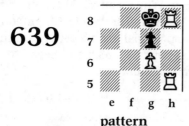

639

pattern

14. ...   **Qe7-e6**
15. Rd1-h1

Threatens 16. Rh8# (the pattern of Diagram 637 — a back-rank mate).

15. ...   **f7-f5**

Making a hole for the King on f7. White's task is to keep the Black King in the mating net by maintaining control over f7 at any cost.

16. Nf3-e5!!

An astoundingly beautiful and strong move! The threat is 16. Rh8# (the mating pattern of Diagram 635 — a back-rank mate). 16. ... g6

does not save Black, because of 17. Rh8+ Kg7 18. R1h7# (mating pattern of diagram 636). If the White pawn manages to reach g6 unpunished, Black will not be able to avoid mate. It is for that reason that Alekhine tries to **deflect** either the Black Queen from controlling g6 or the d6 pawn from being able to interpose on the a2-g8 diagonal.

16. ...   **d6xe5**

On 16. ... Qxe5 White wins by 17. Qxe5 dxe5 18. g6 any 19. Rh8# (mating pattern of Diagram 639 — a back-rank mate).

17. g5-g6!

Only now did Black understand the World Champion's brilliant idea. He immediately resigned, since the threat of 18. Rh8# is deadly. The only defense, 17. ... Qxg6, abandons the a2-g8 diagonal and allows the White Queen to deliver a fatal check: 18. Qc4+ Rf7 19. Rh8# (mating pattern of Diagram 638 — a back-rank mate). The final game position is shown in Diagram 640.

640

This game shows the importance of open lines in attacking the enemy King.

Game 92
Fink–Alekhine, Pasadena 1932
Ponziani's Opening

1. e2-e4   **e7-e5**
2. Ng1-f3   **Nb8-c6**
3. c2-c3

This move introduces the opening worked out more than two hundred years ago by the great Italian chessplayer Domenico Ponziani.

3. ...	**d7-d5**

Black, the reigning World Champion, immediately counterattacks in the center.

4. Qd1-a4	**Ng8-f6**

Alekhine plays a gambit variation, sacrificing a pawn but developing rapidly.

5. Nf3xe5	**Bf8-d6**
6. Ne5xc6	**b7xc6**
7. e4-e5	

The first mistake. White could have maintained the equilibrium by 7. d3 0-0 8. Be2, with the idea of 9. Nd2 and 10. 0-0. 7. Qxc6 + Bd7 8. Qa6 would be bad for White because of 8. ... dxe4, with the better game for Black. White decides to return the pawn to gain time for developing his pieces.

7. ...	**Bd6xe5**
8. d2-d4	**Be5-d6**
9. Qa4xc6 + ?	

White should have resisted this temptation and instead thought about developing his pieces!

9. ...	**Bc8-d7**
10. Qc6-a6	**0-0**

Black has finished his development while his opponent has in effect been moving only his Queen. White has a lost position in spite of his extra pawn.

11. Bf1-e2	**Rf8-e8**
12. Nb1-d2	

White was afraid to castle, as Black pieces were looking straight at his Kingside.

12. ...	**Ra8-b8**
13. a2-a4	

Parrying the threat of 13. ... Bb5, winning the pinned Bishop. 13. 0-0 would not help, because of 13. ... Rb6 14. Qd3 Bb5, winning a piece.

13. ...	**Qd8-e7**

The World Champion prepares the mating pattern shown in Diagram 641.

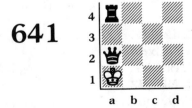

641

14. Nd2-f1?
White can save himself only by playing

14. Kd1, unpinning the bishop, although he would still be in a bad state because of his hopelessly retarded development.

14. ...	**Bd7-b5!**

The tactical motif of **interference.** Now the White Queen can no longer defend the Bishop.

15. a4xb5	**Qe7xe2#**

The mating pattern of Diagram 641. The final game position is shown in Diagram 642.

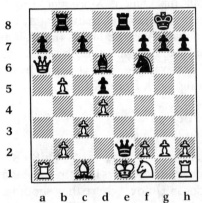

642

White received a good lesson! You must play with **all** your pieces, and not just your Queen.

Game 93
Alekhine–DeCassio, 1944
Vienna Game

1. e2-e4	**e7-e5**
2. Nb1-c3	

This introduces an opening worked out by a group of Viennese chessplayers in the 19th century.

2. ...	**Bf8-c5**
3. Bf1-c4	**Ng8-e7?**

The Knight is passively placed here. You should generally try to place it on f6, from where it controls many important squares.

4. d2-d3
World Champion Alekhine was playing this game blindfolded.

4. ...	**Nb8-c6**
5. Qd1-h5!	

Threatens 6. Qxf7#. This is the "Scholar's Mate" pattern shown in Diagram 643.

643

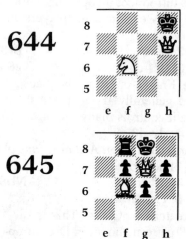

Why can the World Champion bring his Queen out early in the game while we are advised not to do so? The reason is that in this case Black made a poor move, 3. ... Ne7, and only after that did Alekhine allow himself to bring out his Queen. Moreover, the World Champion foresaw a mating attack many moves ahead. And the fact is that it is not so easy for Black to gain time by attacking the Queen. For example, 5. ... g6 is met by 6. Qh6, preventing Black from castling.

5. ...	**0-0**
6. Bc1-g5	

Pinning the Knight.

6. ...	**Qd8-e8?**

Black of course knows **how** the pieces move, but he doesn't know **where** they should go. He had to pin the **dangerous** White Knight by 6. ... Bb4, and then neutralize White's **dangerous** light-square Bishop by 7. ... d6 and 8. ... Be6.

7. Ng1-f3	**Ne7-g6?**

It was still not too late to play 7. ... Bb4.

8. Nc3-d5!	

Though blindfolded, the Grandmaster sees several potential mating patterns (Diagrams 644 and 645) and begins to set up a combination.

644

645

8. ...	**Bc5-b6**

All of White's minor pieces as well as his Queen are taking part in his attack, while the Black pieces are placed passively and are unable to help their King.

9. Nd5-f6 + !	**g7xf6**

Forced. 10. Qxh7# (mating pattern of Diagram 644) was threatened.

10. Bg5xf6	

White has the double threat of 11. Ng5 followed by 12. Qxh7# (mating pattern of Diagram 644) and 11. Qh6 followed by 12. Qg7# (mating pattern of Diagram 645). Since Black cannot defend against both threats, he resigned. The final game position is shown in Diagram 646.

646

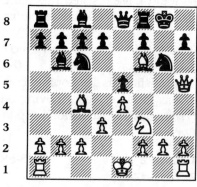

The World Champion's opponent played aimlessly and was routed right at the start of the game.

Game 94
Mardle–Gaprindashvili, Hastings 1965
Sicilian Defense

1. e2-e4	**c7-c5**
2. Ng1-f3	**Nb8-c6**

The Women's World Champion Nona Gaprindashvili played this game in a men's tournament.

2. d2-d4	**c5xd4**
3. Nf3xd4	**e7-e6**
4. Bc1-e3	**Ng8-f6**
5. Nb1-d2	

A passive move! 6. Bd3 is stronger. Also possible is 6. Nc3, but White didn't like the pin arising after 6. ... Bb4.

6. ...	**e6-e5**

Black can allow herself to make two moves with the e-pawn in the opening because White's last move was weak.

7. Nd4xc6	**d7xc6**

Opening a diagonal for the Bishop.

8. f2-f3

Preventing Black from playing her Knight to g4.

8. ...	**Bf8-e7**
9. Bf1-c4	**0-0**
10. 0-0	**Nf6-h5**

With the idea of exchanging Bishops after 11. ... Bg5.

11. Nd2-b3

Safer is 11. g3.

11. ...	**Be7-g5**
12. Be3-c5	

12. Qxd8 is of course bad because of the **in-between** check 12. ... Bxe3 +, winning a piece.

12. ...	**Qd8-f6**

The Women's World Champion sees a possibility of creating a "Greco's Mate" pattern (Diagram 647), and so she leaves her Rook en prise.

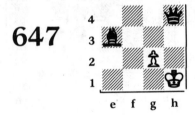

647

13. Bc5xf8?

White does not notice the trap. He had to play 13. f4 Nxf4 14. Bxf8, with a double-edged position.

13. ...	**Bg5-e3 +**
14. Kg1-h1??	

Mate could have been prevented only by 14. Rf2.

14. ...	**Nh5-g3 +!**

White resigns. 15. hxg3 Qh6# is a "Greco's mate" (pattern of Diagram 647). The final game position is shown in Diagram 648.

648

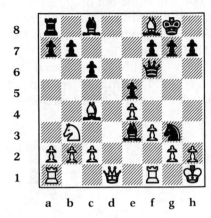

The Women's World Champion wasn't playing specially to catch her opponent in a trap, and it wasn't her fault if he voluntarily fell into the trap and got mated!

Game 95
Gaprindashvili–Servati, Germany 1974
Sicilian Defense

1. e2-e4	**c7-c5**
2. Ng1-f3	**Nb8-c6**
3. d2-d4	

White was Nona Gaprindashvili, Women's World Champion from 1962 to 1978.

3. ...	**c5xd4**
4. Nf3xd4	**g7-g6**

The Dragon Variation.

5. c2-c4

Controlling d5.

5. ...	**Bf8-g7**
6. Bc1-e3	**Ng8-f6**
7. Nb1-c3	**Nf6-g4**
8. Qd1xg4	

8. Nxc6 is unsatisfactory because of 8. ... Nxe3 9. Nxd8 Nxd1 10. Nxd1 Kxd8, with the better game for Black.

8. ...	**Nc6xd4**
9. Qg4-d1	**e7-e5**

9. ... Ne6 would give better chances of equalizing.

10. Nc3-b5	**0-0**
11. Bf1-e2	**Qd8-h4?**

Black had to play 11. ... Nxb5 12. cxb5 d6 13. Bc4 Be6, with an approximately equal game.

12. Nb5xd4	**e5xd4**
13. Be3xd4	**Qh4xe4**

233

14. Bd4xg7   Qe4xg2?

No good can come out of greediness. Black should have played 14. ... Kxg7, although even then White has the freer game after 15. 0-0.

15. Qd1-d4!

A pretty double-Rook sacrifice! The Women's World Champion sees the potential mating pattern shown in Diagram 649.

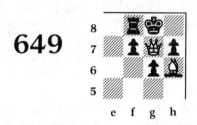

15. ...   Qg2xh1 +
16. Ke1-d2   Qh1xa1?

Again Black is greedy. He still had some chances of saving his game by playing 16. ... Qxh2, controlling h6.

17. Qd4-f6!

Black only now realized that he was in a trap, and capitulated. There is no defense to be seen against White's threat of 18. Bh6 followed by 19. Qg7# (mating pattern of Diagram 649). The immediate 17. Bh6 would not have worked, because of 17. ... f6, defending against the mate. The final game position is shown in Diagram 650.

650

Black made a mistake in his calculation of the variations. He overlooked the Women's World Champion's last move, which made it impossible for Black to save himself.

Game 96
Shamkovich–Ivashin, 1946
Ruy Lopez

1. e2-e4	e7-e5
2. Ng1-f3	Nb8-c6
3. Bf1-b5	a7-a6
4. Bb5-a4	d7-d6
5. c2-c4	

With the idea of strengthening his control over b5 and d5.

5. ...	Ng8-e7
6. Nb1-c3	Bc8-g4

Pinning the Knight.

7. d2-d4

White sacrifices a pawn with the aim of developing his pieces as rapidly as possible.

7. ...	e5xd4
8. Nc3-d5	

The well-known Grandmaster playing White anticipated several possible mating patterns at this point (see Diagrams 651–656).

651

652

234

653

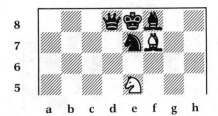

654

655

656

8. ...   **Ra8-b8**

Black prepares the move ... b5 to try and free his Knight from the pin. 8. ... g6 was not possible, because of 9. Nf6# (pattern of Diagram 651 — a smothered mate).

9. Bc1-g5	**b7-b5**
10. c4xb5	**a6xb5**
11. Ba4-b3	**Nc6-e5?**

Delighted at being unpinned, the Black Knight rushes to attack the pinned White

Knight. However, Black should have instead been thinking of how to unpin his other Knight (the one on e7) and prepare for castling. 11. ... f6 immediately, though, would not work, because of 12. Bxf6 gxf6 13. Nxf6# (mating pattern of Diagram 652).

12. Nf3xe5!

This move had been overlooked by Black.

12. ...   **Ne7xd5**

A pretty mate would have resulted after 12. ... Bxd1 13. Nf6+! gxf6 14. Bxf7# (mating pattern of Diagram 653). If instead Black plays 12. ... dxe5, he will remain a piece down after 13. Qxg4.

13. Qd1xg4	**f7-f6**
14. Bg5xf6!!	

Black can take the Bishop in any one of three ways, but in each case he gets mated.

If he takes with the pawn by 14. ... gxf6, then 15. Qh5+ Ke7 16. Qf7# (pattern of Diagram 654 — an epaulette mate).

If he takes with the Knight by 14. ... Nxf6, then 15. Bf7+ Ke7 16. Qe6# (pattern of Diagram 655 — an epaulette mate).

Finally, if he takes with the Queen by 14. ... Qxf6, then 15. Qd7# (pattern of Diagram 656).

So **Black resigned.** The final game position is shown in Diagram 657.

657

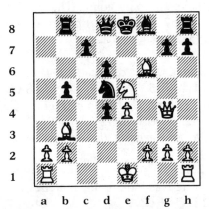

Black started active operations before completing his development and underestimated his opponent's threats. As a result, he deservedly lost.

Game 97
Marshall–Burn, Paris 1900
Queen's Gambit Declined

This pretty game, which we take from Frank Marshall's book *Marshall's Best Games of Chess*, is annotated by the grandmaster in an original and amusing way: "I attribute the win largely to the fact that my opponent never had time to get his pipe lit! . . . Britisher Amos Burn was a very conservative player and liked to settle down for a long session of close, defensive chess. He loved to smoke his pipe while he studied the board. As I made my second move, Burn began hunting through his pockets for his pipe and tobacco."

1. d2-d4	d7-d5
2. c2-c4	e7-e6
3. Nb1-c3	Ng8-f6
4. Bc1-g5	Bf8-e7

"Not much thought needed on these moves, but Burn had his pipe out and was looking for a pipe cleaner."

5. e2-e3	0-0
6. Ng1-f3	b7-b6
7. Bf1-d3	Bc8-b7
8. c4xd5	e6xd5

"He began filling up his pipe. I speeded up my moves."

9. Bg5xf6	Be7xf6
10. h2-h4	

"Made him think on that one — and he still didn't have the pipe going. The threat is 11. Bxh7+ Kxh7 12. Ng5+, known as the Pillsbury attack."

10. ...	g7-g6

(A mistake. 10. ... c5 is better —Pelts).

11. h4-h5	Rf8-e8

(A loss of time. He had to play 11. ... Qe7 and answer 12. hxg6 with 12. ... fxg6, allowing the Queen to take part in the defense of the King —Pelts).

12. hxg6	hxg6

"Now he was looking for matches."

13. Qd1-c2	Bf6-g7

(A serious mistake, for now the Bishop no longer controls the important g5 square. It was necessary to play 13. ... Kg7 14. 0-0-0 Nd7, when Black would have good defensive chances —Pelts).

14. Bxg6	

(Marshall sees several potential mating patterns [Diagrams 658–660] and makes an absolutely

sound sacrifice of a Bishop for two pawns —Pelts).

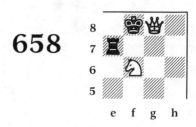

658

659

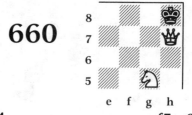

660

14. ...	f7xg6

"He struck a match, appeared nervous. The match burned his fingers and went out."

15. Qc2xg6	Nb8-d7

"Another match was on its way." *(15. ... Re7 would not save Black, because of 16. Ng5 [threatening 17. Rh8+! followed by 18. Qh7# — the mating pattern of Diagram 660], and 16. ... Kf8 would be met by 17. Nh7+ Kg8 18. Nf6+ Kf8 19. Rh8+ Bxh8 20. Qg8# — the mating pattern of Diagram 658 —Pelts.)*

16. Nf3-g5	

(Threatens 17. Qf7# — the mating pattern of Diagram 659 —Pelts).

16. ...	Qd8-f6

"He was puffing away and lighting up at last. No time left."

17. Rh1-h8+	Resigns

"For if 17. ... Kxh8, 18. Qh7#." *(Mating pattern of Diagram 660. The final game position is shown in Diagram 661. —Pelts).*

661

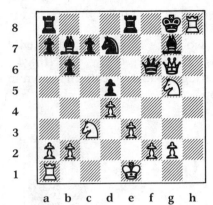

"Poor Burn. I think I swindled him out of that one. If he could only have got that pipe going, it might have been a different story. He took it good-naturedly and we shook hands. Then his pipe went out."

To these comments by the great Marshall we can only add that he played the game brilliantly, while his opponent helped him by underestimating White's attack.

Game 98
Keres–Meeke, Correspondence, 1933
King's Gambit

1. e2-e4	e7-e5
2. f2-f4	

White was a sixteen-year-old Estonian chessplayer who later became one of the top players in the world.

2. ...	e5xf4
3. Nb1-c3	Qd8-h4 +
4. Ke1-e2	d7-d5!

The opponents are playing a very sharp opening variation that gives chances to win to both sides. With his last move, Black returns the pawn in order to gain time.

5. Nc3xd5	Bc8-g4 +
6. Ng1-f3	Nb8-c6

Sacrificing a Rook to launch a dangerous attack against the White King, which is stranded in the center. In such sharp positions, a single mistake can lead to a catastrophe.

7. Nd5xc7 +	Ke8-d8
8. Nc7xa8	Nc6-e5

This sets up the possibility of 9. ... Nxf3 10. gxf3 Bxf3 +! 11. Kxf3 Qh5 + 12. any Qxd1.

9. h2-h3!

White is prepared to return some material in order to weaken Black's attack. Now 9. ... Nxf3 can be met by 10. hxg4 Nd4 + 11. Kd3 Qxh1 12. Kxd4, and White's position is better, since he can later hide his King on c2 after the preliminary move c2-c3.

9. ...	Bg4-h5

Also possible was 9. ... Bxf3 + 10. gxf3 Qg3 11. d3, with unclear play.

Black, however, has in mind the mating pattern shown in Diagram 662 and so decides to keep his Bishop.

662

10. Rh1-g1?

The decisive mistake! A loss of valuable time! White must instead sacrifice his Queen to maintain approximate equality: 10. d4! Nxf3 11. gxf3 Bxf3 + 12. Kxf3 Qh5 + 13. Kg2 Qxd1 14. Bd3.

10. ...	Qh4-g3

Now the Knight on f3 cannot be defended.

11. Qd1-e1

Only 11. d3 would prevent mate, but after 11. ... Nxf3 12. gxf3 Qxf3 + White would suffer huge material losses.

11. ...	Bh5xf3 +
12. g2xf3	Qg3xf3#

The mating pattern of Diagram 662. The final game position is shown in Diagram 663.

663

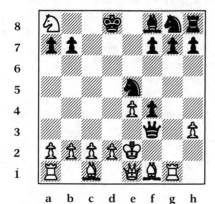

a b c d e f g h

White lost even though he just made one mistake!

Game 99
Johner–Tartakower, 1928
Sicilian Defense

1. e2-e4   **c7-c5**

Black was a famous grandmaster.

2. Ng1-f3   **Ng8-f6**

A rare move.

3. Nb1-c3

3. e5 would be met by 3. ... Nd5, with chances for both sides.

3. ...   **d7-d5**

4. e4xd5

4. e5 is not dangerous for Black in view of 4. ... d4 5. exf6 dxc3 6. fxg7 cxd2+, with an even game.

4. ...   **Nf6xd5**

5. Nc3-e4

It would be better to bring fresh forces into play. For example, 5. Bb5+ Bd7 6. Ne5 Bxb5 7. Qf3 f6 8. Nxb5 fxe5 9. Qxd5 Qxd5 10. Nc7+, with advantage to White.

5. ...   **e7-e6**
6. d2-d4   **c5xd4**
7. Nf3xd4   **Bf8-e7**
8. Bf1-b5+   **Bc8-d7**
9. c2-c4   **Nd5-f6**
10. Ne4-c3   **0-0**
11. 0-0   **Qd8-c7**

The position is even. Both sides have finished their development without difficulty.

12. Qd1-e2   **Nb8-c6**
13. Nd4-f3

It would be more logical to exchange Knights

instead of losing time by retreating.

13. ...   **Rf8-e8**

Preparing to push the e-pawn.

14. Bc1-g5

Safer would be 14. h3, controlling g4.

14. ...   **Nf6-g4!**

Preparing the mating pattern shown in Diagram 664.

664

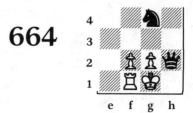

e f g h

15. Bg5xe7?

Johner does not suspect anything and decides to exchange Bishops. If he had discovered White's threat, he would have replied 15. g3.

15. ...   **Nc6-d4!**

An **in-between** move! Instead of capturing the Bishop, Black makes use of the tactical motif of **deflection. White resigned** since 16. Nxd4 would be met by 16. ... Qxh2# (pattern of Diagram 664) and 16. Qd3 would fail to 16. ... Nxf3+ 17. ... Qxh2# (pattern of Diagram 664). The final game position is shown in Diagram 665.

665

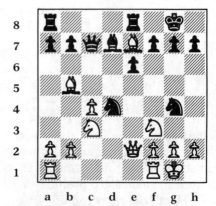

a b c d e f g h

White lost because he did not see Black's threat in time.

Game 100
Serebryanskii–van Gompel
Correspondence, 1973
Queen's Pawn Game

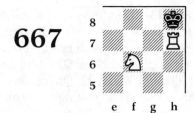

667

1. d2-d4	d7-d5
2. Ng1-f3	Ng8-f6
3. e2-e3	e7-e6
4. Bf1-d3	c7-c5
5. 0-0	Nb8-c6
6. b2-b3	Bf8-d6
7. Bc1-b2	0-0
8. Nf3-e5	

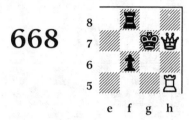

668

This quiet opening is known as the Queen's Pawn Game. Sometimes White plays 8. a3 here, depriving the Black Knight of the b4 square.

| 8. ... | Qd8-c7 |
| 9. f2-f4 | |

With the idea of transferring the Rook to the Kingside via f3.

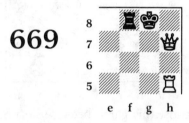

669

9. ...	c5xd4
10. e3xd4	Nc6-b4
11. Nb1-c3	Nb4xd3

Eliminating the dangerous Bishop that was pointed at Black's Kingside.

| 12. Qd1xd3 | a7-a6 |

Depriving the White Knight of the b5 square.

13. Rf1-f3!

White has completed his development and is ready to attack the enemy King.

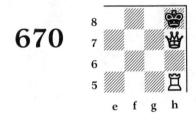

670

| 13. ... | b7-b5 |

Black's desire to bring out his light-square Bishop is understandable, but it was more important to see to the safety of his King by playing 13. ... g6, with the idea of 14. ... Ne8 and 15. ... f5.

| 14. Rf3-h3 | Bc8-b7?? |

Black suspects nothing. 14. ... g6 was obligatory. The position is now ripe for combinational play and White visualizes several potential mating patterns (Diagrams 666–670).

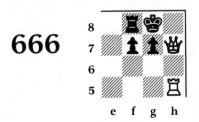

666

| 15. Ne5-g4! | |

To **deflect** the Knight from the defense of h7.

| 15. ... | Nf6-e4 |

Blocking the Queen's path. 15. ... Nxg4 would of course allow 16. Qxh7# (pattern of Diagram 666).

| 16. Nc3xe4! | |

Eliminating the Knight, which was controlling f6.

| 16. ... | d5xe4 |
| 17. Ng4-f6 + ! | |

Exposing the King.

| 17. ... | g7xf6 |

Else 18. Rxh7# (pattern of Diagram 667 — an Arabian mate).

239

| 18. Qd3-g3 + | Kg8-h8 |
| 19. Qg3-h4 | Resigns |

For there is no satisfactory defense against the threat of 20. Qxh7# (if 20. ... h6 or ... h5, then 21. Qxh6(5) + and 22. Qh7#). Black must succumb to one of the mating patterns shown in Diagrams 668 (epaulette mate), 669, and 670. The final position is shown in Diagram 671.

671

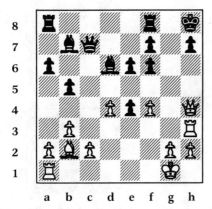

Black lost this game because he underestimated White's attack.

Lesson Twelve

672

White to play and draw.

_____

_____

_____

674

White to play and mate in two moves.

_____

_____

_____

673

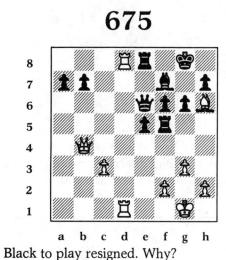

Black to play. Can he avoid losing a piece?

_____

_____

_____

675

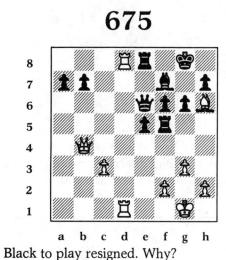

Black to play resigned. Why?

_____

_____

_____

676

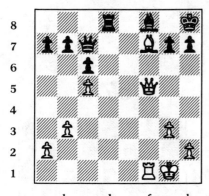

White to play. Find his strongest continuation.

_____

_____

_____

677

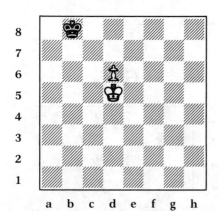

How does White queen his pawn if it is his turn to play? And if it is Black's turn?

_____

_____

_____

678

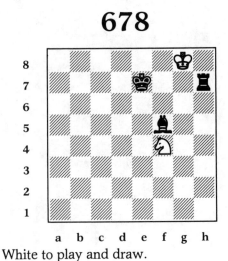

White to play and draw.

_____

_____

_____

680

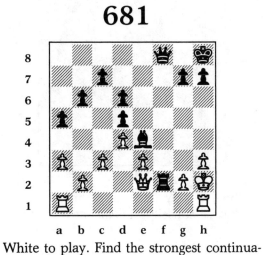

Black to play and win a piece.

_____

_____

_____

679

White to play. Why did he resign?

_____

_____

_____

681

White to play. Find the strongest continuation.

_____

_____

_____

682

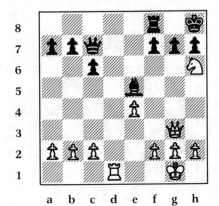

White to play and win a piece.

_____

_____

_____

683

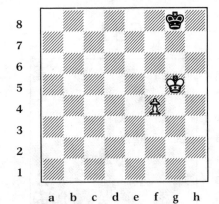

White to play and queen his pawn. Can Black save himself if it is his move?

_____

_____

_____

Test Three
Write your answers below.

684

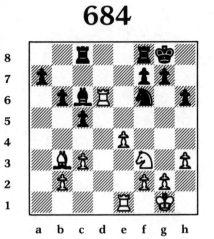

Black to play. Can he win the pawn on e4?

_____

_____

_____

686

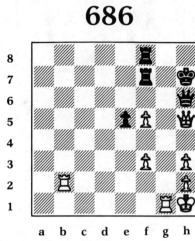

White to play and win a piece.

_____

_____

_____

685

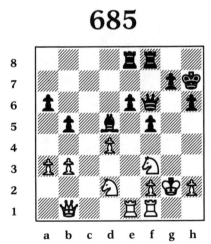

Black to play and win a piece.

_____

_____

_____

687

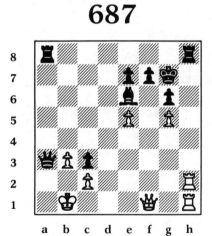

White to play and mate in three moves.

_____

_____

_____

688

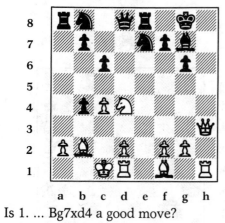

a b c d e f g h

Is 1. ... Bg7xd4 a good move?

_____

_____

_____

689

a b c d e f g h

Black to play and queen a pawn.

_____

_____

_____

690

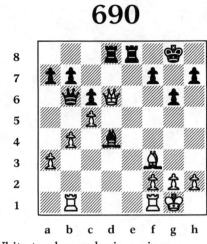

White to play and win a piece.

_____

_____

_____

692

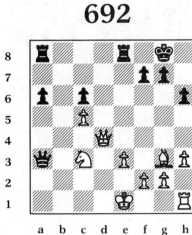

Black to play and win a piece.

_____

_____

_____

691

White to play and win a piece.

Is 1. ... Bd5-e4 (double attack) a good move?

_____

_____

_____

693

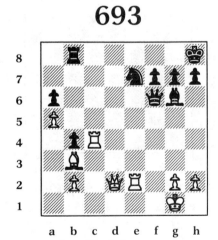

White to play. Find the strongest continuation.

_____

_____

_____

694

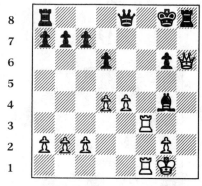

White to play and mate in three moves.

_____

_____

_____

695

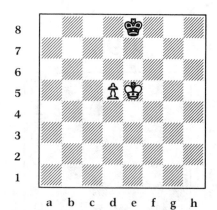

White to play and queen his pawn. Can Black save himself if it is his turn to play?

_____

_____

_____

696

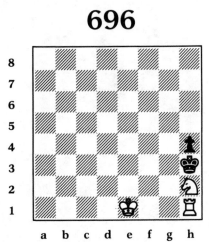

White to play and mate in two moves. (The White King and Rook have not moved in the game so far.)

_____

_____

_____

698

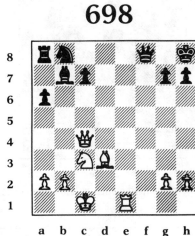

White to play and win a piece.

_____

_____

_____

697

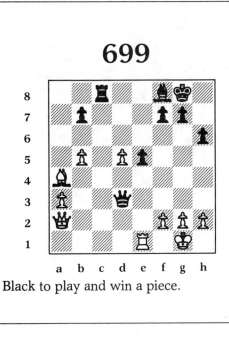

Black to play and win a piece.

_____

_____

_____

699

Black to play and win a piece.

_____

_____

700

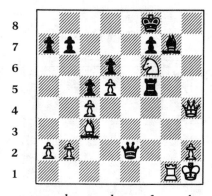

White to play and mate in three moves.

_____

_____

_____

701

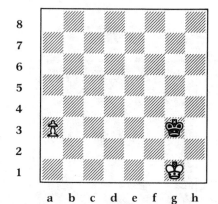

White to play. Can he queen his pawn? Can Black stop the pawn if it is his turn to play?

_____

_____

_____

Test Six
Write your answers below.

702

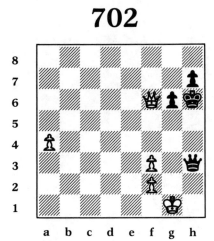

Black to play. What is his strongest continuation?

_____

_____

_____

704

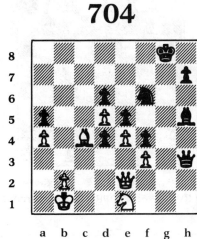

Black to play and win a pawn.

_____

_____

_____

703

Black to play. Why did he resign?

_____

_____

_____

705

White to play and win a Rook.

_____

_____

_____

706

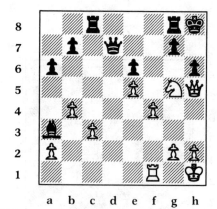

White to play and mate in two moves.

_____

_____

_____

707

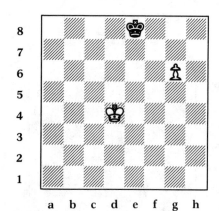

White to play and queen his pawn.

_____

_____

_____

708

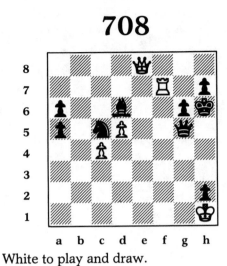

White to play and draw.

_____

_____

_____

710

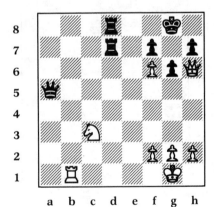

White to play. How can he avoid losing a piece?

_____

_____

_____

709

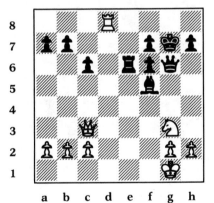

White to play and win a piece.

_____

_____

_____

711

Black to play and mate in three moves.

_____

_____

_____

712

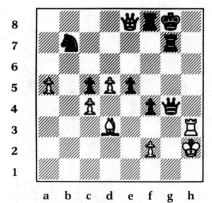

White to play and mate in three moves.

_____

_____

_____

713

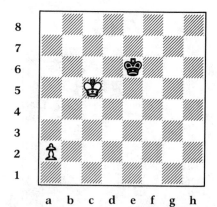

White to play and queen his pawn. Black to play and draw.

_____

_____

_____

254

714

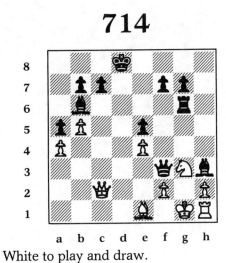

White to play and draw.

_____

_____

_____

716

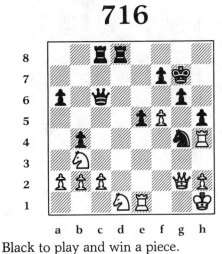

Black to play and win a piece.

_____

_____

_____

715

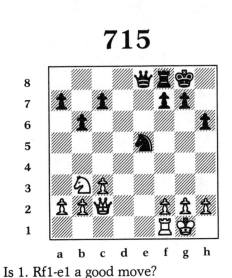

Is 1. Rf1-e1 a good move?

_____

_____

_____

717

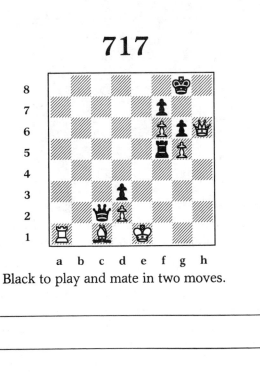

Black to play and mate in two moves.

_____

_____

_____

718

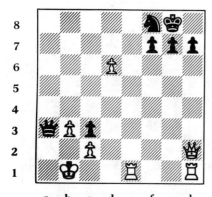

White to play and mate in four moves.

_____

_____

_____

719

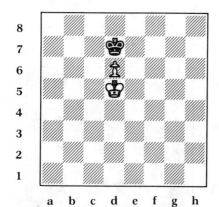

Show that the result should be a draw no matter who moves first.

_____

_____

_____

256

Test Nine
Write your answers below.

720

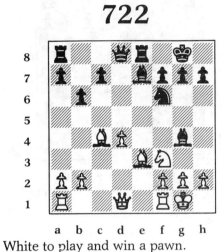

Black to play. How should the game end?

_____

_____

_____

722

Black to play. How should the game end?

White to play and win a pawn.

_____

_____

_____

721

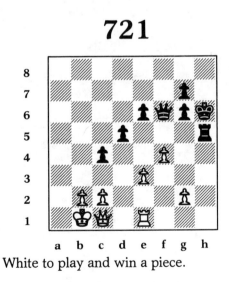

White to play and win a piece.

_____

_____

_____

723

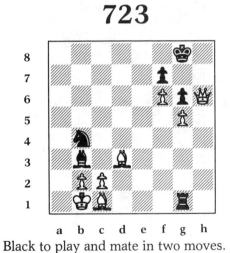

Black to play and mate in two moves.

_____

_____

_____

724

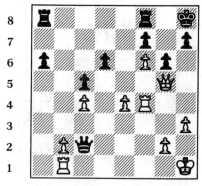

a b c d e f g h

White to play. Find his strongest continuation.

_____

_____

_____

725

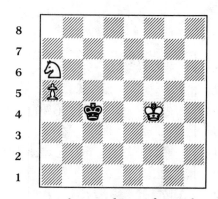

a b c d e f g h

White to play and queen his pawn.

_____

_____

_____

726

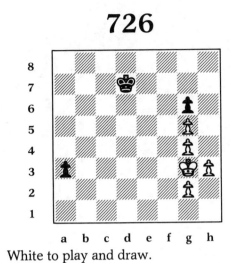

White to play and draw.

_____

_____

_____

728

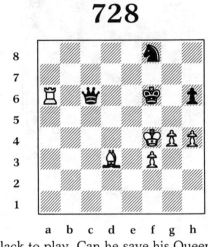

Black to play. Can he save his Queen?

_____

_____

_____

727

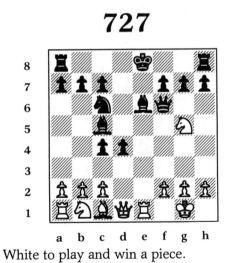

White to play and win a piece.

_____

_____

_____

729

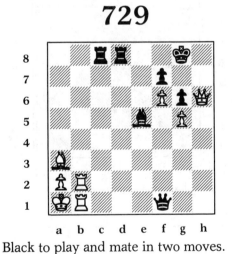

Black to play and mate in two moves.

_____

_____

_____

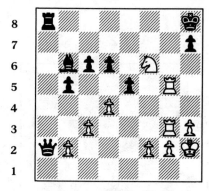

White to play and mate in three moves.

_____

_____

_____

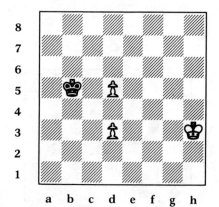

White to play and queen a pawn.

_____

_____

_____

732

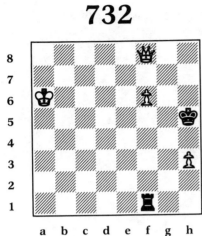

Black to play and draw.

_____

_____

_____

734

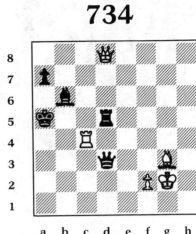

White to play and win material.

_____

_____

_____

733

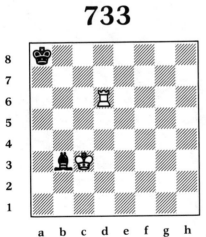

Black to play. Can he save his Bishop?

_____

_____

_____

735

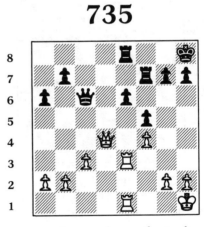

White to play and win material.

_____

_____

_____

736

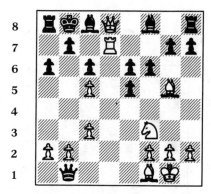

White to play and mate in two moves.

_____

_____

_____

737

How should the game end if it is White's turn to play? And if it is Black's turn?

_____

_____

_____

738

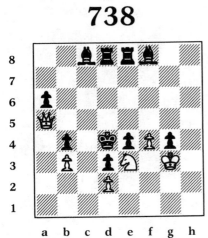

Black to play. Show how White mates Black in one move after each of Black's possible moves.

_____

_____

_____

740

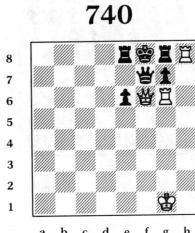

White to play and mate in two moves.

_____

_____

739

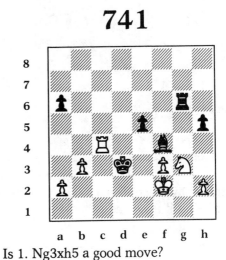

Black to play. Find his strongest continuation.

_____

_____

741

Is 1. Ng3xh5 a good move?

_____

_____

_____

263

742

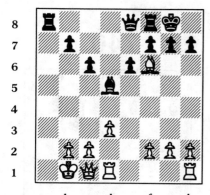

The player whose turn it is to move wins.

_____

_____

_____

743

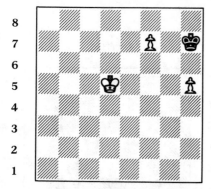

White to play and queen a pawn. Can Black save himself if it is his move?

_____

_____

_____

744

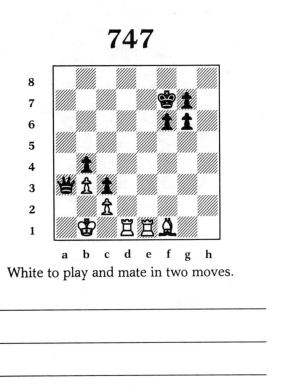

White to play and win Black's Queen.

_____

_____

_____

746

White to play. Find his strongest continuation.

_____

_____

_____

745

Black to play and win White's Queen.

_____

_____

_____

747

White to play and mate in two moves.

_____

_____

_____

748

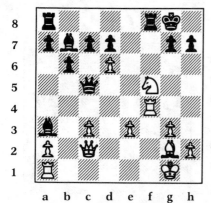

Is 1. ... Bb7xg2 a good move?

_____

_____

_____

749

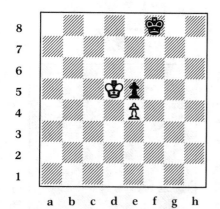

White to play. Can Black save himself?

_____

_____

_____

Test Fourteen
Write your answer below.

750

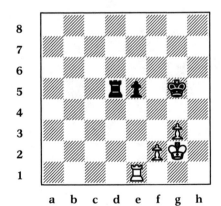

White to play. How should the game end?

_____

_____

_____

752

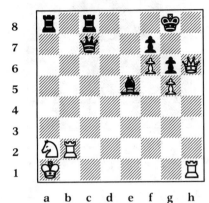

Black to play and mate in two moves.

_____

_____

_____

751

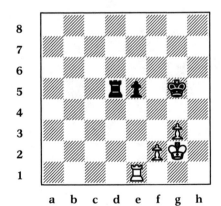

White to play. Find his strongest continuation.

_____

_____

_____

753

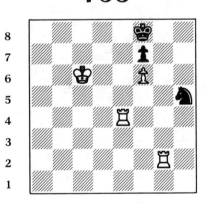

White to play and mate in two moves.

_____

_____

_____

754

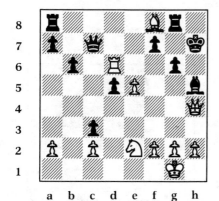

White to play and mate in two moves.

_____

_____

_____

755

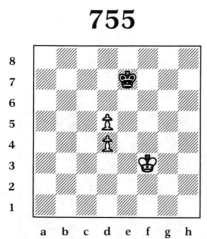

White to play and queen a pawn.

_____

_____

_____

Test Fifteen
Write your answers below.

756

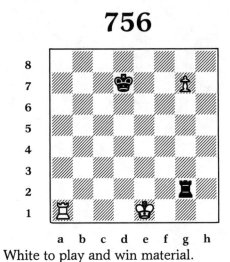

White to play and win material.

_____

_____

_____

757

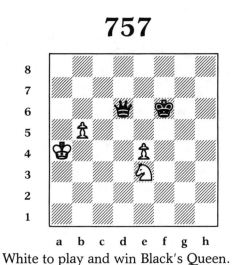

White to play and win Black's Queen.

_____

_____

_____

758

White to play and mate in two moves.

_____

_____

_____

759

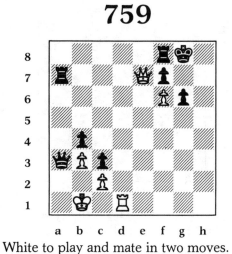

White to play and mate in two moves.

_____

_____

_____

760

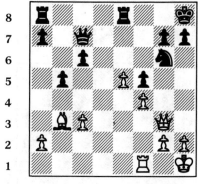

White to play. Find his strongest continuation.

_____

_____

_____

761

Can White win if it is his turn to play? What would happen if it were Black's turn?

_____

_____

_____

762

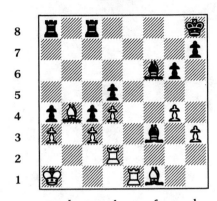

White to play. Can he win a piece?

_____

_____

_____

764

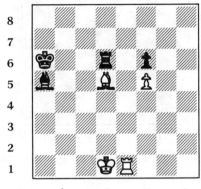

Can White to play avoid losing a piece?

_____

_____

_____

763

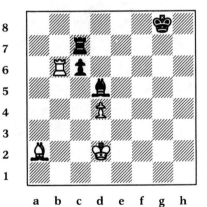

White to play and win material.

_____

_____

_____

765

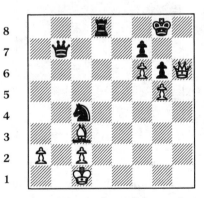

Black to play and mate in two moves.

_____

_____

_____

766

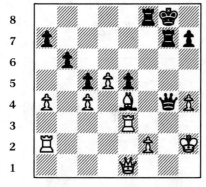

Black to play. Find a winning combination for him.

_____

_____

_____

767

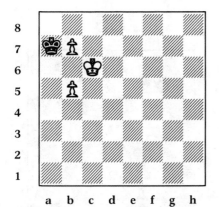

White to play and queen a pawn. Can Black save himself if it is his turn to play?

_____

_____

_____

Test Seventeen
Write your answers below.

768

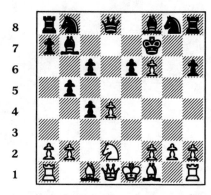

White to play. Find his strongest continuation.

_____

_____

_____

769

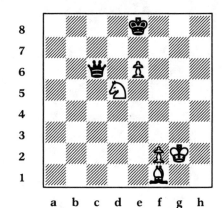

White to play and win Black's Queen.

_____

_____

_____

770

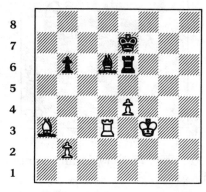

White to play and win a piece.

_____

_____

_____

771

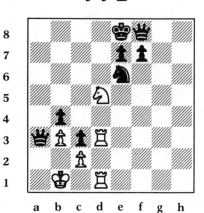

White to play and mate in two moves.

_____

_____

_____

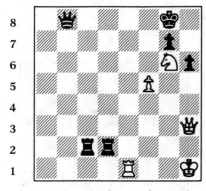

White to play. Find a winning combination for him.

_____

_____

_____

773

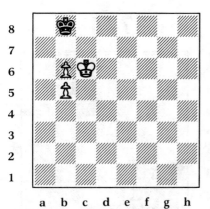

White to play and queen a pawn. Could Black save himself if it were his turn to play?

_____

_____

_____

Test Eighteen
Write your answers below.

774

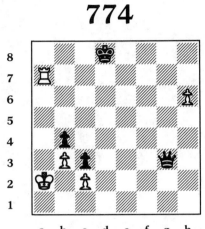

a b c d e f g h

White to play and win material.

_____

_____

_____

776

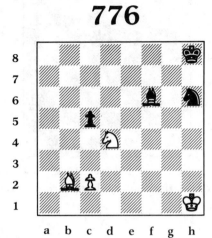

a b c d e f g h

White to play. Can he avoid losing a piece?

_____

_____

_____

775

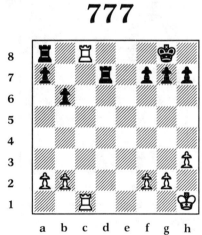

a b c d e f g h

White to play. Find a winning combination for him.

_____

_____

777

a b c d e f g h

Can Black avoid getting mated on the back rank?

_____

_____

_____

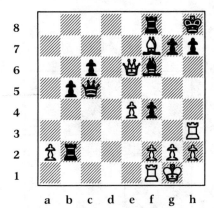

Show how the player whose turn it is to play wins.

_____

_____

_____

779

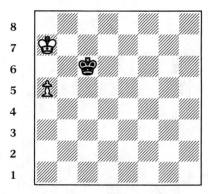

Show how the game is drawn no matter who moves first.

_____

_____

_____

780

White to play and win material.

_____

_____

_____

782

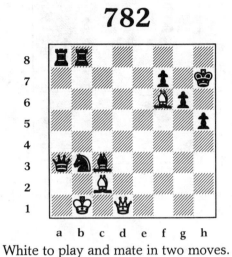

White to play and mate in two moves.

_____

_____

_____

781

White to play. Find his strongest continuation.

_____

_____

_____

783

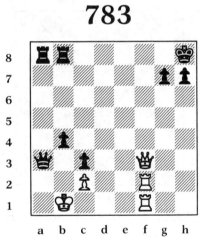

White to play and mate in three moves.

_____

_____

_____

784

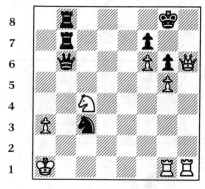

Black to play and mate in three moves (two solutions.)

_____

_____

_____

785

Show that the game should be drawn no matter who moves first.

_____

_____

_____

Test Twenty
Write your answers below.

786

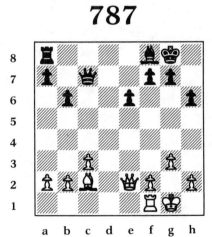

Black to play and win material.

_____

_____

_____

788

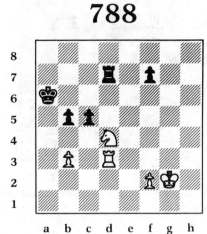

White to play. Can he avoid losing a piece?

_____

_____

_____

787

White to play. Find his strongest continuation.

_____

_____

_____

789

White to play and mate in two moves.

_____

_____

_____

790

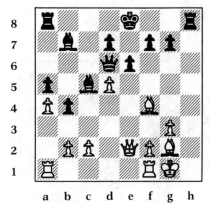

Black to play. Find a winning combination for him.

_____

_____

_____

791

Show that White wins no matter who moves first.

_____

_____

_____

Test One Answers

Diagram 672 **1. Bd1-c2 +!** (Double attack) **1. ... Qb1xc2; 2. Nf1-e3 +** (fork) **2. ... Bf4xe3** stalemate.

Diagram 673 Ilyin-Zhenevsky–Levenfish, Moscow 1936. Black avoids losing a piece as follows: **1. ... Qd7-d4! 2. Bb5xc6 + b7xc6 3. Qe4xd4** (if 3. Qxc6+, then 3. ... Kf7) **3. ... Ne3-c2 +** (fork) **4. any Nc2xd4.**

Diagram 674 **1. Qf1-f8 + Re8xf8 2. Rc8xf8#** (a back-rank mate).

Diagram 675 Pelts–Fauzi, Chess Olympics, Lucerne 1982. White is threatening 1. Qf8 + Rxf8 2. Rxf8#. If **1. ...Kh8**, then **2. R1d7** (threatening 3. Qf8 + Rxf8 4. Rxf8 + Bg8 5. Bg7#) **2. ... Rxd8 3. Rxd8 + Bg8 4. Qf8** and Black cannot avoid mate.

Diagram 676 Reti–Bogoljubow, New York 1924. **1. Bf7-e8!** Black resigned.

If 1. ... Rxe8, then 2. Qxf8 + Rxf8 3. Rxf8# (back-rank mate);

if 1. ... Be7, then 2. Qf8 Bxf8 3. Rxf8# (back-rank mate);

if 1. ... h6, then 2. Qxf8 + Kh7 3. Bg6 + Kxg6 4. Qf5#;

if 1. ... h5, then 2. Qxf8 +, and White is up a Bishop.

Diagram 677 White to play: **1. Kd5-e6 Kb8-c8 2. Ke6-e7** and the pawn queens by force.

Black to play: **1. ...Kb8-c8 2. Kd5-c6** (or 2. Ke6) **2. ... Kc8-d8 3. d6-d7** etc.

Test Two Answers

Diagram 678 **1. Nf4-g6 +! Bf5xg6** (or else 2. Kxh7 follows) **stalemate.**

Diagram 679 Leonhardt–Englund, Stockholm 1908. Black threatens **1. ...Rxh2 + Kxh2 Rh8 + 3. Bh6 Rxh6#** (Anastasia's mate). If 1. h3, then **1. ...Rxh3#**, while on 1. Bf4 the reply **1. ... Nxf4** is decisive.

Diagram 680 Bogoljubow–Capablanca, New York 1924. **1. ... Rc8xc5!** White re-

signed. If 2. Rxc4, then 2. ... Rxc4, while 2. dxc5 is followed by 2. ... Qxc5 + (double attack) 3. any Rxc1.

Diagram 681 **1. Ra1-f1 (or 1. Rh1-f1)** *a pin.* If now 1. ... Rxg2 +, then 2. Qxg2 Bxg2 3. Rxf8# is a back-rank mate.

Diagram 682 Capablanca–Tanarov, New York 1910. **1. Qg3xe5! Qc7xe5 2. Nh6xf7 +** (double attack) **2. ... Kh8-g8** (if 2. ... Rxf7, then 3. Rd8 + Qe8 4. Rxe8 + Rf8 5. Rxf8# is a a back-rank mate). **3. Nf7xe5** and Black resigned.

Diagram 683 White to play wins as follows: **1. Kg5-f6 Kg8-f8 2. f4-f5 Kf8-e8** (if 2. ... Kg8, then 3. Ke7) **3. Kf6-g7** and the pawn will queen by force.

Black to play draws: **1. ... Kg8-g7!** (taking the opposition) **2. Kg5-f5 Kg7-f7** (again the opposition) **3. Kf5-e5 Kf7-e7** (still keeping the opposition) **4. f4-f5 Ke7-f7 5. f5-f6 Kf7-f8 6. Ke5-e6 Kf8-e8** (the opposition) **7. f6-f7 + Ke8-f8 8. Ke6-f6 stalemate.**

Test Three Answers

Diagram 684 No, Black cannot win the pawn on e4; if **1. ... Nf6xe4**, then **2. Rd6xc6! Rc8xc6 3. Re1xe4** (an equal trade); if **1. ... Bc6xe4**, then **2. Rd6xf6! g7xf6 3. Re1xe4**, and again the trade has been equal, each side having lost six points forth of material.

Diagram 685 Hasenfus–Flohr, Latvia 1937. **1. ... Qf6-g5 + 2. Kg2-h1** (if 2. Kh3, then 2. ... Qg4#) **2. ... Qg5xd2** (the N on f3 is pinned; White resigned).

Diagram 686 Stahlberg–Saemisch. **1. Qh5-g6 +!** Black resigned, since if 1. ... Qxg6 (or else 2. Qxh6 + follows), then 2. f5xg6 + (fork) 2. ... any 3. g6xf7.

Diagram 687 **1. Qf1-f6 +! e7xf6 2. e5xf6 +** (or 2. gxf6+) **2. ... Kg7-g8 3. Rh2xh8#.**

Diagram 688 Eve–Loman, Rotterdam 1923. **1. ... Bg7xd4?? 2. Qh3-h8 + Bd4xh8 3. Rh1xh8#.**

Diagram 689 1. ... Kc5-c4 (putting White in Zugzwang) **2. Kb2-a1 b3-b2 +!! 3. Ka1xa2** (if 3. Kxb2, then 3. ... a1Q+ 4. Kxa1 Kb3 5. Kb1 — taking the opposition — 5. ... Ka3 6. Ka1 — keeping the opposition — 6. ... b3 7. Kb1 b2 8. Kc2 Ka2 and Black wins) **3. ... b2-b1Q +! 4. Ka2xb1 Kc4-b3** (taking the opposition) **5. Kb1-c1** (if 5. Ka1, then 5. ... Kc2) **5. ... Kb3-a2** and the pawn will queen by force.

Test Four Answers

Diagram 690 **1. Qd6xd4!** (if 1. Qxd8, then 1. ... Qxd8; if 1. cxb6, then 1. ... Rxd6) **1. ... Rd8xd4 2. c5xb6.**

Diagram 691 **1. ... Bd5-e4?** (double attack) **2. Rh7-h8 +** (an in-between check) **2. ... Kb8-b7 3. Nb5-d6 +** (fork) **any 4. Nd6xe4.**

Diagram 692 Pirc–Stolz, Prague 1931. **1. ... Qa3-a1 +** (a skewer) **White resigned.**
If 2. Ke2, then 2. ... Qxh1;
if 2. Qd1, then 2. ... Qxc3 +;
if 2. Nd1, then 2. ... Qxd4 (the pawn on e3 is pinned).

Diagram 693 Keres–Levenfish, Moscow 1949. **1. Qd2xb4! Black resigned.**
If 1. ... Rxb4, then 2. Rc8 + Ng8 (or 2. ... Nxc8 3. Re8# — a back rank mate) 3. Re8xg8 +! Kh8xg8 4. Re2-e8# (a back-rank mate).
If 1. ... Re8, then 2. Qxe7 Rxe7 3. Rc8 + Re8 4. Rxe8#

Diagram 694 Morphy–Amateur, New York 1857. **1. Rf3-f8 +! Qe8xf8 2. Rf1xf8 + Ra8xf8 3. Qh6xg6#** (an epaulette mate).

Diagram 695 White to play: **1. Ke5-e6!** (taking the opposition) **1. ... Ke8-d8** (if 1. ... Kf8, then 2. Kd7 Kf7 3. Kc7) **2. Ke6-d6** (opposition) **2. ... Kd8-c8** (if 2. ... Ke8, then 3. Kc7) **3. Kd6-e7** and the pawn queens by force.
Black to move draws: **1. ... Ke8-e7!** (taking the opposition) **2. d5-d6 + Ke7-d7 3. Ke5-d5 Kd7-d8! 4. Kd5-e6** (if 4. Kc6, then 4. ...Kc8!, keeping the opposition) **4. ... Kd8-e8!** (opposition) **5. d6-d7 + Ke8-d8 6. Ke6-d6 stalemate.**

Test Five Answers

Diagram 696 **1. 0-0 Kh3-g3 2. Rf1-f3#**

Diagram 697 Makogonov–Chehover. **1. ... Qg4-h4 +!** (a double attack; the White Queen is pinned). White resigned, since after 2. any there follows 2. ... Qxf6.

Diagram 698 Morphy–Mongredien, Paris 1859. **1. Qc4-b4!** (a double attack). Black resigned, since if 1. ... Nd7 (1. ... Qxb4 leads to a back-rank mate: 2. Re8 + Qf8 3. Rxf8#), then 2. Qxb7.

Diagram 699 Alekhine–Bogoljubow, Match, Berlin 1929. **1. ... Qd3-e4!** (a double attack). White resigned, since if 2. Rxe4, then 2. ... Rc1 + 3. Re1 Rxe1# is a back-rank mate, while 2. Qb1 is met by 2. ... Qxa4.

Diagram 700 Vladimirov–Bobotsov, 1966. **1. Qh4-h8 +!.** Black resigned, since if 1. ... Bxh8 (if 1. ... Ke7, then 2. Qe8#), then 2. Rg8 + Ke7 3. Re8#.

Diagram 701 White to play wins by **1. a3-a4,** since the Black King cannot enter the square of the pawn: **1. ... Kg3-f4 2. a4-a5 Kf4-e5 3. a5-a6 Ke5-d5 4. a6-a7 Kd5-c6 5. a7-a8Q +.**
Black to play will stop the pawn since his King can enter the square of the pawn by **1. ... Kg3-f3,** e.g.: **2. a3-a4 Kf3-e4 3. a4-a5 Ke4-d5 4. a5-a6 Kd5-c6 5. a6-a7 Kc6-b7 6. a7-a8Q + Kb7xa8.**

Test Six Answers

Diagram 702 Keres–Holmov, Moscow 1948. **1. ... Qh3-g4 +!** (double attack) **2. f3xg4 stalemate** (or else Black plays 2. ... Qxa4, winning back his pawn, after which the game should be a draw).

Diagram 703 Morphy–Bogier, Paris 1858. Black is faced with a double attack on the Bishop on d7 and the pawn on h6; if he saves the Bishop by 1. ... Bxe6, then 2. Rxh6 + gxh6 3. Qxh6#.

Diagram 704 Chekhover–Kasparyan, Moscow 1936. **1. ... Nf6xe4!** The pawn on f3 is pinned: if 2. fxe4, then 2. ... Bxe2. If 2. Qxe4, then 2. ... Bg6 pins and wins the White Queen.

Diagram 705 **1. Kf6-e6!** (a double attack! The Rook is attacked and 2. Rh8# is threatened at the same time!) **1. ... Ke8-f8 2. Ke6xd5.**

Diagram 706 Romanovski–Rohlin, Moscow 1927. **1. Qh5-g6!** (threatening 2. Qh7#). Black resigned.
If 1. ... hxg5, then 2. Qh5#;
if 1. ... Qd3, then 2. Nf7#.

Diagram 707 **1. Kd4-e5 Ke8-e7** (opposition: if 1. ... Kf8, then 2. Kf6 with the opposition) **2. Ke5-f5 Ke7-e8 3. Kf5-e6** (opposition) **3. ... Ke8-f8 4. Ke6-f6** (opposition) **4. ... Kf8-g8 5. g6-g7 Kg8-h7 6. Kf6-f7** and the pawn will queen by force.

Test Seven Answers

Diagram 708 Gurgenidze–Suetin, Moscow 1961. **1. Rf7xh7+! Kh6xh7 2. Qe8-h8+! Kh7xh8 stalemate.**

Diagram 709 Chigorin–Janowski, Paris 1900. **1. Qc3-c5!** Black resigned because of the double threat of capturing the Bishop on f5 and 2. Qf8#.

Diagram 710 **1. Rc5-d5!** 1. Rc4 would not save the piece, because of 1. ... c5 2. Rxc5 Rxd4+) **1. ... c6xd5 2. Bd4xf6+** (the unpinned Bishop makes a double attack) **2. ... any 3. Bf6xd8.**

Diagram 711 **1. ... Rd7-d1+! 2. Rb1xd1** (if 2. Nxd1, then 2. ... Qe1# — a back-rank mate) **2. ... Rd8xd1+ 3. Nc3xd1 Qa5-e1#** (a back-rank mate).

Diagram 712 Johanson–Rey, 1935. **1. Rh3-h8+! Kg8xh8 2. Qe8xf8+ Rg7-g8 3. Qf8-h6#.**

Diagram 713 White to play wins as follows: **1. Kc5-c6** (opposition) **1. ... Ke6-e7 2. Kc6-b7 Ke7-d6 3. a2-a4** and the pawn will queen by force.

Black to play draws as follows: **1. ...Ke6-d7 2. Kc5-b6 Kd7-c8 3. Kb6-a7** (if 3. a4, then 3. ... Kb8 [opposition] 4. a5 Ka8 5. a6 Kb8 [opposition] 6. a7+ Ka8 7. Ka6 stalemate) **3. ... Kc8-c7** (opposition) **4. a2-a4 Kc7-c8 5. a4-a5 Kc8-c7** (opposition) **6. a5-a6 Kc7-c8 7. Ka7-a8** (opposition) **7. ... Kc8-c7 8. a6-a7 Kc7-c8 stalemate.**

Test Eight Answers

Diagram 714 Troitzky–Foht, 1896. **1. Qc2-d1+!!** (double attack) **1. ... Qf3xd1 stalemate** (or else 2. Qxf3).

Diagram 715 **1. Rf1-e1?** (pin) **1. ... Ne5-f3+** (double attack) **2. g2xf3 Qe8xe1+.**

Diagram 716 Stolyar–Averbakh, Leningrad 1938. **1. ... Rd8xd1! 2. Re1xd1** (if 2. Qxc6, then 2. ... Rxe1+ 3. Kg2 Rxc6) **2. ... Qc6xg2+ 3. Kh1xg2 Ng4-e3+** (fork) **4. any Ne3xd1.**

Diagram 717 **1. ... Qc2-d1+! 2. Ke1xd1 Rf5-f1#** (back-rank mate).

Diagram 718 **1. Qh2xh7+! Nf8xh7 2. Re1-e8+ Nh7-f8 3. Re8xf8+ Kg8xf8 4. Rh1-h8#** (a back-rank mate).

Diagram 719 White to play: **1. Kd5-e5 Kd7-d8! 2. Ke5-e6 Kd8-e8!** (opposition) **3. d6-d7+ Ke8-d8 4. Ke6-d6 stalemate.**

Black to play: **1. ... Kd7-d8! 2. Kd5-c6 Kd8-c8** (opposition) **3. d6-d7+ Kc8-d8 4. Kc6-d6 stalemate.**

Test Nine Answers

Diagram 720 Emanuel Lasker–Lisitsyn, Moscow 1935. Black draws by perpetual check: **1. ... Qf4xf2+ 2. Kg1-h1 Qf2-h4+ 3. Kh1-g1 Qh4-e1+ 4. Kg1-h2 Qe1-h4+** (if Black doesn't take the perpetual check, White will queen his pawn on d7.)

Diagram 721 **1. g2-g4** A double attack. The Rook is attacked and at the same time the fork 2. g5+ is threatened.

Diagram 722 1. Bc4xf7 + ! Kg8xf7 2. Nf3-e5 + (the Knight escapes from the pin and forks the White King and Bishop) 2. ... any 3. Ne5xg4 Nf6xg4 4. Qd1xg4.

Diagram 723 1. ... Bb3-a2 + 2. Kb1-a1 Rg1xc1# (A back-rank mate.)

Diagram 724 Bronstein–Keres, Budapest 1950. 1. Qg5-h6!. Black resigned. 2. Qg7# is threatened, and 1. ... Qxb1 + would be met by 2. Kh2 Rg8 3. Qxh7 + ! Kxh7 4. Rh4#.

Diagram 725 1. Na6-b4!! (Black was threatening a double attack by 1. ...Kb5. If 1. Nb8, then 1. ... Kb5 2. a6 Kb6 3. Ke5 Ka7 — again a double attack. If 1. Nc7, then 1. ... Kc5 2. Ke5 Kc6 3. N-any Kb5 and the pawn is lost.) 1. ... Kc4-b5 (If 1. ... Kxb4, then 2. a6 and the pawn will queen.) 2. a5-a6 Kb5-b6 3. Kf4-e5 Kb6-a7 4. Ke5-d6 Ka7-b6 (opposition) 5. Kd6-d7 Kb6-a7 6. Kd7-c6 Ka7-a8 (opposition) 7. Kc6-b6 Ka8-b8 (opposition) 8. Nb4-d5 Kb8-a8 9. Nd5-c7 + Ka8-b8 (opposition) 10. a6-a7 + and the pawn will queen.

Test Ten Answers

Diagram 726 1. Kg3-h4! any 2. g2-g3! any stalemate.

Diagram 727 1. Ng5xe6 f7xe6 2. Qd1-h5 + (double attack) 2. ... any 3. Qh5xc5.

Diagram 728 Black can save his Queen after 1. ... Nf8-e6 + (an in-between check).

Diagram 729 1. ... Qf1xb1 + ! 2. Ka1xb1 (the Rook on b2 is pinned) 2. ... Rd8-d1# (a back-rank mate).

Diagram 730 Verlinski–Yuhtman, USSR 1949. 1. Rg5-g7! Black resigned. The threat is 2. Rxh7# (Arab mate). 1. ... Qb1 would be met by 2. Rg8 + Rxg8 3. Rxg8# (Arab mate), while if 1. ... Ra7, then 2. Rg8 + Qxg8 3. Rxg8#, again with an Arab mate.

Diagram 731 1. d3-d4! (If 1. Kg4, then 1. ... Kc5 2. Kf5 Kxd5 and Black should draw with

correct play) 1. ... Kb5-b6 2. Kh3-g4 Kb6-c7 3. Kg4-f5 Kc7-d6 4. Kf5-e4 Kd6-d7 5. Ke4-e5 Kd7-e7 (opposition) 6. d5-d6 + Ke7-d7 7. Ke5-d5 (opposition) 7. ... Kd7-d8 8. Kd5-c6 Kd8-c8 9. d6-d7 + Kc8-d8 10. d4-d5! Kd8-e7 11. Kc6-c7 and the pawn will queen.

Test Eleven Answers

Diagram 732 1. ... Rf1xf6 + (double attack) 2. Qf8xf6 stalemate (or else 2. ... Rxf8 would follow).

Diagram 733 Black loses in Bishop in all variations:
   1. ... Ba2 (or 1. ... Ba4) 2. Ra6 + (double attack);
   1. ... Bf7 2. Rd8 + any 3. Rd7 + (double attack);
   1. ... Bg8 2. Rd8 + (double attack).

Diagram 734 1. Rc4-c5 + (a double attack; the Bishop on b6 is pinned) 1. ... Rd5xc5 (or else 2. Qxd5) 2. Qd8xd3 (the Rook on d5 was also pinned. Black has lost a Queen for a Rook).

Diagram 735 1. Re3xe6! Rf7-f8! (if 1. ... Rxe6, then 2. Qd8 + Qe8 3. Qxe8 + Rxe8 4. Rxe8 + Rf8 5. Rxf8# [a back-rank mate]) 2. Qd4-e5 and White has won a pawn. But White must not play 2. Rxc6, for Black would then win a Rook by 2. ... Rxe1 + 3. Qg1 Rxg1 + 4. Kxg1 bxc6.

Diagram 736 Kramstov–Vaisberg, USSR 1938. 1. Rd7xb7 + ! Kb8xb7 (the Bishop on c8 was pinned) 2. Qd8-b6# (an epaulette mate).

Diagram 737 With White to play, the game should be drawn: 1. Kf6-g5 (or 1. g7 + Kg8 2. Kg6 stalemate; or 1. Kf7 stalemate) 1. ... Kh8-g7 2. Kg5-h5 Kg7-g8 3. Kh5-h6 Kg8-h8 (opposition) 4. g6-g7 + Kh8-g8 5. Kh6-g6 stalemate.
   With Black to play, White wins: 1. ... Kh8-g8 2. g6-g7 Kg8-h7 3. Kf6-f7 and the pawn will queen.

Test Twelve Answers

Diagram 738 This is a problem by Sam

Loyd. Black is in Zugzwang — every move of his allows White to mate him immediately:

1. **1. ... Bb7 2. Nf5#;**
2. **1. ... Bd7 2. Qd5#;**
3. **1. ... Be6 1. Qe5#;**
4. **1. ... Bf5 2. Nxf5#;**
5. **1. ... Rd7 2. Nf5#;**
6. **1. ... Rd6 2. Qxb4#;**
7. **1. ... Rd5 2. Qxd5#;**
8. **1. ... Re7 2. Qxb4#;**
9. **1. ... Re6 2. Nf5#;**
10. **1. ... Re5 2. Qxe5#;**
11. **1. ... Bc5 2. Qa1#;**
12. **1. ... Bd6 2. Qd5#;**
13. **1. ... Be7 2. Qe5#;**
14. **1. ... Bg7 2. Qb6#;**
15. **1. ... Bh6 2. Qb6#.**

Diagram 739 Mikenas—Pelts, Leningrad 1969. **1. ... Qd8xd4!** (double attack on the Bishop and the pawn on b2) **2. Qd3xd4 Ne3xc2 +** (fork) **3. any Nc2xd4.**

Diagram 740 **1. Rg6xg7!** (the Black Queen and the Rook on g8 are pinned) **1. ... Rg8xh8** (or else 2. Rhxg8#) **2. Qf6xf7#.**

Diagram 741 Taimanov–Kotov, Moscow 1948. **1. Ng3xh5?? Bf4-e3 +** White resigned. (2. any Rg1#).

Diagram 742 White to play: **1. Qc1-g5! g7-g6 2. Qg5-h6 Ra8-a1 + 3. Kb1xa1 Qe8-a8 + 4. Ka1-b1 Qa8-a2 + 5. Kb1-c1 Qa2-a1 + 6. Kc1-d2 Qa1-a5 + 7. c2-c3 Qa5xc3 + 8. b2xc3 any 9. Qh6-g7#.**

Black to play: **1. ... Ra8-a1 +! 2. Kb1xa1 Qe8-a8 + 3. Ka1-b1 Qa8-a2#.**

Diagram 743 White to play: **1. Kd5-e6 Kh7-g7 2. Ke6-e7 Kg7-h7 3. Ke7-f6** (3. f8Q?? is stalemate) **3. ... Kh7-h6 4. f7-f8Q +** etc.

Black to play draws: **1. ... Kh7-g7 2. Kd5-e6 Kg7-f8** (White is now in Zugzwang) **3. Ke6-f5** (3. Kf6 or 3. h6 is stalemate) **3. ... Kf8xf7** (opposition) **4. h5-h6 Kf7-g8 5. Kf5-g6** (opposition) **5. ... Kg8-h8 6. h6-h7** stalemate.

Test Thirteen Answers

Diagram 744 **1. Nb7-c5 +** (or 1. Nd6 +) **1. ...**

Ke4-d5 2. Qc3-f3 +! (skewer) **2. ... any 3. Qf3xa8.**

Diagram 745 Amateur–Leonhardt, Leipzig 1903. **1. ... Bc5xf2 +! 2. Qg3xf2** (if 2. Kxf2, then 2. ... Nxe4 + [fork] 3. any Nxg3) **2. ... Ne5-d3 +** (fork) **3. any Nd3xf2.**

Diagram 746 **1. Kh3-g4! Rh8xh6 3. Kg4-g5!** (double attack) **2. ... Rh6-h2 3. Kg5xg6.**

Diagram 747 **1. Bf1-c4 + Kf7-f8 2. Rd1-d8#.**

Diagram 748 Kan–Alatortsev, Leningrad 1951. If **1. ... Bxg2??**, then **2. Ne7 +! Kh8 3. Qxh7 +! Kxh7 4. Rh4 + Qh5 5. Rxh5#** (Anastasia's mate).

Diagram 749 The position is drawn no matter who plays first. **1. Kd5xe5 Kf8-e7!** (opposition) **2. Ke5-d5 Ke7-d7** (opposition) **3. e4-e5 Kd7-e7 4. e5-e6 Ke7-e8 5. Kd5-d6 Ke8-d8** (opposition) **6. e6-e7 + Kd8-e8 7. Kd6-e6** stalemate.

Test Fourteen Answers

Diagram 750 White draws by perpetual check:

1. **Qh3-c8 +**	**Rb7-b8**
2. **Qc8-c6 +**	**Rb8-b7**
3. **Qc6-c8 +**	**Rb7-b8**
4. **Qc8-c6**	**Rb8-b7**
5. **Qc6-c8 +**	

Diagram 751 **1. Re1xe5 +** (double attack) **1. ... Rd5xe5 2. f2-f4 +!** (fork) **2. ... Kg5-f5 3. f4xe5 Kf5xe5 4. Kg2-h3! Ke5-f5** (opposition) **5. Kh3-h4! Kf5-g6 6. Kh4-g4!** and with correct play White should win, since his King has the opposition in front of his pawn.

Diagram 752 **1. ... Qc7-c1 +! 2. Rh1xc1** (the Knight and Rook on b2 are pinned) **2. ...Rc8xc1#** (a back-rank mate).

Diagram 753 **1. Re4-e8 +! Kf8xe8 2. Rg2-g8#** (a back-rank mate).

Diagram 754 Duras–Olland, Karlsbad 1907. **1. Qh4xh5 +! g6xh5 2. Rd6-h6#.**

Diagram 755 **1. Kf3-f4!** (if 1. Ke4, then 1. ... Kd6 puts White in Zugzwang: 2. any Kxd5 and Black should draw with correct play.) **1. ... Ke7-d6** (opposition) **2. Kf4-e4** (now it is Black who is in Zugzwang) **2. ... Kd6-d7 3. Ke4-e5 Kd7-e7** (opposition) **4. d5-d6 + Ke7-d7 5. Ke5-d5 Kd7-d8 6. Kd5-e6 Kd8-e8** (opposition) **7. d6-d7 + Ke8-d8 8. d4-d5!** (a waiting move) **8. ...Kd8-c7 9. Ke6-e7** and the pawn will queen by force.

Test Fifteen Answers

Diagram 756 **1. Ra1-a8!** (threatening 2. g8Q) **1. ... Rg2xg7 2. Ra8-a7 +** (skewer) **2. ... any 3. Ra7xg7.**

Diagram 757 **1. e4-e5 +** (a fork) **1. ... Qd6xe5** (or 1. ... Kxe5 2. Nc4 + [fork] 2. ... any 3. Nxd6) **2. Ne3-g4 +** (fork) **2. ... any 3. Ng4xe5.**

Diagram 758 **1. Qh5-g6!** (the pawn on f7 is pinned) **1. ... any 2. Qg6-h7#.**

Diagram 759 **1. Qe7xf8 + ! Kg8xf8** (or else 2. Qg7# would follow) **2. Rd1-d8#** (a back-rank mate).

Diagram 760 Kolisch–Loyd, Paris 1867. **1. Qg3xg6!!** h7xg6? **2. Rf1-f3** Black resigned, since 3. Rh3# (Greco's mate) is threatened and if 2. ... Re6, then 3. Bxe6 Qf7 4. Bxf7 any 5. Rh3# (Greco's mate).

Diagram 761 This is a position of mutual Zugzwang. If White starts, Black draws, while if Black moves first, White queens his pawn and wins.

With White to move: **1. Kh7-h8 Kf7-f8!** (opposition) **2. f6-f7** (or 2. h7 Kf7 stalemate) **2. ... Kf8xf7 3. Kh8-h7** (opposition; if 3. h7, then 3. ... Kf8 stalemate) **3. ... Kf7-f8 4. Kh7-g6 Kf8-g8** (opposition) **5. h6-h7 + Kg8-h8 6. Kg6-h6 stalemate.**

With Black to move: **1. ... Kf7-f8** (or 1. ... Kxf6 2. Kg8) **2. Kh7-g6 Kf8-g8** (opposition) **3. f6-f7 + Kg8-f8 4. h6-h7** and the h-pawn will queen.

Test Sixteen Answers

Diagram 762 No, White cannot win a piece. If 1. Rf2? (skewer), then 1. ... Bh4 (counter skewer) 2. Rxf3 Bxe1 and White has lost an Exchange.

Diagram 763 **1. Rb6xc6! Rc7-d7** (the Bishop on d5 is pinned, while 1. ... Rxc6 is met by the fork 2. Bxd5 + winning a Bishop and a Rook. If 1. ... Bxa2, then 2. Rxc7) **2. Rc6-c8 +** (White has won a pawn by his combination).

Diagram 764 **1. Re1-e6!** (a counter pin) saves the piece.

Diagram 765 **1. Qb7-b1 +! Kc1xb1 Rd8-d1#** (a back-rank mate).

Diagram 766 Delva–Pelts, Ottawa 1981. **1. ... Rf8-f3!!** White resigned. 2. Bxf3 is met by 2. ... Qxh4# and 2. Rxf3 by 2. ... Qg2#.

Diagram 767 White to play: **1. b7-b8Q +!** (not 1. Kc7 stalemate or 1. b6 + Kb8 2. Kc5 Kxb7 3. Kb5 Kb8 4. Kc6 Kc8 [opposition] 5. b7 + Kb8 6. Kb6 stalemate) **1. ... Kxb8 2. Kc6-b6!** (opposition) **2. ... Kb8-a8** (or 2. ...Kc8 3. Ka7) **3. Kb6-c7** and the pawn queens by force.

Black to play draws: **1. ... Ka7-b8** (White is now in Zugzwang) **2. Kc6-c5** (if 2. Kb6 or 2. b6 it is stalemate) **2. ... Kb8xb7 3. b5-b6 Kb7-b8 4. Kc5-c6 Kb8-c8** (opposition) **5. b6-b7 + Kc8-b8 6. Kc6-b6 stalemate.**

Test Seventeen Answers

Diagram 768 **1. Qd1-h5 + Kf7xf6 2. Qh5-h4 + !** (skewer) **2. ... any 3. Qh4xd8.**

Diagram 769 **1. Bf1-b5!** (pin) **1. ... Qc6xb5 2. Nd5-c7 +** (fork) **2. ... any 3. Nc7xb5.**

Diagram 770 **1. Rd3xd6! Re6xd6** (now the Rook is pinned) **2. e4-e5 any 3. Ba3xd6.**

Diagram 771 **1. Nd5-c7 + ! Ne6xc7 2. Rd3-d8#** (back-rank mate).

Diagram 772 1. Qh3-b3 + !! Qb8xb3 (or 1. ... Kh7 2. Qxb8 Rh2+ 3. Qxh2 Rxh2+ 4. Kxh2) 2. Re1-e8 + Kg8-f7 (or 2. ... Kh7 3. Rh8#) 3. Re8-f8#.

Diagram 773 White to play: 1. b6-b7 Kb8-a7 2. b7-b8Q + ! (not 2. Kc7 stalemate or 2. b6+ Kb8 3. Kc5 Kxb7 4. Kb5 Kb8 5. Kc6 Kc8 [opposition] 6. b7+ Kb8 7. Kb6 stalemate) 2. ... Ka7xb8 3. Kc6-b6! (opposition) 3. ... Kb8-a8 (or 3. ... Kc8 4. Ka7) 4. Kb6-c7 and the pawn will queen by force.

Black to play draws: 1. ... Kb8-a8 (or 1. ... Kc8) 2. b6-b7 + (2. Kc7 gives a stalemate) 2. ... Ka8-b8 (White is now in Zugzwang) 3. Kc6-c5 (after 3. Kb6 or 3. b6 it is stalemate) 3. ... Kb8xb7 4. b5-b6 Kb7-b8 5. Kc5-c6 Kb8-c8 (opposition) 6. b6-b7 + Kc8-b8 7. Kc6-b6 stalemate.

Test Eighteen Answers

Diagram 774 1. h6-h7 Qg3-h2 2. h7-h8Q + ! Qh2xh8 3. Ra7-a8 + (skewer) 3. ... any 4. Ra8xh8.

Diagram 775 1. Qc4xe6! Qd7xe6 (or else 2. Qe8 followed by 3. f8Q) 2. f7-f8N + ! any 3. Nf8xe6.

Diagram 776 White saves the piece by playing 1. Nd4-f5!. Then 1. ... Bxb2 is met by 2. Nxh6 (an even trade) while 1. ...Nxf5 is met by 2. Bxf6 + (also an even trade).

Diagram 777 Black can defend his back rank by playing 1. ... Rd7-d8! and now 2. Rc8xa8 can be met by 2. ... Rd8xa8 while if 2. Rc8xd8, then 2. ... Ra8xd8. But 1. ... Rxc8 would lose to 2. Rxc8 + Rd8 3. Rxd8# (back-rank mate).

Diagram 778 Composed by Kubbel. White to play: 1. Rh3xh7 + ! Kh8xh7 2. Qe6-h3 + Bf6-h4 3. Qh3xh4 + Qc5-h5 4. Qh4xh5# (Greco's mate).

Black to play: 1. ... Qc5xf2 + !! 2. Rf1xf2 (or else 2. ... Qxf1# [back-rank mate]) 2. ... Rb2-b1 + 3. Rf2-f1 Bf6-d4 + 4. Rh3-e3 Bd4xe3 + 5. Kg1-h1 Rb1xf1# (back-rank mate).

Diagram 779 White to play: 1. Ka7-a6 (opposition; if 1. Ka8 or 1. Kb8, then 1. ...Kb5, while if 1. a6, then 1. ... Kc7 [opposition] 2. Ka8 Kc8 [opposition] 3. a7 Kc7 stalemate) 1. ... Kc6-c7 2. Ka6-b5 2. ... Kc7-b7 (opposition) 3. a5-a6 + Kb7-a7 4. Kb5-a5 Ka7-b8 5. Ka5-b6 (opposition) 5. ... Kb8-a8 6. a6-a7 stalemate.

Black to play: 1. ... Kc6-c7 (opposition) 2. a5-a6 (if 2. Ka8, then 2. ...Kc8 [opposition]; if 2. Ka6, then 2. ...Kc6 [opposition]) 2. ... Kc7-c8 3. Ka7-b6 (if 3. Ka8 [opposition], then 3. ...Kc7 4. a7 Kc8 stalemate) 3. ... Kc8-b8 (opposition) 4. a6-a7 + Kb8-a8 5. Kb6-a6 stalemate.

Test Nineteen Answers

Diagram 780 1. Bc1-g5 + (skewer) 1. ... f7-f6 (or else 2. Rxd8#) 2. e5xf6 + g7xf6 (if 2. ... Ke8, then 3. f7+ [in-between check] followed by 4. Rxd8) 3. Bg5xf6 + ! Ke7xf6 4. Rd1xd8 and White has won the Exchange and a pawn.

Diagram 781 1. Nh4-g6 + Kh8-h7 2. Ng6-f8 + (fork) 2. ... Kh7-h8 3. Nf8xe6 (fork).

Diagram 782 1. Qd1xh5 + (the pawn on g6 is pinned) 1. ... Kh7-g8 2. Qh5-h8#.

Diagram 783 1. Qf3-f8 + ! Rb8xf8 2. Rf2xf8 + Ra8xf8 3. Rf1xf8# (back-rank mate).

Diagram 784
solution a): 1. ... Qb6-b1 + 2. Rg1xb1 Rb7xb1 + 3. Rh1xb1 Rb8xb1#.
solution b): 1. ... Qb6xg1 + ! 2. Rh1xg1 Rb7-b1 + 3. Rg1xb1 Rb8xb1#.

Diagram 785 White to play: 1. Kf4-e5 (or 1. Kf5 Kg7 and White is in Zugzwang: 2. any Kxg6 and Black should draw with correct play) 1. ... Kg8-g7 2. Ke5-f5 Kg7-g8! 3. Kf5-f6 Kg8-h8 (or 3. ...Kf8 [opposition]) 4. g6-g7 + (or 4. Kf7 stalemate) 4. ... Kh8-g8 5. Kf6-f5 (after 5. g6 or 5. Kg6 it is stalemate) 5. ... Kg8xg7 6. g5-g6 Kg7-g8 7. Kf5-f6 Kg8-h8 (or 7. ... Kf8 [opposition]) 8. g6-g7 + (or 8. Kf7 stalemate) 8. ... Kh8-g8 9. Kf6-g6 stalemate. Black to play draws in an analogous manner.

287

Diagram 786 1. ...Rc7-c2! (pin) 2. Qd2xc2 Qb8-h2 + (skewer) 3. any Qh2xc2.

Diagram 787 1. Qe2-e4! (with the double threat of 2. Qh7# and 2. Qxa8) 1. ... g7-g6 2. Qe4xa8.

Diagram 788 White saves his pinned Knight as follows: 1. Nd4-e6! Rd7xd3 (or 1. ... fxe6 2. Rxd7) 2. Ne6xc5 + (fork) 2. ... any 3. Nc5xd3.

Diagram 789 1. Rc8-h8 + Bg7xh8 2. Qe5xh8#.

Diagram 790 Gutop–Roshal, Moscow 1963. 1. ... Qd6xd5!! (threatening 2. ... Qxg2#) 2. Bg2xd5 Bb7xd5 (the pawn on f2 is pinned and so White has no defense against 3. ... Rh1#). White resigned.

Diagram 791 White to play: 1. Ke4-f5 Kg8-g7 2. Kf5-g5 (2. g5? leads to a draw) 2. ... Kg7-g8 3. Kg5-h6 Kg8-h8 (opposition) 4. g6-g7 + Kh8-g8 5. g4-g5! (a waiting move: the immediate 5. Kg6 gives stalemate) 5. ... Kg8-f7 6. Kh6-h7 and the pawn will queen by force.

Black to play: 1. ... Kg8-g7 2. Ke4-f5 Kg7-h6! 3. g6-g7! (3. Kf6 gives stalemate; 3. g5? leads to a drawn position after 3. ... Kg7) 3. ... Kh6xg7 4. Kf5-g5 (opposition) 4. ... Kg7-f7 (or 4. ... Kh7 5. Kf6) 5. Kg5-h6 Kf7-g8 6. g4-g5 Kg8-h8 (opposition) 7. g5-g6 Kh8-g8 8. g6-g7 Kg8-f7 9. Kh6-h7 and the pawn queens by force.

MOVING ON TO EXPERT AND MASTER

Students who complete Volumes I and II of *Comprehensive Chess Course* frequently ask a compelling question, "What do I do next?" Which is another way of asking, how does one consolidate knowledge gained and move on to the next level of strength?

As already noted, *Comprehensive Chess Course* is part of a multi-year course of study long and successfully employed in the former Soviet Union. This ambitious course is designed to make masters out of rank beginners. Volumes I and II contain materials which, if completely mastered, bring most players up to what we call the Class A level. The task is now that of, as stated in the title of this chapter, "Moving On to Expert and Master."

FM Roman Pelts and GM Lev Alburt, the authors of the book you are now reading, initially intended to publish a third volume designed to advance players toward the level of 2000 to 2100. But this good intention has encountered the reality of the economics of publishing. Readers will notice that Volume I contained 124 pages and Volume II, 288 pages. Both volumes together contained nearly 1,100 diagrams. The increase in pages from Volume I to Volume II is no accident. It is a function of the increased knowledge required to ascend from level to level in chess strength and the in-creased ability of players to absorb information as they grow stronger.

We estimate that Level III in our *Comprehensive Chess Course* will require about 1,000 pages and nearly 3,000 diagrams. Thus, we're producing it in several books. The first of these, *Chess Tactics for the Tournament Player*, appeared last December, with books on Attack & Defense, Strategy, Endings and Openings to follow soon.

The current chapter — though it presents chess positions to illustrate certain points — is **not** instructional in nature and does not contain questions to answer, problems to solve and tests to take. Rather, it is meant to provide concrete advice on how to create a regimen of self-study and self-training that will make *you* a stronger chess player.

In what follows, we recommend several books by other authors. These recommendations by no means exhaust the pantheon of good chess books. It may happen, for example, that a given student will find a particular work on endgames more useful than our own recommendations. That is completely natural, and students should feel no hesitation in consulting works other than those mentioned here.

BEGINNING ANEW?

The first step for you on the road to expert and master may be a variation on the old Leninist theme about taking one step backward in order to take two steps forward. Be brutally honest with yourself: Have you really mastered the material presented in Volumes I and II? By which we mean, can you readily apply in practice what you have learned in theory?

Quick, what color is the g5 square? Quick, what color is c6? There should be no hesitation in your answers. Okay, here is an easy one: White has pawns on a6 and b6 and a King on e2; Black has a Rook on c5 and a King on g5. With the second player to move, can he stop the pawns? Yes or no, quickly!

The preceding questions concern material presented in Volume I, and they deal with knowledge of the board and the endgame. If you cannot answer these questions readily, then you ought to consider beginning anew. In fact, even as you read this chapter, turn back to Diagram 168, which contains the Rook and pawn ending mentioned in the preceding paragraph. Also take a look at Diagram 51, in which the Rook fights three connected passed pawns, and at Diagram 52, in which the Bishop must fight two connected passed pawns. And what about Diagram 55, in which the Rook is matched against four pawns, and Diagram 16, in which pawns are scattered everywhere? Don't forget to recheck the review questions in Lesson Four. Can you provide instant answers? (All the above refers to Volume I).

Believe us, knowing the basics and knowing the chessboard like you know the multiplication tables is useful knowledge up to the master level and well beyond. Indeed, it is essential knowledge. Most A and B players do not see the chessboard clearly and, therefore, often fail to analyze lines correctly to their conclusion. To use a phrase of George Bush's, the "vision thing" in chess is crucial, and it must be developed early by mastering the chessboard and by studying tactics.

Our advice is that except for those tests covering material that you know very well indeed, retake the examinations in both Volumes I and II. Grade the results not only on whether you answer the questions correctly but also on whether you answer them quickly. Do you *feel* this knowledge in your fingertips? And do these fingertips move naturally to the correct piece?

Or, even better, are you able to take the tests without using a board and pieces?

If you cannot complete the tests with virtually no errors and well within the one hour allotted for each examination, then peruse the relevant lessons in Volumes I and II. These are the lessons that contain knowledge which is not yet active in your mind and which you cannot yet apply automatically.

For those students who can truthfully state that they easily handle the material in Volumes I and II, we recommend that they read over Jose Capablanca's *Chess Fundamentals* and *Last Lectures*, two wonderful books by the man regarded by many as chess history's greatest genius. Capablanca also had a genius for making the complex, simple — perhaps because for him, it was simple. He understood the *reasons* for things and could relate those reasons in clear language.

STUDY THE SOUL OF CHESS

Most readers have limited time for study; therefore, how that time is used becomes crucial. We recommend that students devote two-thirds to three-quarters of their time studying tactics, which are the soul of chess. "Chess is 99 percent tactics," Savielly Tartakower either said or ought to have said.

The importance of tactics in chess is obvious. (We beg students who are addicted to opening manuals to remember that most players who spend their time studying theory never reach A-level.) Every student should remember how he struggles constantly during most games to wend his way through tactical complications.

In chess, strategy is based on what is tactically feasible, which is to say, positional ideas must always survive tactical examinations before they are played. Black often wants to play ... d6-d5 in the Sicilian, but the timing of this positionally useful advance is strictly a function of specific tactical considerations. Learning all of the positional "oughts" in chess is useless if these rules cannot be accurately applied.

Laying down a solid tactical foundation is, then, absolutely necessary. In *Comprehensive Chess Course* we introduce numerous tactical ideas and provide hundreds of exercises. Assuming that the student has mastered this subject matter, the time has come to study other books. Some of our favorites include Moe Moss and Ian Mullin's *Blunders and Brilliancies*, Yasser Seirawan's *Flash Tactics*, August Livshitz's *Test Your Chess IQ*, Nikolai Krogius' *Encyclopedia of Middlegames: Combinations*, Vladimir Vukovic's *The Art of Attack*, Leonid Shamkovich's *The Tactical World of Chess*, Fred Reinfeld's hardy perennials, *1001 Brilliant Ways to Checkmate* and *1001 Winning Sacrifices and Combinations*, and, of course, our own Level III books on tactics and attack.

Students who aim for the expert and master levels should study tactics in order to learn new ideas. Training is secondary at this stage. The best way to approach, say, Krogius' *Encyclopedia* is to move from one chapter to another, solving only two or three positions, which proceed from the simple to the complex, in each chapter. After going through all of the chapters — there are 16 thematic categories of combinations — go back another time and look at positions that you have yet to solve. Our advice is not to spend more than five or 10 minutes on each position, then look at the solution. Your objective is not primarily to train yourself to solve positions but to try to understand the solution so that you will recognize the idea on the next occasion. Use these positions to learn more about such combinative themes as double attacks and deflection, overloading and X-rays, etc.

The positions in the *Encyclopedia* are frequently rather difficult. The positions in Reinfeld's *1001* books are easier and can be used to refresh your mind about simpler combinational ideas and motives. The Reinfeld volumes are excellent for warming up on the way to a tournament without tiring oneself by playing five-minute chess. Here is a neat *petite* combination, using a pinning theme: *[See the diagram at the top of the next column.]*

White wins immediately with **1. Qg8 + !**. On 1. ... Kxg8, White forces mate by 2. Ng6, threatening 3. Rh8, mate. In the game Black lost quickly after **1. ... Ke7 2. Qxf7 + Kd8 3. Ng6 Qxb2 4. Rd1 + Bd7 5. Qxe8 + , Black resigns**. With proper tactical study, shots like **1. Qg8 + !** should suggest themselves as readi-

ly to the eye as 2. ... Qh4, mate after 1. f3 e5 2. g4.

**Gerald Abrahams–Thynne
Liverpool 1930**

The more proficient a student becomes in handling tactical themes, the more instruction he can obtain from the Vukovic and Shamkovich volumes, which contain complete games and which cover complex tactical ideas such as the intuitive sacrifice. And while on the subject of intuitive sacrifices, Mikhail Tal's autobiographical *The Life and Games of Mikhail Tal* offers both instruction and entertainment. Indeed, hard study becomes unadulterated fun with the Tal volume.

Self-training in calculating variations is largely a matter of method combined with a willingness to concentrate over extended periods. Take an *Informant* and spend an evening looking for positions in the combination section with solutions running between five and eight moves. Write down the numbers of these positions, along with the first move of each solution, and return to them at a later date. Remember, your aim now is purely training in calculation.

Our advice is to spend, if necessary, from 30 minutes to an hour on each position. Depending on how successfully you perform, handling from three to six such positions at a sitting provides a fine workout and a good test of where you stand. (If you do not own any *Informants*, then an inexpensive substitute is *Flash Tactics*, especially the "Advanced" series.)

As your friends expend their limited study time on plowing through opening monographs written by grandmasters for grandmasters, just remember that players in the process of development in the former Soviet Union and Eastern Europe received relatively little opening theory and a great deal of training in tactics and the endgame.

And these players from former Communist lands, who have often been exposed to far less opening theory than Western players, now participate in Western Swiss events and are regarded as "monsters." They seem to play middlegames and endings as if they were geniuses. In reality, they are merely formidably schooled in the basics.

THE IMPORTANCE OF STUDYING ENDGAMES

Few players need to be convinced of the utility of knowing how to win or draw King and pawn versus King endgames. Such positions occur so often in their games that the practical value of studying them is obvious. Nonetheless, they regard endings as dry and act as if they were of little practical importance by imagining that they will win in the opening or middlegame.

The fact that most players are woefully ignorant of endgames is one of the best reasons for *you* to study them. Such work will prove one of the most efficient ways of increasing your strength in absolute terms and in relation to others. Moreover, the stronger a player and his competition become, the more often endgames occur. The player who studies endings will be able to win even positions and draw inferior and lost positions.

Another reason to study endings is that while opening theory constantly changes and players often switch openings as they grow stronger, endgame theory remains relatively stable and, of course, players do not have the option of switching endgames. To study endings, especially Rook endings, which are the most common of all endgames, is an efficient use of time because these endings or slight variations tend to repeat themselves. If memorizing complicated opening traps may net a player an occasional quick point, studying Rook endings will garner hundreds of extra points and half-points over the years.

Studying pared down endings or miniatures

is also very helpful for tactical thinking. Many endings illustrate chessboard geometry in particularly stark fashion. The common theme of interposing the Queen against an opponent's Queen check, while simultaneously checking the opponent's King, is a good example. Here is another:

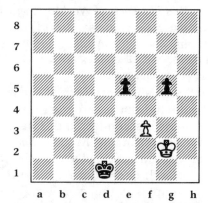

White to move. Can he save the game?

Yes, White can save the game. But the solution is far from obvious for those who are unacquainted with opposition in the endgame. White has only one move to hold the draw: **1. Kh1!**. Please note that there are no extraneous pieces to clutter up some very clear ideas.

"Clear ideas?" — what do we mean by this phrase? Unlike openings and middlegames, endings are ultimately easier to study because the vast majority of positions yield to definite evaluations. Too, the importance of move order is demonstrable in endings — and never more so than in King and pawn endings where the weaker side must maintain the opposition.

Two of our favorite books for studying the endgame are an old classic, Capablanca's *Chess Fundamentals,* and Bruce Pandolfini's modern classic, *Pandolfini's Endgame Course.* The latter volume contains within its beautifully organized pages every basic bit of knowledge that a player requires to handle endings like an expert or even a master. It perfectly complements our **Comprehensive Chess Course**.

Other books to consult include Edmar Mednis' *Practical Rook Endings,* Jon Speelman and August Livshitz's *Test Your Endgame Ability* and Mikhail Shereshevsky's *Endgame Strategy.* Once again, we note that our list is far from exhaustive, and some players may prefer Irving

Chernev's *Capablanca's Best Chess Endings* as an advanced primer rather than the Shereshevsky volume. Or, perhaps, some players may find the miniature studies in Chernev's *Practical Chess Endings* so fascinating as to awake a passion for endgames — even though the book itself is not designed as a teaching tool.

Readers will note the obvious absence of GM Reuben Fine's *Basic Chess Endings* from our list of recommended works. This book is a product of genius by a genius. There is nothing "basic" about it. Wait a few years, develop a bit more, then purchase this masterpiece. Use Fine's book primarily as a reference tool.

The ideal solution for would-be experts and masters with endgame disabilities is to work with a chess trainer. But if this kind of intensive care is impractical, then the student does best to investigate systematically the 200 or so basic positions isolated in *Pandolfini's Endgame Course*.

THE ART OF PYTHON–THINKING

We also advise students to make a concerted effort to reorient their thinking when playing endgames. Which is to say, the most common pitfall in endgame thinking is to mistake endings for middlegames and to act like a tiger pouncing on its prey rather than a python slowly squeezing out resignations. At the highest level, this fundamental misconception may constitute the defining distinction between a fine endgame player like Mikhail Tal and a supreme virtuoso like Mikhail Botvinnik. Certainly, in their 1961 world title match, Botvinnik repeatedly took advantage of Tal's tigerish impatience in the final part of the game. And as is true of politics, so it is of chess: In any contest between power and patience, always bet on patience.

The objective in practical endgames is to transfer to basic ending positions which are known to be winning. Trading one advantage for another is a typical technique. In the following position, GM Bent Larsen tries to keep a two-pawn advantage at all costs instead of shifting into a known win: *(See the diagram at the top of the next column.)*

White plays **78. Rc7** in order to keep both pawns. Objectively, the move is okay. But GM

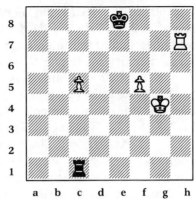

Bent Larsen–Eugenio Torre
Leningrad (St. Petersburg) Interzonal, 1973
White to move

Larsen fails to transfer into a known win, which he could have done with 78. Kg5 Rxc5 79. Kg6, threatening 80. Rh8 + . Black must lose because his King is on the long side of the board, while his Rook cannot effectively play lateral checks on the White King which is on the short side.

The point is that GM Larsen knew that 78. Kg5 was a theoretical win, and had he played this move, the game would have been *de facto* over. But after the text, it is still a game. Play continued: **78. ... Kd8 79. Rc6 Kd7 80. Rd6 + Ke7.** White could still have won with 81. Re6 + Kf7 82. c6, but Larsen fell into a draw with **81. f6 + ? Kf7 82. c6 Kg6 83. Kf3 Re1!.** The White King is cut off from both pawns.

Another practice to adopt when playing endings is the simple act of remaining alert for tempo gains. Many players blindly push ahead with their pawns and plans even when they notice good opportunities to pick up tempos. "Why bother?" they ask themselves.

Here's why:

P.S. Leonhardt–Rudolf Spielmann
San Sebastian, 1912; **Black to move**

Spielmann played **1. ... Kxd4**, and Leonhardt held a draw after **2. g6 Kd3 3. Rd7 d4 4. g7.** Black could have scored the full point by executing an elementary maneuver to win two tempos: 1. ... Kc3 2. Rc7+ (White relieves the mate threat) 2. ... Kxd4 (the first tempo) 3. Rg7 Kc3 4. Rc7+ Kd3 (the second tempo) 5. Rg7 d4 6. g6 Rc2+ 7. Kb1 Rc6 8. Rb7 Rxg6 9. Rxb4 Kc3 10. Rb8 Rg1+ 11. Ka2 d3, and Black wins.

The significance of the above example is not that Spielmann failed to win a superior ending or that he missed the win of two tempos. Not at all. The point is that Spielmann could certainly have essayed the above maneuver if not for a desire to avoid apparent digressions in the pursuit of his plan. He was thinking like a tiger rather than a python, who would have clamped on the big squeeze by gaining two insurance tempos.

Python-thinking is a kind of prophylaxis, which is the anticipation and prevention of an opponent's threats. The python wraps all of its coils around the prey, whether such overkill is needed or not. Chess pythons are never in a hurry and always take time to pick up tempos — not because they are thwarting specific threats but because they can never get too much of a good thing.

To develop a feel for python-practice, play through the endgames of Jose Capablanca and Akiba Rubinstein. Start with their numerous Rook-and-pawn endings, if only because this category of ending occurs most often in over-the-board play.

LAST AND LEAST

Studying the openings ought to occupy much less time in a player's work regimen than studying tactics and endgames. Still, the openings are obviously part of chess — at the highest levels, a big part of chess — and do merit investigation. But those players who aspire to reach expert and master levels ought to conduct their individual investigations differently from international level players. Yet . . . .

Much of the chess-book publishing business is built on opening manuals written by professionals for professionals, but bought and studied mainly by Class A and B players. The *Informant* series, the *Encyclopedia of Chess Open-*ings and nearly every other "serious" treatise on openings conclude individual lines with obscure symbols such as a plus sign over an equals sign (White has some unspecified microscopic edge).

As chess teachers, we often observe Class A and B players adopting opening lines unsuitable for their level of development. These players see an advantage awarded to White in, say, the Catalan and blindly follow the given variations. But their results are poor against opponents of similar strength, and these players conclude that the Catalan does not accord with their "style." They move on to a new opening, thereby forfeiting an immense amount of previous study time.

The truth is that certain lines in the Catalan in which White gains a Queenside pawn majority are objectively superior for the first player, but these lines are unsuitable for players below the master level because Black's crude, though often effective counterchances in the center are easier to exploit than the long-range advantage of a Queenside pawn majority.

Another typical mistake of developing players — especially those rated 1500 and below — is to head blindly for certain theoretically favorable positions in which they enjoy the advantage of a Bishop for a Knight or what Bobby Fischer calls "the minor exchange." Once again, however, the advantage evaporates in their hands, and more often than not the non-linear movements of the Knight prove more dangerous in practice than the more easily envisaged diagonal sweeps of the Bishop.

The general principle behind our advice for studying openings is that students will achieve the best practical results not by memorizing variations but by mastering the ideas of respective openings. In purely practical terms, it is better for a player to have an inferior position in which he understands what to do than to enjoy a better game without a clue of where to move next.

When selecting books for opening study, avoid opening manuals with columns of variations. A rational, though not infallible practice, is to purchase books with a large preponderance of words over variations, especially if these words are penned by reliable writers.

Remember: Variations seldom repeat themselves, but ideas do. It is better to play over one well-annotated contest than 10 variation-engorged games from an *Informant*. With these thoughts in mind, some of our favorite opening books are Reuben Fine's *Ideas Behind the Chess Openings*, Edmar Mednis' *How to Play Good Opening Moves*, Larry Evans' (*et alia*) *How to Open a Chess Game* (in particular, Lajos Portisch's chapter, "Developing an Opening Repertoire"), and as an example of a model work on a single opening, Robert Bellin and Pietro Ponzetto's *Mastering the King's Indian Defense*.

In opening play and chess style, conventional wisdom says that players ought to begin as gambiteers and progress toward more positional openings. For once, conventional wisdom has much to recommend it. By all means, try out the King's Gambit, the Goering Gambit and the Scotch Game to sharpen tactical awareness. Explore the open game before wrapping yourself in closed positions. When an opponent plays 1. e4, do not be afraid to try 1. ... e5.

A natural progression from the slam-bang chess of classic gambits is toward the pawn-based chess of Andre Philidor. The French Defense is a natural opening choice, since pawn structures are so important in many variations of this debut.

Only later in a player's development, do we suggest that he move to openings and ideas developed by the likes of Reti and Nimzovich — openings such as the Reti, the Nimzo-Indian and Alekhine's Defense.

After sampling openings ranging from the ancient Muzio Gambit to the Modern Defense, most students discover personal preferences. Some do not mind sacrificing material, and gambits are often for them; others prefer solid, grinding play, and the exchange variation of the Ruy Lopez may be their cup of tea. In either case — and for the many cases in between — the next steps are to master the main tactical and positional ideas of the opening and, of course, to play it in training games against friends and computers.

Following each game, a student should analyze what happened and try to discover where mistakes were made. If a student simply gets a better position and presses the advantage home, then he must understand clearly the reasons for such success. When a student finally plays an opening in tournaments, then *ECOs* and *Informants* have a role in concrete preparation against specific opponents or as reference works to discover alternative lines of play from what occurred.

ALL DRESSED UP, NOWHERE TO GO?

Most players find themselves stranded at one point or another on a performance plateau. They work ever harder, spending hundreds of hours with noses burrowed in middens of *BCOs*, *ECOs* and *MCOs*. They succeed in reaching excellent positions out of the opening but cannot find or decide upon a good middlegame plan. They are all dressed up but with nowhere to go.

Sound familiar? The cause is simple: These players know their opening lines cold but lack a positional feel for emerging middlegame positions. Players who constantly snag themselves on the cusp between opening and middlegame ought first to analyze their choice of openings. Here is a suggested method:

1. Compile results according to opening.
2. Break down the resulting numbers into sub-results against opponents of different rating levels.
3. When tabulating results for seldom-played openings, check to discover whether the outcome of individual games was decided in the opening or later on.
4. Examine early middlegame play in various openings to evaluate one's "feel" for emerging middlegame positions.
5. Draw appropriate conclusions, discarding some opening variations and researching additions to one's repertoire.

Another piece of advice — and an important one — is to start looking for one's own ideas. Forget the fear of playing something unbooked or little-booked. For, in fact, the best way to ensure smooth passage from opening to middlegame is to work out pet opening variations. Never make a book move that you do not understand; if you feel that you have a better idea, then try it.

The player who progresses from memorizing lines to creating ideas is a player who cannot help but grow, because to see value in an opening idea is to apprehend at least part of its long-term potential. Nor is the creative act in chess restricted to internationally ranked players. GM Yevgeny Sveshnikov was only an expert when he began working on novel ideas in what has become known as the Sveshnikov Sicilian (**1. e4 c5 2. Nf3 Nc6 3. d4 cxd4 4. Nxd4 Nf6 5. Nc3 e5**). Richard Moody, a correspondence student of Lev Alburt, came up with a very interesting idea in the King's Gambit (**1. e4 e5 2. f4 exf4 3. Qe2**) that contains plenty of pitfalls for the second player.

The beauty of developing one's own ideas is that even when they are mediocre or frankly inferior, they stand a good chance of doing well over the board. In most instances, a player who invents an idea has reasons for it and will make the most of his practical chances, which can be considerable.

Except at the highest levels of chess (where punishment of error is almost automatic), the secret behind successful opening play is to understand what one is doing, even when it turns out to be the wrong thing! Why? Because in understanding — not in rote application of theoretically correct moves — lies the seed of future improvement.

THE STUDY OF STRATEGY

Although we make no bones about emphasizing the study of tactics and endgames as the most productive use of limited study time, the student should devote some time to strategy, which in chess is the art of ascertaining the best kind of position one can achieve in a given situation and then getting the job done.

Emanuel Lasker's *Manual of Chess* and Siegbert Tarrasch's *Dreihundert Schachpartien* and *The Game of Chess* are classic teaching volumes for strategy — three works which have survived the test of time. More modern treatments are Robert Bellin and Pietro Ponzetto's *Test Your Positional Play* and Lev Alburt's *Test and Improve Your Chess*. For those with time to study strategy in depth, we recommend Max Euwe's *The Middle Game* (2 vols.) and Ludek Pachman's *Modern Chess Strategy*.

KNOW THYSELF IN CHESS

In *Hamlet*, William Shakespeare nearly wrote, "This above all: to thine own chess self be true." Which means, first and foremost, getting to know your chess self. But most students never take the time to assess carefully their chess play.

In the former Soviet Union, one of the most effective, though demanding methods for conducting personal chess assessments was to assign numerical values to the facets of one's game and to the play of others. On an ascending scale of zero to 10, assign yourself an overall playing strength of five. This part is easy because in this system, everyone from a Class A player to the world champion starts out at five.

The part that is not so easy is to determine the other number values. Begin by searching your memory to get a sense of your play, and jot down some rough ratings for your strength in such broad categories of practical play as the opening, middlegame, endgame, strategy, tactics, and attacking and defensive skills. Later on, there will be time to refine these rough impressions. Predictably, your strength in some areas will exceed the value of five assigned to your overall level, and in other areas, it will lag.

Now, this practice of attaching numbers to one's attacking or defensive play is easy to parody. Yet over the years, practice has shown that the zero-to-10 scale is highly effective, especially if one extends it beyond the major departments of over-the-board play. One player broke down hundreds of his games to discover how well he handled the two Bishops, conducted pawn storms, played positions with Kings castled on opposite wings, exercised technique in favorable positions, negotiated the rigors of time pressure, and so on. Eventually, he generated ratings to express his performance in these and other areas. Remember: The important thing is not to calculate absolutely accurate numbers but to compare one's strength in specific categories with one's overall strength and, if possible, with the strength of likely opponents.

Startling discoveries can be made about one's play. One player discovered that he was too apt to opt for the two Bishops. In a line of the

English (1. c4 Nf6 2. Nc3 e6 3. Nf3 Bb4 4. Qc2 0-0 5. a3 Bxc3 6. Qxc3 d5), he often courted trouble in the early middlegame by dropping tempos to keep his clerics. Simply becoming aware of this weakness was half the battle, and this player began to check more carefully those moves designed to obtain Bishops for Knights.

Another helpful practice is to assign numerical values to the overall strengths of likely opponents and to specific areas of their play — the kind of analysis that Mikhail Botvinnik made of his opponents at the 1948 world championship tournament. Among other things, Botvinnik discovered that former world champion Max Euwe relentlessly sought attacking positions and open files, paid too little attention to square weaknesses and too much to King safety, and — charmingly — tended to overlook long moves.

The player who takes apart his games, evaluates hundreds of important decisions, charts his overall performance in important areas, and does the same for likely opponents is on his way to major improvement. He will soon be shaping his opening repertoire to achieve middle and endgame positions in which he excels.

PREPARING FOR
SPECIFIC OPPONENTS

Players who are experts and masters know that the only way to reach their respective levels is to defeat their peers. They know that more efficient disposal of lower-rated players is not enough to bridge the gap which separates the Class A or B player from journeymen experts and masters.

And so, inevitably, ambitious players must prepare against individual opponents — especially if they do not live in one of a half-dozen urban chess centers and have, therefore, only a few targets to knock off.

The task of preparation ought to be easier than many players make it. The problem is that they are trapped in a time warp. Their concept of preparation is exhausted by the famous story of how Harry Nelson Pillsbury lost to Emanuel Lasker at St. Petersburg 1895-96, discovered an improvement (1. d4 d5 2. c4 e6 3. Nc3 Nf6 4. Nf3 c5 5. Bg5 cxd4 6. Qxd4 Nc6 7. *Bxf6!* rather than his earlier 7. Qh4), analyzed it exhaustively, and sprang the new idea on Lasker at Cambridge Springs 1904. Pillsbury won the game brilliantly, and generations have grown up reading all about it.

That's fine. But if Pillsbury, as the legend goes, really spent nine years analyzing the above line, then he squandered his time. There is, of course, nothing wrong with finding an opening improvement and springing it on an opponent; our point is only that there is ever so much more to preparation than trapping someone in an opening line.

Players of all strengths should find partners with whom to collaborate. A Class A player who wants to move higher should approach a local expert and ask to work with him.

Work with the hated competition, divulge one's precious thoughts? Absolutely. Strong players are too often reluctant to work together because they see only relatively minuscule negatives (letting slip an opening idea or stylistic preference) instead of the huge dividends that come from fruitful collaboration. Just ask Artur Yusupov and Sergei Dolmatov or Mikhail Botvinnik, who worked with the late Vyacheslav Ragozin. The idea behind chess cooperation is to concentrate on one's own improvement rather than worrying about silly "secrets." Players who grow stronger have no problem detecting the rough edges of their competitors and no need to worry about an occasional lost "secret."

In the preceding section of this chapter, we spoke of learning to know your chess self and suggested using a rating scale of zero to 10 by which to guage performance in the varied elements of chess play. To the extent that one wants to concentrate on the opposition, it should be in conjunction with using this scale. Aspiring experts, for example, ought to play over a local expert's games and discover how well the latter handles, say, the rigors of time pressure or positions with Kings castled on opposite wings. Break down an opponent's game into its constituent parts and compare his strengths with your own.

OLEG ROMANISHIN: A CASE STUDY

One day back in 1978, GM Lev Alburt — one of the authors of this chapter — was leafing through a notebook containing his past games with a fellow grandmaster, Oleg Romanishin. Still a Soviet citizen, the future U.S. chess champion was *not* hunting for opening novelties to spring on GM Romanishin. He was attempting *a la* Botvinnik to understand the chess psychology of his potential opponent.

Alburt discovered that he and Romanishin were a lot alike: Both players pursued complex, unbalanced positions, searched for exceptions to general rules, and willingly gave or grabbed material. Contrary to the common assumption, Romanishin was not so much an attacking master per se but rather a player seeking unbalanced positions whether in attack or defense. Alburt also noticed that in his games with Romanishin, the side sacrificing material fared better than the side accepting debatable gifts.

Only after analyzing Romanishin's play in detail did Alburt develop an overall game plan which involved sacrificing material. He began to think about possible openings and knew that Romanishin liked to play the Black side of the Queen's Gambit Accepted. What possibilities did White have to offer a pawn for an initiative?

QUEEN'S GAMBIT ACCEPTED
W: GM Lev Alburt
B: GM Oleg Romanishin
Vilnius, 1978

1. d4 d5 2. c4 dxc4 3. e4 e5 4. Nf3 Bb4 + At the time, a novelty. But Alburt keeps to his pregame plan. **5. Nc3** White cannot play 5. Nbd2 because of 5. ... c3! and has no interest in the slightly better ending that could arise after 5. Bd2. Before playing the text, Alburt analyzed the game continuation and was not surprised that Romanishin played 6. ... Qe7 and 7. ... Qxe4 + . There was no immediate punishment in sight for Black, and the capture led to a dynamic, unbalanced position. **5. ... exd4 6. Nxd4 Qe7 7. Bxc4 Qxe4 +** Here it is: Romanishin is true to his style — after thinking for 40 minutes. After 7. ... Nf6, White has only a slight advantage. **8. Kf1! Bxc3 9. bxc3 Be6 10. Qb3! Bxc4 11. Qxc4 Nc6 12. Bg5**

The obvious threat is 13. Re1. **12. ... Qg6 13. Re1 + Kf8 14. Nxc6 bxc6** The capture, 14. ... Qxc6, is met by the same move as in the game.

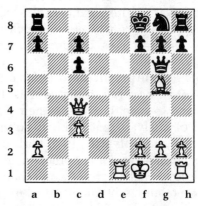

15. Qb4 + Qd6 16. Qb7 Rd8 The alternative is 16. ... Re8 17. Rxe8 + Kxe8 18. Qc8 + Qd8 19. Qxd8, mate. **17. Bxd8 Qxd8 18. Qxa7, and White wins** The first player is an exchange and, in effect, a pawn up.

Real preparation is more than finding a hole in opening analysis or setting a trap. It is coming to understand how an opponent thinks at the chessboard, which is seldom a random process with most strong players. When GM Alburt assumed that GM Romanishin would unbalance the position, he was not inveigling his opponent into a trap but drawing a behavioral conclusion based on close study.

HOW TO THINK DURING A GAME
In his *Think Like a Grandmaster*, Alexander Kotov explained the thought processes of himself and perhaps other grandmasters during chess combat. He recommended that players identify candidate moves in a given position, analyze these moves each in their turn (without, in general, returning to check calculations), and then make a move.

Kotov's candidate-move method has value if only because it offers an orderly way to analyze positions. Less intellectual static buzzes in the brain when one ceases jumping from move to move — and then back again and again. Yet a warning label must be attached to Kotov's method: Avoid rigid adherence. If after considering, say, three candidate moves, do not be afraid to look at other ideas as they occur. Further, if after rejecting candidate move "A," you notice that an idea involved with candidate move "B" could prove useful in line "A," then do not hesitate to reconsider the latter.

"Flexibility" is the byword.

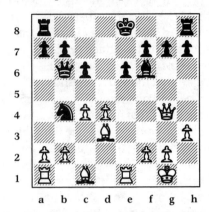

GM Mikhail Tal–GM Lajos Portisch
1965 Candidates' Match, Game 2; White to Move

In the above position, Tal won quickly after **16. Rxe6 + ! fxe6 17. Qxe6 + Kf8 18. Bf4 Rd8 19. c5 Nxd3 20. cxb6 Nxf4 21. Qg4 Nd5 22. bxa7 Ke7?! 23. b4! Ra8 24. Re1 + Kd6 25. b5! Rxa7? 26. Re6 + Kc7 27. Rxf6!, Black resigns.** On move 17, Black had two other alternatives: 17. ... Kd8 and 17. ... Be7. The first idea would have resulted in a draw by perpetual via 18. Qd6 + Ke8 19. Qe6 + , etc. When playing **16. Rxe6 + !**, Tal suspected that Portisch would eschew this line in search of a refutation to the sacrifice. At first glance, one such refutation is 17. ... Be7.

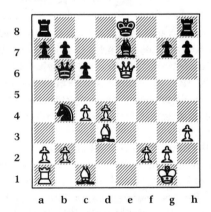

GM Mikhail Tal–GM Lajos Portisch
White to move

White has two candidate moves that suggest themselves, 18. Bg5 and 18. Bf5. Following Kotov's method by rote, one treats the two

moves as equals and analyzes both of them. But a more natural way to approach the position is simply to look at the obvious and promising 18. Bg5. One discovers that Black wins after 18. ... Qc7 19. Re1 Nxd3! 20. Bxe7 Qd7!. White would like to play 21. Qg6, mate, but the pawn on h7 prevents it. Ah, ha! Is there any trick that frees up the g6 square? The answer is a third possibility at move 18 that would never enter the mind until after analyzing 18. Bg5. White can play 18. Bg6 + , and Black cannot reply with 18. ... hxg6 because of 19. Bg5 Qc7 20. Re1. White's threats are decisive. Therefore, Black must try 18. ... Kd8, with a complex position that is difficult for both sides.

Kotov teaches us not to jump unnecessarily from move to move when analyzing. That's good. But do not fear searching for exceptions to general rules and do not avoid natural methods of thought.

In a sentence, the problem with Kotov's method of thinking is that in complex positions, it is often impossible to identify candidate moves immediately. These moves appear as you analyze other moves, *e.g.* the above Tal-Portisch example. In over-the-board play, a more subtle organization of thinking is the following method:

1. Establish the goal of calculation, *e.g.* can I get a perpetual check?
2. Search for ideas to reach the goal, and begin calculating the move most likely to lead to the goal.
3. Calculate the moves in order of their seeming strength.

The above method of thinking in complex positions saves time over the Kotov method while maintaining intellectual discipline in analysis. (See also a chapter on calculation in our *Tactics*).

THE ROLE OF CREATIVITY IN CHESS
"I have always a slight feeling of pity," wrote Siegbert Tarrasch in *The Game of Chess*, "for the man who has no knowledge of chess, just as I would pity the man who has remained ignorant of love. Chess, like love, like music, has the power to make men happy."

Tarrasch was on to something. Chess is, after all, an art. And the player who recognizes this element of the game will not only find chess more satisfying and enjoyable but will also improve his over-the-board results.

Improve one's over-the-board results? In an age when brilliancy prizes are *toute passe* and ratings the single ticket to peer validation, the idea of approaching chess as an art seems impractical, if not suicidal. The idea of tossing away rating points by essaying brilliant sacrificial combinations that go bust seems crazy.

Yet the young Mikhail Tal did not worry about losing games because of sacrificial over-exuberance. He understood as a young player struggling to raise his game that he could do no better for himself than to stretch his limits by playing both winning and imaginative chess. Many students do not understand that striving to play artistically contains practical, long-term benefits, but those players who are alert to these benefits possess what has sadly become a secret weapon.

Here, for example, is a combination played by Ted Field, sponsor of the New York leg of the 1990 World Championship. Field, who is not a tournament player, performs at about master level. He did not have to play the sacrifice at move 24 and could have chosen a quiet and strong, though less conclusive positional line. But no player improves unless he stretches his limits and strives for the very best continuation.

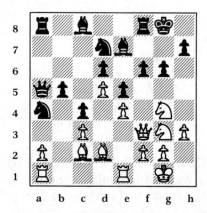

Ted Field–Lev Alburt
Training Game, 1991

23. Re3! This position has developed from the Tchigorin Variation of the Ruy Lopez. In the postmortem, White stated that he was proud of this move—and rightly so. Indeed, world champion

Gary Kasparov, who played over this game, praised the Rook lift as showing true mastery by patiently building an attack, while simultaneously shutting down Black's Queenside demonstration. White's key insight — based on a *positional* understanding of Ruy Lopez formations — was that his contemplated attack probably required the services of the King Rook. The move, 23. Re3!, is a known maneuver to those who study the ideas behind openings. **23. ... Ndc5** By this time, Black knew that his position was worse but still expected to confuse the issue with this move, followed by a timely pawn sacrifice on d3. **24. Nf5!!** At the time, Black feared this shot to the head less than the positional body punches of h3-h4 and h4-h5. Events show that in this instance the more direct course is also the stronger. **24. ... gxf5** If 24. ... Bxf5, White gains a crushing position without material investment after 25. exf5 g5 26. h4. **25. exf5 Kh8** Black now realized that he was in big trouble. White threatens to play Nh6, Qg4, and Rg3, intending to mate on either g7 or g8. If the Black monarch attempts to escape with 25. ... Kf7, he is cut down by 26. Nxe5+ dxe5 (if 26. ... Ke8, White has 27. Qh5+ Kd8 28. Nc6+) 27. Qh5+. **26. Nh6 Rg8 27. Qh5!** Black's last hope was that the first player would grab the Rook on g8. The text threatens 28. Nf7+ Kg7 29. Rg3+ Kf8 30. Bh6+, etc. **27. ... Rf8 28. Rg3** One threat is 29. Qg4. But there is another. **28. ... Qd8 29. Qf7!, Black resigns** Of course, if 29. ... Rxf7, then White plays 30. Nxf7, mate.

Players who seek beauty in chess are not afraid to lose because they can admire both their moves and those of the opponent. Not being chess cowards, they die but once. Players who approach chess as an art believe that there is a point to playing the game and are, therefore, more likely to have the courage to dare.

We all know the practical value of courage in chess, which is an expression of a strong, if not always a moral personal character. We all know smooth, well-schooled players who seem to fall apart when the going gets tough. We all know other players who lift a piece into the air — their hand shaking with tension — and somehow put it down on the right square.

The point is not that every chess tough guy is a conscious chess artist; the point is that testing one's creative limits is an excellent way to learn to play better chess. Making creative demands on oneself builds confidence, which in turn develops the capability to do the right thing even when it appears unlikely.

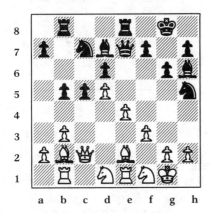

GM Svetozar Gligoric–GM Mikhail Tal
1959 Candidates' Tournament; Black to Move

In the above position, Tal plays a surprising, if soundly based sacrifice. White's position seems solid enough, but Black rips open the pawn center with **18. ... Nxd5!** Tal has in mind the position which arises after **19. exd5 Bf5 20. Qc3 Bg7 21. Qc1 Bxb1 22. Bxg7 Kxg7 23. Qxb1 Nf4 24. Nde3 Qe5**, when he threatens ... Qd4. Gligoric counters with **25. Bxb5! Rxb5 26. Nf5+ gxf5 27. Rxe5 Rxe5**, and the position is about equal because Black's Queen Rook is poorly placed.

At first glance, Black's sacrifice seems to violate general principles because White appears to have a solid position. Yet Tal never risked losing equality and posed difficult problems for Gligoric to solve. He had the confidence to play an unlikely and correct line because he trusted in his judgment.

None of us are born with the capacity to believe in and act upon our better judgment. We learn to do the right thing in chess by extending our creative limits, which means taking some lumps along the way. The young Bobby Fischer of the late 1950s was often criticized for stubbornly adhering to opening lines even when they yielded poor immediate results. He was, in fact, paying creative dues for the stunning and easy elegance of his maturity.

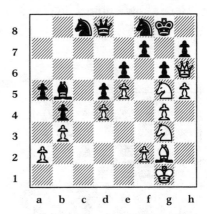

GM Bobby Fischer–GM Oscar Panno
Buenos Aires, 1970; White to move

Fischer plays a misprint, **28. Be4!!**, with the idea of adding a Bishop to his Kingside attack. Black cannot capture the Bishop because of 28. ... dxe4 29. N3xe4, threatening 30. Nf6 + Kh8 31. Nxf7, mate. The game quickly concluded after **28. ... Qe7 29. Nxh7! Nxh7 30. hxg6 fxg6 31. Bxg6 Ng5** (Black lands in a hopeless ending with 31. ... Qg7 32. Bxh7+ Kh8 33. Qxg7+ Kxg7 34. Bb1 Ne7 35. f4 Nc6 36. Kf2.) **32. Nh5 Nf3+ 33. Kg2 Nh4+ 34. Kg3 Nxg6 35. Nf6+ Kf7 36. Qh7+, Black resigns.**

GOOD TO THE LAST MOVE
Bobby Fischer and Mikhail Tal are not the only chess artists around. Akiba Rubinstein, who won some Rook-and-pawn endings that still look like witchcraft, is as different from Tal as anyone could be. Yet he, too, is a chess artist whose games are good to the last move. Unlike many of us, players like Fischer, Tal and Rubinstein seldom relax in winning positions because a chess game is seen as an artistic whole. Alexander Alekhine, too, was famous for ruthlessly exploiting won positions. Inaccuracies — even meaningless mistakes that do not affect the outcome — are viewed as pox on alabaster.

The player who cares about chess as an art is never bored by a position, and this quality in conjunction with a determination to play intensely from the opening through the mopping-up stage is of tremendous practical value. The common complaint about drawing or losing a "hopelessly won position" is not so common among players motivated to maintain maximum concentration until the opponent's resignation. Here's how Rubinstein won a "hope-lessly boring position" against a man who once beat Alekhine:

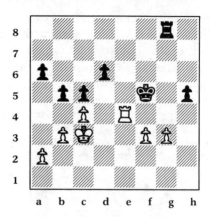

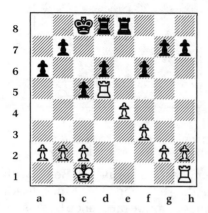

Hermanis Mattison–Akiba Rubinstein
Carlsbad 1929; Black to move

18. ... Re5 19. Rhd1?! This move appears to be above reproach: White doubles his Rooks and bears down on the seemingly weak and backward Queen pawn. But he ought to play 19. Rxe5 dxe5 to achieve a clear draw. The charm of this ending is that Black ought to lose based on rote positional ideas. Not only does the second player have a backward Queen pawn, he will later isolate his Kingside pawns and permit White a passed f-pawn. **19. ... Rxd5 20. Rxd5 Kd7 21. c4 g6 22. Kc2 Ke6 23. Kc3 f5!** Black has now a slight edge because of a more active King and more mobile Rook. **24. exf5+ gxf5 25. Rd2 b5 26. b3** White needs to get active with 26. b4. **26. ... h5 27. g3 f4! 28. Re2+ Kf5 29. Re4 fxg3 30. hxg3 Rg8**

31. Rf4+? White had to try 31. g4+ hxg4 32. Rxg4 Rh8!, when Black keeps a strong initiative. Of course, Black must avoid both 32. ... b4+ 33. Kd3 Rxg4 34. fxg4+ Kxg4 35. Ke4 and 32. ... Rxg4 33. fxg4+ Kxg4 34. cxb5 axb5 35. a4. **31. ... Ke6 32. Re4+ Kd7 33. g4 Rf8! 34. Re3** White does not save himself with 34. gxh5 Rxf3+ 35. Kc2 Rh3. **34. ... h4 35. a4 bxa4 36. bxa4 Re8! 37. Kd2** Another way to lose is 37. Rd3 h3 38. Kc2 Re2+ 39. Kc3 Rf2!. **37. ... Rxe3 38. Kxe3 d5!, White resigns** The filigree-like delicacy of Rubinstein's concluding pawn push beautifully complements the artistic economy of moves and means that he has exhibited throughout this ending.

Much more can be said about how an appreciation for the beauty of chess improves one's over-the-board play. The sheer joy of satisfaction is probably the chess artist's greatest practical reward. At the board he remains ever hungry for the intellectual high afforded by creative endeavor.

And this chess hunger means more rating points.

SELECTED BIBLIOGRAPHY

Most of the books listed below are easily available. An exception is Siegbert Tarrasch's *Dreihundert Schachpartien*, which has yet to be published in English. Among well-known mail-order outlets for books and chess equipment are the U.S. Chess Federation (186 Route 9W, New Windsor, N.Y. 12553; phone: 800-388-5464); PBM International Corporation (504 Bloomfield Avenue, Montclair, New Jersey 07042; phone: 800-726-4685); Chess Digest Incorporated (P.O. Box 59029; Dallas, Texas 75229; phone: 800-462-3548); and Dewain Barber (524 S. Avenida Fara, Anaheim, California 92807; phone: 714-998-5508). To procure the Tarrasch volume, contact dealers in used chess books. One well-known and respected dealer is Fred Wilson — Books (80 East 11th Street, Suite 334, New York, N.Y. 10003; phone: 212-533-6381).

The books listed under each subhead are arranged in ascending order of difficulty, though such a ranking can only be approximate.

BOOKS FOR STUDYING OPENINGS
1. Edmar Mednis, *How to Play Good Opening Moves*
2. Reuben Fine, *Ideas Behind the Chess Openings*
3. Robert Bellin and Pietro Ponzetto, *Mastering the King's Indian Defense*
4. Larry Evans *et al., How to Open a Chess Game*
5. *Encyclopedia of Chess Openings* and *Chess Informants*

BOOKS FOR STUDYING CHESS STRATEGY
1. Jose Capablanca, *Chess Fundamentals*
2. Emanuel Lasker, *Manual of Chess*
3. Jose Capablanca, *Last Lectures*
4. Ludek Pachman, *Modern Chess Strategy*
5. Andrew Soltis, *Pawn Structure Chess*
6. Robert Bellin and Pietro Ponzetto, *Test Your Positional Play*
7. Lev Alburt, *Test and Improve Your Chess*
8. Siegbert Tarrasch, *The Game of Chess*
9. Siegbert Tarrasch, *Dreihundert Schachpartien*
10. Max Euwe, *The Middle Game* (two volumes)

BOOKS FOR STUDYING TACTICS
1. Fred Reinfeld, *1001 Brilliant Ways to Checkmate* and *1001 Winning Sacrifices and Combinations*
2. August Livshitz, *Test Your Chess IQ*
3. Moe Moss and Ian Mullin, *Blunders and Brilliancies*
4. Vladimir Vukovic, *The Art of Attack*
5. Garry Kasparov, *Kasparov Teaches Chess*
6. Leonid Shamkovich, *The Tactical World of Chess*
7. Mikhail Tal, *The Life and Games of Mikhail Tal*
8. Yasser Seirawan, *Flash Tactics* (Advanced series)
9. Nikolai Krogius, *Encyclopedia of Middlegames: Combinations*
10. *Chess Informants* (see the chapter on "Combinations" at the back of each volume)

BOOKS FOR STUDYING ENDGAMES
1. Jose Capablanca, *Chess Fundamentals* and *Last Lectures*
2. Edmar Mednis, *Practical Rook Endings*
3. Bruce Pandolfini, *Pandolfini's Endgame Course*
4. Irving Chernev, *Capablanca's Best Chess Endings*
5. Hans Kmoch, *Rubinstein's Chess Masterpieces*
6. August Livshitz and Jonathan Speelman, *Test Your Endgame Ability*
7. Irving Chernev, *Practical Chess Endings*
8. Mikhail Shereshevsky, *Endgame Strategy*
9. Reuben Fine, *Basic Chess Endings*

Alexander Kotov's *Think Like a Grandmaster* is an important work for studying and evaluating this famous grandmaster-author's advice about how to calculate variations during a game. And, of course, read *Comprehensive Chess Course, Level III* books (see "How to Order" page.)

ROMAN PELTS

Born in Odessa, Ukraine, on August 11, 1937, Roman Pelts holds the rank of FIDE master. But he is best known as one of the most respected chess trainers in the world. Since founding the Roman Pelts Chess Studio, first in Montreal and later in Toronto, he has taught hundreds of students and is commonly regarded as Canada's top chess teacher.

FM Pelts left the former Soviet Union in 1977, taking with him the notes on which *Comprehensive Chess Course* is based. During his years in the Soviet Union, he quickly gained name as a coming young master, finishing second in the Russian Championship for Young Masters. But he soon found teaching chess to be more fulfilling and challenging than playing the game.

In 1959, FM Pelts founded in Odessa a chess school, and among his first pupils were several children, who later became famous grandmasters, including Lev Alburt (the co-author of *Comprehensive Chess Course*), Semyon Palatnik and Vladimir Tukmakov. He was awarded the prestigious title of "Honored Coach." In 1971, he served as coach for the Soviet national student team, which included among its members future FIDE world champion Anatoly Karpov and future title candidate Alexander Beliavsky.

Along with Mark Dvoretsky, FM Pelts is among the most innovative of chess teachers and trainers. He instructs children and adults who are just beginning in chess and top-rated players who need the services of an experienced coach. "One of the most important teaching principles," states FM Pelts, "is to provide students only the knowledge they need at their given level of development. Give them too much, they bog down in detail; give them too little, they do not receive proper training in the basics."

FM Pelts is in demand as a chess teacher and lecturer throughout both Canada and the United States. He is a leading proponent of putting chess into Canada's public schools and has organized numerous tournaments for children. "I firmly believe," he states, "that chess sharpens the minds of kids and contains a value beyond its role of being, quite simply, the world's premier game."

LEV ALBURT

Grandmaster Lev Alburt was born in Orenburg, Russia, on August 21, 1945. For many years, he lived in Odessa, a Ukrainian city located on the Black Sea. A three-time champion of the Ukraine (1972-74), he became European Cup champion in 1976. In 1979, while in West Germany for a chess competition, he defected. Since 1979, GM Alburt has made his home in New York City. In his adopted country, he continues to play chess and "to enjoy the best Russian food anywhere in the United States." He has also returned to his earlier love of teaching chess to those who wish to learn the royal game.

This three-time U.S. Champion (1984, 1985, and 1990), who first taught chess in the former Soviet Union under the direction of many-time world champion Mikhail Botvinnik, nowadays conducts classes at chess camps, teaches and trains some of America's strongest young players under the auspices of the American Chess Foundation, and lectures at clubs throughout the United States. In addition, GM Alburt conducts clinics for scholastic coaches on how better to teach chess to their students. One memorable high point was a speech to the Harvard Russian Research Center on the role of chess in Soviet politics.

As a teacher, GM Alburt is at the forefront of finding new ways to teach chess to students ranging from young children to adults who wish to take up the game. *Comprehensive Chess Course* is one of the products of what is sometimes called "the new chess pedagogy." He frequently works on lessons with IM Mark Dvoretsky, who is commonly regarded as the world's outstanding chess trainer.

Currently GM Alburt often conducts chess lessons by both telephone and mail — having developed course plans for both kinds of instruction. He can be reached by writing to Lev Alburt, P.O. Box 534, Gracie Station, New York, N.Y. 10028.

Other books by GM Alburt include *Test and Improve your Chess*, published by Pergamon Press, and *The Alekhine for the Tournament Player* (co-authored with Eric Schiller), published by Batsford.

"Chess is a game for life," GM Alburt says, " and that means children who learn chess not only improve their ability to reason clearly but also have a pastime that will never fail them as they grow older."

a note from GM Lev Alburt ...

To Order Additional Books:

Contact your local Bookseller or complete the form below

Please send me the following items:

❑ *Comprehensive Chess Course (Volumes I and II come* in one large book!)   *$42.00*

❑ *Comprehensive Chess Course Vol. I* (Learn Chess in 12 Lessons)   *$16.95*

❑ *Comprehensive Chess Course Vol. II* (From Beginner to Tournament Player)

    $28.95

❑ *Chess Tactics for the Tournament Player*   *$19.95*

❑ *The King in Jeopardy* (The Best Techniques for Attack and Defense)   *$19.95*

Add $4.00 per order for shipping. *All orders will be shipped the same/next day by second-day delivery Priority Mail.*

Send books to:

_____
Name

_____
Street

_____
City   State   Zip Code

To receive an autographed copy, please print name and desired inscription on the following line:

_____

Mail your order and check to:

Lev Alburt
P.O. Box 534 Gracie Station • New York, NY 10028-0005

For credit card orders, call toll-free at (800) 247-6553. Unfortunately, autographs are not available on credit card orders.

Lev Alburt teaches students of all ages and strengths and is available for lessons by telephone, mail or in-person. For further information contact GM Alburt at the above address or phone him at (212) 794-8706.